THE VIKING BOOK OF

FOLK BALLADS

OF THE ENGLISH-SPEAKING WORLD

The Viking Book of

FOLK BALLADS

of the English-Speaking World

Edited by Albert B. Friedman

The Viking Press, New York

VIKING COMPASS EDITION
Issued in 1963 by The Viking Press, Inc.
625 Madison Avenue, New York, N.Y. 10022

Distributed in Canada by
The Macmillan Company of Canada Limited

Library of Congress catalog card number: 56-7084

Printed in the U.S.A. by
The Colonial Press Inc.

Fifth printing November 1968

The editor thanks the following publishers for the use of ballad versions from books by them (the author names are used here, as in the headnotes in the book, to refer to full listings by author and title in the Bibliography, p. 459).

J. J. Augustin: Eddy, Henry; Boosey & Hawkes: McGill (copyright 1917 by Boosey & Co. Ltd.); Duke University Press: Brown; Harcourt, Brace & World, Inc.: Sandburg; Harvard University Press: Cox, Davis, MacKenzie, Rickaby, Scarborough, White (copyright respectively 1925 by Harvard University Press, 1929 by The President and Fellows of Harvard College and 1957 by Arthur Kyle Davis, Jr., 1928 by The President and Fellows of Harvard College and 1956 by William Roy MacKenzie, 1926 by Harvard University Press and 1954 by Lillian Rickaby Dykstra, 1925 by Harvard University Press and 1953 by Mary McDaniel Parker, 1928 by The President and Fellows of Harvard College); Indiana University Press: Brewster (copyright 1940 by Indiana University); McGraw-Hill Book Company: Hubbard (copyright © 1945 by Freeman H. Hubbard); W. W. Norton & Company: Colcord (copyright 1938 by W. W. Norton & Company); University of Florida Press: Morris (copyright 1950 by University of Florida Press); University of North Carolina Press: Judson, Johnson, Odum and Johnson (copyright respectively 1936, 1929, 1925 by University of North Carolina Press); Yale University Press: Barry (copyright 1929 by Yale University Press). Thanks also to Barthold Fles for "Zebra Dun" from Larkin (copyright 1931 by Alfred A. Knopf, Inc.); to the Estate of Charles J. Finger for "Sam Bass" from Finger (copyright 1927 by Doubleday & Company); Folkways Music Publishers, Inc., for "De Ballit of Boll Weevil" from Lomax (copyright 1936 Folkways Music Publishers, Inc., New York, N.Y.); to Mrs. Charles H. Linscott for "Captain Kidd" from Linscott (copyright 1939 by The Macmillan Company); and to Shapiro, Bernstein and Co., Inc. for "The Wreck of the Old 97" (copyright 1924, 1940 by F. Wallace Rega, 1939 by R.C.A. Mfg. Co., Inc., assigned to and copyright 1944 by Shapiro, Bernstein & Co., Inc.) and "Casey Jones" (copyright 1909, 1936, assigned to and copyright 1937 by Shapiro, Bernstein & Co., Inc.). Gratitude is also due the many individual scholars, collectors, and journals whose contributions are duly acknowledged in the headnotes and the Bibliography.

CONTENTS

V. PASTOURELLES   148

VI. DOMESTIC TRAGEDIES   156

VII. TABLOID CRIME   178

VIII. CRIMINALS' GOODNIGHTS   218

IX. BALLADS OF THE SCOTTISH BORDER   233

X. HISTORICAL BALLADS   276

INTRODUCTION

SIR WALTER SCOTT thought to flatter an old Scotswoman from whose singing he had taken down a number of ballads by showing her the printed texts of the pieces she had sung to him. But the old woman was more annoyed than amused. He had spoiled them altogether, she complained. "They were made for singing and no for reading, but ye hae broken the charm now and they'll never be sung mair. And the warst thing o' a', they're nouther right spell'd, nor right setten down." This last phrase may have been a slash at Scott's tactful doctoring of his ballads. But would old Mrs. Hogg have been any happier even if the texts had been exactly reproduced? Probably not. There are people who hate to see wild flowers in a vase or animals in cages, and ballads in static print may well seem equally unnatural. Most of us, however, would remain blissfully ignorant of the folk ballads if to hear them meant a field trip for song-catching in the Appalachians. And the folk ballads of the olden times that got sporadically recorded in manuscripts and old ballad books would have been utterly lost if those who preserved them had felt the way Mrs. Hogg did. Nonetheless, the testy old woman's scruples bring to the fore a key fact about balladry—simply this: ballads are songs or performances, not poems. They are not literature, but illiterature.

Balladry vs. literary poetry. Poetry usually gains by being read aloud, and certain essential features of a poem—rhythm, rhyme, euphony—appeal to the ear, but poems from their first conception are destined for the printed page and for the eye. The folk ballad, on the other hand, is an oral phenomenon; its style, as we shall see, is largely explained by the necessities of oral transmission. Originally and naturally ballads were preserved in the memory of peoples whose culture was traditional, word-of-mouth, preserved without benefit of paper and ink. So it is that though a poem has a fixed form, standing as the poet left it when he gave it to a scribe or to the press, ballads alter with every singer, the more popular ones appearing in innumerable versions and variants, some of which are less good than others, but all—theoretically, at least—of equal authority.

Poetry and balladry differ in another important way. The poet subjectively expresses himself in his work; his study is to find the novel phrases, the unique, evocative figures that will convey his personal, particularistic thoughts and feelings. Ballads, significantly, are anonymous. There may be an "I," but it is as fictitious as the editorial "we." Any rare or subtle figurative expression in a ballad would make its genuineness suspect, for the language of ballads is a tissue of commonplaces, stock figures, stock symbols, and formulaic phrasing. Whatever poetic triumphs one encounters in balladry are to be credited to the general ballad style and the ballad way of looking at things, not to any one ballad maker. And the feeling expressed is community feeling, the individual singer being merely the deputy of the public voice.

Why call balladry "illiterature"? The answer is implicit in what has already been said. The physical medium of literary poetry is the written or printed letter (*litera*), whereas balladry, in the period in which its nature was determined, was strictly oral and existed only in the collective memory of the ballad folk. Moreover, the ballad flourishes best and natively among people of unlettered culture—illiterates. In our society illiteracy is common only in depressed areas or in the backwoods; elsewhere illiterates are usually mentally deficient. But in the Middle Ages, when the ability to read and write was limited almost entirely to clerics, the persons who heard and shaped ballads came from all social strata, and thus the ballads were created by a greater pool of talent and judged by a higher and more refined standard of taste than could be expected of a modern illiterate community.

The Child ballad as norm. The generalizations that have just been spun out apply in a strict sense only to the central and most important kind of ballads in English, the British "folk," "popular," "traditional" ballads that are gathered in Francis James Child's monumental collection of *English and Scottish Popular Ballads* (1882–1898). Child, who was a professor at Harvard, had acquired from deep, sustained study of the various European balladries an almost infallible instinct for detecting the true ballad note which popular origin and oral transmission stamp into traditional song. Winnowing through the narrative songs

recorded in manuscripts and published in the books of British
collectors such as Bishop Percy (1729–1811), Joseph Ritson
(1752–1803), Sir Walter Scott (1771–1832), Robert Jamieson
(1780–1844), and William Motherwell (1797–1835), Child
found three hundred and five distinct ballads in British tradition, some in as many as twenty-five versions. His thick five-volume collection is the basic repository of the folk ballad in English, and it is customary in ballad books to refer to a Child-type
ballad by the number it bears in Child's collection, even though
the title may vary from his and the version may be one he did
not know. In our collection Child numbers are indicated in
parentheses after the titles of appropriate ballads. Since Child's
death only about a dozen additional ballads which satisfy
what seem to have been his canons of admission have been discovered, but it would be no exaggeration to say that many more
than a thousand new texts of ballads Child recognized have been
taken down from folk singers and printed in the sixty years since
his work was published.

Child knew that the British ballads had been brought to this
country; he himself printed several pieces he had recorded in
Massachusetts or which had been sent to him from correspond-
ents in the South. Still, he would have been overwhelmed to
learn how lively the ballad tradition imported from the old country really was. All the while Gavin Greig was gleaning the last
leaves of traditional balladry in Scotland and a whole school of
enthusiasts was gathering the withered remnants of folksong in
England and Ireland, collectors such as Phillips Barry (New
England), H. M. Belden (Missouri), the Englishman Cecil
Sharp (Appalachian states), F. C. Brown (North Carolina), J.
A. Lomax (Texas), Mary Eddy (Ohio), Vance Randolph (Oz-
arks), W. R. Mackenzie (Nova Scotia), and many others were
abundantly documenting the survival of the British ballads in
twentieth-century America. In fact, thanks to the diligence of
the American collectors, it is now clear that the Child ballad
survives more numerously in the United States and Canada than
in the countries of its origin.

Only a part of the great mass of ballads collected before and
after Child belongs to the kind of ballad he isolated and
described. Very different in manner and tone are the "vulgar"
ballads derived from British broadsides and songsters. The native

American ballads, notably the songs of cowboys and lumberjacks and sensational murder and outlaw ballads, also stand
apart. These and other non-Child ballads are fully represented
in this book and will be duly treated. In discussing ballad theory
and style, however, it is best to take the Child ballad as the norm.
For one thing, the Child ballad has a more distinctive style and
one that is fairly general in all its examples. Also the Child ballad, not the others, has been the battleground of the contro-
versies we shall have to look at briefly. Most important, perhaps,
it is the Child ballad that is our representative in international
balladry, since it is the nearest counterpart in English-speaking
countries to the folk ballads of Denmark, Spain, France, Italy,
and other European ballad areas.

What is a folk ballad? It is harder to define than to recognize
a folk ballad, for after very little experience one develops a tact
for appreciating the genuine ballad style. Even amateurs can
spot the spurious passages in otherwise bona fide examples. A
somewhat unwieldy but inclusive definition describes the ballad
as a short, traditional, impersonal narrative told in song, transmitted orally from generation to generation, marked by its own
peculiar structure and rhetoric, and uninfluenced by literary
conventions. "Short" here means compressed; the best ballads
avoid extensive descriptions or mere decoration, and even the
story proper is stripped to its essentials. "Narrative" also needs
limiting; certainly it must not be taken to imply the "and then
. . . and then" method of storytelling in which the emphasis is
on continuity.

To enlarge upon "the peculiar structure and rhetoric" of the
ballads, we might do well to follow G. H. Gerould and canvass
the three basic characteristics that Child ballads have in common
with European folk ballads. First, we note that ballads focus on
a single situation, usually a single scene. Events that lead up to
this central situation, no matter how important to the story, are
only hurriedly, though firmly, sketched in. Any activity after
the culminating episode on which the ballad has concentrated
is also handled sketchily. Another important constant: ballads are
told in a peculiarly effective dramatic manner. We are not told
about things happening; we are shown them happening. This
immediacy and intensity is produced by treating the central
episode as a dramatic scene or set of scenes and having the

characters speak in their own persons. Dialogue, therefore, bulks large in ballads ("Edward," for example, is all dialogue), and it is the kind of dialogue that furthers action, not the kind that is introduced to exhibit or develop the characters of the participants. For—and here we come to the third constant—ballads show no interest in the subtleties of character or in psychological motive-mongering. The attitude of the narrator is impersonal, in the sense that he never moralizes and rarely allows his subjective attitude toward the action to intrude.

Ballad Style

The ballad method of narration is unique, and until one gets used to it, it can be disconcerting. Characteristically a ballad breaks into its story at a moment when the train of action is decisively pointed toward the catastrophe. Setting, time, the appearance of the persons involved, the background, are indicated by a few light strokes or a few casual hints. Characters pop out of nowhere just at the moment they are needed and are dropped with equal suddenness. We shift from place to place abruptly, scene after scene flashing by without connectives or explanation. Sometimes one scene opens out of another almost by sleight-of-hand, as in the transition from palace to sea strand in "Sir Patrick Spence":

> The king has written a braid letter,
> And sign'd it wi' his hand,
> And sent it to Sir Patrick Spence,
> Was walking on the sand.

But though rapid movement is the rule, the ballads occasionally linger at some stages of the action in order to underline a fact or to enhance an emotional effect. Thus, for all its economy, "Sir Patrick Spence" luxuriates for two stanzas in the pathos of the ladies awaiting the return of their drowned lovers:

> O lang, lang may their ladies sit,
> Wi' thair fans into their hand,
> Or eir they se Sir Patrick Spence
> Cum sailing to the land.

> O lang, lang may the ladies stand,
>   Wi' thair gold kems in their hair,
> Waiting for thair ain deir lords,
>   For they'll se thame na mair.

The shift from narrative to dialogue invariably comes at a crucial and strategic point in the story to make one of the ballad's heightened moments. And, in keeping with the brisk pace of the narration, the dialogue is terse and telling. No words are wasted in comment on the tone of delivery; tags relating the speaker to his speech are perfunctory and kept to a minimum. Often, indeed, we are left to infer the speaker from what is being said.

Language. Because in a ballad the story is the thing, the language is formalized, and seldom does a striking expression draw our attention away from the action. A limited stock of images, epithets, and descriptive terms does service for all the ballads. Horses are always steeds, and if white, milk-white, if brown, berry-brown, if gray, dapple-gray. They are regularly shod with silver before and gold behind. Knights are always gallant, swords royal, ladies gay (even when in tragic circumstances), beds soft and narrow, sheets inevitably of the finest Holland linen. A man's lips are described as "ruby red" although he has just bled to death; similarly, "true lover" becomes so fixed a phrase that a mountain ballad can speak of a "false true lover"! As one might expect, the ballad world is drenched in primary colors, and the colors are likened to simple, obvious things—as red as wine, roses, blood, rubies; lily-white, milk-white, snow-white. Whole speeches as well as phrases float from ballad to ballad. Innumerable ballad heroes in haste to get somewhere call out to their grooms in the urgent rhythms of

> "Go saddle me the black, the black,
>   Go saddle me the brown;
> Go saddle me the swiftest steed
>   That ever rode frae a town."

To indicate that night has fallen, too many ballads fall back on the same vapid cliché:

> When bells were rung, and mass was sung,
>   And a' men bound to bed . . .

And at least a dozen ballads of tragic love conclude with the sentimental vignette of having a rambling rosebush grow out of one lover's grave, a briar out of the other's:

> They grew as high as the church-top,
>   Till they could grow no higher;
> And then they grew in a true lover's knot,
>   Which made all people admire.

Perhaps the commonplaces are not completely explained by saying they are purposely used, in preference to richer language, in order to help us keep our mind on the story. They have also the positive value of contrasting with the eruptive vigor of the story line.

Repetition. However we explain them, these formulas and stereotypes should not deceive us into thinking the ballads artless. On the contrary, they are molded by a high order of folk art, a fact which strikes one most forcibly when he comes to analyze the ballads' extensive and ingenious use of repetition and parallelism. Any compressed narrative of sensational doings told at a high pitch of feeling is bound to repeat words and phrases in order to accommodate the emotion that cannot be exhausted in one saying. David's lament for Absalom—"O my son Absalom, my son, my son Absalom! would God I had died for thee, O Absalom, my son, my son!"—shows this natural device operating in Hebrew narrative. We meet such repetition everywhere in ballads, where it extends even to stanzas, as in the mourning scene in "Sir Patrick Spence" just quoted. Not all repeated phrases of course are emotional. Many of them merely reinforce a rhythmical pattern or match a repeated figure in the music. No great emotion, for example, is at work in

> "Lie still, lie still, my own dear son,
>   Lie still and take a sleep . . ."
>   ("The Lass of Roch Royal")

—the lines of a cold-hearted mother.

Some repetition is doubtless an aid to memory. Ballads are oral: a hearer cannot turn back a page to recover a vital detail that slipped by in a moment of inattention. Essential facts in the ballad story therefore must be incised in the memory, and here repetition is functional as well as poetic in itself. Thus instructions given in a speech are faithfully repeated in the resulting action:

> "Oh brither dear, take me on your back,
>   Carry me to yon kirkyard,
> And dig a grave baith wide and deep,
>   And lay my body there."

> He's ta'en him up upon his back,
>   Carried him to yon kirkyard,
> And dug a grave both deep and wide,
>   And laid his body there.
>   ("The Twa Brothers")

Answers parody the form of the questions that elicited them:

> "But wha will bake my bridal bread,
>   Or brew my bridal ale?
> And wha will welcome my brisk bride,
>   That I bring o'er the dale?"

> "It's I will bake your bridal bread,
>   And brew your bridal ale,
> And I will welcome your brisk bride,
>   That you bring o'er the dale."
>   ("Fair Annie")

Still another repetitive formula used by singers creates suspense by emitting a fact piecemeal. Instead of saying, "He had not even gone three miles," the ballad has:

> He had not gone a mile, a mile,
>   A mile but barely three . . .

As a British critic (Hodgart) points out, here we have a device analogous to the movie technique of "montage." Instead of skipping from the place of departure to the three-mile mark, we are given three rapid "shots," one at one mile, one at two miles, one at three miles. The statement of distance traveled could not be put in a more subtly dynamic way.

Incremental repetition. Most distinctive of all rhetorical schemes used in ballads is the technique known as "incremental repetition." "Incremental" does not mean accumulative: we are not dealing with the device employed in "The House that Jack Built" or "Old Macdonald Had a Farm," where each later stanza repeats the string of items accumulated thus far in the song and adds another. In incremental repetition a phrase or stanza is repeated several times with some small but material substitution at the same crucial spot. With each repetition and its new substituted element, suspense mounts powerfully until we come at last to the critical substitution that bursts the pattern, marking the climax and with it a release of tension. Sometimes a sequence of incremental repetition is the entire structural principle of a ballad, as in "Lord Randal." The classic example is "The Maid Freed from the Gallows." A girl on the point of being hanged begs the hangman (in some versions a judge) to wait for a while—she sees her father approaching:

> "Oh father, oh father, a little of your gold,
>   And likewise of your fee!
> To keep my body from yonder grave,
>   And my neck from the gallows-tree."

The father refuses. Parallel requests are made of mother, brother, and sister. All refuse, using the pattern of the girl's plea in their refusals:

> "None of my gold now shall you have,
>   Nor likewise of my fee;
> For I am come to see you hang'd,
>   And hangèd you shall be."

Last to ride up is the girl's "true love." He ransoms the girl and breaks the series of refusals:

> "For I am come to see you saved,
>   And savèd you shall be."

Incremental repetition is particularly effective in protracting a tense moment. Fair Annie in the ballad of that title steels herself to the ordeal she must face when her lover comes ashore with his new bride. Leaving her tower, she advances painfully toward the humiliating encounter:

> And she gaed down, and farther down,
>   Her love's ship for to see,
> And the topmast and the mainmast
>   Shone like the silver free.
>
> And she's gane down, and farther down,
>   The bride's ship to behold;
> And the topmast and the mainmast
>   They shone just like gold.

The span of incremental repetition used for this lingering effect may extend over no more than a stanza. Little Musgrave as he lies in bed with Lady Barnard is suspensefully devious in confessing his fear that the lady's husband may break in on them:

> "Methinks I hear the thresel-cock,
>   Methinks I hear the jaye;
> Methinks I hear my lord Barnard,
>   And I would were away."

The seduction of Mary Hamilton is built up to in a similar way:

> He's courted her in the kitchen,
>   He's courted her in the ha',
> He's courted her in the laigh cellar,
>   And that was warst of a'!

In ballads of a heavy supernatural cast, extended passages of repetition set up a rocking motion that lends the proceedings the glamor of ritual incantation.

Hyperbole and understatement. Other stylistic traits the ballad shares with literary poetry. Hyperbole is everywhere. A bride arrives with a dowry of seven shiploads of gold. We are not surprised to learn that the vessels have sails of taffeta. And where halls are paved in gold, it is only fitting that the ladies that tread the floor should be so laden with diamonds that no other illumination is necessary. In literary poetry hyperbole is strained—a willful, conscious exaggeration. Hyperbolic expressions in balladry are less deceptive, more genuinely naïve, for these are peasants describing royal palaces they have never seen, and, as in fairy tales, the imagined splendors rampantly surpass anything the architects of reality can build.

laigh, low.

Directly opposed to hyperbole is understatement. Sometimes the singers intend it to be ironical or merely humorous. Most of the time, however, whether the singers intended it or not, understatements point up the tragic conception of life held by the ballad folk. Both women and men in the ballads suffer horrors in stoical silence and bear their grief dry-eyed. Heroics there are, but they are muted. One of the noblest utterances in all poetry is Sir Andrew Barton's speech inspiriting his men as he lies dying of an arrow wound:

> "Ffight on my men," sayes Sir Andrew Bartton,
> "I am hurt, but I am not slaine;
> I'le lay mee downe and bleed a-while,
> And then I'le rise and ffight againe."

Surely it is frivolous to regard as a mere figure of speech what is so palpably the unconscious reflection of a way of life in which violence, feud, barbaric cruelty, and impulses of revenge and lust work themselves out with elemental boldness.

Ballad narration analyzed. The narrative techniques and the idiosyncrasies of tone and language we have been talking about can be neatly shown at work in the somewhat untypical ballad "The Bonny Earl of Murray," which laments the slaying of the popular earl in 1592 at the hands of his enemy Huntly, who was acting on a commission from the king of Scotland to apprehend Murray. The folk by whom the ballad was sung had an immediate relation to the event; there was thus little need for the historical information that a modern reader requires. We begin with a wailing dirge wonderfully enhanced by the lambent heaviness of the melody:

> Ye Highlands, and ye Lawlands,
> Oh where have you been?
> They have slain the Earl of Murray,
> And they layd him on the green.

The narrator here speaks for the grief-stricken admirers of the earl. The second stanza jumps without explanation from the green at Leith to the palace at Edinburgh. Though the speaker is not named, from what is being said we easily deduce that it is the king addressing Huntly.

"Now wae be to thee, Huntly!
    And wherefore did you sae?
I bade you bring him wi' you,
    And forbade you him to slay."

Next follows a passage of incremental repetition (stanzas 3–5).
We are lulled into taking the first stanza as mere reminiscence
and eulogy, but as soon as the repetition begins, we are caught
up in a train of suspense that intensifies with each line and cul-
minates in the ballad's surprise denouement:

He was a braw gallant,
    And he rid at the ring;
And the bonny Earl of Murray,
    Oh he might have been a king!

He was a braw gallant,
    And he play'd at the ba';
And the bonny Earl of Murray
    Was the flower amang them a'.

He was a braw gallant,
    And he play'd at the glove;
And the bonny Earl of Murray,
    Oh he was the Queen's love!

Sung at slower pace and with emphasis, the last line insinuates
that the king had purposefully sent Huntly, notoriously Murray's enemy, to arrest the earl because he was jealous of the
queen's love for Murray and wanted him slain. The final stanza
invites pathos by turning to the grief of the widowed Countess
of Murray:

Oh lang will his lady
    Look o'er the castle Down,
Eer she see the Earl of Murray
    Come sounding thro the town!

Ballad Subjects

By far the largest group of ballads deals with the stuff of
tabloid journalism—sensational tales of lust, revenge, and do-

mestic crime. Unwed mothers slay their newborn babes; lovers unwilling to marry their pregnant mistresses brutally murder the poor women, for which, without fail, they are justly punished. Slighted mistresses take cruel revenge, as do husbands who discover their wives unfaithful. Brothers kill one another out of jealousy or in rivalry over a girl. "The Cruel Brother" stabs his sister because she neglected to consult him before she married. Incest, accidental or conscious, is surprisingly frequent. Family opposition to the course of true love accounts for the conflict in dozens of song-stories, tragic or otherwise. In such contests the Freudian paradigm holds: fathers oppose the marriage of their daughters; mothers attempt to frustrate their sons, or, if overridden, torment their unwelcome daughters-in-law.

Native American ballads, interestingly enough, show a predilection for the same themes, though naturally they swathe the old plots in modern circumstances. Few if any native ballads, however, treat the relations of supernatural beings and human folk, which is the concern of some of the finest British ballads. Ballads on religious subjects are hardly more common in Child's collection than they are in modern balladries. In the Middle Ages they were probably the dominant species, but after the Reformation the Protestant folk must have found their tone uncongenial. As for humorous ballads, these with monotonous regularity have to do with the shabby dealings of incompatible married couples: the cuckold, the shrewish wife, the discontented spouse who is frustrated in his or her attempt to "do in" the other partner.

Ballad Meter, Refrains, Music

Meter. Ballads in English are strophic—that is, they are written in stanzas rather than in uninterrupted series of lines. The tune rounds itself over the stanza, being repeated as many times as there are stanzas. Two stanza types account for most Child ballads: the stanza composed of two lines of four beats each, considered by Child the older form, and the stanza of four lines with four beats, three beats, four beats, three beats, only the second and fourth lines rhyming.

> (1) He's got consent frae her kin each one,
> But forgot to spiek to her brother John.
> (2) There lived a wife at Usher's Well,
> And a wealthy wife was she;
> She had three stout and stalwart sons,
> And sent them o'er the sea.

Gerould has argued that the second form is really a two-line stanza of seven beats to the line, basing his argument on the fact that the musical phrase spreads itself over lines 1 and 2 without observing the line break, then repeating itself for lines 3 and 4. This can be demonstrated by noting the correspondence of musical phrase to words in Greig's modern Scottish "Barbara Allen" (page 90 in this book), which happens to be Gerould's example. The fact that lines 1 and 3 are regularly rhymeless also recommends Gerould's theory. Unfortunately, the relation of the music to the verbal units so frequently contradicts Gerould that the printing of the ballads in four-line stanzas is still justified. Uncontestable, though not fully understood, is another Gerould observation: the beats or stresses are not of uniform weight in the ballad line, but rather are heavy and light in strict alternation. This phenomenon is probably explained by the fact that ballad tunes are in compound time, and therefore each bar has a medial beat as well as a main beat at the beginning.

Refrains. More ballads had refrains than the printed copies show because early recorders and collectors saw no point to these flourishes in texts not printed with music and sloughed them. Even now it is customary to print an inorganic refrain, one that is separable from the story lines, only with the first stanza, knowing that the reader will understand that the refrain also goes with the subsequent stanzas. In some ballads the refrain is merely the repetition of the last line of the stanza, whatever it may be, occasionally with slight embellishment—see, notably, "Lord Lovel." Not a few ballads have the very same last line for each stanza and only vary this refrain line a little at the beginning so that it connects with the earlier lines.

Nonsense refrains ("Fa la la diddle," "Hey derry, derry, down,"

"Lillumwham, lillumwham") appear frequently in ballads. Some scholars have tried to show that these strings of syllables were once sensible lines that have since been corrupted. "Hey derry, derry, down," for example, has been traced incredibly to a Druid call to prayer. Admittedly these nonsensical phrases look silly in cold print, but if one studies them in conjunction with the music, it becomes apparent that in these refrains the singers have simply chosen, without reference to sense, those random vocables on which the musical phrases are best projected.

Nonsense refrains are somewhat different from irrelevant refrains, lines which are sensible in themselves but have no connection with the story being told, such as the interspersed refrain of "The Cruel Brother":

> There was three ladies play'd at the ba',
> *With a hey ho and a lillie gay*
> There came a knight and play'd o'er them a'.
> *As the primrose spreads so sweetly.*

To say irrelevant refrains have no connection with the story, however, may be a mistake. The flower refrains we find in some love ballads—"Parsley and sage, rosemary and thyme" (see "The Elfin Knight," B)—are not merely decorative; these are all herbs that have magical properties for lovers, and to people who understood herbal lore, the continued recital of the line probably had the force of incantation. Also, certain apparently irrelevant lines have considerable atmospheric value. One thinks immediately of the gloomy, moaning refrain stanza in "Captain Car":

> *Syck, sike, and to-towe sike,*
> *And sike, and like to die;*
> *The sikest nighte that ever I abode,*
> *God lord have mercy on me!*

Whatever the work of the refrain, its function is primarily lyrical and never advances the story.

Ballad music. Ballad tunes were neglected by the early collectors, who were primarily interested in texts. They wrote expressively of the music's charm, but few of them were musically expert enough to record the songs that pleased them so greatly.

to-towe, too, too.

Even those rare ballads that did get captured on paper were incompetently noted down, because the peculiar rhythmic and tonal organization of folk music baffled musicians trained in art music. Only since the 1890s and the collecting and writing of Cecil Sharp, Anne Geddes Gilchrist, and Phillips Barry have accurate transcriptions of the tunes and trustworthy theoretical explanations become available.

The principal difference between folk and art music is that folk song is based on an archaic system of modes, a system finally discarded by sophisticated musicians upon the advent of common-practice harmony in the baroque era. Instead of the chromatic scale and the stable major and minor modes of modern music, folk songs use the six diatonic modes, to which musicians give Greek titles though they hardly conform to ancient Greek practice. These modes can be formed by playing from C to C on the white notes of the piano (Ionian, the modern major), D to D (Dorian), E to E (Phrygian), F to F (Lydian), G to G (Mixolydian), A to A (Aeolian, the natural minor). Actually, the folk music which is least affected by learned influences does not use the full seven tones of these scales, but employs gapped scales, either pentatonic (five tones) or hexatonic (six tones). Thus in a tune whose tonic is C, gaps will be detected between D and F and between A and C (pentatonic), or perhaps only one of the gaps will be open (hexatonic). Close analysis of phonograph recordings of songs which have been transcribed as using all seven tones of a modal scale often reveals that the notes which fill the gaps are "weak," showing that in reality the singer's ear was tuned to a gapped scale.

Rhythmical peculiarities are more readily detectable. Mixed time occurs frequently; note, for example, the vacillation in "James Harris; or, The House Carpenter" (page 16)—3/2, 9/4, 3/2, 5/4, 4/4. Time-measures, too, are often irregular, bars of five and seven beats being scattered among regular bars of two or four beats. Syncopation, the shifting of the accent in a measure to a note normally unaccented, would be a more striking feature in folk music if ragtime and jazz had not made such rhythmical aberrations ordinary.

As to performance, folk ballads are meant to be sung by one voice, though a group may join in the refrain. Harmonic singing, natural or arranged, has seldom been reported. In the best periods of balladry, the folk singer was unaccompanied, but this has not always been true in recent years. European singers occasionally accompany themselves with a harp or fiddle (held against the chest), or sing to someone else's accompaniment on these instruments. In America, the guitar or banjo is the favorite "backing," though some Kentuckians prefer the dulcimer—a zither-like instrument of German origin, only one of whose strings is fretted to yield a melody. But whether the ballad is accompanied or not, and whatever the quality of the singer's voice, the tune adds a great deal to the ballad, reinforcing emphatic phrases, adding richness and color to otherwise thin and insipid passages, intensifying the emotional effects. Music is especially important to the American versions of the Child ballads, since the texts have suffered badly in transmission and are often the dullest doggerel, whereas the music has maintained its quality even better than among British singers.

Once the music of the ballads was neglected; now there is danger that its importance relative to the words will be overrated. Unless music had constantly aided the folk memory, the traditional preservation of the ballads might not have been possible. But for all this, the collectors bring us back decisive evidence that the singer does not think of himself as projecting a melody. He is primarily intent on telling his story in the most straightforward and effective way within the conventions of his traditional art. If asked to hum a ballad tune without using the words, the folk singer is stymied, since to his mind the melody is simply the vehicle of the narrative.

The Varieties of Ballads

Thus far our discussion of ballad style has been based on Child ballads collected in Britain and America. It is time now to widen our survey.

Minstrel ballads. Child's collection is not all of one piece. Among his ballads are some which were not in the possession of the folk when they were recorded; they were included because they preserved certain interesting folk touches. The minstrel ballads are one such group. The medieval minstrel, a professional entertainer who catered mainly to nobles and clerics, should properly have had no connection with folk balladry, the self-created entertainment of the peasantry. But apparently minstrels condescended on occasion to spin out tales in verse for the humbler classes. Their ballads affect some of the traits of their folk audience's usual poetic fare, but on the whole the minstrel product is a far fancier thing. Impersonality goes by the board; the narrator constantly intrudes, commenting on the action or assuring us that he is not lying. Frequently he is the outspoken partisan of a noble family or a class, as in the older Robin Hood ballads, which exalt the virtues of the small landowners, the yeomanry. (Similar propaganda ballads, though more blatantly didactic, were turned out in the 1920s and 1930s by folk singers in the employ of unions.) Instead of abrupt changes of scene, we are given advance notice of the shifts and even occasional descriptions of settings; and instead of focusing on a single scene, the minstrel ballad tends to be rambling and episodic. But the minstrel's hallmarks are sufficiently analyzed in the notes to the Robin Hood ballads (see page 326). Here it is only necessary to mention that the minstrel ballads descend to us through manuscripts, not through tradition. They were too long and too diffuse to be carried in memory. And almost certainly they were recited rather than sung.

The broadside ballad. Shortly after printing presses were set up in England, vendors of broadside ballads took up their pitches in the streets of London and provincial towns. The ballads they sold for a penny or half-penny apiece were printed in three to six columns on one side of a sheet of paper, about the size of a handbill, called a broadsheet or broadside. At the top the ballad sheet was decorated with a crude woodcut, and below the title appeared a line advising that the ballad was to be sung "To the tune of . . ." (specifying a popular melody known to everyone). Broadsides were thus the urban counterpart of the folk ballads. For centuries a whole tribe of hack rhymers were kept busy grinding them out for the broadside press. Gradually the format shrunk, until in the mid-nineteenth century the broadside had dwindled to a single-column slip. London dominated the broadside world, but the "flying leaves" were printed in most large towns in the British Isles for distribution in the countryside as well as among city people. Colonial Boston supported several broadside presses. During the heyday of American broadside printing—about 1840 to 1880—broadsides and songbooks made up of broadside material were the stock in trade of several prosperous publishers in New York and Philadelphia as well as Boston. Southern Negro communities before World War I were the last American stronghold of the broadside or slip ballads; Dublin seems to have been the latter-day European center.

Few people now living have ever seen or handled broadsides, but they were for several hundred years the staple poetry and song of the semi-literate masses. News ballads, rhymed accounts of current events with heavy editorial comment, took the place of newspapers, and, like newspapers, they were extremely ephemeral. Metrical journalism of this kind made up the largest part of the broadside production, but the whole gamut of themes found in folk ballads, particularly criminal cases, also appeared on broadsides, along with human-interest pieces about poor girls who managed to snare rich husbands, lovers who outwitted their families, and infinite variations on the theme of lovers parting and reuniting. A comparatively small number of broadsides—Robin Hood tales mainly and tear-jerkers like "The Babes in the Woods"—were perennial favorites and were always in print. In addition, the more lasting pieces appeared in cheap garlands and songsters, interspersed among popular love songs and patriotic ditties.

Any ballad that got printed on a broadsheet or slip may be called a broadside, but a common style and a common outlook does emerge from the mass. As we should expect, the broadsides exploit every excuse for sensationalism. They are drenched in sentimentality; cheap pathos mars many of them; a tawdry optimism based on conventional piety and material coziness suffuses the lot. As poetry the broadsides, to be frank, are trash. The rhymers seldom rose in metrical competence or in the shaping of expression to anywhere near the level of art poetry, though they attempted it, and of course lost the simplicity of folk poetry in the attempt. The story is told in a perfunctory way, undramatically, diffusely. And, unlike the Child ballads, the broadsides are full of names, dates, places, and other pedestrian circumstance by way of attesting the novelty and veracity of the story.

Though to us the broadsides seem a world removed from folk ballads, country people both in Britain and America cherished these city cousins of their own traditional songs and were probably from the very first the chief customers of the poetical peddlers who sold them. Taken up from the printed sheet into the singer's memory, certain broadsides were submitted to traditional re-creation, a process to be described shortly, and became in the course of time genuine folk ballads. Perhaps a third of the ballads in this book have this history, as individual notes point out, and one whole genre, the "goodnight," was borrowed from broadside balladry.

Imported American balladry. Imported ballads make up the core of the American ballad repertory. In the main the imported songs are Child ballads brought to this country by English, Scottish, and Irish immigrants in the eighteenth century. The changes these ballads have undergone in the course of being naturalized into a new social environment are fascinating to study, and, in order to encourage comparisons along this line, numerous American versions have been placed in our collection side by side with their British ancestors and crucial divergences have been brought out in the headnotes. In the section on supernatural ballads, for instance, the ballads are selected to show how American singers rationalized the elf lovers and miraculous doings in which they could no longer believe. Elsewhere ("The Lass of Roch Royal") we find American singers excerpting a lyrical passage from an older ballad and treating it as an independent song. In general the naturalization process was one of giving the ballad event a local habitation and local names—as when Lord Randal becomes Johnny Randolph in Virginia—or of supplanting archaic words and old country folkways with modern phrases and equivalent American customs. British broadsides as well as traditional ballads were imported, brought over both in print and in memory, and were subjected in a similar way to American adaptation.

Native American balladry. The recent folk-song revival has commendably focused attention on ballads of native origin dealing with incidents that happened in America. Throughout our history, folk singers bred in the older ballad tradition must continually have been framing songs about unusual love affairs or murder cases or outbreaks of feud rivalry that had occurred in their neighborhoods. Of the thousands of such compositions, a few "caught on" and spread beyond the districts in which they had originated, to become eventually a part of the American songbag. All the while, the American broadside press—including not only the publishers in the large cities but also job printers who had been hired by town minstrels to make up copies of their compositions for them to peddle—was setting afloat a massive quantity of ballads, a small number of which were also taken up into tradition. Other of our native ballads derive from poems by known authors that were disseminated through songbooks and the poetry corners of newspapers before folk balladry absorbed them. But perhaps the most curious provenience is that of certain cowboy ballads ("The Buffalo Skinners," "The Cowboy's Lament," "The Lone Prairie"), which are reworkings of ballads and sentimental songs carried to the West by forty-niners and traveling troupes from eastern music halls. Australian stockmen pilfered their tunes and verse patterns from similar sources (Irish broadsides and English music-hall ditties), and occasionally, on the plains down under, an American favorite like "Billy Barlow" or T. D. English's "Ben Bolt" was the ground for a parody.

Except for the nearly complete disappearance of supernatural characters and the trappings of chivalry, American balladry occupies itself with much the same subjects as the older balladry, specifically crime, outlawry, feuds, intrafamilial conflicts, love, and lust. Incest and patricide, to be sure, are taboo in the New World (the American "Edward" kills his brother-in-law rather than his father) and sexual motives are prudishly glossed over. "The Jealous Lover," for example, is driven to murder because he does not want to marry the girl whom he has "gotten into trouble." His motivation, vital as it is to the story, has to be inferred from the vaguest hints because Fair Florella, his victim, would seem infinitely less pathetic according to American folk mores if we knew that she had lapsed from virtue. Industrial society has introduced a few stories that are basically new, such as mine disasters, railroad wrecks, bursting dams, and the tragedy of men such as John Henry who heroically compete with machines. And of course the older ballads have nothing to match the tales of occupational hazards and off-duty pranks that are the standard content of cowboy, lumberjack, whaling, and sailor ballads. Yet behind even the most American ballads, the sentiments of the ancient pieces still show through. Jesse James and Robin Hood both robbed from the rich and gave

to the poor, and the Wells Fargo men sitting atop their boxes
of gold in the baggage cars that the James boys robbed bear a
curious resemblance to the fat abbots whose packhorses Robin
relieved of their golden burden. One leaves for the historian to
decide whether the image of the railroad in the folk mind of
the 1880s can be equated with the attitude of the English peasantry of the 1280s toward the Church hierarchy.

The native ballads come from so many different sources and
have been in tradition so short a time—too short a time to be
completely made over—that they fall into a perplexing variety
of metrical forms and seem governed by no single system of
poetic conventions. Broadsides, however, have been quite definitely the strongest influence. American ballads tell their stories
with full journalistic detail, poetic effects are clumsily managed,
little is left to the imagination. The texture of the language is
generally poor and thin, though a spirited or otherwise charm-
ing tune often compensates for the poverty of the words. At
the opposite extreme in the matter of language are numerous
nineteenth-century pieces that are shot through with an archaic
vein of high-flown phraseology. "Fuller and Warren" is notorious
in this respect. The heroic Fuller, "handsome in deportment,"
courts the "choicest of the fair." He accosts Warren in melo-
dramatic accents:

"Young man, you know you've injured me to gratify your cause,
  By reporting I have left a prudent wife . . ."

And on the scaffold, as "the smiling gods of love" look down
on the proceedings, he pompously "bids the world adieu." These
fustian expressions, paradoxically, sometimes have the same
quaint ring to our ears as that of the naïvely simple phrases of
better folk ballads. Rarely do the rhetorical devices of the Child
ballads make an appearance in the native songs, and few substitute graces have been evolved in their place. Most striking
of all the differences between the British and American ballads
is the supplanting of the impersonal narrator by one who pro-
fesses to have been a participant in the story, and who tells it
therefore at embarrassingly close range and is always at hand
with subjective and pious reflections.

There are ready and valid explanations for the poorer poetic
quality of the American ballads. The youngest Child ballads,

one should always remember, are older than the oldest American ballads. Our ballads are the products of a moribund tradition; besides, they have grown up in a semi-literate atmosphere uncongenial to folk art and in competition with school poetry, vaudeville, sheet music, and, lately, the ephemeral lyrics purveyed by radio and juke box. Another unfortunate factor: those who concocted the original versions of the American ballads, as well as the folk singers who have transmitted them, have not had a single standard of poetic practice in their minds. Their tastes rather have been contaminated by the style of school poems and stage songs; they have thus tended to produce mediocre art poetry which is folk poetry only because it is in the possession of the folk. But few of us are deeply bothered by the poetic lameness of the native ballads because our attention is diverted by their extrinsic charms—their tunes, their naïveté, their value as Americana, the strange light they throw on American folkways and history. And perhaps we are right in refusing to try these pieces by the strictest poetic standards, just as we would not think of comparing a country-made rocker with a museum Chippendale or the hooked rugs of the state fair with Persian Ispahans.

Negro ballads. American Negro ballads deserve a special word. They have not been set apart in this book because, for one thing, most of them are sung by both Negro and white singers; for another, the finest of them—"John Henry," "Frankie and Albert," "Casey Jones"—are the joint creation of both races. There is admittedly a distinct Negro ballad style, as I have tried to illustrate by contrasting the Negro and white versions of "Dupree." Judging from the field collections of Negro song, the typical Negro ballad is a loose arrangement of stanzas interspersed with occasional lines, excellent in themselves but irrelevant to the story, which have floated in from other songs. Negro singers appear to be little interested in shaping their stories toward an effective climax, and their ballads therefore lack cohesiveness and design. Well-organized ballads such as "Frankie and Albert" or "Casey Jones" are radically untypical of Negro balladry in this respect, and even if we did not have certain knowledge that the popular forms of these ballads had been put together by persons trained in the white folk-song tradition, we could infer the fact.

But having noted the Negro singers' lack of constructive power, one must concede their superiority in most other departments. Of all American ballads, those of Negro origin are the only ones which match the old-world ballads in vigor and violence. They also resemble the older ballads in having evolved a rhetoric of repetition and in using ellipsis suggestively. And musically, of course, Negro folk songs are the most interesting we have.

Other ballad areas. Although British and American ballads preponderate, our collection fairly represents, I think, the other English-speaking countries of the world. "America" and "American" in this book should in most cases be understood to include Canada, for the ballads do not recognize political boundaries. Nova Scotia and Newfoundland, which furnish us at least a dozen fine texts, make up one ballad area with New England; the shanty songs in the lumber camps of Maine and Michigan are interchangeable with those sung in Northern Ontario. Symbolically, Young Monroe, the hero of the most popular shanty-boy ballad among singers in the United States, was probably a Canadian. Since French songs could not be included, we have not of course done justice to Canadian folk song as a whole. For a similar reason, Ireland and the Scottish Isles, whose best singers use Gaelic, come off less well than they deserve, even though a great number of our pages are flavored with brogue and the dialect of the Lowlands. To complement the continental Negro tradition, the West Indies have been drawn on for a few texts. Our Australian samples were chosen to show how much alike were the responses of cowboy and stockman to the lonely business of herding the world's cattle.

Ballad Origins and Transmission

Much hard language has passed between scholars over the question of ballad origins. Two camps have kept up the word-battle, communalists and individualists. Communalists speculate that the prototype of the older traditional ballads originated during choral dances among the medieval folk and were composed spontaneously by the assembled dancing throng. Their opponents argue that nothing of any artistic worth could be produced in this fashion: a ballad is the creation of some anonymous entertainer, perhaps even a learned poet, which fell among the folk and became folk song through some vague process of erosion.

Neither theory is wholly adequate. Communalists have to admit that no extant ballad was composed by the method they reconstruct; nonetheless, their conjectures throw interesting light on the refrains, which undoubtedly have some connection with the dance, and their interpretation of structural repetition as an outgrowth of choral singing is also convincing. The error of the individualists is not in their insistence that each ballad had an individual author, but rather in their tendency to consider folk songs as nothing more than degenerate relics of older, sophisticated songs. If the Child ballads were miscellaneous cast-offs, we would not be able to discover in them—as we do—a standard, generic style significantly unlike anything in sophisticated verse. For ballad tradition is not, as some individualists seem to think, simply a means of transmitting ballads. And the result of such transmission need not always be degeneration. Tradition in the healthy days of balladry was a constructive, creative process. Guided by a superintending pattern, it was capable of remaking all manner of diverse material into ballads. This pattern, the essential traits of ballad style, is balladness; the origin of this pattern, not the origin of any individual ballad, is the proper concern of theories about ballad origins.

How then, putting theory into practice, did a ballad come into being? An individual singer or minstrel commemorated a local event in song. Most such songs hardly outlasted the memory of the events that occasioned them, but our hypothetical song is one of the few that the community happened to adopt. Each time the story was sung, new variations crept in, since the communal memory was not restrained by a fixed, written text. Variations that lived up to the community standard of taste were incorporated in the embryo ballad; the others were discarded. Always the tendency of variation was to mold the song as an individual expression toward the ballad as a communal expression. After only a few generations, or after only spreading through a few communities laterally in one generation, the ballad was radically altered. But as long as a ballad remains in tradition, its form never sets; variation is constantly working on it, improving or corrupting. Nor does the fact that a ballad gets recorded by a collector inhibit further variation. It is for this reason that ballads, unlike poems, exist in so many versions and variants, each of which captures in print the ballad only as it was at one place and at one moment in its protean existence.

All post-medieval balladry is the product of a progressively deteriorating tradition. The broadsides were probably the first blow. They flooded the countryside in such numbers that traditional balladry was overwhelmed. And they not only competed with the folk ballads as entertainment, but, more insidiously, they undermined the folk art itself by planting a competing pattern of storytelling in the folk singer's mind, thus confusing the traditionalizing process. Broadsides, as I have mentioned before, were frequently made over into folk ballads; in general, however, they resisted transformation. One reason they could not be transformed was that popular broadsides were constantly being reprinted. A folk singer who had in memory a broadside-become-traditional-ballad would see a fresh reprint of the original broadside, and—such is the tyranny of print—would relearn the ballad as it appeared on the sheet. In this way, the changes the broadside had undergone during its tour in tradition would be wiped out. But even if the broadside had never been invented, folk balladry was doomed. Communities in which conditions congenial to the making and singing of ballads prevail have steadily decreased everywhere. Universal education has weakened the communal memory and easier communications have acquainted the folk with other and more passive forms of entertainment: in addition to the broadsides and songbooks, one must arraign the newspaper, radio, and phonograph. And so it has come about that the modern folk are content with the debased leavings of higher culture in place of arts and diversions of their own making. "We don't sing many of the old songs now," a Tennessee singer confessed to a collector (Coffin, p. 12). "Radio has come in and we have to keep up with 'Flat Foot Floogie' . . ."

In the last decade there has been a sudden burst of interest in folk song, as anyone who has recently browsed in a bookstore or record shop must have observed. But one must not be misled by the word "revival" into thinking that this interest means the coming to life again of traditional folk balladry. On

its own proper level and as a living art, balladry has almost
ceased to exist and could only be revived by setting back the
clock and civilization several hundred years. What we call the
folk-song revival is actually the translation of folk song from
an active life on the folk level to a sort of museum life on the
sophisticated level. This being the case, a ballad editor should
think of himself as a lepidopterist preparing and labeling specimens for exhibit cases. A mounted butterfly is a poor thing beside a hovering one and a ballad in a book is a poor substitute
for one sung in an authentic folk gathering, but perhaps there
is some merit in setting out a display of species before the genus
becomes extinct.

Acknowledgments

In putting together this collection I have been helped by a
number of friends whose kindness must not go unacknowledged.
Anthony Saletan worked through hundreds of tunes and gave
me the benefit of his unfailing musical taste. Robert Keppel
ran down some rare texts that eluded me; Gaynor Bradish cheer-
fully shared the arduous business of proofreading. The burden
of collating manuscripts was much alleviated by the assistance
of Pascal Covici, Jr. My greatest debt, however, is to the instruc-
tion of Bartlett Jere Whiting, who has helped me to the best
ideas I have about the ballads.

THE VIKING BOOK OF

FOLK BALLADS

OF THE ENGLISH-SPEAKING WORLD

Note to the Reader

Ballads were composed and sung by illiterate or semi-literate folk, and they were often written down by persons whose education was also very limited. The reader must therefore be prepared to find many instances of bad grammar, misspellings and inconsistent spellings, though seldom should these blemishes interfere with his reading pleasure. The editor has tampered with the texts as little as possible. Only when the inconsistencies or grammatical lapses obscured the meaning have the recorded words been altered; and all such changes, as well as interpolations, have been marked by square brackets.

❀◇

1: BALLADS
OF THE SUPERNATURAL

The older British ballads, like fairy tales, owe part of their charm to the peculiar twilight atmosphere in which the stories unfold. At bottom the ballad folk have a firm grasp on facts and things; they are impelled by elemental desires; they conceive the world as a violent place and their own roles in it as unavoidably tragic. But for all this toughness and concreteness, the ballads obviously stem from a culture rich in folk beliefs and dominated by several orders of supernatural beings, some benevolent, more of them diabolic—beings in constant commerce with human folk. Charms and enchantments are common and potent; jewels, flowers, trees, in fact all natural objects, possess magical properties. Latter-day singers have not always understood these primitive beliefs or the relics of the lower mythology fossilized in the ballads, and have altered them into poor sense or nonsense. Supernatural elements in the ballads suffered particularly in the transatlantic crossing, often being sadly corrupted, discarded, or rationalized in America.

Riddles Wisely Expounded (1) [1]

In a fifteenth-century manuscript at Oxford is found the oldest version of this dialogue between the devil and a maiden. But that version lacks the wonderfully ironic conclusion of our text A (from Motherwell's MS., p. 647). In the Oxford ballad, the maiden is aware that the man accosting her is the devil and that she must answer the riddles in order to escape his power. The maiden in A, however, thinks she will secure a husband by answering the riddles. It so happens that in solving the final riddle she names "Clootie," and since to name the devil to his face is to send him down in flames, she is accidentally saved.

[1] Numbers given after the titles of certain ballads are the numbers these ballads bear in Francis J. Child's five-volume thesaurus (see *Bibliography*).

Most fairy-tale heroines caught in a riddle duel have some advance intelligence as to the solutions from a creature they have befriended. The ballad maidens, like Oedipus in the paws of the Sphinx, have only mother wit to rely upon.

The diabolic element has evaporated from later British and American versions of the ballad, the devil's place being taken by a bona fide suitor and the maiden winning a husband by her cleverness. The B text from Maine (*Bulletin*, 10:8) is representative of the modern rationalized type.

❧◊ A ◊❧

1   There was a knicht riding frae the east,
      Sing the Cather banks, the bonnie brume
    Wha had been wooing at monie a place.
      And ye may beguile a young thing sune.

2   He came unto a widow's door,
    And speird whare her three dochters were.

3   The auldest ane's to a washing gane,
    The second's to a baking gane.

4   The youngest ane's to a wedding gane,
    And it will be nicht or she be hame.

5   He sat him doun upon a stane,
    Till thir three lasses came tripping hame.

6   The auldest ane's to the bed making,
    And the second ane's to the sheet spreading.

7   The youngest ane was bauld and bricht,
    And she was to lye wi' this unco knicht.

8   "Gin ye will answer me questions ten,
    The morn ye sall be made my ain.

9   "O what is heigher nor the tree?
    And what is deeper nor the sea?

10   "Or what is heavier nor the lead?
    And what is better nor the breid?

speir, inquire. *unco,* strange. *gin,* if.

11 "O what is whiter nor the milk?
    Or what is safter nor the silk?

12 "Or what is sharper nor a thorn?
    Or what is louder nor a horn?

13 "Or what is greener nor the grass?
    Or what is waur nor a woman was?"

14 "O heaven is higher nor the tree,
    And hell is deeper nor the sea.

15 "O sin is heavier nor the lead,
    The blessing's better nor the bread.

16 "The snaw is whiter nor the milk,
    And the down is safter nor the silk.

17 "Hunger is sharper nor a thorn,
    And shame is louder nor a horn.

18 "The pies are greener nor the grass,
    And Clootie's waur nor a woman was."

19 As sune as she the fiend did name,
    He flew awa in a blazing flame.

❧ B ❧

1   'Twas of a gay young cavalier,
        Of honor and renown;
    All for to seek a lady fair,
        He rode from town to town.

2   'Twas at a widow woman's door,
        He drew his rein so free;
    For by her side the knight espied
        Her comely daughters three.

3   Small marvel if his gallant heart
        Beat quick within his breast;
    'Twas hard to choose, yet hard to lose,
        Which might he wed the best.

waur, worse. *pie*, green (French) woodpecker.

4 "Come, maidens, pretty maidens,
       Come read my riddles three;
   And she who reads the best of all,
       My loving bride shall be;

5 "Oh, tell me what is longer
       Than the longest path there be;
   And tell me what is deeper
       Than is the deepest sea.

6 "And tell me what is louder
       Than is the loudest horn;
   And tell me what is sharper
       Than is the sharpest thorn

7 "And tell me what is greener
       Than the grass on yonder hill,
   And tell me what is crueller
       Than a wicked woman's will."

8 The eldest and the second maid,
       They sat and thought a while;
   The youngest she looked up to him,
       And said with a merry smile;

9 "Love, surely it is longer
       Than the longest path there be;
   And Hell, they say is deeper
       Than is the deepest sea;

10 "Thunder, I know is louder
       Than is the loudest horn;
   And hunger it is sharper
       Than is the sharpest thorn;

11 "I know a deadly poison, greener
       Than the grass on yonder hill;
   And a foul fiend is crueller
       Than a wicked woman's will."

12 Now scarcely had she spoke those words,
       When the youth was at her side;
   'Twas all for what she answered him
       He claimed her for his bride.

13 The eldest and the second maid,
They pondered and were dumb;
And they, perchance, are waiting yet,
Some other one to come.

14 Now maidens, pretty maidens,
Be neither coy nor shy,
But always, when a lover speaks,
Look kindly and reply.

The Elfin Knight (2)

Here the elfin knight sets his prospective bride a series of impossible tasks; she counters (beginning at stanza 10 in A) with a series equally impossible. The burden or refrain of A, "My plaid awa," etc., is unique, as Child points out, in being longer than the stanza it accompanies. From numerous Scottish lyrics which use the plaid-blown-away motif, one deduces that the line refers covertly to the surrender of chastity. Ballad elves, it hardly needs saying, are full-grown, lusty men, not the diminutive, sexless creatures of nursery stories. Though preserved as a Scottish black-letter broadside of about 1670, the A text (from Motherwell, *Minstrelsy,* appendix) is indisputably folk ballad in style.

The B text, recorded in Boston in 1895 (*JAF,* 7:228), again shows modern tradition rejecting the supernatural element and deflating the elfin knight to a flirtatious lover. The refrain, "Let ev'ry rose grow merry in time," is a corruption of "rosemary and thyme." Both these herbs have magical properties for lovers: "Rosemary," as Ophelia says in her mad scene, "that's for remembrance"; thyme represents sexual vigor or the strength that comes with abstinence.

❀◇ A ◇❀

My plaid awa, my plaid awa,
And ore the hill and far awa,
And far awa to Norrowa,
My plaid shall not be blown awa.

1 The elphin knight sits on yon hill,
      Ba, ba, ba, lilli ba
   He blaws his horn both lowd and shril.
      The wind hath blown my plaid awa

2 He blowes it east, he blowes it west,
   He blowes it where he lyketh best.

3 "I wish that horn were in my kist,
   Yea, and the knight in my armes two."

4 She had no sooner these words said,
   When that the knight came to her bed.

5 "Thou art over young a maid," quoth he,
   "Married with me thou il wouldst be."

6 "I have a sister younger than I,
   And she was married yesterday."

7 "Married with me if thou wouldst be,
   A courtesie thou must do to me.

8 "For thou must shape a sark to me,
   Without any cut or heme," quoth he.

9 "Thou must shape it [knife]-and-sheerlesse,
   And also sue it needle-threadlesse."

10 "If that piece of courtesie I do to thee,
   Another thou must do to me.

11 "I have an aiker of good ley-land,
   Which lyeth low by yon sea-strand.

12 "For thou must eare it with thy horn,
   So thou must sow it with thy corn.

13 "And bigg a cart of stone and lyme,
   Robin Redbreast he must trail it hame.

14 "Thou must barn it in a mouse-holl,
   And thrash it into thy shoes' soll.

kist, chest. *sark,* shirt. *ley,* fallow. *eare,* plow. *bigg,* build.

15   "And thou must winnow it in thy looff,
     And also seck it in thy glove.

16   "For thou must bring it over the sea,
     And thou must bring it dry home to me.

17   "When thou hast gotten thy turns well done,
     Then come to me and get thy sark then."

18   "I'l not quite my plaid for my life;
     It haps my seven bairns and my wife."
          The wind shall not blow my plaid awa

19   "My maidenhead I'l then keep still,
     Let the elphin knight do what he will."
          The wind's not blown my plaid awa

❦◇ B ◇❦

1   As I walked out in yonder dell,
         Let ev'ry rose grow merry in time;
    I met a fair damsel, her name it was Nell;
         I said, "Will you be a true lover of mine?

2   "I want you to make me a cambric shirt,
         Let ev'ry rose grow merry in time;
    Without any seam or needlework,
         And then you shall be a true lover of mine.

3   "I want you to wash it on yonder hill,
         Let ev'ry rose grow merry in time;
    Where dew never was nor rain never fell,
         And then you shall be a true lover of mine.

4   "I want you to dry it on yonder thorn,
         Let ev'ry rose grow merry in time;
    Where tree never blossomed since Adam was born,
         And then you shall be a true lover of mine."

5   "And since you have asked three questions of me,
         Let ev'ry rose grow merry in time;
    And now I will ask as many of thee,
         And then I will be a true lover of thine.

looff, palm of the hand.   *seck,* sack.   *hap,* cover.

6   "I want you to buy me an acre of land,
      Let ev'ry rose grow merry in time;
    Between the salt sea and the sea sand,
      And then I will be a true lover of thine.

7   "I want you to plough it with an ox's horn,
      Let ev'ry rose grow merry in time;
    And plant it all over with one kernel of corn,
      And then I will be a true lover of thine.

8   "I want you to hoe it with a peacock's feather,
      Let ev'ry rose grow merry in time;
    And thrash it all out with the sting of an adder,
      And then I will be a true lover of thine."

Lady Isabel and the Elf-Knight (4)

The motive of the elf-knight who lures the enchanted princess
to the greenwood—or Wearie's Well, or a sea cliff—is somewhat
obscure in the older forms of this ballad. Probably he is merely
a demoniac Bluebeard with whom the murdering of young
maidens has become habitual. If he is a water sprite, as some
scholars suggest, it seems odd that he should drown in his own
element. Later versions supply a motive—robbery—and the elf
is humanized into a false knight. Lacking the magic horn of his
elf predecessor, false Sir John entices the girl with promises of
wealth and castles. The ruse by which the girl turns the tables
on the knight is also altered. In A, in which the supernatural
atmosphere is still strong, she charms him to sleep and stabs him
with his own dagger. (The heroine of a Danish version gets the
knight to put his head in her lap by promising to delouse him!)
The heftier Lady Isabel or Pretty Polly or May Colvin of the
later versions persuades the villain to turn away while she is
undressing, and, catching him unawares, pitches him into the
sea. Analogues to this ballad are found in virtually all European
languages.

Buchan (I, 22) supplies text A, which is Scottish; B is from
Missouri (Belden, p. 8).

❀❖ A ❖❀

1   Fair lady Isabel sits in her bower sewing,
      Aye as the gowans grow gay
    There she heard an elf-knight blawing his horn.
      The first morning in May

2   "If I had yon horn that I hear blawing,
    And yon elf-knight to sleep in my bosom."

3   This maiden had scarcely these words spoken,
    Till in at her window the elf-knight has luppen.

4   "It's a very strange matter, fair maiden," said he,
    "I canna blaw my horn but ye call on me.

5   "But will ye go to yon greenwood side?
    If ye canna gang, I will cause you to ride."

6   He leapt on a horse, and she on another,
    And they rode on to the greenwood together.

7   "Light down, light down, lady Isabel," said he,
    "We are come to the place where ye are to die."

8   "Hae mercy, hae mercy, kind sir, on me,
    Till ance my dear father and mother I see."

9   "Seven king's-daughters here hae I slain,
    And ye shall be the eight o them."

10   "O sit down a while, lay your head on my knee,
    That we may hae some rest before that I die."

11   She stroakd him sae fast, the nearer he did creep,
    Wi' a sma charm she lull'd him fast asleep.

12   Wi' his ain sword-belt sae fast as she ban him,
    Wi' his ain dag-durk sae sair as she dang him.

13   "If seven king's-daughters here ye hae slain,
    Lye ye here, a husband to them a'."

gowan, daisy. *luppen*, leaped. *ban*, bound. *dag-durk*, dagger.
dang, struck.

❧❖ B ❖❧

1   "Go steal your father's weight in gold,
    Likewise your mother's fee,
    And two of the best horses that there are,
    For there stands thirty-three."

2   She stole her father's weight in gold,
    And likewise her mother's fee,
    And two of the best horses that there were,
    For there stood thirty-three.

3   She mounted on a milk-white steed
    And he upon a bay;
    They rode, they rode through the merry green woods
    Till they came to the side of the sea.

4   "Dismount, dismount, my pretty fair maid,
    Dismount, dismount, I say.
    There are six king's daughters I've drowned here
    And you the seventh shall be.

5   "You must take off those costly robes
    And lay them down by me.
    They are too costly, ah! by far
    To rot in the bottom of the sea."

6   "If I take off these costly robes
    And lay them down by thee,
    You must turn yourself all round and round
    All for to face that tree."

7   He turned himself all round and round
    All for to face the tree;
    And manfully she picked him up
    And flung him into the sea.

8   "Lie there, lie there, you false villain,
    Lie there instead of me.
    If there are six king's daughters you've drowned here,
    Go, keep them company."

9   "O, give me hold [of] your lily-white finger,
     Or give me your whole hand,
     And you shall be the lady of my house
     And own one half of my land."

10   "I will not give you my lily-white finger,
     I won't give you my whole hand;
     I will not be the lady of your house
     Or own one half of your land."

11   She mounted on the milk-white steed,
     But now she led the bay.
     She rode, she rode through the merry green woods
     Till she came to the parrot's tree.

12   "O Polly, Polly, pretty Polly,
     Don't tell any tales on me.
     And your cage shall be lined with the yellow bea[ten] gold
     And locked with a silver key."

13   The old man heard the parrot's cry
     And unto her did say,
     "O Polly, Polly, pretty Polly,
     What makes you cry so long today?"

14   "The old cat came to my cage door,
     And that's what worried me.
     I called upon your pretty Caroline
     For to drive the old cat [a]way."

James Harris (The Demon Lover;
The House Carpenter) (243)

The Pepys broadside of about 1675 from which come the older traditional versions of this ballad has been neatly synopsized by Child (IV, 361):

Jane Reynolds and James Harris, a seaman, had exchanged vows of marriage. The young man was pressed as a sailor, and after three years was reported as dead; the young woman married a ship-carpenter, and they lived together happily for four years, and had children. One night when the carpenter was absent from home, a spirit rapped at the window and announced himself as James Harris, come after an absence of seven years to claim the woman for his wife. She explained the state of things, but upon obtaining assurance that her long-lost lover had the means to support her—seven ships upon the sea—consented to go with him, for he was really *much* like a man. "The woman-kind" was seen no more after that; the carpenter hanged himself.

Scott's version, our A, elevates the demon lover to the devil himself and includes visions of heaven and hell. But, as we should expect, the demoniac character of the lover does not survive the transatlantic crossing; even the visions have largely disappeared. Instead, the American ballad, which, incidentally, is among the best-known British ballads in this country, has become a warning piece showing the retribution exacted from adulterous elopers.

Texts: A, Scott, *Minstrelsy*, ed. 1812, II, 427 (omitting stanzas considered spurious by Child); B, with tune, Columbia 15654D (1930), a Southern text.

✛✣ A ✣✛

1   "O where have you been, my long, long love,
        This long seven years and mair?"
    "O I'm come to seek my former vows
        Ye granted me before."

2   "O hold your tongue of your former vows,
        For they will breed sad strife;
    O hold your tongue of your former vows,
        For I am become a wife."

3   He turned him right and round about,
        And the tear blinded his ee:
    "I wad never hae trodden on Irish ground,
        If it had not been for thee.

4   "I might hae had a king's daughter,
        Far, far beyond the sea;

I might have had a king's daughter,
　　Had it not been for love o thee."

5 "If ye might have had a king's daughter,
　　Yer sel ye had to blame;
　Ye might have taken the king's daughter,
　　For ye kend that I was nane.

6 "If I was to leave my husband dear,
　　And my two babes also,
　O what have you to take me to,
　　If with you I should go?"

7 "I hae seven ships upon the sea—
　　The eighth brought me to land—
　With four-and-twenty bold mariners,
　　And music on every hand."

8 She has taken up her two little babes,
　　Kiss'd them baith cheek and chin:
　"O fair ye weel, my ain two babes,
　　For I'll never see you again."

9 She set her foot upon the ship,
　　No mariners could she behold;
　But the sails were o the taffetie,
　　And the masts o the beaten gold.

10 They had not sailed a league, a league,
　　A league but barely three,
　When dismal grew his countenance,
　　And drumlie grew his ee.

11 They had not sailed a league, a league,
　　A league but barely three,
　Until she espied his cloven foot,
　　And she wept right bitterlie.

12 "O hold your tongue of your weeping," says he,
　　"Of your weeping now let me be;
　I will shew you how the lilies grow
　　On the banks of Italy."

drumlie, gloomy.

13 "O what hills are yon, yon pleasant hills,
    That the sun shines sweetly on?"
  "O yon are the hills of heaven," he said,
    "Where you will never win."

14 "O whaten mountain is yon," she said,
    "All so dreary wi frost and snow?"
  "O yon is the mountain of hell," he cried,
    "Where you and I will go."

15 He strack the tap-mast wi his hand,
    The fore-mast wi his knee,
  And he brake that gallant ship in twain,
    And sank her in the sea.

win, achieve.

❖◇ **B** ◇❖

"Well met, well met," said an old true love, "Well met, well met," said he; "I'm just re-turn-ing from the salt, salt sea, And it's all for the love of thee."

1 "Well met, well met," said an old true love,
  "Well met, well met," said he;
  "I'm just returning from the salt, salt sea,
  And it's all for the love of thee."

2 "Come in, come in, my old true love,
  And have a seat with me.
  It's been three-fourths of a long, long year
  Since together we have been."

3 "Well I can't come in or I can't sit down,
   For I haven't but a moment's time.
   They say you're married to a house carpenter,
   And your heart will never be mine.

4 "Now it's I could have married a king's daughter dear;
   I'm sure she'd a married me;
   But I've forsaken her crowns of gold,
   And it's all for the love of thee.

5 "Now will you forsaken your house carpenter
   And go along with me?
   I'll take you where the grass grows green
   On the banks of the deep blue sea."

6 She picked up her little babe,
   And kisses gave it three.
   Says, "Stay right here, my darling little babe,
   And keep our poppa company."

7 Well he hadn't been on ship but about two weeks—
   I'm sure it was not three—
   Till his true love begin to weep and mourn
   And to weep most bitterly,

8 Says, "Are you weeping for my silver or my gold?"
   Says, "Are you weeping for my store?
   Are you weeping for that house carpenter
   Whose face you'll never see any more?"

9 "No, it's I'm not a-weeping for your silver or your gold,
   Or neither for your store;
   I am weeping for my darling little babe
   Whose face I'll never see any more."

10 Well he hadn't been on ship but about three weeks—
   I'm sure it was not four—
   Till they sprung a leak in the bottom of the ship
   And sunk for to rise no more.

Willie's Lady (6)

Willie's lady has the misfortune of having a witch for a mother-in-law, and because of the complicated series of charms with which the old woman has surrounded her, she cannot be delivered of her child. Willie's entreaties are of no use, but luckily Belly Blind, a kindly household spirit, advises Willie how to undo his mother's mischief.

The unique version is printed here from Ritson's transcript of William Tytler's Brown MS. at Harvard.

1   Willie's taen him o'er the fame,
    He's woo'd a wife and brought her hame.

2   He's woo'd her for her yellow hair,
    But [hi]s mother wrought her meikle care.

3   And meikle dolor gar'd her dree,
    For lighter she can never be.

4   But in her bow'r she sits wi' pain,
    And Willie mourns o'er her in vain.

5   And to his mother he has gane,
    That vile rank witch o' vilest kind.

6   He says: "My lady has a cup,
    Wi' gowd and silver set about.

7   "This goodly gift shall be your ain,
    And let her be lighter o' her young bairn."

8   "Of her young bairn she's never be lighter,
    Nor in her bow'r to shine the brighter.

9   "But she shall die and turn to clay,
    And you shall wed another may."

10 "Another may I'll never wed,
    Another may I'll neer bring hame."

meikle, much. *gar,* make. *dree,* suffer. *may,* maiden.

11   But sighing says that weary wight,
"I wish my life were at an end."

12   "Ye doe [ye] unto your mother again,
That vile rank witch of vile[st] kind.

13   "And say your ladie has a steed,
The like o'm's nae in the lands of Leed.

14   "For he is golden shod before,
And he is golden shod behind.

15   "An' at ilka tet of that horse's main,
There's a golden chess and a bell ringing.

16   "This goodly gift shall be your ain,
And let me be lighter of my young bairn."

17   "Of her young bairn she's never be lighter,
Nor in her bow'r to shine the brighter.

18   "But she shall die and turn to clay,
And ye shall wed another may."

19   "Another may I'll never wed,
Another may I'll neer bring hame."

20   But sighing said that weary wight,
"I wish my life were at an end."

21   "Ye doe [ye] unto your mother again,
That vile rank witch of vile[st] kind.

22   "And say your ladie has a girdle,
It's red gowd unto the middle.

23   "And ay at every silver hem,
Hangs fifty silver bells and ten.

24   "That goodlie gift shall be [your] ain,
An' lat me be lighter o' my young bairn."

25   "Of her young bairn she's never be lighter,
Nor in her bow'r to shine the brighter.

o'm's, of him is.   *ilka,* each.   *tet,* lock.

26   "But she shall die and turn to clay,
        And you shall wed another may."

27   "Another may I'll never wed,
        Another may I'll neer bring hame."

28   But sighing says that weary wight,
        "I wish my life were at an end."

29   Then out and spake the Belly Blind;
        He spake ay in good time.

30   "Ye doe ye to the market place,
        And there ye buy a loaf o' wax.

31   "Ye shape it bairn and bairnly like,
        And in twa glassen een ye pit;

32   "And bid her come to your boy's christening;
        Then notice weel what she shall do.

33   "And do you stand a little fore bye,
        And listen weel what she shall say."

34   "Oh wha has loosed the nine witch knots
        That was amo' that lady's locks?

35   "And wha has ta'en out the kaims of care
        That hangs amo' that lady's hair?

36   "And wha's ta'en down the bush o' woodbine
        That hangs atween her bower and mine?

37   "And wha has killed the master kid
        That ran beneath that lady's bed?

88   "And wha has loosed her left-foot shee,
        And latten that lady lighter be?"

39   O Willie's loosed the nine witch knots
        That was amo' that lady's locks.

40   And Willie's ta'en out the kaims o' care
        That hang amo' that lady's hair.

een, eyes.

41   And Willie's ta'en down the bush o' woodbine
      That hang atween her bower and thine.

42   And Willie has killed the master kid
      That ran beneath that lady's bed.

43   And Willie has loosed her left-foot shee,
      And latten his lady lighter be.

44   And now he's gotten a bonny young son,
      And mickle grace be him upon.

Kemp Owyne (34)

Kemp Owyne (Owen the Champion) figures in the Grail romances, but no such adventure as this ballad relates is attributed to him. The stages of his disenchantment of dove Isabel are measured out by incremental repetition, a rhetorical device to which the ballad owes much of its effectiveness.

Text: Motherwell, *Minstrelsy*, p. 374.

1   Her mother died when she was young,
         Which gave her cause to make great moan;
     Her father married the warst woman
         That ever lived in Christendom.

2   She served her with foot and hand,
         In every thing that she could dee;
     Till once, in an unlucky time,
         She threw her in ower Craigy's sea.

3   Says, "Lie you there, dove Isabel,
         And all my sorrows lie with thee;
     Till Kemp Owyne come ower the sea,
         And borrow you with kisses three,
     Let all the warld do what they will,
         Oh borrowed shall you never be!"

4   Her breath grew strang, her hair grew lang,
         And twisted thrice about the tree,

borrow, ransom.

And all the people, far and near,
　　Thought that a savage beast was she.

5　Thi[s] news did come to Kemp Owyne,
　　Where he lived, far beyond the sea;
He hasted him to Craigy's sea,
　　And on the savage beast lookd he.

6　Her breath was strang, her hair was lang,
　　And twisted was about the tree,
And with a swing she came about:
　　"Come to Craigy's sea, and kiss with me.

7　"Here is a royal belt," she cried,
　　"That I have found in the green sea;
And while your body it is on,
　　Drawn shall your blood never be;
But if you touch me, tail or fin,
　　I vow my belt your death shall be."

8　He stepped in, gave her a kiss,
　　The royal belt he brought him wi';
Her breath was strang, her hair was lang,
　　And twisted twice about the tree,
And with a swing she came about:
　　"Come to Craigy's sea, and kiss with me.

9　"Here is a royal ring," she said,
　　"That I have found in the green sea;
And while your finger it is on,
　　Drawn shall your blood never be;
But if you touch me, tail or fin,
　　I swear my ring your death shall be."

10　He stepped in, gave her a kiss,
　　The royal ring he brought him wi';
Her breath was strang, her hair was lang,
　　And twisted ance about the tree,
And with a swing she came about:
　　"Come to Craigy's sea, and kiss with me.

11   "Here is a royal brand," she said,
        "That I have found in the green sea;
     And while your body it is on,
        Drawn shall your blood never be;
     But if you touch me, tail or fin,
        I swear my brand your death shall be."

12   He stepped in, gave her a kiss,
        The royal brand he brought him wi';
     Her breath was sweet, her hair grew short,
        And twisted nane about the tree,
     And smilingly she came about,
        As fair a woman as fair could be.

The Three Ravens (The Twa Corbies) (26)

What was once common belief among the folk now frequently
has the force and wonder of poetry. We are tempted to find in
the tender devotion of the fallow doe in the ballad a mystical or
at least symbolic value. Actually we are dealing with primitive
superstition. Perhaps in the folk mind the doe is the form the
soul of a human mistress, now dead, has taken. Or it may be
that the doe was considered an animal-paramour of the dead
knight. Most probably the knight's beloved was understood to
be an enchanted woman who was metamorphosed at certain
times into an animal.

"The Twa Corbies" (B) has been called a "cynical variation"
of "The Three Ravens." The final degradation of the ballad
comes in the American comic ballad, a product of the minstrel
stage, called "The Three Crows," from which the knight and
doe have disappeared altogether.

Texts: A, Ravencroft's *Melismata*, 1611; B, Scott, *Minstrelsy,*
III, 239 (1803); C, from Indiana, Brewster, p. 55.

❀◊ A ◊❀

1   There were three ravens sat on a tree,
        Downe a downe, hay down, hay downe
brand, sword.

There were three ravens sat on a tree,
With a downe
There were three ravens sat on a tree,
They were as blacke as they might be,
With a downe derrie, derrie, derrie, downe, downe.

2 The one of them said to his mate,
"Where shall we our breakfast take?"

3 "Down in yonder greene field,
There lies a knight slain under his shield.

4 "His hounds they lie downe at his feete,
So well they can their master keepe.

5 "His haukes they flie so eagerly,
There's no fowle dare him come nie."

6 Downe there comes a fallow doe,
As great with yong as she might goe.

7 She lift up his bloudy hed,
And kist his wounds that were so red.

8 She got him up upon her backe,
And carried him to earthen lake.

9 She buried him before the prime,
She was dead herselfe ere even-song time.

10 God send every gentleman
Such haukes, such hounds, and such a leman.

❀◇ B ◇❀

1 As I was walking all alane,
I heard twa corbies making a mane;
The tane unto the t'other say,
"Where sall we gang and dine to-day?"

2 "In behint yon auld fail dyke,
I wot there lies a new-slain knight;

mane, moan. *lake,* pit. *tane,* one. *fail,* turf.

And naebody kens that he lies there,
But his hawk, his hound, and his lady fair.

3 "His hound is to the hunting gane,
His hawk, to fetch the wild-fowl hame,
His lady's ta'en another mate,
So we may mak our dinner sweet.

4 "Ye'll sit on his white hause-bane,
And I'll pike out his bonny blue een.
Wi' ae lock o' his gowden hair,
We'll theek our nest when it grows bare.

5 "Mony a one for him makes mane,
But nane sall ken whare he is gane;
O'er his white banes, when they are bare,
The wind sall blaw for evermair."

❖◇ C ◇❖

1 There were three crows sat on a tree,
O Billy McGee, McGaw;
There were three crows sat on a tree,
O Billy McGee, McGaw.
There were three crows sat on a tree,
And they were as black as crows could be;
And they all flapped their wings and cried,
"Caw! Caw! Caw!"
And they all flapped their wings and cried,
"Caw! Caw! Caw!"

2 One crow said to the other mate,
"What shall we do for grub to eat?"

3 "There is an old horse in yonder lane,
Whose body has been lately slain.

4 "We'll sit upon his old dry bones,
And pick his eyes out one by one."

5 O maybe you think there's another verse,
But there isn't.

hause-bane, neck. *theek,* thatch.

Molly Bawn

The folk versions of "Molly Bawn" are mainly traceable to nineteenth-century Irish broadsides. The story the ballad tells, however, though sadly rationalized, goes back to the dawn of European culture. For Molly Bawn is a swan-maiden, a woman under enchantment who assumes at times the form of a swan. From the emphasis on the setting of the sun in the ballad, one gathers that she became a swan each evening. While in her bird state, Molly was unwittingly shot by her hunter lover. Metamorphosis of this kind was beyond the imagination of later singers; therefore they invented the rain, the apron drawn over Molly's head, the cringing in the bushes, in order to explain her being taken for a swan. But the supernaturalism is not altogether lost—Molly's ghost returns to secure her lover's acquittal.

Text: *JAF*, 30:360, sung by a Kentuckian.

1   Jimmie Randall was a-hunting, a-hunting in the dark;
    He shot at Molly Bawn O and he missed not his [mark].
    Molly Bawn O was a-walking when the shower came down;
    She sat under a green tree the shower to shun;
    With her apron pinned around her he took her for a swan;
    He shot her and he killed her, it was poor Molly Bawn.

2   He runnèd up to her with his gun in his hand:
    "Dear Molly, dear Molly, you're the joy of my life:
    For I always intended to make you my wife."
    He went to his uncle with his locks all so gray:
    "Dear uncle, dear uncle, I've killed Molly Bawn:
    With her apron pinned around her I took her for a swan.

3   "I shot her, I killed her; it was poor Molly Bawn."
    "Stay at home, Jimmie, and don't run away;
    They never shall hang you, and I'll spend my whole farm."
    On the day of Jimmie's trial young Molly did appear,
    Saying, "Judges and jury, Jimmie Randall come clear!
    With my apron pinned around me he took me for a swan,
    And through his misfortune it was poor Molly Bawn."

The Great Silkie of Sule Skerry (113)

The folklore of the Hebrides and Orkneys—Sule or Shule Skerry is a western Orkney islet—is rich in tales of the silkies or seal-folk. Enchanted creatures, they dwell in the depth of the sea, but they occasionally come upon land, after doffing their sealskins, and pass as ordinary men, like the silkie of the ballad, who has begot a child upon an "eartly nourris," a mortal woman. Many families in the Scottish islands trace their ancestry to sealmen, and, because of a totemic taboo, will not taste seal meat. Though the denouement of this ballad may seem a contrived literary device, the Orkney islanders would consider the prophecy in keeping, because the silkies are noted for their power of foretelling the future.

Texts: A, *Proceedings, Society of Antiquaries of Scotland*, I (1852), 86; B, R. M. Fergusson, *Rambling Sketches in the Far North*, 1883, p. 140. The haunting melody for B was collected in Orkney by Professor Otto Andersson of Helsinki.

✺◊ A ◊✺

1   An eartly nourris sits and sings,
        And aye she sings, "Ba, lily wean!
    Little ken I my bairnis father,
        Far less the land that he staps in."

2   Then ane arose at her bed-fit,
        An' a grumly guest I'm sure was he:
    "Here am I, thy bairnis father,
        Although that I be not comelie.

3   "I am a man, upo the lan,
        An' I am a silkie in the sea;
    And when I'm far and far frae lan,
        My dwelling is in Sule Skerrie."

4   "It was na weel," quo the maiden fair,
        "It was na weel, indeed," quo she,

ba, lily wean, (lullaby croon).   *stap*, stop, live.   *grumly*, fierce.

"That the Great Silkie of Sule Skerrie
Suld hae come and aught a bairn to me."

5   Now he has taen a purse of goud,
And he has pat it upo her knee,
Sayin, "Gie to me my little young son,
An' tak thee up thy nourris-fee.

6   "An' it sall come to pass on a simmer's day,
When the sin shines het on evera stane,
That I will tak my little young son,
An' teach him for to swim the faem.

7   "An' thu sall marry a proud gunner,
An' a proud gunner I'm sure he'll be,
An' the very first schot that ere he schoots,
He'll schoot baith my young son and me."

aught . . . to, had . . . by.

❀◊ B ◊❀

In Nor-way lands there lived   a maid, "Bal
loo,   my babe," this_ maid be-gan;   "I
know not where   your   fa-ther is,   Or   if
land   or   sea   he   tra-vels   in."

1   In Norway lands there lived a maid,
"Balloo [my babe]," this maid began;

"I know not where [your] father is,
[Or if] land or sea he travels in."

2 It happened on a certain day,
When this fair lady fell fast asleep,
That in cam' a good grey selchie,
And set him doon at her bed feet,

3 Saying, "Awak', awak' my pretty fair maid,
For oh! how sound as thou dost sleep!
An' I'll tell thee where thy baby's father is;
He's sittin' close at thy bed feet."

4 "I pray, come tell to me thy name,
Oh! tell me where does thy dwelling be?"
"My name it is good Hein Mailer,
An' I earn my livin' oot o' the sea.

5 "I am a man upon the land;
I am a selchie in the sea;
An' whin I'm far frae every strand,
My dwellin' is in Shool Skerrie."

6 "Alas! alas! this woeful fate!
This weary fate that's been laid for me!
That a man should come frae the Wast o' Hoy,
To the Norway lands to have a bairn wi' me."

7 "My dear, I'll wed thee with a ring,
With a ring, my dear, I'll wed wi' thee."
"Thoo may go wed thee weddens wi' whom thoo wilt;
For I'm sure thoo'll never wed none wi' me."

8 "Thoo will nurse my little wee son
For seven long years upo' thy knee,
An' at the end o' seven long years
I'll come back an' pay the norish fee."

9 She's nursed her little wee son
For seven long years upo' her knee,
An' at the end o' seven long years
He cam' back wi' gold an' white monie.

10   She says, "My dear, I'll wed thee wi' a ring,
        With a ring, my dear, I'll wed wi' thee."
    "Thoo may go wed thee weddens wi' whom thoo will;
        For I'm sure thoo'll never wed none wi' me.

11   "But I'll put a gold chain around his neck,
        An' a gey good gold chain it'll be,
    That if ever he comes to the Norway lands,
        Thoo may hae a gey good guess on hi'.

12   "An' thoo will get a gunner good,
        An' a gey good gunner it will be,
    An' he'll gae oot on a May mornin'
        An' shoot the son an' the grey selchie."

13   Oh! she has got a gunner good,
        An' a gey good gunner it was he,
    An' he gaed oot on a May mornin',
        An' he shot the son and the grey selchie.

14   "Alas! alas! this woeful fate!
        This weary fate that's been laid for me!"
    An' ance or twice she sobbed and sighed,
        An' her tender heart did brak in three.

Clerk Colvill (42)

Scandinavian analogues of "Clerk Colvill" straighten out a
story which all versions in English tell rather confusedly. The
mermaid was once Clerk Colvill's love. By marrying a human
woman, he has angered her. The painful, fatal sark is her revenge.
Colvill, thus, is not being punished for adultery but rather for
unfaithfulness to his mermaid mistress.

The text is from Herd, ed. 1769, p. 302. The interpolated lines,
from William Tytler's Brown MS., have never before been
printed.

1   Clerk Colvill and his lusty dame
        Were walking in the garden green;

The belt around her stately waist
    Cost Clerk Colvill of pounds fifteen.

2   "O promise me now, Clerk Colvill,
    Or it will cost ye muckle strife,
  Ride never by the wells of Slane,
    If ye wad live and brook your life."

3   "Now speak nae mair, my lusty dame,
    Now speak nae mair of that to me;
  Did I neer see a fair woman,
    But I wad sin with her body?"

4   He's taen leave o his gay lady,
    Nought minding what his lady said,
  And he's rode by the wells of Slane,
    Where washing was a bonny maid.

5   "Wash on, wash on, my bonny maid,
    That wash sae clean your sark of silk;"
  ["It's a' for you, ye gentle knight,
    My skin is whiter than the milk."]

5* [He's taen her by the milk-white hand,
    And likewise by the grass-green sleeve,
  And laid her down upon the green,
    Nor of his lady speer'd he leave.]

6   Then loud, loud cry'd the Clerk Colvill,
    "O my head it pains me sair;"
  "Then take, then take," the maiden said,
    "And frae my sark you'll cut a gare."

7   Then she's gied him a little bane-knife,
    And frae her sark he cut a share;
  She's ty'd it round his whey-white face,
    But ay his head it aked mair.

8   Then louder cry'd the Clerk Colvill,
    "O sairer, sairer akes my head."
  "And sairer, sairer ever will,"
    The maiden crys, "till you be dead."

sark, gown. *speer,* ask. *gare,* strip of cloth.

9   Out then he drew his shining blade,
        Thinking to stick her where she stood,
     But she was vanished to a fish,
        And swam far off, a fair mermaid.

10   "O mother, mother, braid my hair;
        My lusty lady, make my bed;
     O brother take my sword and spear,
        For I have seen the false mermaid."

The Unquiet Grave (78)

The tranquillity of the dead is ruffled by the excessive grief of mourners. Cecil Sharp collected this unusually full version in the west of England (*One Hundred English Folksongs*, 1916, No. 24). He has also preserved the tune, which is one of the most beautiful English folk melodies.

Cold blows the wind to my — true love, And gen-tly drops — the rain, — I nev-er had — but one — sweet-heart, And in green - wood she — lies slain, And in green - wood she — lies slain. —

1   Cold blows the wind to my true love,
        And gently drops the rain,

I never had but one sweetheart,
   And in greenwood she lies slain,
   And in greenwood she lies slain.

2 I'll do as much for my sweetheart
   As any young man may;
  I'll sit and mourn all on her grave
   For a twelvemonth and a day.

3 When the twelvemonth and one day was past,
   The ghost began to speak;
  "Why sittest here all on my grave,
   And will not let me sleep?"

4 "There's one thing that I want, sweetheart,
   There's one thing that I crave;
  And that is a kiss from your lily-white lips—
   Then I'll go from your grave."

5 "My breast it is as cold as clay,
   My breath smells earthly strong;
  And if you kiss my cold clay lips,
   Your days they won't be long.

6 "Go fetch me water from the desert,
   And blood from out of a stone;
  Go fetch me milk from a fair maid's breast
   That a young man never had known."

7 "O down in yonder grove, sweetheart,
   Where you and I would walk,
  The first flower that ever I saw
   Is wither'd to a stalk.

8 "The stalk is wither'd and dry, sweetheart,
   And the flower will never return;
  And since I lost my own sweetheart,
   What can I do but mourn?

9 "When shall we meet again, sweetheart?
   When shall we meet again?"

> "When the oaken leaves that fall from the trees
>   Are green and spring up again,
>   Are green and spring up again."

The Wife of Usher's Well (79)

A mother's uncontrolled grief over her recently dead sons disturbs their repose. They return for a visit, not as incorporeal wraiths but as flesh-and-blood, living corpses—the typical ballad revenants. Only their birch hats—birch protects ghosts against the influence of the living—and their compulsion to be off before daylight mark the sons as ghostly visitors.

Text A, from Scott's *Minstrelsy*, II, 111, has often been praised. Especially poignant is the hint in the last line that one of the sons is leaving behind a sweetheart as well as a mother. B, from Shropshire (*Shropshire Folk-Lore*, ed. C. S. Burne, 1883, p. 541), paints out the pagan superstitions with a heavy coat of Christian coloring; while C, from North Carolina (Child, V, 294; compare *JAF*, 13:119), makes the whole visit a dream, thus deleting the supernatural altogether. One odd feature of many American versions of this ballad is a pair of stanzas in which one of the sons chides his mother, as she makes the bed and sets the table, for her excessive pride:

> She spread a downy bed for them,
>   And on it spread clean sheets;
> And on it she spread a golden spread,
>   That they might for the better sleep.

> "Take it off, take it off," the oldest said,
>   " 'Tis vanity and sin;
> And woe, woe be to this wicked world,
>   Since pride has so entered in." (Cox, p. 89)

Observe also that the sons of the older versions have become babes in America.

❊◊ A ◊❊

1   There lived a wife at Usher's Well,
       And a wealthy wife was she;
     She had three stout and stalwart sons,
       And sent them o'er the sea.

2   They hadna been a week from her,
       A week but barely ane,
     Whan word came to the carline wife
       That her three sons were gane.

3   They hadna been a week from her,
       A week but barely three,
     Whan word came to the carlin wife
       That her sons she'd never see.

4   "I wish the wind may never cease,
       Nor [fashes] in the flood,
     Till my three sons come hame to me,
       In earthly flesh and blood."

5   It fell about the Martinmass,
       When nights are lang and mirk,
     The carlin wife's three sons came hame,
       And their hats were o' the birk.

6   It neither grew in syke nor ditch,
       Nor yet in ony sheugh;
     But at the gates o Paradise,
       That birk grew fair eneugh.

7   "Blow up the fire, my maidens!
       Bring water from the well!
     For a' my house shall feast this night,
       Since my three sons are well."

8   And she has made to them a bed,
       She's made it large and wide,

carline, peasant.   *fashes,* troubles, storms.   *birk,* birch.   *syke,* rivulet
sheugh, trench.

And she's ta'en her mantle her about,
    Sat down at the bed-side.

9   Up then crew the red, red cock,
      And up and crew the gray;
    The eldest to the youngest said,
      "'Tis time we were away."

10   The cock he hadna craw'd but once,
      And clapp'd his wings at a',
    When the youngest to the eldest said,
      "Brother, we must awa'.

11   "The cock doth craw, the day doth daw,
      The channerin' worm doth chide;
    Gin we be mist out o' our place,
      A sair pain we maun bide.

12   "Fare ye weel, my mother dear!
      Fareweel to barn and byre!
    And fare ye weel, the bonny lass
      That kindles my mother's fire!"

❖◇ **B** ◇❖

1   There was a widow-woman lived in far Scotland,
      And in far Scotland she did live,
    And all her cry was upon sweet Jesus,
      Sweet Jesus so meek and mild.

2   Then Jesus arose one morning quite soon,
      And arose one morning betime,
    And away He went to far Scotland,
      And to see what the good woman want.

3   And when He came to far Scotland,

    .   .   .   .   .

    Crying, "What, O what, does the good woman want,
      That is calling so much on Me?"

4   "It's You go rise up my three sons,
      Their names, Joe, Peter, and John,

channerin', fretting, gnawing.   *gin*, if.   *byre*, cowhouse.

And put breath in their breast,
  And clothing on their backs,
And immediately send them to far Scotland,
  That their mother may take some rest."

5 Then He went and rose up her three sons,
  Their names, Joe, Peter, and John,
And did immediately send them to far Scotland,
  That their mother may take some rest.

6 Then she made up a supper so neat,
  As small, as small, as a yew-tree leaf,
  But never one bit they could eat.

7 Then she made up a bed so soft,
  The softest that ever was seen,
And the widow-woman and her three sons
  They went to bed to sleep.

8 There they lay. About the middle of the night,
  Bespeaks the youngest son:
"The white cock he has crowed once,
  The second has, so has the red."

9 And then bespeaks the eldest son:
"I think, I think it is high time
  For the wicked to part from their dead."

10 Then they [led] her along a green road,
  The greenest that ever was seen,
Until they came to some far chaperine,
  Which was builded of lime and sand;
Until they came to some far chaperine,
  Which was builded with lime and stone.

11 And then He opened the door so big,
  And the door so very wide;
Said He to her three sons, "Walk in!"
  But told her to stay outside.

12 "Go back, go back!" sweet Jesus replied,
  "Go back, go back!" says He;
"For thou hast nine days to repent
  For the wickedness that thou hast done."

13   Nine days then was past and gone,
          And nine days then was spent,
      Sweet Jesus called her once again,
          And took her to Heaven with Him.

                         ✿◇ C ◇✿

1   There was a lady fair and gay,
          And children she had three;
      She sent them away to some northern land,
          For to learn their grammaree.

2   They hadn't been gone but a very short time,
          About three months to a day,
      When sickness came to that land,
          And swept those babes away.

3   There is a king in the heavens above,
          That wears a golden crown;
      She prayed that he would send her babies home
          To-night or in the morning soon.

4   It was about one Christmas time,
          When the nights was long and cool,
      She dreamed of her three little [lonely] babes,
          Come running in their mother's room.

5   The table was fixed and the cloth was spread,
          And on it put bread and wine:
      "Come sit you down, my three little babes,
          And eat and drink of mine."

6   "We'll neither eat your bread, dear mother,
          Nor we'll neither drink your wine;
      For to our Saviour we must return
          To-night or in the morning soon."

7   The bed was fixed in the back room;
          On it were some clean white sheet,
      And on the top was a golden cloth,
          To make those little babies sleep.

8 "Wake up! wake up!" says the oldest one,
      "Wake up! it's almost day.
   And to our Saviour we must return
      To-night or in the morning soon.

9 "Green grass grows at our head, dear mother,
      Green [moss] grows at our feet;
   The tears you shed for us three babes,
      [They] wet our winding sheet."

Thomas Rymer (37)

According to a venerable Scottish legend, Thomas Rymer of
Erceldoune, a thirteenth-century poet, spent seven years in elfland. At the end of his sojourn he won from the fairy queen the
gift of prophecy that eventually made him as famous a seer as
Merlin.

Text: Jamieson, II, 7, compared with A. F. Tytler's Brown MS.

1 True Thomas lay o'er yond grassy bank,
      And he beheld a lady gay,
   A lady that was brisk and bold,
      Come riding o'er the fernie brae.

2 Her skirt was of the grass-green silk,
      Her mantel of the velvet fine,
   At ilka tate o' her horse's mane
      Hung fifty siller bells and nine.

3 True Thomas he took off his hat,
      And bowed him low down till his knee:
   "All hail, thou mighty Queen of Heaven!
      For your like on earth I never did see."

4 "O no, O no, True Thomas," she says,
      "That name does not belong to me;
   I am but the queen of fair Elfland,
      And I am come here for to visit thee.

fernie brae, fern-covered bank. *ilka,* each. *tate,* lock.

5   "But ye maun go wi' me now, Thomas,
       True Thomas, ye maun go wi' me,
    For ye maun serve me seven years,
       Thro weel or wae, as may chance to be."

6   She turned about her milk-white steed,
       And took True Thomas up behind,
    And aye whene'er her bridle rang,
       The steed flew swifter than the wind.

7   For forty days and forty nights
       He wade thro red blude to the knee,
    And he saw neither sun nor moon,
       But heard the roaring of the sea.

8   O they rade on, and farther on,
       Until they came to a garden green:
    "Light down, light down, ye ladie free,
       Some of that fruit let me pull to thee."

9   "O no, O no, True Thomas," she says,
       "That fruit maun not be touched by thee,
    For a' the plagues that are in hell
       Light on the fruit of this countrie.

10   "But I have a loaf here in my lap,
       Likewise a bottle of claret wine,
    And now ere we go farther on,
       We'll rest a while, and ye may dine."

11   When he had eaten and drunk his fill,
       "Lay down your head upon my knee,"
    The lady sayd, "ere we climb yon hill,
       And I will show you ferlies three.

12   "O see not ye yon narrow road,
       So thick beset wi' thorns and briers?
    That is the path of righteousness,
       Tho after it but few enquires.

13   "And see not ye yon braid braid road,
       That lies across yon lilly leven?

ferlies, wonders.   *leven,* glade.

That is the path of wickedness,
    Tho some call it the road to heaven.

14   "And see not ye that bonny road,
        Which winds about the fernie brae?
    That is the road to fair Elfland,
        Whe[re] you and I this night maun gae.

15   "But Thomas, ye maun hold your tongue,
        Whatever you may hear or see,
    For gin ae word you should chance to speak,
        You will neer get back to your ain countrie."

16   He has gotten a coat of the even cloth,
        And a pair of shoes of velvet green,
    And till seven years were past and gone
        True Thomas on earth was never seen.

Tam Lin (39)

Few ballads carry forward so much ancient folklore as "Tam Lin." The setting is the taboo grounds of Carterhaugh. Janet plucks a rose, a flower under the special protection of elves and fairies, and this mild provocation gains her an interview with Tam Lin. Though the ballad becomes purposefully vague at this point (after stanza 7), it is clear that a serious amorous encounter takes place. Pregnancy follows. Janet wants a father for her child; Tam Lin is no less anxious to return to the human world from which he was stolen. Every seven years the elves are required to pay a tithe to hell—an elf plump for sacrifice. To save one of their own number, they usually pass off an abducted mortal on the devil. Being "full of flesh," Tam Lin fears that he will be the next victim. To disenchant her lover, Janet must pull him from his horse while he rides in the fairy troop and hold him fast as he passes through a series of repulsive shapes. (Peleus won Thetis, the mother of Achilles, in a similar kind of wrestling match.) A bath completes Tam Lin's redemption.

The final stanza may require a word of explanation. It is not revenge that stirs the queen of fairy to wish that she had torn

gin. if.

out Tam Lin's eyes and given him wooden ones. By failing to
take this security precaution, she has allowed Tam Lin to return to the human world with all the secrets of fairyland.

Robert Burns contributed the present text to James Johnson's
Scots Musical Museum (1787-1803), No. 411.

1   O I forbid you, maidens a',
  That wear gowd on your hair,
 To come or gae by Carterhaugh,
  For young Tam Lin is there.

2   There's nane that gaes by Carterhaugh
  But they leave him a wad,
 Either their rings, or green mantles,
  Or else their maidenhead.

3   Janet has [kilted] her green kirtle
  A little aboon her knee,
 And she has broded her yellow hair
  A little aboon her bree,
 And she's awa to Carterhaugh,
  As fast as she can hie.

4   When she came to Carterhaugh
  Tam Lin was at the well,
 And there she fand his steed standing,
  But away was himsel.

5   She had na pu'd a double rose,
  A rose but only twa,
 Till up then started young Tam Lin,
  Says, "Lady, thou's pu nae mae.

6   "Why pu's thou the rose, Janet,
  And why breaks thou the wand?
 Or why comes thou to Carterhaugh
  Withoutten my command?"

7   "Carterhaugh, it is my ain,
  My daddie gave it me;

wad, forfeit. *kilt,* tuck up. *kirtle,* petticoat. *bree,* brow.

I'll come and gang by Carterhaugh,
  And ask nae leave at thee."

8 Janet has kilted her green kirtle
     A little aboon her knee,
   And she has snooded her yellow hair
     A little aboon her bree,
   And she is to her father's ha',
     As fast as she can hie.

9 Four and twenty ladies fair
     Were playing at the ba',
   And out then cam the fair Janet,
     Ance the flower among them a'.

10 Four and twenty ladies fair
      Were playing at the chess,
    And out then cam the fair Janet,
      As green as onie glass.

11 Out then spak an auld grey knight,
      Lay o'er the castle wa',
    And says, "Alas, fair Janet, for thee
      But we'll be blamed a'."

12 "Haud your tongue, ye auld fac'd knight,
      Some ill death may ye die!
    Father my bairn on whom I will,
      I'll father nane on thee."

13 Out then spak her father dear,
      And he spak meek and mild;
    "And ever alas, sweet Janet," he says,
      "I think thou gaes wi' child."

14 "If that I gae wi' child, father,
      Mysel maun bear the blame;
    There's neer a laird about your ha'
      Shall get the bairn's name.

15 "If my love were an earthly knight,
      As he's an elfin grey,

maun, must.

I wad na gie my ain true-love
   For nae lord that ye hae.

16 "The steed that my true-love rides on
     Is lighter than the wind;
  Wi' siller he is shod before,
     Wi' burning gowd behind."

17 Janet has kilted her green kirtle
     A little aboon her knee,
  And she has snooded her yellow hair
     A little aboon her bree,
  And she's awa to Carterhaugh,
     As fast as she can hie.

18 When she cam to Carterhaugh,
     Tam Lin was at the well,
  And there she fand his steed standing,
     But away was himsel.

19 She had na pu'd a double rose,
     A rose but only twa,
  Till up then started young Tam Lin,
     Says, "Lady, thou pu's nae mae.

20 "Why pu's thou the rose, Janet,
     Amang the groves saw green,
  And a' to kill the bonnie babe,
     That we gat us between?"

21 "O tell me, tell me, Tam Lin," she says,
     "For's sake that died on tree,
  If eer ye was in holy chapel,
     Or Christendom did see?"

22 "Roxbrugh he was my grandfather,
     Took me with him to bide,
  And ance it fell upon a day
     That wae did me betide.

23 "And ance it fell upon a day,
     A cauld day and a snell,
  When we were frae the hunting come,

snell, frosty.

That frae my horse I fell;
The Queen o Fairies she caught me,
    In yon green hill to dwell.

24 "And pleasant is the fairy land,
    But, an eerie tale to tell,
Ay at the end of seven years
    We pay a tiend to hell;
I am sae fair and fu o flesh,
    I'm feard it be mysel.

25 "But the night is Halloween, lady,
    The morn is Hallowday;
Then win me, win me, an ye will,
    For weel I wat ye may.

26 "Just at the mirk and midnight hour
    The fairy folk will ride,
And they that wad their true-love win,
    At Miles Cross they maun bide."

27 "But how shall I thee ken, Tam Lin,
    Or how my true-love know,
Amang sae mony unco knights
    The like I never saw?"

28 "O first let pass the black, lady,
    And syne let pass the brown,
But quickly run to the milk-white steed,
    Pu ye his rider down.

29 "For I'll ride on the milk-white steed,
    And ay nearest the town;
Because I was an earthly knight
    They gie me that renown.

30 "My right hand will be glovd, lady,
    My left hand will be bare,
Cockt up shall my bonnet be,
    And kaimd down shall my hair,
And thae's the takens I gie thee,
    Nae doubt I will be there.

tiend, tithe, tax. *unco,* strange. *syne,* then. *thae,* these.

31   "They'll turn me in your arms, lady,
      Into an esk and adder;
    But hold me fast, and fear me not,
      I am your bairn's father.

32   "They'll turn me to a bear sae grim,
      And then a lion bold;
    But hold me fast, and fear me not,
      As ye shall love your child.

33   "Again they'll turn me in your arms
      To a red hot gaud of airn;
    But hold me fast, and fear me not,
      I'll do to you nae harm.

34   "And last they'll turn me in your arms
      Into the burning gleed;
    Then throw me into well water,
      O throw me in wi' speed.

35   "And then I'll be your ain true-love,
      I'll turn a naked knight;
    Then cover me wi' your green mantle,
      And cover me out o sight."

36   Gloomy, gloomy was the night,
      And eerie was the way,
    As fair Jenny in her green mantle
      To Miles Cross she did gae.

37   About the middle o the night
      She heard the bridles ring;
    This lady was as glad at that
      As any earthly thing.

38   First she let the black pass by,
      And syne she let the brown;
    But quickly she ran to the milk-white steed,
      And pu'd the rider down.

39   Sae weel she minded what he did say,
      And young Tam Lin did win;

gaud of airn, iron bar. *gleed,* coal.

Syne coverd him wi' her green mantle,
    As blythe's a bird in spring.

40   Out then spak the Queen o Fairies,
    Out of a bush o broom:
"Them that has gotten young Tam Lin
    Has gotten a stately groom."

41   Out then spak the Queen o Fairies,
    And an angry woman was she:
"Shame betide her ill-far'd face,
    And an ill death may she die,
For she's taen awa the boniest knight
    In a' my companie.

42   "But had I kend, Tam Lin," she says,
    "What now this night I see,
I wad hae taen out thy twa grey een,
    And put in twa een o tree."

Sweet William's Ghost (77)

Sweet William, killed apparently in some foreign war, cannot rest until he has recovered the troth plighted to Lady Margret. Like most ballad ghosts, William is not distinguishable from a living man and must convince his beloved that he can no longer answer her passion. Margret gives back the troth in A by striking the corpse's breast; in another Scottish version (Herd MSS.— Child II, 230), a more primitive custom is preserved—the troth is symbolically transferred to an intermediate object, a wand:

Up she has tain a bright long wand,
And she has straked her trouth thereon;
She has given [it] him out at the shot-window,
Wi' many a sad sigh and heavy groan.

In version B, from *The Green Mountain Songster*, Sandgate, Vermont, 1823, the symbols at the graveyard are given a fuller allegorical interpretation.

een, eyes.   *tree,* wood.
strake, stroke.

Texts: A, Ramsay, *Tea-Table Miscellany*, ed. 1750, p. 324; B,
as above.

✿◇ A ◇✿

1 There came a ghost to Margret's door,
       With many a grievous groan,
   And ay he tirled at the pin,
       But answer made she none.

2 "Is that my father Philip,
       Or is't my brother John?
   Or is't my true-love, Willy,
       From Scotland new come home?"

3 " 'Tis not thy father Philip,
       Nor yet thy brother John;
   But 'tis thy true-love, Willy,
       From Scotland new come home.

4 "O sweet Margret, O dear Margret,
       I pray thee speak to me;
   Give me my faith and troth, Margret,
       As I gave it to thee."

5 "Thy faith and troth thou's never get,
       Nor yet will I thee lend,
   Till that thou come within my bower,
       And kiss my cheek and chin."

6 "If I should come within thy bower,
       I am no earthly man;
   And should I kiss those rosy lips,
       Thy days will not be lang.

7 "O sweet Margret, O dear Margret,
       I pray thee speak to me;
   Give me my faith and troth, Margret,
       As I gave it to thee."

8 "Thy faith and troth thou's never get,
       Nor yet will I thee lend,

tirled . . . , rattled at the latchpin.

Till you take me to yon kirk,
And wed me with a ring."

9 "My bones are buried in yon kirk-yard,
Afar beyond the sea,
And it is but my spirit, Margret,
That's now speaking to thee."

10 She stretched out her lily-white hand,
And, for to do her best,
"Hae, there's your faith and troth, Willy,
God send your soul good rest."

11 Now she has kilted her robes of green,
A piece below her knee,
And a' the live-lang winter night
The dead corp followed she.

12 "Is there any room at your head, Willy?
Or any room at your feet?
Or any room at your side, Willy,
Wherein that I may creep?"

13 "There's no room at my head, Margret,
There's no room at my feet:
There's no room at my side, Margret,
My coffin's made so meet."

14 Then up and crew the red, red cock,
And up then crew the gray:
"'Tis time, 'tis time, my dear Margret,
That you were going away."

15 No more the ghost to Margret said,
But, with a grievous groan,
Evanished in a cloud of mist,
And left her all alone.

16 "O stay, my only true-love, stay,"
The constant Margret cry'd;
Wan grew her cheeks, she clos'd her een,
Stretch'd her soft limbs, and dy'd.

❀◇ B ◇❀

1   Lady Margaret sat in her bowry all alone,
And under her bowry east window she heard three pitiful groans;
Oh, is it my father dear, she said, or is it my brother John,
Or is it my loving dear William from Scotland newly come home?

2   It is not your father, he said, nor is it your brother John,
But is your loving dear William from Scotland newly come home.
Oh have you brought me any gold, she said, or have you brought me any fee,
Or have you bro't any fine linnen from Scotland home to me?

3   I have not bro't you any gold, he said, nor have I bro't you any fee,
But I've brought you my winding sheet 'tis rotted off from me;
Give me my troth, Lady Margaret, he said, I'll give thee thine again,
For the longer I tarry and talk with you the sharper'll be my pain.

4   I will not give you your troth, she said, nor you give mine to me,
Until you carry me to fair Scotland your bowry for to see.
My bowry 'tis a poor bowry, it is both deep and dim;
My bowry 'tis a poor bowry to put a fair lady in.

5   I will not give you your troth, she said, nor will I have mine again,
Until you kiss my merry merry lips or wed me with a ring.
I cannot kiss your merry, merry lips, my breath it is so strong,
My face it is all worm-eaten, I am no living man.

bowry, bower.

6   She pulled up her petticoat, almost unto her knee,
    And in a cold and a winter's night the pale ghost follow'd
       she;
    Oh who are these, Sweet William, she said, are standing at
       your head?
    They're three pretty maids, Lady Margaret, he said, that I
       refused to wed.

7   Oh who are these, sweet William, she said, are standing at
       your feet?
    They're three children, Lady Margaret, he said, that I
       refus'd to keep.
    Oh who are these, sweet William, she said, are standing by
       your side?
    They're three pretty maids, Lady Margaret, he said, waiting
       my soul to guide.

8   The first is for my drunkenness, the second's for my pride,
    The third is for my false swearing and wandering in the
       night;
    Give me my troth, Lady Margaret, he said, I'll give thee
       thine again.
    For the longer I tarry and talk with you the sharper'll be
       my pain.

9   She had a handkerchief in her hand, she spread it on the
       ground,
    Saying, here is your faith and troth William, God lay your
       body down;
    She had a willow in her hand, she laid it across his breast,
    Saying, here is your faith and troth, William, I wish your
       soul at rest.

10 So here is your faith and troth, William, and give me mine
      again,
    But if you're dead and gone to hell in hell you must remain.

Fair Margaret and Sweet William (74)

Spontaneous death of a broken heart occurs not uncommonly in ballads, and chiding ghosts are scarcely rarer. The rose-and-briar ending to this tragic piece is likewise a commonplace, the decorative, sentimental conclusion of a score of ballads. In America, Lady Margaret often loses her title, becoming Lydia Margret or Lillie Margaret. Occasional American versions banish superstition by treating the ghost's visit as a dream and syncopating it with the dream of wild swine. Such is the case in a North Carolina text (Brown, II, 83):

> "I dreamt a dream," Sweet William said,
> "That troubles me in my head;
> I dreamt my hall was full of wild swine
> And Lady Margaret was dead."

Text: Harvard Percy Papers, contributed by the Dean of Derry.

1   Sweet William would a-wooing ride,
     His steed was lovely brown;
   A fairer creature than Lady Margaret
     Sweet William could find none.

2   Sweet William came to Lady Margaret's bower,
     And knocked at the ring,
   And who so ready as Lady Margaret
     To rise and to let him in.

3   Down then came her father dear,
     Clothed all in blue:
   "I pray, Sweet William, tell to me
     What love's between my daughter and you?"

4   "I know none by her," he said,
     "And she knows none by me;
   Before tomorrow at this time
     Another bride you shall see."

5 Lady Margaret at her bower-window,
    Combing of her hair,
  She saw Sweet William and his brown bride
    Unto the church repair.

6 Down she cast her iv'ry comb,
    And up she tossed her hair,
  She went out from her bow'r alive,
    But never so more came there.

7 When day was gone, and night was come,
    All people were asleep,
  In glided Margaret's grimly ghost,
    And stood at William's feet.

8 "How d'ye like your bed, Sweet William?
    How d'ye like your sheet?
  And how d'ye like that brown lady,
    That lies in your arms asleep?"

9 "Well I like my bed, Lady Margaret,
    And well I like my sheet;
  But better I like that fair lady
    That stands at my bed's feet."

10 When night was gone, and day was come,
    All people were awake,
  The lady waket out of her sleep,
    And thus to her lord she spake.

11 "I dream'd a dream, my wedded lord,
    That seldom comes to good;
  I dream'd that our bow'r was lin'd with white swine,
    And our brid-chamber full of blood."

12 He called up his merry men all,
    By one, by two, by three,
  "We will go to Lady Margaret's bower,
    With the leave of my wedded lady."

13 When he came to Lady Margaret's bower,
    He knocked at the ring,
  And who were so ready as her brethren
    To rise and let him in.

14   "Oh is she in the parlor," he said,
         "Or is she in the hall?
       Or is she in the long chamber,
         Amongst her merry maids all?"

15   "She's not in the parlor," they said,
         "Nor is she in the hall;
       But she is in the long chamber,
         Laid out against the wall."

16   "Open the winding sheet," he cry'd,
         "That I may kiss the dead;
       That I may kiss her pale and wan
         Whose lips used to look so red."

17   Lady Margaret [died] on the over night,
         Sweet William died on the morrow;
       Lady Margaret died for pure, pure love,
         Sweet William died for sorrow.

18   On Margaret's grave there grew a rose,
         On Sweet William's grew a briar;
       They grew till they join'd in a true lover's knot,
         And then they died both together.

Unfortunate Miss Bailey

George Colman's ditty poking fun at the ballads about venge-
ful ghosts returning to accuse their unfaithful lovers was popular
in London music halls during the Regency and, for all its smart-
ness, has been occasionally recorded from folk singers.
   Text: Broadside by Such of London, 1840.

1   A Captain bold, in Halifax, who dwelt in country quarters,
       Seduced a maid, who hang'd herself, one morning, in her
                     garters,
       His wicked conscience smited him, he lost his stomach daily,
       He took to drinking ratafee, and thought upon Miss Bailey.
         Oh, Miss Bailey! unfortunate Miss Bailey.
ratafee, cordial flavored with fruit kernels.

2   One night betimes he went to rest, for he had caught a
      fever,
    Says he, "I am a handsome man, but I'm a gay deceiver:"
    His candle just at twelve o'clock began to burn quite paley,
    A ghost stepp'd up to his bed side, and said, "Behold Miss
      Bailey!"
      Oh, Miss Bailey! unfortunate Miss Bailey.

3   "Avaunt, Miss Bailey!" then he cried, "your face looks white
      and mealy,"
    "Dear Captain Smith," the ghost replied, "you've used me
      ungenteely;
    The Crowner's Quest goes hard with me, because I've acted
      frailly,
    And Parson Biggs won't bury me, though I am dead Miss
      Bailey."
      Oh, Miss Bailey! unfortunate Miss Bailey.

4   "Dear Corpse," said he, "since you and I accounts must once
      for all close,
    I've really got a one-pound note in my regimental small
      clothes;
    'Twill bribe the sexton for your grave."—The ghost then
      vanish'd gaily,
    Crying, "Bless you, wicked Captain Smith, remember poor
      Miss Bailey."
      Oh, Miss Bailey! unfortunate Miss Bailey.

II: RELIGIOUS BALLADS

Judas (23)

These thirty-six verses, recorded about 1300, compose the oldest traditional ballad in English preserved in writing. It was probably its religious theme that recommended the ballad to the monastic scribe. The explanation of Judas' treachery, however, is unorthodox and has no basis in the Gospels. It seems rather to derive from obscure folk traditions. Child unearthed a Wendish ballad (I, 242) in which Judas gambles away thirty pieces of silver entrusted to him by Christ to buy bread with, and betrays his Master in order not to return to Him empty-handed! Other legends (see *PMLA* 31:181, 481) saddle Judas with a rapacious wife who drives him to steal and to inform upon his leader. From a combination of such elements emerges a ballad in which Judas sins out of simplicity rather than malice. Why Judas in the ballad should insist on only thirty pieces of silver, no more, no less, no gold, may have a symbolic meaning. "Judas," with its eruptive movement, lack of transitions, narration accomplished through dialogue, dramatic repetition, and vivid conciseness, shows how well developed the ballad method of narration was as early as 1300.

Because of the difficulty of the text (from Trinity College, Cambridge MS. 323), a literal translation has been printed between the lines.

1 Hit wes upon a Scere Thorsday that ure Loverd aros;
   [It was upon a Holy Thursday that our Lord arose;]
   Ful milde were the wordes he spec to Judas:
   [Full mild were the words he spoke to Judas:]

2 "Judas, thou most to Jurselem, oure mete for to bugge;
   ["Judas, thou must go to Jerusalem to buy (our) food;]
   Thritti platen of selver thou bere upon thi rugge;
   [Thirty pieces of silver thou bearest upon thy back;]

56

3   "Thou comest fer i the brode stret, fer i the brode strete;
    ["Thou goest far in the broad street, far in the broad
      street;]
    Summe of thin cunesmen ther thou meiht i-mete."
    [Some of thy kinsmen there thou mightest meet."]

4   Imette wid [h]is soster, the swikele wimon.
    [He met his sister, that wicked woman.]
    "Judas, thou were w[u]rthe me stende the wid ston.
    ["Judas, thou wert worth that people stoned thee with
      stones.]

5   "Judas, thou were w[u]rthe me stende the wid ston,
    ["Judas, thou wert worth that people stoned thee with
      stones,]
    For the false prophete that tou bilevest upon."
    [For the false prophet that thou believest on."]

6   "Be stille, leve soster, thin herte the to-breke!
    ["Be still, dear sister, may thy heart burst!]
    Wiste min Loverd Crist, ful wel he wolde be wreke."
    [If my Lord Christ knew it, full well would he be avenged."]

7   "Judas, go thou on the roc, heie upon the ston,
    ["Judas, go thou on the rock, high upon the stone,]
    Lei thin heved i my barm, slep thou the anon."
    [Lay thy head in my lap, go thou to sleep."]

8   Sone so Judas of slepe was awake,
    [As soon as Judas awakened from sleep,]
    Thritte platen of selver from hym weren i-take.
    [Thirty pieces of silver had been taken from him.]

9   He drou hymselve bi the top, that al it lavede a-blode;
    [He pulled out his hair so that (his head) was bathed in
      blood.]
    The Jewes out of Jurselem awenden he were wode.
    [The Jews of Jerusalem thought he was mad.]

10 Foret hym com the riche Jeu that heihte pilatus—
    [Toward him came the rich Jew that was called Pilate—]
    "Wolte sulle thi Loverd that heite Jesus?"
    ["Wilt thou sell thy Lord that men call Jesus?"]

11   "I nul sulle my Loverd for nones cunnes eihte,
      ["I will not sell my Lord for any kind of ware,]
      Bote hit be for the thritti platen that he me bitaihte."
      [Unless it be for the thirty pieces that he entrusted to me."]

12   "Wolte sulle thi Lord Crist for enes cunnes golde?"
      ["Wilt thou sell thy Lord Christ for any kind of gold?"]
      "Nay, bote hit be for the platen that he habben wolde."
      ["Nay, unless it be for the (silver) pieces that he entrusted
          to me."]

13   In him com ur Lord gon, as [H]is postles setten at mete—
      [Our Lord came walking in as His apostles sat at table—]
      "Wou sitte ye, postles, ant wi nule ye ete?
      ["How is it that ye sit, apostles, and why will ye not eat?]

14   "Wou sitte ye, postles, ant wi nule ye ete?
      ["How is it that ye sit, apostles, and why will ye not eat]
      Ic am abouht ant i-sold to-day for oure mete."
      [I am bought and sold today for your food."]

15   Up stod him Judas: "Lord, am I that [frec]?
      [Up stood Judas: "Lord, am I that [man]?]
      I nas never o the stude ther me the evel spec."
      [I was never in the place where people spoke evil of thee."]

16   Up him stod Peter, ant spec wid al [h]is mihte—
      [Up stood Peter, and spoke with all his strength—]
      "Thau Pilatus him come wid ten hundred cnihtes,
      ["Though Pilate himself came with ten hundred knights,]

17   "Thau Pilatus him come wid ten hundred cnihtes,
      ["Though Pilate himself came with ten hundred knights,]
      Yet ic wolde, Loverd, for thi love fihte."
      [Yet I would, Lord, for thy love fight."]

18   "Stille thou be, Peter. Wel I the i-cnowe;
      ["Be still, Peter. Well I know thee;]
      Thou wolt fursake me thrien ar the coc him crowe."
      [Thou wilt forsake me thrice ere the cock crow."]

The Cherry-Tree Carol (54)

Again the folk have preferred a pseudo-gospel's human-interest-drenched account of Christ's life to the inspired biblical narrative. As told by the pseudo-Matthew, the cherry-tree incident occurred on the flight into Egypt and the tree was a palm. Joseph's cruel outburst in stanza 5 reflects a heterodox belief, widely held in the Middle Ages, that Joseph misunderstood the Virgin's pregnancy and accused her of infidelity. Several British and American versions continue the ballad with a set of stanzas in which Joseph takes Mary on his knees and begs mercy of the unborn child. The child is asked when his birthday will be and replies either "on old Christmas morning" or

> "the sixth day of January,
> When the hills and high mountains shall bow unto me."

The text printed from W. Sandys, *Christmas Carols,* 1833, p. 123, is easily adapted to the exquisite melody preserved in J. McGill, *Folk Songs of the Kentucky Mountains,* 1917, p. 60.

Jo - seph was _ an old _ man, and an old man was _

he,   When   he wed - ded Ma - ry,   in the

land   of Gal - i - lee,   When he wed - ded

Ma - ry,   in _ the land   of Gal - i - lee.

1   Joseph was an old man, and an old man was he,
    When he wedded Mary, in the land of Galilee.

2   Joseph and Mary walked through an orchard good,
    Where was cherries and berries, so red as any blood.

3   Joseph and Mary walked, through an orchard green,
    Where was berries and cherries, as thick as might be seen.

4   O then bespoke Mary, so meek and so mild:
    "Pluck me one cherry, Joseph, for I am with child."

5   O then bespoke Joseph, with words most unkind:
    "Let him pluck thee a cherry that brought thee with child."

6   O then bespoke the babe, within his mother's womb:
    "Bow down then the tallest tree, for my mother to have
        some."

7   Then bowed down the highest tree unto his mother's hand;
    Then she cried, "See, Joseph, I have cherries at command."

8   O then bespake Joseph: "I have done Mary wrong;
    But cheer up, my dearest, and be not cast down."

9   Then Mary plucked a cherry, as red as the blood,
    Then Mary went home with her heavy load.

10 Then Mary took her babe, and sat him on her knee,
    Saying, "My dear son, tell me what this world will be."

11 "O I shall be as dead, mother, as the stones in the wall;
    O the stones in the streets, mother, shall mourn for me all.

12 "Upon Easter-day, mother, my uprising shall be;
    O the sun and the moon, mother, shall both rise with me."

The Bitter Withy

Like "Judas," this ballad describes an incident not found in the
canonical sacred writings or in official church legends. Its source
rather is the pseudo-evangelical chronicles of Christ's childhood,
homely little stories in which Jesus often, as He does here, uses

divine power with unbecomingly human motives. The "bridge of sunbeams" miracle has been traced by Phillips Barry from Egypt to Ireland to the medieval saints' lives and finally to the pseudo-gospels (see *JAF* 27:79-89).

Our text, the first full version of "The Bitter Withy" ever published, was contributed to *Notes and Queries* (4th series, I, 53) by Frank Sidgwick in 1905. A slightly different text is set under the tune (Herefordshire, 1908; *JFS*, 4:29).

1   As it fell out on a Holy Day,
        The drops of rain did fall, did fall,
    Our Saviour asked leave of His mother Mary
        If He might go play at ball.

2   "To play at ball, my own dear Son,
        It's time You was going or gone,
    But be sure let me hear no complain of You,
        At night when You do come home."

3   It was upling scorn and downling scorn,
        Oh, there He met three jolly jerdins;
    Oh, there He asked the jolly jerdins
        If they would go play at ball.

4   "Oh, we are lords' and ladies' sons,
        Born in bower or in hall,
    And You are some poor maid's child
        Born'd in an ox's stall."

5   "If you are lords' and ladies' sons,
        Born'd in bower or in hall,
    Then at last I'll make it appear
        That I am above you all."

6   Our Saviour built a bridge with the beams of the sun,
        And over it He gone, He gone He.
    And after followed the three jolly jerdins,
        And drownded they were all three.

7   It was upling scorn and downling scorn,
        The mothers of them did whoop and call,

upling scorn . . . , (vague phrase to express passage of time and movement). *jerdin,* boy?

Crying out, "Mary mild, call home your Child,
For ours are drownded all."

8   Mary mild, Mary mild, called home her Child,
And laid our Saviour across her knee,
And with a whole handful of bitter withy
She gave Him slashes three.

9   Then He says to His mother, "Oh! the withy, oh! the withy,
The bitter withy that causes me to smart, to smart,
Oh! the withy, it shall be the very first tree
That perishes at the heart."

As— it fell out on a high ho-li-day, When

drops of rain did fall, did fall, Then Je-sus ask'd of His

Mo-ther Ma-ry If— He should go and play at the ball.

Sir Hugh (The Jew's Daughter) (155)

Jewish communities in the Middle Ages were regularly pillaged
in revenge for alleged murders of Christian children, whose blood
was needed—or so the charge ran—in the Passover rites. The
little chorister of Chaucer's "Prioress's Tale" was one such victim; Sir Hugh of this ballad was another. For though text A
(Jamieson, I, 151) makes the murder seem purposeless, numerous other versions, including American ones, describe the scour-
ing of a basin in which to catch the victim's blood.

Sir Hugh's directing his mother to his corpse is the miracle
on which the ballad centers. Jamieson's version illustrates the

handling of this incident in the older tradition. The late English version, our text C (M. H. Mason, *Nursery Rhymes and Country Songs,* 1878, p. 46), retains the speaking corpse, but the ballad has been reduced to the prattle of a nursery rhyme. Apparently only on the child's level are such marvels now credible. The American text, B (Victor 401938, 1930), has a gypsy lady (sometimes a jeweler's daughter or a duke's daughter replaces the original Jewess) and in place of a miraculously vocal corpse we have a rationalized, if illogical, scene in which the dying boy discusses funeral arrangements with his murderess.

✿◇ A ◇✿

1 Four and twenty bonny boys
   Were playing at the ba',
   And by it came him, sweet Sir Hugh,
   And he played o'er them a'.

2 He kick'd the ba' with his right foot,
   And catch'd it wi' his knee,
   And throuch-and-thro the Jew's window
   He gard the bonny ba' flee.

3 He's doen him to the Jew's castell,
   And walk'd it round about;
   And there he saw the Jew's daughter,
   At the window looking out.

4 "Throw down the ba', ye Jew's daughter,
   Throw down the ba' to me!"
   "Never a bit," says the Jew's daughter,
   "Till up to me come ye."

5 "How will I come up? How can I come up?
   How can I come to thee?
   For as ye did to my auld father,
   The same ye'll do to me."

6 She's gane till her father's garden,
   And pu'd an apple red and green;

gar, make. *doen him,* betaken himself.

'Twas a' to wyle him, sweet Sir Hugh,
  And to entice him in.

7 She's led him in through ae dark door,
    And sae has she thro' nine;
  She's laid him on a dressing-table,
    And stickit him like a swine.

8 And first came out the thick, thick blood,
    And syne came out the thin;
  And syne came out the bonny heart's blood;
    There was nae mair within.

9 She's row'd him in a cake o' lead,
    Bade him lie still and sleep;
  She's thrown him in Our Lady's draw-well,
    Was fifty fathom deep.

10 When the bells were rung, and mass was sung,
    And a' the bairns came hame,
  When every lady gat hame her son,
    The Lady Maisry gat nane.

11 She's ta'en her mantle her about,
    Her coffer by the hand,
  And she's gane out to seek her son,
    And wander'd o'er the land.

12 She's doen her to the Jew's castell,
    Where a' were fast asleep:
  "Gin ye be there, my sweet Sir Hugh,
    I pray you to me speak."

13 She's doen her to the Jew's garden,
    Thought he had been gathering fruit:
  "Gin ye be there, my sweet Sir Hugh,
    I pray you to me speak."

14 She near'd Our Lady's deep draw-well,
    Was fifty fathom deep:
  "Whare'er ye be, my sweet Sir Hugh,
    I pray you to me speak."

wyle, deceive.   *syne,* then.   *coffer,* box (meaningless here).   *gin,* if.

15 "Gae hame, gae hame, my mither dear,
  Prepare my winding sheet,
And at the back o' merry Lincoln
  The morn I will you meet."

16 Now Lady Maisry is gane hame,
  Made him a winding sheet,
And at the back o' merry Lincoln
  The dead corpse did her meet.

17 And a' the bells o' merry Lincoln
  Without men's hands were rung;
And a' the books o' merry Lincoln
  Were read without man's tongue;
And ne'er was such a burial
  Sin Adam's days begun.

❀◇ B ◇❀

1 It rained, it poured, it rained so hard,
It rained so hard all day,
That all the boys in our school
Came out to toss and play.

2 They tossed their ball again so high,
Then again so low,
They tossed it into a flower garden
Where no one was allowed to go.

3 Up stepped this gypsy lady,
All dressed in yellow and green;
"Come in, come in, my pretty little boy,
And get your ball again."

4 "I won't come in, I shan't come in,
Without my playmates all;
I'll go t' my father 'n' tell him about it⸺
That'll cause tears to fall."

5 She first showed him an apple seed [for sweet?]
Then again a gold ring;
Then she showed him a diamunt,
That enticed him in.

6   She took him by his lily-white hand,
    She led him through the hall,
    She put him into an upper room,
    Where no one could hear him call.

7   "Oh take these finger-rings off my fingers,
    Smoke them with your breath;
    If any of my friends should call for me,
    Tell them that I'm at rest.

8   "Tether [?] the Bible at my head,
    The Testament at my feet;
    If my dear mother should call for me,
    Tell her that I'm asleep.

9   "Tether the Bible at my feet,
    The Testament at my head;
    If my dear father should call for me,
    Tell him that I am dead."

❀◆ C ◆❀

1   Easter Day was a holiday,
        Of all days in the year;
    And all the little schoolfellows went out to play,
        But Sir William was not there.

2   Mamma went to the Jew's wife's house,
        And knocked at the ring,
    Saying, "Little Sir William, if you are there,
        Oh! let your mother in!"

3   The Jew's wife opened the door and said,
        "He is not here to-day;
    He is with the little schoolfellows out on the green,
        Playing some pretty play."

4   Mamma went to the Boyne water,
        That is so wide and deep,
    Saying, "Little Sir William, if you are there,
        Oh! pity your mother's weep!"

5   "How can I pity your weep, mother,
     And I so long in pain?
  For the little penknife sticks close in my heart,
     And the Jew's wife has me slain.

6   "Go home, go home, my mother dear,
     And prepare my winding sheet;
  For to-morrow morning before eight o'clock,
     You with my body shall meet.

7   "And lay my Prayer-book at my head,
     And my grammar at my feet;
  That all the little schoolfellows, as they pass by,
     May read them for my sake."

III: ROMANTIC TRAGEDIES

Earl Brand (The Douglas Tragedy) (7)

"Earl Brand," in story at least, goes back to the days when men stole their not unwilling brides from among the maidens of hostile clans. No extant text in English develops the tale completely, but by using all the clues that the English and Scottish versions and the Scandinavian analogues furnish, one can piece together the ancient details. The lovers elope from the castle of the bride's father, both usually on a single horse. (This inconvenience explains why they are so easily overtaken.) Riding across the moors, they are stopped and recognized by a malicious henchman of the bride's family. The bride urges her lover to kill the knight; the lover prefers bribery. No sooner have the pair resumed their journey than the knight is on his way to betray them to the bride's father. Version A begins at this point.

"Ribold and Guldborg," a Danish ballad that parallels "Earl Brand" closely, fills in a key incident in the fight scene that no version in English retains. As Ribold prepares for the onslaught, he warns his beloved that in no case whatsoever, no matter how hard pressed he appears, is she to call his name. But seeing all her family slaughtered and her lover about to dispatch the final survivor, her youngest brother, Guldborg calls out, "Ribold, Ribold, put up your sword!" At that very moment, Ribold receives his death wound. Operating over this incident is some form of the primitive belief in name taboos. Ribold is fighting with supernatural fury; to call his name is to reduce him to human strength. Also, Ribold's adversary gains magical power over him by learning his personal name.

The Earl Brand and Child Ell of the English versions of the ballad probably represent the Scandinavian hero Hildebrand. In the Scottish versions, such as A (from Motherwell's MS., p. 502), the hero is a scion of the House of Douglas, and the ballad, therefore, is more properly titled "The Douglas Tragedy."

❧ A ❧

1   "Rise up, rise up, my seven brave sons,
     And dress in your armour so bright;
  Earl Douglas will hae Lady Margaret awa
     Before that it be light.

2   "Arise, arise, my seven brave sons,
     And dress in your armour so bright;
  It shall never be said that a daughter of mine
     Shall go with an earl or a knight."

3   "Oh will ye stand, fair Margaret," he says,
     "And hold my milk-white steed,
  Till I fight your father and seven brethren,
     In yonder pleasant mead?"

4   She stood and held his milk-white steed,
     She stood trembling with fear,
  Until she saw her seven brethren fall,
     And her father that loved her dear.

5   "Hold your hand, Earl Douglas," she says,
     "Your strokes are wonderous sair;
  I may get sweethearts again enew,
     But a father I'll ne'er get mair."

6   She took out a handkerchief
     Was made o' the cambrick fine,
  And aye she wiped her father's bloody wounds,
     And the blood sprung up like wine.

7   "Will ye go, fair Margaret?" he said,
     "Will ye now go, or bide?"
  "Yes, I'll go, sweet William," she said,
     "For ye've left me never a guide.

8   "If I were to go to my mother's house,
     A welcome guest I would be;
  But for the bloody deed that's done this day
     I'll rather go with thee."

enew, enough.

9   He lifted her on a milk-white steed
        And himself on a dapple gray;
    They drew their hats out over their face,
        And they both went weeping away.

10 They rode, they rode, and they better rode,
        Till they came to yon water wan;
    They lighted down to gie their horse a drink
        Out of the running stream.

11 "I am afraid, Earl Douglas," she said,
        "I am afraid ye are slain;
    I think I see your bonny heart's blood
        Running down the water wan."

12 "Oh no, oh no, fair Margaret," he said,
        "Oh no, I am not slain;
    It is but the scad of my scarlet cloak
        Runs down the water wan."

13 He mounted her on a milk-white steed
        And himself on a dapple gray,
    And they have reached Earl Douglas' gates
        Before the break of day.

14 "O rise, dear mother, and make my bed,
        And make it braid and wide,
    And lay me down to take my rest,
        And at my back my bride."

15 She has risen and made his bed,
        She made it braid and wide;
    She laid him down to take his rest,
        And at his back his bride.

16 Lord William died ere it was day,
        Lady Margaret on the morrow;
    Lord William died through loss of blood and wounds,
        Lady Margaret died with sorrow.

17 The one was buried in Mary's kirk,
        The other in Mary's quire;

scad, reflection.

> The one sprung up a bonnie bush,
>> And the other a bonny brier.

18 These twa grew, and these twa threw,
>> Till they came to the top,
> And when they could na farther gae,
>> They coost the lovers' knot.

❧◇ B ◇❧

Sentimentality overwhelms the American versions of "Earl Brand." When the girl in a Mississippi text (Hudson, p. 66) sees her father about to be run through, she sud-denly feels a revulsion against her lover:

7 Fair Elinor stood and looked very sad;
>> Not one word did she say
> Till she saw her father's own heart's blood
>> Come flowing down to his knees.

8 "Be mad or pleased," Fair Elinor she said;
>> "Be mad or pleased as you may be.
> I wish myself in old Ireland
>> And you in the middle of the sea."

Glasgerion (67)

Y Bardd Glas Keraint, the Glasgerion of our ballad, occupies the place among legendary Welsh harpers that Orpheus held among Greek musicians. The effect of his playing is beautifully, if hyperbolically, expressed by a Scottish reciter:

> He'd harpit a fish out o' saut water,
>> Or water out o' a stane,
> Or milk out o' a maiden's breast,
>> That bairn had never nane.

Text: Percy Folio MS. (about 1640), I, 248.

threw, twisted.   *coost,* cast, formed into.

1   Glasgerion was a king's owne sonne,
    And a harper he was good,
  He harped in the king's chamber
    Where cup and candle stoode,
  And soe did hee in the queen's chamber
    Till ladies waxed wood.

2   And then bespake the king's daughter,
    And these words thus sayd shee . . .

3   Saide, "Strike on, strike on, Glasgerrion,
    Of thy striking doe not blinne;
  There's never a stroke comes over thine harpe
    But it glads my hart within."

4   "Faire might you fall, lady!" quoth hee,
    "Who taught you now to speake?
  I have loved you, lady, seven yeere;
    My hart I durst neere breake."

5   "But come to my bower, my Glasgerryon,
    When all men are att rest;
  As I am a ladie true of my promise,
    Thou shalt bee a welcome guest."

6   But hom then came Glasgerryon,
    A glad man, Lord, was hee,
  "And come thou hither, Jacke, my boy,
    Come hither unto mee,

7   "For the king's daughter of Normandye
    Her love is granted mee,
  And att her chamber must I bee
    Beffore the cock have crowen."

8   "But come you hither, master," quoth hee,
    "Lay your head downe on this stone,
  For I will waken you, master deere,
    Afore it be time to gone."

9   But upp then rose that lither ladd,
    And did on hose and shoone,

waxed, grew, became,   *wood,* mad.   *blinne,* stop.   *lither,* wicked.

A coller he cast upon his necke,
    Hee seemed a gentleman.

10 And when he came to that lady's chamber,
    He thrild upon a pinn.
    The lady was true of her promise,
      Rose up and lett him in.

11 He did not take the lady gay
    To boulster nor noe bedd,
    But downe upon her chamber flore
      Full soone he hath her layd.

12 He did not kisse that lady gay
    When he came nor when he youd;
    And sore mistrusted that lady gay
      He was of some churl's blood.

13 But home then came that lither ladd,
    And did off his hose and shoone,
    And cast that coller from about his necke—
      He was but a churl's sonne.
    "Awaken," quoth hee, "my master deere,
      I hold it time to be gone,

14 "For I have sadled your horsse, master,
    Well bridled I have your steed;
    Have not I served a good breakfast,
      When time comes I have need."

15 But up then rose good Glasgerryon,
    And did on both hose and shoone,
    And cast a coller about his necke,
      He was a king's sonne.

16 And when he came to that lady's chamber
    He thrild upon a pinn;
    The lady was more then true of promise,
      Rose up and let him in:

17 Saies, "Whether have you left with me
    Your braclett or your glove,

thrild, rattled (at latchpin).   *youd*, went.

Or are you returned backe againe
To know more of my love?"

18   Glasgerryon swore a full great othe
By oake and ashe and thorne,
"Lady! I was never in your chamber
Sith the time that I was borne!"

19   "O then it was your litle foote page
Falsly hath beguiled me,"
And then shee pulld forth a litle pen-kniffe
That hanged by her knee,
Says, "There shall never noe churl's blood
Spring within my body."

20   But home then went Glasgerryon,
A woe man, good [Lord], was hee,
Sayes, "Come hither, thou Jacke my boy!
Come thou hither to me!

21   "For if I had killed a man to-night,
Jacke, I wold tell it thee:
But if I have not killed a man to-night,
Jacke, thou hast killed three!"

22   And he puld out his bright browne sword,
And dryed it on his sleeve,
And he smote off that lither ladds head,
And asked noe man noe leave.

23   He sett the sword's poynt till his brest,
The pumill till a stone:
Thorrow that falsenese of that lither ladd
These three lives werne all gone!

Lady Maisry (65)

Burning, or hanging, was the prescribed penalty in medieval
Scottish law for sexual indulgence by an unmarried woman—
unless her family protected the offender or found a nominal
pumill, pommel, hilt knob.

father for her child. Doubtless the unnatural cruelty of the
brother in the ballad explains why it has disappeared from
modern tradition.

Text: Jamieson's Brown MS., p. 24.

1   The young lords o' the north country
      Have all a wooing gone,
   To win the love of Lady Maisry,
      But o' them she would hae none.

2   O they hae courted Lady Maisry
      Wi' a' kin kind of things;
   An they hae sought her Lady Maisry
      Wi' brotches and wi' rings.

3   An they ha sought her Lady Maisry
      Frae father and frae mother;
   An they ha sought her Lady Maisry
      Frae sister an frae brother.

4   An they ha followd her Lady Maisry
      Thro chamber an thro ha';
   But a' that they could say to her,
      Her answer still was Na.

5   "O had your tongues, young men," she says,
      "An think nae mair o' me;
   For I've gien my love to an English lord,
      An think nae mair o' me."

6   Here father's kitchy-boy heard that,
      An ill death may he dee!
   An he is on to her brother,
      As fast as gang coud he.

7   "O is my father an' my mother well,
      But an' my brothers three?
   Gin my sister Lady Maisry be well,
      There's naething can ail me."

8   "Your father and your mother is well,
      But an' your brothers three;

gin, if.

Your sister Lady Maisry's well,
  So big wi' bairn gangs she."

9   "Gin this be true you tell to me,
  My mailison light on thee!
But gin it be a lie you tell,
  You sal be hangit hie."

10 He's done him to his sister's bowr,
  Wi' meikle doole an care;
An there he saw her Lady Maisry,
  Kembing her yallow hair.

11 "O wha is aught that bairn," he says,
  "That ye sae big are wi'?
And gin ye winna own the truth,
  This moment ye sall dee."

12 She turnd her right an roun about,
  An the kem fell frae her han';
A trembling seizd her fair body,
  An her rosy cheek grew wan.

13 "O pardon me, my brother dear,
  An' the truth I'll tell to thee;
My bairn it is to Lord William,
  An he is betrothd to me."

14 "O coud na ye gotten dukes, or lords,
  Intill your ain country,
That ye draw up wi' an English dog,
  To bring this shame on me?

15 "But ye maun gi' up the English lord,
  Whan youre young babe is born;
For, gin you keep by him an hour langer,
  Your life sall be forlorn."

16 "I will gi' up this English blood,
  Till my young babe be born;
But the never a day nor hour langer,
  Tho my life should be forlorn."

mailison, curse.   *doole,* grief.   *wha is aught,* to whom belongs.

17   "O whare is a' my merry young men,
        Whom I gi' meat and fee,
     To pu' the thistle and the thorn,
        To burn this wile whore wi'?"

18   "O whare will I get a bonny boy,
        To help me in my need,
     To rin wi' hast to Lord William,
        And bid him come wi' speed?"

19   O out it spake a bonny boy,
        Stood by her brother's side:
     "O I would rin your errand, lady,
        O'er a' the world wide.

20   "Aft have I run your errands, lady,
        Whan blawn baith win' and weet;
     But now I'll rin your errand lady,
        Wi' sa't tears on my cheek."

21   O whan he came to broken briggs,
        He bent his bow and swam,
     An whan he came to the green grass growin,
        He slackd his shoone and ran.

22   O whan he came to Lord William's gates,
        He baed na to chap or ca',
     But set his bent bow till his breast,
        An lightly lap the wa';
     An, or the porter was at the gate,
        The boy was i' the ha'.

23   "O is my biggins broken, boy?
        Or is my towers won?
     Or is my lady lighter yet,
        Of a dear daughter or son?"

24   "Your biggin is na broken, sir,
        Nor is your towers won;
     But the fairest lady in a' the lan
        For you this day maun burn."

brigg, bridge.   *baed,* waited.   *chap,* knock.   *biggin,* building.

25   "O saddle me the black, the black,
          Or saddle me the brown;
      O saddle me the swiftest steed
          That ever rade frae a town."

26   Or he was near a mile awa,
          She heard his wilde horse sneeze:
      "Mend up the fire, my false brother,
          It's na come to my knees."

27   O whan he lighted at the gate,
          She heard his bridle ring:
      "Mend up the fire, my false brother,
          It's far yet frae my chin.

28   "Mend up the fire to me, brother,
          Mend up the fire to me;
      For I see him comin hard an fast
          Will soon men 't up to thee.

29   "O gin my hands had been loose, Willy,
          Sae hard as they are boun,
      I would have turnd me frae the gleed,
          And castin out your young son."

30   "O I'll gar burn for you, Maisry,
          Your father an your mother;
      An' I'll gar burn for you, Maisry,
          Your sister an your brother.

31   "An' I'll gar burn for you, Maisry,
          The chief of a' your kin;
      An' the last bonfire that I come to,
          Mysel I will cast in."

The Lass of Roch Royal (76)

Annie's sorrowful history is one of the few long ballads still
sung by folksingers. Particularly pleasing to the folk mind apparently is the rhetorical charm of the opening dialogue. This

gleed, fire.

passage has become an independent song in America, and, as text B illustrates, American delicacy has obliterated any mention of the affair with Lord Gregory or the child. The same stanzas have also wandered into "John Hardy" and "John Henry" and a number of mountain folk lyrics about the sad parting of lovers. One such parting song, "Cold Winter's Night," or "The False True-Lover"—our C—contains, in addition to the "Lass of Roch Royal" borrowing, two stanzas (2 and 6) that are almost identical with parts of Burns' renowned "A Red, Red Rose." This coincidence does not necessarily mean that the Appalachian folk stole from Burns. More probably the mountain singers had preserved the old Scottish folk song that was the basis of Burns' lyric.

Texts: A, Scottish tradition about 1850 (Greig, p. 60), with tune; B, Davis, p. 267; C, *Modern Language Review*, 6:514.

❀◇ **A** ◇❀

She's ta'en her young son in her airms,— An to the door— she's gane, An' lang— she knocked an sair she ca'd,— But an - swer she — got nane.

1 "O wha will lace my shoes sae small?
      An' wha will glove my hand?
   Or wha will lace my middle sae jimp
      With my new made linen band?

2 "Wha will trim my yellow hair
      With my new siller kame?
   An' wha will father my young son
      Till Lord Gregory comes hame?"

jimp, slender.

3   "Your father will lace your shoes sae small;
        Your mother will glove your hand;
    Your sister will lace your middle sae jimp
        With your new made linen band;

4   "Your brother will trim your yellow hair
        With a new made siller kame;
    An' the king o heaven will father your son
        Till Lord Gregory comes hame."

5   "But I will get a bonnie boat,
        An' I will sail the sea,
    For I maun gang to Lord Gregory,
        Since he canna come hame to me."

6   She has gotten a bonnie boat,
        An' sailed upon the main;
    She langed to see her ain true love,
        Since he could nae come hame.

7   "O row your boat, my mariners,
        An' bring me to the land,
    For yonder I see my love's castle
        Close by the saut sea strand."

8   She's taen her young son in her airms,
        An' to the door she's gané,
    An' lang she knocked an' sair she ca'd,
        But answer she got nane.

9   "O open the door, Lord Gregory,
        O open an' lat me in,
    For the wind blaws through my yellow hair,
        An' I'm shiverin to the chin."

[*Lord Gregory's mother impersonates her son*]

10 "Awa, awa, ye wile woman,
        Some ill death may ye dee:
    Ye're but some witch or wile warlock
        Or mermaid o the sea."

wile warlock, vile wizard.

11   "I'm neither a witch or wile warlock,
     Nor mermaid o the sea;
  But I'm fair Annie o Rough Royal,
     O open the door to me."

12   "Gin ye be Annie o Rough Royal,
     As I trust ye canna be,
  Now tell me some o the love tokens
     That passed between you an' me."

13   "O dinna ye mind, Lord Gregory,
     When ye sat at the wine,
  Ye changed the rings fae our fingers?
     An' I can show ye thine.

14   "For yours was good an' very good,
     But aye the best was mine;
  For yours was o the good red gold,
     But mine the diamonds fine.

15   "Don't ye mind, Lord Gregory,
     By bonnie Irwine side,
  When first I owned that virgin love
     I lang lang had denied?

16   "O don't ye mind, Lord Gregory,
     When in my father's ha',
  'Twas there ye got your will o me,
     An' that was worst o a'?"

17   "Awa, awa, ye wile woman,
     For here ye sanna win in;
  Gae drown ye in the ragin sea,
     Or hang on the gallows pin."

18   When the cock did craw, an' the day did daw,
     An' the sun began to peep,
  Then up did rise Lord Gregory,
     An' sair sair did he weep.

19   "I dreamed a dream, my mither dear,
     The thought o't gars me greet;

gin, if. *dinna ye mind,* don't you remember. *sanna,* shall not.
win, make one's way. *gars me greet,* makes me weep.

I dreamed fair Annie o Rough Royal
   Lay caul deid at my feet."

20 "Gin it be for Annie o Rough Royal
     That ye mak a' this din,
  She stood a' last night at our door,
     But I think I letna her in."

21 "O wae betide ye, ill woman,
     Some ill death may ye dee,
  That ye wadna hae latten poor Annie in,
     Or else hae wauken'd me."

22 He's gane down to yon sea shore
     As fast as he could fare:
  He saw fair Annie in her boat,
     An' the wind it tossed her sair.

23 "Hey bonnie Annie, an' How bonnie Annie,
     O Annie, winna ye bide?"—
  But aye the mair bonnie Annie he cried,
     The rougher grew the tide.

24 "Hey bonnie Annie, an' How bonnie Annie,
     O winna ye speak to me?"—
  But aye the mair bonnie Annie he cried,
     The rougher grew the sea.

25 The wind blew loud, an' the sea grew rough,
     An' the boat was dashed on shore;
  Fair Annie floats upon the sea,
     But her young son rose no more.

26 Lord Gregory tore his yellow hair,
     An' made a heavy moan:
  Fair Annie's corpse lay at his feet,
     But his bonnie young son was gone.

27 First he kissed her cherry cheeks,
     An' next he kissed her chin,
  An' saftly pressed her rosy lips
     That there was not breath within.

28   "O wae betide ye, cruel mother,
      An ill death may ye dee,
   For ye turned my true love fae my door,
      When she came sae far to me."

✺◇ B ◇✺

1   "Oh, who will shoe your foot, my dear?
      And who will glove your hand?
   And who will kiss your red rosy lips,
      When I am gone to the far-off land?"

2   "My papa will shoe my foot, my dear;
      My brother will glove my hand;
   My mamma will kiss my red rosy lips,
      When you have gone to the far-off land."

✺◇ C ◇✺

1   As I walked out one cold winter night,
      And drinking good old wine,
   A-thinking of that pretty little girl,
      That stole this heart of mine—

2   And she looks like some pink rose
      That blooms in the month of June,
   And now she's like some instrument
      Been newly put in tune.

3   I asked your mamma for you, my love;
      She said you were too young.
   I wish I'd never seen your face,
      Or had died when I was young.

4   Oh, who will shoe your little feet,
      And who will glove your hand,
   Oh, who will kiss your ruby lips,
      While I'm in a foreign land?

5   Your papa, my dear, will shoe your feet,
      And your mamma will glove your hand;
   And I will kiss your ruby lips,
      When I return again.

6   Fare you well, my own true love,
        Fare you well, for awhile;
     If I go away, I'll come again,
        If I go ten thousand mile.

7   If ever I prove false to you,
        The elements shall mourn;
     If ever I false prove to you,
        The sea would rage and burn.

Lord Thomas and Fair Annet (73)

Among ballad scholars, "Lord Thomas and Fair Annet" ranks
as one of the finest specimens of balladry. This praise is particularly applicable to our text, the best Scottish version, which was
contributed to Percy's *Reliques* (II, 293) by a Scottish judge.
Almost all variants found in American and British tradition have
sprung from a seventeenth-century broadside found in the Roxburghe, Pepys, and other collections.

1   Lord Thomas and fair Annet
        Sate a' day on a hill;
     Whan night was cum, and sun was sett,
        They had not talkt their fill.

2   Lord Thomas said a word in jest,
        Fair Annet took it ill:
     "A, I will nevir wed a wife
        Against my ain friends' will."

3   "Gif ye wull nevir wed a wife,
        A wife wull neir wed yee."
     Sae he is hame to tell his mither,
        And knelt upon his knee.

4   "O rede, O rede, mither," he says,
        "A gude rede gie to mee;
     O sall I tak the nut-browne bride,
        And let fair Annet bee?"

rede, advise, advice.

5   "The nut-browne bride has gowd and gear,
        Fair Annet she has gat nane;
    And the little beauty fair Annet haes
        O it wull soon be gane."

6   And he has till his brother gane:
        "Now, brother, rede ye mee;
    A, sall I marrie the nut-browne bride,
        And let fair Annet bee?"

7   "The nut-browne bride has oxen, brother,
        The nut-browne bride has kye;
    I wad hae ye marrie the nut-browne bride,
        And cast fair Annet bye."

8   "Her oxen may dye i' the house, billie,
        And her kye into the byre,
    And I sall hae nothing to mysell
        Bot a fat fadge by the fyre."

9   And he has till his sister gane:
        "Now, sister, rede ye mee;
    O sall I marrie the nut-browne bride,
        And set fair Annet free?"

10 "I'se rede ye tak fair Annet, Thomas,
        And let the browne bride alane;
    Lest ye sould sigh and say, Alace!
        What is this we brought hame?"

11 "No, I will tak my mither's counsel,
        And marrie me owt o' hand;
    And I will tak the nut-browne bride,
        Fair Annet may leive the land."

12 Up then rose fair Annet's father,
        Twa hours or it were day.
    And he is gane into the bower
        Wherein fair Annet lay.

13 "Rise up, rise up, fair Annet," he says,
        "Put on your silken sheene;

kye, cows, cattle. *billie,* chum. *byre,* cowbarn. *fadge,* drab, slattern. *sheene,* shoes.

Let us gae to St. Marie's kirke,
And see that rich weddeen."

14 "My maides, gae to my dressing-room,
And dress to me my hair;
Whair-eir yee laid a plait before,
See yee lay ten times mair.

15 "My maides, gae to my dressing-room,
And dress to me my smock;
The one half is o' the holland fine,
The other o' needle-work."

16 The horse fair Annet rade upon,
He amblit like the wind;
Wi' siller he was shod before,
Wi' burning gowd behind.

17 Four and twanty siller bells
Wer a' tyed till his mane,
And yae tift o' the norland winde,
They tinkled ane by ane.

18 Four and twanty gay gude knichts
Rade by fair Annet's side,
And four and twanty fair ladies,
As gin she had bin a bride.

19 And whan she cam to Marie's kirk,
She sat on Marie's stean:
The cleading that fair Annet had on
It skinkled in their een.

20 And whan she cam into the kirk,
She shimmerd like the sun;
The belt that was about her waist
Was a' wi' pearles bedone.

21 She sat her by the nut-browne bride,
And her een they wer sae clear,
Lord Thomas he clean forgat the bride,
When fair Annet drew near.

yae, every. *tift,* puff. *gin,* if. *stean,* stone seat. *cleading,* clothing. *skinkled,* sparkled. *een,* eyes.

22 He had a rose into his hand,
        He gae it kisses three,
    And reaching by the nut-browne bride,
        Laid it on fair Annet's knee.

23 Up than spak the nut-browne bride,
        She spak wi' meikle spite:
    "And whair gat ye that rose-water,
        That does mak yee sae white?"

24 "O I did get the rose-water
        Whair ye wull neir get nane,
    For I did get that very rose-water
        Into my mither's wame."

25 The bride she drew a long bodkin
        Frae out her gay head gear,
    And strake fair Annet unto the heart,
        That word spak nevir mair.

26 Lord Thomas he saw fair Annet wex pale,
        And marvelit what mote bee;
    But whan he saw her dear heart's blude,
        A' wood-wroth wexed hee.

27 He drew his dagger, that was sae sharp,
        That was sae sharp and meet,
    And drave it into the nut-browne bride,
        That fell deid at his feit.

28 "Now stay for me, dear Annet," he sed,
        "Now stay, my dear," he cry'd;
    Then strake the dagger untill his heart,
        And fell deid by her side.

29 Lord Thomas was buried without kirk-wa',
        Fair Annet within the quiere,
    And o' the tane thair grew a birk,
        The other a bonny briere.

30 And ay they grew, and ay they threw,
        As they wad faine be neare;

meikle, much.   *wood-wroth,* insanely angry.   *wexed,* grew, became.
tane, one.   *threw,* twisted.

And by this ye may ken right weil
They were twa luvers deare.

Barbara Allen (84)

To hear Mrs. Knipps sing her "little Scotch song of Barbary
Allen" was for Samuel Pepys "perfect pleasure" (*Diary*, 2 January 1666). Judging by the hundreds of variants recorded on both
sides of the Atlantic, the ballad's charm persists, for it is easily
the most widely and frequently sung of all the old ballads. This
is no new phenomenon in America. A Western pioneer, writing
to J. Frank Dobie, reported that "Barbara Allen" was a "favorite
cowboy song in Texas before the pale faces became thick enough
to make the Indians consider a massacre worth while."

The three texts of "Barbara Allen" printed here represent the
major versions discernible among the variants. Text A, from
Ramsay's *Tea-Table Miscellany*, ed. 1750, p. 343, fixes the time
of the tragedy as autumn, identifies the unfortunate lover as Sir
John Graeme, and gives Graeme's slighting of Barbara in a round
of tavern toasts as the motive for her cruelty. Remorse comes
upon Barbara as she hears the death knell. An Aberdeen version,
text B was discovered comparatively recently (Greig, p. 68) and
deserves to be better known. It follows A in general outline but
contains some extremely interesting additions. In stanza 6, the
lover begs a kiss of "Bawbie Allan," but is denied. Nonetheless
(8 and 9) he makes her handsome and symbolic gifts. These two
stanzas are probably misplaced; they are phrased as bequests
and should come in after Barbara Allen leaves the room. A few
American variants show traces of this bequest passage. Apparently unique to this text, however, is the series of stanzas (12-14)
in which successive members of Bawbie's family beg her to
"take" the dying man—they do not know he is dead. With each
refusal, Bawbie's remorse deepens. No other text manages the
heroine's transition from haughtiness to fatal remorse and repentance so poignantly.

Text C from West Virginia (Cox, p. 96) is the typical American version. The narrator sets the events in Scarlet Town where
he was born or bound (apprentice), and gives the time as May

rather than November. The death-bed visit proceeds much as it
does in A, but the final stanzas in which Barbara reasons out her
remorse and warns "ye virgins all" to avoid her fate derive from
broadside reworkings of the ballad, as do many other crude
touches. A rose-and-briar ending, to symbolize the continuance
of the lovers' earthly passion, is so common to variants like C that
it has been supplied in brackets from another West Virginia text.

The tune accompanies B, Greig's version.

❂◇ A ◇❂

1   It was in and about the Martinmas time,
        When the green leaves were a-falling,
    That Sir John Graeme in the west country
        Fell in love with Barbara Allan.

2   He sent his man down through the town,
        To the place where she was dwelling,
    "O haste and come to my master dear,
        Gin ye be Barbara Allan."

3   O hooly, hooly rose she up,
        To the place where he was lying,
    And when she drew the curtain by—
        "Young man, I think you're dying."

4   "O it's I'm sick, and very, very sick,
        And 'tis a' for Barbara Allan."
    "O the better for me ye's never be,
        Tho' your heart's blood were a-spilling.

5   "O dinna ye mind, young man," said she,
        "When ye was in the tavern a-drinking,
    That ye made the healths gae round and round,
        And slighted Barbara Allan."

6   He turn'd his face unto the wall,
        And death was with him dealing:
    "Adieu, adieu, my dear friends all,
        And be kind to Barbara Allan."

gin, if.   *hooly,* slowly, softly.   *dinna ye mind,* don't you remember.

7   And slowly, slowly raise she up,
         And slowly, slowly left him;
     And sighing, said she cou'd not stay,
         Since death of life had reft him.

8   She had not gane a mile but twa,
         When she heard the dead-bell ringing,
     And every jow that the dead-bell geid,
         It cry'd, Woe to Barbara Allan.

9   "O mother, mother, make my bed,
         O make it saft and narrow,
     Since my love died for me today,
         I'll die for him tomorrow."

jow, stroke.

❀◇ B ◇❀

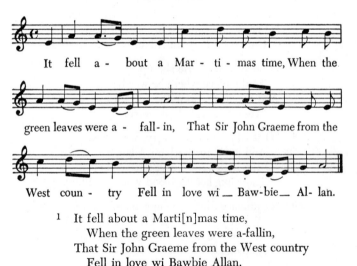

It fell a - bout a Mar - ti - mas time, When the
green leaves were a - fall- in, That Sir John Graeme from the
West coun - try Fell in love wi ⎯ Baw-bie ⎯ Al- lan.

1   It fell about a Marti[n]mas time,
         When the green leaves were a-fallin,
     That Sir John Graeme from the West country
         Fell in love wi Bawbie Allan.

2   He sent his men down through the town
         To the place where she was dwallin;
     "O haste an' come to my master dear,
         Gin ye be Bawbie Allan."

gin, if.

3   O hooly, hooly, rase she up,
        Till she cam where he was lyin,
    An' when she drew the curtains roun,
        Said, "Young man, I think ye're dyin."

4   "I am sick an' very very sick,
        An' it's a' for Bawbie Allan."—
    "But the better for me ye never shall be
        Though your heart's blood were a-spillin.

5   "O don't you mind, young man," she said,
        "When in the tavern callin,
    Ye made the toasts gang roun an' roun,
        But ye slighted Bawbie Allan."

6   "A kiss o you would do me good,
        My bonnie Bawbie Allan."—
    "But a kiss o me ye sanna get,
        Though your heart's blood were a-spillin."

7   He's turned his face untae the wa',
        For death was wi him dealin,
    Said, "Fare ye weel, my kind friends a',
        But be kind to Bawbie Allan.

8   "Put in your han' at my bedside,
        An' there ye'll find a warran',
    Wi my gold watch an' my prayer book,
        Gie that to Bawbie Allan.

9   "Put in your han' at my bedside,
        An' there ye'll find a warran',
    A napkin full o my heart's blood,
        Gie that to Bawbie Allan."

10 Slowly, slowly, rase she up,
        An' slowly, slowly, left him,
    An' sighin said she could not stay,
        Since death o life had reft him.

11 She hadna gane a mile but ane,
        When she heard the dead bell knellin,

hooly, slowly, quietly.   *sanna,* shall not.   *warran',* deed of gift.

An' ilka toll that the dead bell gae
  Said, Woe to Bawbie Allan.

12   In then cam her father dear,
       Said, "Bonnie Bawbie, tak him."—
     "It's time to bid me tak him noo
       When ye know his coffin's makin."

13   In then cam her brother dear,
       Said, "Tak him, Bawbie, tak him."—
     "It's time to bid me tak him noo
       When his grave-claes is a-makin."

14   Then in cam her sisters dear,
       Said, "Bonnie Bawbie, tak him."—
     "It's time to bid me tak him noo,
       When my heart it is a-brakin.

15   "O mother dear, O mak my bed,
       An' mak it saft an' narrow;
     My love has died for me to-day,
       I'll die for him to-morrow."

❦◇ C ◇❦

1   In Scarlet town, where I was born,
      There was a fair maid dwelling,
    Made every youth cry "Well away!"
      Her name was Barbara Allen.

2   All in the merry month of May,
      When green buds they are swelling,
    Young Jimmy Green on his death bed lay
      For the love of Barbara Allen.

3   He sent his man unto her there,
      To the town where she was dwelling;
    "O you must come to my master dear,
      If your name be Barbara Allen.

4   "For death is printed on his face
      And o'er his heart is stealing;

ilka, each.   *claes,* clothes.

O haste away to comfort him,
O lovely Barbara Allen!"

5 "If death is printed on his face
And o'er his heart is stealing,
Yet little better shall he be
For the love of Barbara Allen."

6 So, slowly, slowly, she came up,
And slowly she came nigh him;
And all she said when there she came,
"Young man, I think you're dying."

7 He turned his face unto her straight,
With deadly sorrow sighing:
"O lovely maid, come pity me!
I'm on my death bed lying."

8 "If on your death bed you do lie,
What need the tale you're telling?
I cannot keep you from your death:
Farewell," said Barbara Allen.

9 He turned his face unto the wall,
And deadly pains he fell in:
"Adieu, adieu, adieu to all,
Adieu to Barbara Allen."

10 As she was walking o'er the fields,
She heard the bell a-knelling;
And every stroke it seemed to say,
"Unworthy Barbara Allen."

11 She turned herself around about
And spied the corpse a-coming:
"Lay down, lay down the corpse," said she,
"That I may look upon him."

12 With scornful eyes she did look down,
Her cheeks with laughter swelling;
While all her friends cried out amen [*for* amain],
"Unworthy Barabara Allen!"

13   When he was dead and laid in grave,
     Her heart was struck with sorrow:
     "O mother, mother, make my bed,
     For I shall die to-morrow.

14   "Hard-hearted creature him to slight,
     He who loved me so dearly!
     O had I been more kind to him,
     When he was alive and near me!"

15   On her death bed as she did lay,
     She begged to be buried by him,
     And sorely repented of that day
     That she e'er did deny him.

16   "Farewell, ye virgins all," she said,
     "And shun the fault I've fell in;
     Henceforward take warning by the fall
     Of cruel Barbara Allen."

16* [One was buried in the high churchyard,
     The other in the choir;
     On one there grew a red rose bush,
     On the other there grew a brier.

17* They grew and they grew to the high steeple top,
     Till they could grow no higher;
     And there they locked in a true-lover's knot,
     For true lovers to admire.]

Clerk Saunders (69)

Unlike the heroines of most tragic ballads, Clerk (or Lord) Saunders' mistress chooses rigorous mourning rather than suicide. The opening two stanzas, lacking in the Motherwell MS. (p. 196), from which our text comes, have been interpolated from another version (Child, II, 160 from Herd MSS.).

1* [Clerk Saunders and a gay lady
     Was walking in yonder green,
     And heavy, heavy was the love
     That fell this twa lovers between.

2* "A bed, a bed," Clerk Saunders said,
    "And ay a bed for you and me;"
"Never a ane," said the gay lady,
    "Till ance we twa married be.]

1 "O I have seven bold brethren,
    And they are all valiant men,
If they knew a man that would tread my bower
    His life should not go along wi him."

2 "Then take me up into your arms,
    And lay me low down on your bed,
That ye may swear, and keep your oath clear,
    That your bower-room I did na tread.

3 "Tie a handkerchief round your face,
    And you must tye it wondrous keen,
That you may swear, and keep your oath clear,
    Ye saw na me since late yestreen."

4 But they were scarsley gone to bed,
    Nor scarse fa'n owre asleep,
Till up and started her seven brethren,
    Just at Lord Saunders' feet.

5 Out bespoke the first brither,
    "Oh but love be wondrous keen!"
Out bespoke the second brither,
    "It's ill done to kill a sleeping man."

6 Out bespoke the third brither,
    "We had better gae and let him be;"
Out bespoke the fourth brither,
    "He'll no be killed this night for me:"

7 Out bespoke the fifth brither,
    "This night Lord Saunders he shall die;
Tho there were not a man in all Scotland,
    This night Lord Saunders he shall die."

8 He took out a rusty rapier,
    And he drew it three times thro the strae;

owre, over.

Between Lord Saunders' short rib and his side
    He gard the rusty rapier gae.

9   "Awake, awake, Lord Saunders," she said,
    "Awake, awake, for sin and shame!
For the day is light, and the sun shines bricht,
    And I am afraid we will be taen.

10   "Awake, awake, Lord Saunders," she said,
    "Awake, awake, for sin and shame!
For the sheets they are asweat," she said,
    "And I am afraid we will be taen.

11   "I dreamed a dreary dream last night,
    I wish it may be for our good,
That I was cutting my yellow hair,
    And dipping it in the wells o blood."

12   Aye she waukened at this dead man,
    Aye she put on him to and fro;
Oh aye she waukened at this dead man,
    But of his death she did not know.

13   "It's I will do for my love's sake
    What many ladies would think lang;
Seven years shall come and go
    Before a glove go on my hand.

14   "And I will do for my love's sake
    What many ladies would not do;
Seven years shall come and go
    Before I wear stocking or shoe.

15   "There'll neer a shirt go on my back,
    There'll neer a kame go in my hair,
There'll never coal nor candle-light
    Shine in my bower nae mair."

gar, make.   *waukened,* tried to waken.

Lord Lovel (75)

The monotonously thumping melody to which this ballad is sung and the light-hearted style of the refrain hardly suit the tragic theme. For this reason, many American singers regard the piece as a burlesque and deliver it with mocking exaggerations. Parodies of "Lord Lovel" also abound. Perhaps the most interesting of them, a Southern taunting of Lincoln on his military reverses, is reproduced here.

Texts: A, *Hadaway's Select Songster*, Philadelphia, 1840, p. 13; B, Davis, p. 258.

⊛◇ A ◇⊛

1 Lord Lovel he stood at his castle gate,
      Combing his milk-white steed:
  When up came lady Nancy Bell,
      To wish her lovier good speed, speed, speed,
      Wishing her lovier good speed.

2 "Where are you going, Lord Lovel?" she said,
      "Oh, where are you going," said she,
  "I'm going, my lady Nancy Bell,
      Strange countries for to see, see, see . . ."

3 "When will you be back, Lord Lovel," she said,
      "Oh, when will you be back," said she,
  "In a year or two, or three at most,
      I'll return to my fair Nancy-cy-cy . . ."

4 But he had not been gone a year and a day,
      Strange countries for to see,
  When languishing thoughts came into his head,
      Lady Nancy Bell he would go see, see, see . . .

5 So he rode and rode on his milk-white horse,
      Till he came to London town,
  And there he heard St. Pancras's bells,
      And the people all mourning round, round,
      round . . .

6   "Oh, what is the matter?" Lord Lovel he said,
      "Oh, what is the matter?" said he;
    "A Lord's lady is dead," the woman replied,
      "And some call her lady Nancy-cy-cy . . ."

7   So he ordered the grave to be opened wide,
      And the shroud to be turned down;
    And there he kiss'd her clay cold lips,
      Till the tears came trickling down, down, down . . .

8   Lady Nancy she died as it might be to day,
      Lord Lovel he died [on the] morrow;
    Lady Nancy she died out of pure, pure grief,
      Lord Lovel he died out of sorrow, row, row . . .

9   Lady Nancy was laid in St. Pancras's Church,
      Lord Lovel was laid in the choir,
    And out of her bosom there grew a red rose,
      And out of her lovier's a briar, riar, riar . . .

10   It grew, and it grew, to the church steeple top,
      And then it could grow no higher;
    So there entwined in a true lovier's knot,
      For all true lovier's to admire, ire, ire . . .

❈◆ B ◆❈

1   Abe Lincoln stood at the White House gate
      Combing his milk-white steed,
    When along came Lady Lizzie Tod,
      Wishing her lover good speed, speed, speed,
      Wishing her lover good speed.

2   "Where are you going, Abe Lincoln?" she said.
      "Where are you going?" said she.
    "I'm going, my dearest Lizzie Tod,
      O'er Richmond for to see, see, see . . ."

3   "When will you be back, Abe Lincoln?" she said.
      "When will you be back?" said she.
    "In sixty or ninety days at the most,
      I'll return to my Lady Lizzie, -zie, -zie . . ."

4   He hadn't been gone more than one or two days
        O'er Richmond for to see,
    When back to the White House gate he came,
        All tattered and torn was he, he, he . . .

5   "How do you flourish, Abe Lincoln?" she said.
        "How do you flourish?" said she.
    "The rebels have killed my old Scotch horse
        And I have skedaddled, -dee, -dee, -dee, -dee . . ."

6   Abe Lincoln rode his Burnside horse
        Which started at the rebels' fire.
    He threw the baboon heels over head,
        And there he stuck tight in the mire, -ire, -ire . . .

The Braes o' Yarrow (214)

Ballads frequently begin well along in the story they are telling; the hearers are supposed to make out what has happened
earlier by alert use of the hints dropped along the way. In "The
Braes o' Yarrow," for example, we learn obliquely that the husband has accepted a challenge to fight his wife's brothers. They
had insulted him, apparently at some tavern bout, by saying
he was not their sister's social equal.

Text: Edinburgh, 1770 (Harvard Percy Papers).

1   "I dreamed a dreary dream this night,
        That fills my heart wi sorrow;
    I dreamed I was pouing the heather green
        Upon the braes of Yarrow.

2   "O true-luve mine, stay still and dine,
        As ye ha done before, O;"
    "O I'll be hame by hours nine,
        And frae the braes of Yarrow."

3   "I dreamed a dreary dream this night,
        That fills my heart wi sorrow;

pouing, pulling. *brae,* bank.

I dreamed my luve came headless hame,
    O frae the braes of Yarrow!

4   "O true-luve mine, stay still and dine,
    As ye ha done before, O;"
   "O I'll be hame by hours nine,
    And frae the braes of Yarrow."

5   "O are ye going to hawke," she says,
    "As ye ha done before, O?
   Or are ye going to weild your brand,
    Upon the braes of Yarrow?"

6   "O I am not going to hawke," he says,
    "As I have done before, O,
   But for to meet your brother John,
    Upon the braes of Yarrow."

7   As he gade down yon dowy den,
    Sorrow went him before, O;
   Nine well-wight men lay waiting him,
    Upon the braes of Yarrow.

8   "I have your sister to my wife,
    [Ye] think me an unmeet marrow;
   But yet one foot will I never flee
    Now frae the braes of Yarrow."

9   [Than] four he killd and five did wound,
    That was an unmeet marrow!
   [And he had weel nigh wan the day
    Upon the braes of Yarrow.]

10 [Bot] a cowardly [loon] came him behind,
    Our Lady lend him sorrow!
   And wi a rappier pierced his heart,
    And laid him low on Yarrow.

11 [Now Douglas] to his sister's gane,
    Wi meikle dule and sorrow:

brand, sword. *dowy,* sad. *den,* glen. *well-wight,* stalwart. *unmeet,* unworthy, unequal. *marrow,* mate. *loon,* rogue. *dule,* grief.

"Gae to your luve, sister," he says,
  "He's sleeping sound on Yarrow."

12 As she went down yon dowy den,
      Sorrow went her before, O;
    She saw her true-love lying slain
      Upon the braes of Yarrow.

13 She swoond thrice upon his breist
      That was her dearest marrow;
    Said, "Ever alace and wae the day
      Thou wentst frae me to Yarrow!"

14 She kist his mouth, she kaimed his hair,
      As she had done before, O;
    She [wiped] the blood that trickled doun
      Upon the braes of Yarrow.

15 Her hair it was three quarters lang,
      It hang baith side and yellow;
    She tied it round [her] white hause-bane,
      [And tint her life on Yarrow.]

Jamie Douglas (204)

In 1681, after eleven years of marriage, James, Marquis of
Douglas, head of the great Scottish family, formally put aside
his wife. The ballad of "Jamie Douglas" registers the marchioness's complaint against James Lockhart of Blackwood (in
reality William Lawrie, called Blackwood), whom she accuses
of having maliciously alienated her husband from her. The
ballad's dramatic first-person style deserves comment, but of
greater interest is the curious connection between "Jamie
Douglas" and the lyric complaint "Waly, Waly, But Love Be
Bonny" (B). As many as four stanzas of the lyric have infiltrated
certain versions of the ballad. Since the lyric is so much more
smoothly integrated than the ballad, one deduces that this
moving lament of an abandoned girl about to become a mother

hause-bane, neck. *tint,* caused to perish.

is the older song. Seemingly the girl's situation was so much like that of the discarded marchioness that borrowing was inevitable.

Texts: A, Kinloch MSS., I, 93, via Child, IV, 93; B, Ramsay's *Tea-Table Miscellany*, ed. 1750, p. 170.

❀◇ **A** ◇❀

1   I was a lady of high renown
      As lived in the north countrie;
   I was a lady of high renown
      Whan Earl Douglas loved me.

2   Whan we cam through Glasgow toun,
      We war a comely sight to see;
   My gude lord in velvet green,
      And I myself in cramasie.

3   Whan we cam to Douglas toun,
      We war a fine sight to behold;
   My gude lord in cramasie,
      And I myself in shining gold.

4   Whan that my auld son was born,
      And set upon the nurse's knee,
   I was as happy a woman as eer was born,
      And my gude lord he loved me.

5   But oh, an my young son was born,
      And set upon the nurse's knee,
   And I mysel war dead and gane,
      For a maid again I'll never be!

6   There cam a man into this house,
      And Jamie Lockhart was his name,
   And it was told to my gude lord
      That I was in the bed wi' him.

7   There cam anither to this house,
      And a bad friend he was to me;
   He put Jamie's shoon below my bed-stock
      And bade my gude lord come and see.

cramasie, crimson.   *an,* if only.

8   O wae be unto thee, Blackwood,
        And ae an ill death may ye dee!
    For ye was the first and the foremost man
        That parted my gude lord and me.

9   Whan my gude lord cam in my room,
        This grit falsehood for to see,
    He turnd about, and, wi' a gloom,
        He straucht did tak farewell o me.

10 "O fare thee well, my once lovely maid!
        O fare thee well, once dear to me!
    O fare thee well, my once lovely maid!
        For wi' me again ye sall never be."

11 "Sit doun, sit doun, Jamie Douglas,
        Sit thee doun and dine wi' me,
    And I'll set thee on a chair of gold,
        And a silver towel on thy knee."

12 "Whan cockle-shells turn silver bells,
        And mussels they bud on a tree,
    Whan frost and snaw turns fire to burn,
        Then I'll sit down and dine wi' thee."

13 O wae be unto thee, Blackwood,
        And ae an ill death may ye dee!
    Ye war the first and the foremost man
        That parted my gude lord and me.

14 Whan my father he heard word
        That my gude lord had forsaken me,
    He sent fifty o his brisk dragoons
        To fesh me hame to my ain countrie.

15 That morning before I did go,
        My bonny palace for to leave,
    I went into my gude lord's room,
        But alas! he wad na speak to me.

16 "Fare thee well, Jamie Douglas!
        Fare thee well, my ever dear to me!

straucht, straightway.   *fesh*, fetch.

Fare thee well, Jamie Douglas!
Be kind to the three babes I've born to thee."

❀◇ B ◇❀

1   O waly, waly up the bank!
   And waly, waly, down the brae!
And waly, waly yon burn-side,
   Where I and my love wont to gae!

2   I lean'd my back unto an aik,
   I thought it was a trusty tree;
But first it bow'd, and syne it brak,
   Sae my true-love did lightly me.

3   O waly, waly! but love [be] bonny
   A little time, while it is new;
But when 'tis auld, it waxeth cauld,
   And fades away like morning dew.

4   O wherefore shou'd I busk my head?
   Or wherefore shou'd I kame my hair?
For my true-love has me forsook,
   And says he'll never love me mair.

5   Now Arthur-Seat shall be my bed,
   The sheets shall neer be fyl'd by me;
Saint Anton's well shall be my drink,
   Since my true-love has forsaken me.

6   Martinmas wind, when wilt thou blaw,
   And shake the green leaves off the tree?
O gentle death, when wilt thou come?
   For of my life I am weary.

7   'Tis not the frost that freezes fell,
   Nor blawing snaw's inclemency;
'Tis not sic cauld that makes me cry,
   But my love's heart grown cauld to me.

brae, bank, hillside. *burn*, brook. *aik*, oak. *syne*, then. *busk*,
decorate. *Arthur-Seat*, desolate hill in Edinburgh.

8 When we came in by Glasgow town,
   We were a comely sight to see;
   My love was cled in the black velvet,
   And I my sell in cramasie.

9 But had I wist, before I kiss'd,
   That love had been sae ill to win,
   I'd lock'd my heart in a case of gold,
   And pin'd it with a silver pin.

10 Oh, oh, if my young babes were born,
   And set upon the nurse's knee,
   And I my sell were dead and gane!
   For a maid again I'll never be.

The Gypsy Laddie (Johnny Faa) (200)

A gypsy chieftain bearing the common Romany name of Johnny Faa was executed by Scottish officials in 1624, but no connection between this unfortunate, or any other gypsy, and a wife of the Earl of Cassilis has ever been established. The numerous American variants of "The Gypsy Laddie" (e.g., "Black Jack David," "Gypsum Davey"), unlike the Scottish versions, leave the principals unnamed. A comparison of our text A (*Scots Magazine*, 80:309) with text B, from North Carolina (Brown, II, 165) points up other differences as well. The American text, for example, incorporates a snatch of a folk song, "I'm Seventeen Come Sunday." Scottish "lord" becomes "landlord," the only lord the mountain folk know. In Scotland the husband recovers his wife and hangs the abductor and his accomplices. No American ballad has this ending. Rather, the lady scoffs at her husband and refuses to return, though upon reflection she comes to feel none too happy with her new lot.

cramasie, crimson.

❦ A ❦

1 The gypsies they came to my lord Cassilis' yett,
    And O but they sang bonnie!
They sang sae sweet and sae complete
    That down came our fair ladie.

2 She came tripping down the stairs,
    And all her maids before her;
As soon as they saw her weel-far'd face,
    They coost their glamourie owre her.

3 She gave to them the good wheat bread,
    And they gave her the ginger;
But she gave them a far better thing,
    The gold ring off her finger.

4 "Will ye go with me, my hinny and my heart?
    Will ye go with me, my dearie?
And I will swear, by the staff of my spear,
    That your lord shall nae mair come near thee."

5 "Gar take from me my silk manteel,
    And bring to me a plaidie,
For I will travel the world owre
    Along with the gypsie laddie.

6 "I could sail the seas with my Jockie Faa,
    I could sail the seas with my dearie;
I could sail the seas with my Jockie Faa,
    And with pleasure could drown with my dearie."

7 They wandred high, they wandred low,
    They wandred late and early,
Until they came to an old tenant's-barn,
    And by this time she was weary.

8 "Last night I lay in a weel-made bed,
    And my noble lord beside me,

weel-far'd, well-favored. *coost*, cast. *glamourie*, magic spell
hinny, honey. *gar*, do.

And now I must ly in an old tenant's-barn,
And the black crew glowring owre me."

9 "O hold your tongue, my hinny and my heart,
O hold your tongue, my dearie,
For I will swear, by the moon and the stars,
That thy lord shall nae mair come near thee."

10 They wandred high, they wandred low,
They wandred late and early,
Until they came to that wan water,
And by this time she was wearie.

11 "Aften have I rode that wan water,
And my lord Cassilis beside me,
And now I must set in my white feet and wade,
And carry the gypsie laddie."

12 By and by came home this noble lord,
And asking for his ladie,
The one did cry, the other did reply,
"She is gone with the gypsie laddie."

13 "Go saddle to me the black," he says,
"The brown rides never so speedie,
And I will neither eat nor drink
Till I bring home my ladie."

14 He wandred high, he wandred low,
He wandred late and early,
Until he came to that wan water,
And there he spied his ladie.

15 "O wilt thou go home, my hinny and my heart,
O wilt thou go home, my dearie?
And I'll close thee in a close room,
Where no man shall come near thee."

16 "I will not go home, my hinny and my heart,
I will not go home, my dearie;
If I have brewn good beer, I will drink of the same,
And my lord shall nae mair come near me.

17 "But I will swear, by the moon and the stars,
        And the sun that shines so clearly,
    That I am as free of the gypsie gang
        As the hour my mother did bear me."

18 They were fifteen valiant men,
        Black, but very bonny,
    And they lost all their lives for one,
        The Earl of Cassilis' ladie.

❀◊ B ◊❀

1 Black Jack David come ridin' through the woods,
   Singin' so loud and merry
   That the green hills all around him ring,
   And he charmed the heart of a lady,
   And he charmed the heart of a lady.

2 "How old are you, my pretty little miss,
   How old are you, my lady?"
   She answered him with a "Tee, hee, hee,
   I'll be sixteen next summer."

3 "Come, go with me, my pretty little miss,
   Come, go with me, my lady;
   I'll take you across the deep blue sea
   Where you never shall want for money.

4 "Won't you pull off those high heeled shoes
   All made of Spanish leather;
   Won't you put on some low heeled shoes?
   And we'll ride off together."

5 She soon pulled off those high heeled shoes
   All made of Spanish leather;
   She put on those low heeled shoes
   And they rode off together.

6 'Twas late at night when the land-lord come
   Inquirin' for his lady.
   He was posted by a fair young maid:
   "She's gone with Black Jack David."

7 "Go saddle me my noble steed,
Go bridle me my derby;
I'll ride to the east, I'll ride to the west,
Or overtake my lady."

8 He rode till he came to the deep below;
The stream was deep and muddy.
Tears came tricklin' down his cheeks,
For there he spied his lady.

9 "How can you leave your house and land,
How can you leave your baby,
How can you leave your husband dear
To go with Black Jack David?"

10 "Very well can I leave my house and land,
Very well can I leave my baby,
Much better can I leave my husband dear
To go with Black Jack David.

11 "I won't come back to you, my love,
Nor I won't come back, my husband;
I wouldn't give a kiss from David's lips
For all your land and money.

12 "Last night I lay on a feather bed
Beside my husband and baby;
Tonight I lay on the cold damp ground
Beside the Black Jack David."

13 She soon run through her gay clothing,
Her velvet shoes and stockings;
Her gold ring off her finger was gone,
And the gold plate off her bosom.

14 "Oh, once I had a house and land,
A feather bed and money,
But now I've come to an old straw pad,
With nothing but Black Jack David."

The Butcher Boy

Widely popular in Britain and America, "The Butcher Boy" is an amalgam of several English broadsides-become-folk-songs. The second stanza, for example, will be recognized as the opening of the old college song "There Is a Tavern in the Town," which was itself drawn from an English folk song "There Is an Alehouse in Yonder Town." "London town" in the Nova Scotia text we print (Mackenzie, p. 157) is more commonly "Jersey City" in the United States. The uniformity of the American variants indicates strict descent from the standard version found in pre-Civil-War songsters. Most versions of the ballad have the abrupt but necessary shift from first to third person just before the discovery scene—a grave aesthetic error in a literary composition, but forgivable in a folk ballad.

1   In London town where I did dwell,
    A butcher boy I loved him well.
    He courted me for many a day;
    He stole from me my heart away.

2   There is an inn in that same town,
    And there my love he sits him down;
    He takes a strange girl on his knee
    And tells her what he wouldn't tell me.

3   The reason is, I'll tell you why,
    Because she's got more gold than I.
    But gold will melt and silver fly,
    And in time of need be as poor as I.

4   I'll go upstairs and make my bed.
    "There is nothing to do," my mother said.
    My mother she has followed me,
    Saying, "What is the matter, my daughter dear?"

5   "O mother dear, you little know
    What pains or sorrow or what woe!

Go get a chair and sit me down,
With pen and ink I'll write all down."

6 She wrote a letter, she wrote a song,
She wrote a letter, she wrote it long;
On every line she dropped a tear,
At every verse cried, "Willy dear!"

7 Her father he came home that night
Enquiring for his heart's delight;
He went upstairs, the door he broke,
He found her hanging on a rope.

8 He took a knife and cut her down,
And in her bosom these lines he found:
"O what a foolish girl was I
To hang myself for a butcher's boy.

9 "Go dig my grave both wide and deep,
Put a marble stone at my head and feet,
And on my grave place a turtle dove
To show the world that I died for love."

IV: LOVE AND SENTIMENT

Hind Horn (17)

Three medieval romances, one in French, describe in detail the protracted series of adventures that won Hind (Young) Horn his renown. The ballad focuses on only one incident, the return of Hind Horn to claim his betrothed, although by way of preparation we are told very briefly of the bestowal of the talisman ring and the warning it gave. Similarities between Horn's homecoming and Ulysses' are apparent; even more closely related are the German ballads of "The Noble Moringer" cycle.

All copies of Hind Horn recovered have come from Scotsmen or from Canadians of Scottish extraction. Our text is from Motherwell's MS., p. 106.

1   In Scotland there was a babie born,
    Lill lal, etc.
  And his name it was called young Hind Horn.
    With a fal lal, etc.

2   He sent a letter to our king
  That he was in love with his daughter Jean.

3   He's gien to her a silver wand,
  With seven living lavrocks sitting thereon.

4   She's gien to him a diamond ring,
  With seven bright diamonds set therein.

5   "When this ring grows pale and wan,
  You may know by it my love is gane."

6   One day as he looked his ring upon,
  He saw the diamonds pale and wan.

7   He left the sea and came to land,
  And the first that he met was an old beggar man.

lavrock, lark.

112

8   "What news, what news?" said young Hind Horn;
     "No news, no news," said the old beggar man.

9   "No news," said the beggar, "no news at a',
     But there is a wedding in the king's ha'.

10 "But there is a wedding in the king's ha',
     That has halden these forty days and twa."

11 "Will ye lend me your begging coat?
     And I'll lend you my scarlet cloak.

12 "Will you lend me your beggar's rung?
     And I'll gie you my steed to ride upon.

13 "Will you lend me your wig o' hair,
     To cover mine, because it is fair?"

14 The auld beggar man was bound for the mill,
     But young Hind Horn for the king's hall.

15 The auld beggar man was bound for to ride,
     But young Hind Horn was bound for the bride.

16 When he came to the king's gate,
     He sought a drink for Hind Horn's sake.

17 The bride came down with a glass of wine,
     When he drank out the glass, and dropt in the ring.

18 "O got ye this by sea or land?
     Or got ye it off a dead man's hand?"

19 "I got not it by sea, I got it by land,
     And I got it madam out of your own hand."

20 "O I'll cast off my gowns of brown,
     And beg wi' you frae town to town.

21 "O I'll cast off my gowns of red,
     And I'll beg wi' you to win my bread."

22 "Ye needna cast off your gowns of brown,
     For I'll make you lady o' many a town.

rung, staff.

23 "Ye needna cast off your gowns of red,
    It's only a sham, the begging o' my bread."

24 The bridegroom he had wedded the bride,
    But young Hind Horn he took her to bed.

Fair Annie (62)

It seems hardly credible that Annie's heartless lover would claim his bride from the very family from which, a few years before, he had stolen his faithful concubine, but a single improbability is a minor flaw in this most touching and lyrical of ballads. Scott's *Minstrelsy* (II, 102) furnishes the classic text, which is our A. Under B are printed two alternative endings. These illustrate how a few older Scottish versions have tried to make Annie's lord more worthy of her devotion by having him repudiate the new bride of his own will. Version C from West Virginia (Combs, p. 129) retells the story in a pioneer setting, introducing Indians, riverboats, banjos, and salt licks.

❀◇ A ◇❀

1 "It's narrow, narrow, make your bed,
    And learn to lie your lane,
  For I'm ga'n o'er the sea, Fair Annie,
    A braw bride to bring hame;
  Wi' her I will get gowd and gear;
    Wi' you I ne'er got nane.

2 "But wha will bake my bridal bread,
    Or brew my bridal ale?
  And wha will welcome my brisk bride,
    That I bring o'er the dale?"

3 "It's I will bake your bridal bread,
    And brew your bridal ale,
  And I will welcome your brisk bride,
    That you bring o'er the dale."

braw, brave, fine.

4 "But she that welcomes my brisk bride
    Maun gang like maiden fair;
She maun lace on her robe sae jimp,
    And braid her yellow hair."

5 "But how can I gang maiden-like,
    When maiden I am nane?
Have I not born seven sons to thee,
    And am with child again?"

6 She's tane her young son in her arms,
    Another in her hand,
And she's up to the highest tower,
    To see him come to land.

7 "Come up, come up, my eldest son,
    And look o'er yon sea-strand,
And see your father's new-come bride,
    Before she come to land."

8 "Come down, come down, my mother dear,
    Come frae the castle wa'!
I fear, if langer ye stand there,
    Ye'll let yoursell down fa'."

9 And she gaed down, and farther down,
    Her love's ship for to see,
And the topmast and the mainmast
    Shone like the silver free.

10 And she's gane down, and farther down,
    The bride's ship to behold;
And the topmast and the mainmast
    They shone just like gold.

11 She's ta'en her seven sons in her hand,
    I wot she didna fail;
She met Lord Thomas and his bride,
    As they came o'er the dale.

12 "You're welcome to your house, Lord Thomas,
    You're welcome to your land;

maun, must.   *jimp,* slender.

You're welcome with your fair ladye,
    That you lead by the hand.

13   "You're welcome to your ha's, ladye,
    You're welcome to your bowers;
   You're welcome to your hame, ladye,
    For a' that's here is yours."

14   "I thank thee, Annie, I thank thee, Annie,
    Sae dearly as I thank thee;
   You're the likest to my sister Annie,
    That ever I did see.

15   "There came a knight out o'er the sea,
    And steal'd my sister away;
   The shame scoup in his company,
    And land where'er he gae!"

16   She hang ae napkin at the door,
    Another in the ha',
   And a' to wipe the trickling tears,
    Sae fast as they did fa'.

17   And aye she served the lang tables,
    With white bread and with wine;
   And aye she drank the wan water,
    To had her colour fine.

18   And aye she served the lang tables,
    With white bread and with brown;
   And ay she turned her round about,
    Sae fast the tears fell down.

19   And he's ta'en down the silk napkin,
    Hung on a silver pin,
   And aye he wipes the tear trickling
    A' down her cheik and chin.

20   And aye he turn'd him round about,
    And smil'd amang his men;
   Says, "Like ye best the old ladye,
    Or her that's new come hame?"

scoup, fly. *had,* hold, fix.

21   When bells were rung, and mass was sung,
    And a' men bound to bed,
  Lord Thomas and his new-come bride
    To their chambers they were gaed.

22   Annie made her bed a little forbye,
    To hear what they might say;
  "And ever alas!" Fair Annie cried,
    "That I should see this day!

23   "Gin my seven sons were seven young rats,
    Running on the castle wa',
  And I were a grey cat mysell,
    I soon would worry them a'.

24   "Gin my seven sons were seven young hares,
    Running o'er yon lilly lee,
  And I were a gre[y]hound mysell,
    Soon worried they a' should be."

25   And wae and sad Fair Annie sat,
    And drearie was her sang,
  And ever, as she sobb'd and grat,
    "Wae to the man that did the wrang!"

26   "My gown is on," said the new-come bride,
    "My shoes are on my feet,
  And I will to Fair Annie's chamber,
    And see what gars her greet.

27   "What ails ye, what ails ye, Fair Annie,
    That ye make sic a moan?
  Has your wine barrels cast the girds,
    Or is your white bread gone?

28   "O wha was't was your father, Annie,
    Or wha was't was your mother?
  And had ye ony sister, Annie,
    Or had ye ony brother?"

29   "The Earl of Wemyss was my father,
    The Countess of Wemyss my mother;

gin, if.   *greet, grat,* weep, wept.   *gars,* makes.   *gird,* hoop.

And a' the folk about the house
　　To me were sister and brother."

30 "If the Earl of Wemyss was your father,
　　I wot sae was he mine;
And it shall not be for lack o' gowd
　　That ye your love sall tine.

31 "For I have seven ships o' mine ain,
　　A' loaded to the brim,
And I will gie them a' to thee,
　　Wi' four to thine eldest son;
But thanks to a' the powers in heaven
　　That I gae maiden hame!"

❧◇ **B** ◇❧

[From Jamieson, II, 375.]

19 "Rise up, rise up, my bierly bride,
　　I think my bed's but cald;
I wadna hear my lady lament
　　For your tocher ten times tald.

20 "O seven ships did bring you here,
　　And ane sall tak you hame;
The leave I'll keep to your sister Jane,
　　For tocher she gat nane."

[From Motherwell, *Minstrelsy*, p. 334.]

29 "Come to your bed, my sister dear,
　　It ne'er was wrang'd for me,
Bot an ae kiss of his merry mouth,
　　As we cam owre the sea."

30 "Awa, awa, ye forenoon bride,
　　Awa, awa frae me;
I wudna hear my Annie greet,
　　For a' the gold I got wi' thee."

tine, lose.
bierly, stately.　*tocher,* dowry.　*leave,* remainder.　*wrang'd for,*
wronged by.　*ae,* single.　*greet,* weep.

31   "There were five ships of gay red gold
        Cam owre the seas with me,
     It's twa o' them will tak me hame,
        And three I'll leave wi' thee.

32   "Seven ships o' white monie
        Came owre the seas wi' me,
     Five o' them I'll leave wi' thee,
        And twa will take me hame;
     And my mother will make my portion up
        When I return again."

❧❀ C ❀❧

1   The Indians stole fair Annie
        As she walked by the sea,
     But Lord Harry for her a ransom paid,
        In gold and silver money.

2   She lived far away with him,
        And none knew whence she came;
     She lived in a mansion-house with her love,
        But never told her name.

3   "Now make your bed all narrow,
        And learn to lie alone;
     For I'm going far away, Annie,
        To bring my sweet bride home.

4   "I'm going far over the river
        To bring my sweet bride home;
     For she brings me land and slaves,
        And with you I can get none.

5   "But who will spread the wedding feast,
        And pour the red red wine?
     And who will welcome my sweet bride,
        My bonny bride so fine?"

6   "O I will spread the wedding feast,
        And I will pour the red red wine,
     And I will welcome your sweet bride,
        Your bonny bride so fine."

7   "But she who welcomes my sweet bride
         Must look like a maiden fair,
     With lace on her robe so narrow,
         And flowers among her hair.

8   "Do up, do up, your yellow hair,
         And knot it on your neck,
     And see you look as maiden-like
         As when I met you first."

9   "How can I look so maiden-like,
         When maiden I am none?
     Have I not had six sons by thee,
         And am with child again?"

10   Four months were past and gone,
         And the word to fair Annie came
     That the boat was back from the river,
         With the sweet bonny bride at home.

11   She took her young son on her hip,
         A second by the hand,
     And she went out on the upper porch
         To see if the boat did land.

12   "Come down, come down, O mother dear,
         Come down from the porch so tall;
     For I fear if longer you stand there,
         You will make yourself fall."

13   She took her young son on her arm,
         A second by the hand,
     And with the keys about her waist
         Out to the gate has gone.

14   "O welcome home, my good Lord,
         To your mansion and your farm;
     O welcome home, my good Lord,
         And you are safe from harm.

15   "O welcome home, my fair lady,
         For all that's here is yours;
     O welcome home, my fair lady,
         And you are safe with yours."

16 "Who is that lady, my Lord,
       That welcomes you and me?
   Before I'm long about the place,
       Her friend I mean to be."

17 Fair Annie served the wedding feast,
       And smiled upon them all;
   But before the healths went round
       Her tears began to fall.

18 When night was late and dance was done,
       All the guests were off for bed;
   After the groom and the bonny bride
       In one bed they had laid,

19 Fair Annie took a banjo in her hand
       To play the two to sleep;
   But ever as she played and sang,
       O sorely did she weep.

20 "But if my sons were seven rats
       Running over the milk-house wall,
   And I were a great gray cat,
       How I would worry them all!

21 "But if my sons were seven grey-foxes
       Running over those brushy hills,
   And I myself a good fox hound,
       I soon would chase their fill.

22 "But if my sons were seven buck deer
       Drinking at the old salt-lick,
   And I myself a good hunting dog,
       I soon would see them kick."

23 Then up did speak the bonny bride
       From the bride-bed where she lay;
   "That's like my sister Annie," said she;
       "Who is it that sings and plays?

24 "I'll slip on my dress," said the new-come bride,
       "And draw my shoes over my feet;
   I will see who so sadly sings,
       And what it is that makes her grief.

25   "O what is it ails my housekeeper,
         That you make such a to-do?
     Have you lost the keys from your belt,
         Or is all your wedding feast gone?"

26   "It isn't because my keys are lost,
         Or because my feast is gone;
     But I have lost my own true-love,
         And he has wedded another one."

27   "Who was your father, tell me,
         And who then was your mother?
     And had you any sister?" she says,
         "And had you any brother?"

28   "The Lord of Salter was my father,
         The Lady of Salter was my mother;
     Young Susan was my dear sister,
         And Lord James was my brother."

29   "If the Lord of Salter was your father,
         I'm sure he so was mine;
     And you're O, my sister Annie,
         And my true-love is thine.

30   "Take your husband, my sister dear;
         You were never wronged by me,
     More than a kiss from his dear mouth,
         As we came up the bay.

31   "Seven ships well loaded
         Brought all my dowry with me;
     And one of them will carry me home,
         And six I will give to thee."

Child Waters (63)

The morality of "Child Waters," stemming as it does from the harsh and tragic view of life held by the medieval ballad folk, generally repels modern hearers. For like Fair Annie, Fair Ellen endures so much needless persecution before winning

through to moderate happiness that we see her as irretrievably
pathetic and even find something morbid in her acceptance of
her trials. And the persecutor-lover of this Patient Griselda is
so exquisitely diabolic in his cruelty that marriage to him hardly
seems the glorious consummation that the ballad makes it out
to be. Without doubt the offense to modern moral sensibilities
explains why this ballad has disappeared from living tradition.
    Text: Percy Folio MS., II, 269.

1   Childe Watters in his stable stoode,
         And stroaket his milk-white steede;
     To him came a ffaire young ladye
         As ere did weare woman's wee[de].

2   Sais, "Christ you saue, good Chyld Waters!"
         Sayes, "Christ you saue and see!
     My girdle of gold, which was too longe,
         Is now to[o] short ffor mee.

3   "And all is with one chyld of yours,
         I ffeele sturre att my side;
     My gowne of greene, it is to[o] strayght;
         Before it was to[o] wide."

4   "If the child be mine, faire Ellen," he said,
         "Be mine, as you tell mee,
     Take you Cheshire and Lancashire both,
         Take them your owne to bee.

5   "If the child be mine, ffaire Ellen," he said,
         "Be mine, as you doe sweare,
     Take you Cheshire and Lancashire both,
         And make that child your heyre."

6   Shee saies, "I had rather haue one kisse,
         Child Waters, of thy mouth,
     Then I wold haue Cheshire and Lancashire both,
         That lyes by north and south.

7   "And I had rather haue a twinkling,
         Child Waters, of your eye,

weede, clothing.

> Then I wold haue Cheshire and Lancashire both,
>> To take them mine oune to bee."

8 "To-morrow, Ellen, I must forth ryde
>> Soe ffarr into the north countrye;
> The ffairest lady that I can ffind,
>> Ellen, must goe with mee."
> "And euer I pray you, Child Watters,
>> Your ffootpage let me bee!"

9 "If you will my ffootpage be, Ellen,
>> As you doe tell itt mee,
> Then you must cutt your gowne of greene
>> An inche aboue your knee.

10 "Soe must you doe your yellow lockes,
>> Another inch aboue your eye;
> You must tell noe man what is my name;
>> My ffootpage then you shall bee."

11 All this long day Child Waters rode,
>> Shee ran bare ffoote by his side;
> Yett was he neuer soe curteous a knight
>> To say, "Ellen, will you ryde?"

12 But all this day Child Waters rode,
>> Shee ran barffoote thorow the broome;
> Yett he was neuer soe curteous a knight
>> As to say, "Put on your shoone."

13 "Ride softlye," shee said, "Child Watters;
>> Why doe you ryde soe ffast?
> The child which is no man's but yours
>> My bodye itt will burst."

14 He sayes, "Sees thou yonder water, Ellen,
>> That fflowes from banke to brim?"
> "I trust to God, Child Waters," she said,
>> "You will neuer see mee swime."

15 But when shee came to the waters side,
>> Shee sayled to the chinne:
> "Except the lord of heuen be my speed.
>> Now must I learne to swime."

speed, help.

16   The salt waters bare vp Ellen's clothes,
     Our ladye bare vpp he[r] chinne,
  And Child Waters was a woe man, good Lord,
     To ssee faire Ellen swime.

17   And when shee ouer the water was,
     Shee then came to his knee:
  He said, "Come hither, ffaire Ellen,
     Loe yonder what I see!

18   "Seest thou not yonder hall, Ellen?
     Of redd gold shine the yates;
  There's four and twenty ffayre ladyes,
     The ffairest is my wordlye make.

19   "Seest thou not yonder hall, Ellen?
     Of redd gold shineth the tower;
  There is four and twenty ffaire ladyes,
     The fairest is my paramoure."

20   "I doe see the hall now, Child Waters,
     That of redd gold shineth the yates;
  God giue good then of your selfe,
     And of your wordlye make!

21   "I doe see the hall now, Child Waters,
     That of redd gold shineth the tower;
  God giue good then of your selfe,
     And of your paramoure!"

22   There were four and twenty ladyes,
     Were playing att the ball,
  And Ellen, was the ffairest ladye,
     Must bring his steed to the stall.

23   There were four and twenty faire ladyes
     Was playing att the chesse;
  And Ellen, shee was the ffairest ladye,
     Must bring his horsse to grasse.

24   And then bespake Child Water's sister,
     And these were the words said shee:

wordlye make, earthly mate.

"You haue the prettyest ffootpage, brother,
    That euer I saw with mine eye;

25 "But that his belly it is soe bigg,
        His girdle goes wonderous hye;
    And euer I pray you, Child Waters,
        Let him goe into the chamber with mee."

26 "It is more meete for a little ffootpage,
        That has run through mosse and mire,
    To take his supper vpon his knee
        And sitt downe by the kitchen fyer,
    Then to goe into the chamber with any ladye
        That weares soe [rich] attyre."

27 But when they had supped euery one,
        To bedd they took the way;
    He sayd, "Come hither, my little footpage,
        Harken what I doe say.

28 "And goe thee downe into yonder towne,
        And low into the street;
    The ffairest ladye that thou can find,
        Hyer her in mine armes to sleepe,
    And take her vp in thine armes two,
        For filinge of her ffeete."

29 Ellen is gone into the towne,
        And low into the streete;
    The fairest ladye that shee cold find
        Shee hyred in his armes to sleepe,
    And tooke her in her armes two,
        For filing of her ffeete.

30 "I pray you now, good Child Waters,
        That I may creepe in att your bedd's feete;
    For there is noe place about this house
        Where I may say a sleepe."

31 This [night] and itt droue on affterward
        Till itt was neere the day:

filinge, defiling.

He sayd, "Rise vp, my litle ffoote-page,
    And giue my steed corne and hay;
And soe doe thou the good blacke oates,
    That he may carry me the better away."

32   And vp then rose ffaire Ellen,
    And gaue his steed corne and hay,
And soe shee did and the good blacke oates,
    That he might carry him the better away.

33   Shee layned her backe to the manger side,
    And greiuouslye did groane;
And that beheard his mother deere,
    And heard her make her moane.

34   Shee said, "Rise vp, thou Child Waters,
    I thinke thou art a cursed man;
For yonder is a ghost in thy stable,
    That greiuouslye doth groane,
Or else some woman laboures of child,
    Shee is soe woe begone.

35   But vp then rose Child Waters,
    And did on his shirt of silke;
Then he put on his other clothes
    On his body as white as milke.

36   And when he came to the stable-dore,
    Full still that hee did stand,
That hee might heare no faire Ellen,
    How shee made her monand.

37   Shee said, "Lullabye, my owne deere child!
    Lullabye, deere child, deere!
I wold thy father were a king,
    Thy mother layd on a beere!"

38   "Peace now," he said, "good faire Ellen,
    And be of good cheere, I thee pray,
And the bridall and the churching both,
    They shall bee vpon one day."

monand, moaning.

Young Beichan (Lord Bateman) (53)

Virtually every ballad community of recent times has reported at least one variant of "Young Beichan," or, to use the English title, "Lord Bateman." American texts show great uniformity, perhaps because the frequent printing of the ballad in nine-teenth-century songbooks and on broadsides had the effect of standardizing the verses. Few of the modern recordings, whether American or British, do justice to the story. For one thing, the ballad's length strains the modern singer's memory. More im-portant, the ballad is somewhat episodic and requires an unusual amount of scene shifting. A few rare locutions have also given difficulty. Because the "tree" put through the hole bored in Beichan's shoulder (stanza 2) is not understood as "draught-tree" (the pole by which a cart is pulled), it is altered in some variants to "key" or "rope." Other texts, among them the commonest English traditional version, solve the problem by placing a flourishing tree in Beichan's prison and chaining him to it!

Legend has it that Gilbert Becket, the father of St. Thomas of Canterbury, actually went through the adventures ascribed to Beichan, but history insists that the saint's mother was a burgher-woman of Caen and not a Saracen princess.

Text: Jamieson's Brown MS., p. 13.

1   In London city was Bicham born,
        He longd strange countries for to see,
     But he was ta'en by a savage Moor,
        Who handld him right cruely.

2   For thro' his shoulder he put a bore,
        And thro the bore has pitten a tree,
     An he's gard him draw the carts o wine,
        Where horse and oxen had wont to be.

3   He's casten [him] in a dungeon deep,
        Where he coud neither hear nor see;

gar, make.

He's shut him up in a prison strong,
    An he's handld him right cruely.

4 O this Moor he had but ae daughter,
    I wot her name was Shusy Pye;
She's doen her to the prison-house,
    And she's calld Young Bicham one word by.

5 "O hae ye ony land or rents,
    Or citys in your ain country,
Coud free you out of prison strong,
    An coud mantain a lady free?"

6 "O London city is my own,
    An other citys twa or three,
Coud loose me out o prison strong,
    An coud mantain a lady free."

7 O she has bribed her father's men
    Wi meikle goud and white money,
She's gotten the key o the prison doors,
    An she has set Young Bicham free.

8 She's gi'n him a loaf o good white bread,
    But an a flask o Spanish wine,
An she bad him mind on the ladie's love,
    That sae kindly freed him out o pine.

9 "Go set your foot on good ship-board,
    An haste you back to your ain country,
An before that seven years has an end,
    Come back again, love, and marry me."

10 It was long or seven years had an end
    She longd fu sair her love to see;
She's set her foot on good ship-board,
    An turnd her back on her ain country.

11 She's saild up, so has she doun,
    Till she came to the other side;
She's landed at Young Bicham's gates,
    An I hop this day she sal be his bride.

doen her, betaken herself.   *meikle,* much.

12 "Is this Young Bicham's gates?" says she,
  "Or is that noble prince within?"
 "He's up the stairs wi his bonny bride,
  An monny a lord and lady wi him."

13 "O has he taen a bonny bride,
  An has he clean forgotten me!"
 An sighing said that gay lady,
  "I wish I were in my ain country!"

14 But she's pitten her han in her pocket,
  An gin the porter guineas three;
 Says, "Take ye that, ye proud porter,
  An bid the bridegroom speak to me."

15 O whan the porter came up the stair,
  He's fa'n low down upon his knee:
 "Won up, won up, ye proud porter,
  An what makes a' this courtesy?"

16 "O I've been porter at your gates
  This mair nor seven years an three,
 But there is a lady at them now
  The like of whom I never did see.

17 "For on every finger she has a ring,
  An on the mid-finger she has three,
 An there's as meikle goud aboon her brow
  As woud buy an earldome o lan to me."

18 Then up it started Young Bicham,
  An sware so loud by Our Lady,
 "It can be nane but Shusy Pye,
  That has come oer the sea to me."

19 O quickly ran he down the stair,
  O' fifteen steps he has made but three;
 He's tane his bonny love in his arms,
  An a wot he kissd her tenderly.

20 "O hae you tane a bonny bride?
  An hae you quite forsaken me?

---

a wot, I know, assuredly.

An hae ye quite forgotten her
That gae you life an liberty?"

21 She's lookit oer her left shoulder
To hide the tears stood in her ee;
"Now fare thee well, Young Bicham," she says,
"I'll strive to think nae mair on thee."

22 "Take back your daughter, madam," he says,
"An a double dowry I'll gi her wi;
For I maun marry my first true love,
That's done and suffered so much for me."

23 He's take his bonny love by the han,
And led her to yon fountain stane;
He's changd her name frae Shusy Pye,
An he's cald her his bonny love, Lady Jane.

The Maid Freed from the Gallows (95)

Why the maid should be in jeopardy of her life is neither answered nor even so much as hinted at in most versions of the ballad. In Sicilian, Catalan, and German analogues, the girl has been carried off by pirates or Moors and the fee she begs of her relatives is her ransom. Another explanation for the girl's plight is implied by recent English traditional texts and a few Negro versions: the girl has lost a golden ball (cup, key) left in her safekeeping. Hanging seems an extreme punishment for so trivial a crime until we realize that the golden ball symbolizes chastity and that hanging or—as in "Lady Maisry"—burning was the normal ballad punishment for the unchaste. Only the lover can restore the girl's honor (see *JFS*, 5:231). A. H. Krapp traces the story to the Greek bride sacrifice (*Speculum*, 16:236).

Under the titles "The Gallows Tree" or "The Gallus Pole," the ballad is a favorite among Southern Negroes; it is widely sung by Negroes in the Bahamas and Jamaica as well (Smith, pp. 80-94). The stanzaic repetition, unaltered except for the substitution of a different relative, resembles the structure of

Negro spirituals. This fact and the dramatic quality of the piece probably account for its great appeal. The story is told in Negro folk tales and in *cante-fables* (compositions partly folk tale, partly ballad—our text C, for example), and dramatizations by Negro children have also been reported. English children have long used the ballad as a game song.

The distinctiveness of "The Maid Freed from the Gallows" lies in its starkly simple structure; once begun, its development is inevitable.

Texts: A, from Kent, 1770 (Harvard Percy Papers); B, Yorkshire, 1866 (Child, II, 353); C, *PMLA,* 39:475, traditional in Jamaica. The rarity of a woman's being hanged in the United States has given rise to versions in which the victim is a man. Text D from North Carolina (Brown, II, 148), a patchwork of phrases from convict songs, is one such ballad.

❖◇ A ◇❖

1 "O good Lord Judge, and sweet Lord Judge,
      Peace for a little while!
   Methinks I see my own father,
      Come riding by the stile.

2 "Oh father, oh father, a little of your gold,
      And likewise of your fee!
   To keep my body from yonder grave,
      And my neck from the gallows-tree."

3 "None of my gold now you shall have,
      Nor likewise of my fee;
   For I am come to see you hangd,
      And hangèd you shall be."

4 "Oh good Lord Judge, and sweet Lord Judge,
      Peace for a little while!
   Methinks I see my own mother,
      Come riding by the stile.

5 "Oh mother, oh mother, a little of your gold,
      And likewise of your fee,
   To keep my body from yonder grave,
      And my neck from the gallows-tree!"

6   "None of my gold now shall you have,
     Nor likewise of my fee;
  For I am come to see you hangd,
     And hangèd you shall be."

7   "Oh good Lord Judge, and sweet Lord Judge,
     Peace for a little while!
  Methinks I see my own brother,
     Come riding by the stile.

8   "Oh brother, oh brother, a little of your gold,
     And likewise of your fee,
  To keep my body from yonder grave,
     And my neck from the gallows-tree!"

9   "None of my gold now shall you have,
     Nor likewise of my fee;
  For I am come to see you hangd,
     And hangèd you shall be."

10   "Oh good Lord Judge, and sweet Lord Judge,
     Peace for a little while!
  Methinks I see my own sister,
     Come riding by the stile.

11   "Oh sister, oh sister, a little of your gold,
     And likewise of your fee,
  To keep my body from yonder grave,
     And my neck from the gallows-tree!"

12   "None of my gold now shall you have,
     Nor likewise of my fee;
  For I am come to see you hangd,
     And hangèd you shall be."

13   "Oh good Lord Judge, and sweet Lord Judge,
     Peace for a little while!
  Methinks I see my own true-love,
     Come riding by the stile.

14   "Oh true-love, oh true-love, a little of your gold,
     And likewise of your fee,
  To save my body from yonder grave,
     And my neck from the gallows-tree."

15   "Some of my gold now you shall have,
        And likewise of my fee,
     For I am come to see you saved,
        And savèd you shall be."

❀◊ **B** ◊❀

1   "Stop, stop!
     I think I see my mother coming . . .

2   "Oh mother, hast brought my golden ball,
     And come to set me free? . . ."

3   "I've neither brought thy golden ball,
     Nor come to set thee free,
     But I've come to see thee hung,
     Upon this gallows-tree."

4   "Stop, stop!
     I think I see my father coming . . .

5   "Oh father, hast brought my golden ball,
     And come to set me free? . . ."

6   "I've neither brought thy golden ball,
     Nor come to set thee free,
     But I have come to see thee hung,
     Upon this gallows-tree."

7   "Stop, stop!
     I see my sweet-heart coming . . .

8   "Sweet-heart, hast brought my golden ball,
     And come to set me free? . . ."

9   "Aye, I have brought thy golden ball,
     And come to set thee free;
     I have not come to see thee hung,
     Upon this gallows-tree."

❀◊ **C** ◊❀

   Deh was a princess propose to be married. During de time
she was going on to de day of marriage, she do somet'ing against

de rule and regulation of her royalty dat cause her to be brought
up in trial, found guilty, an' sentenced to be hung. What she
did was against de family rule, so none of dem prepare any
help to escape her from de gallows.

De day come fo' her execution. De hour is at hand. She
said to de hang-man, "My time is at han'; save me five an'
twenty minute mo'!" She look off an' see her fader was coming.

> Ay! ay! deh come me only fader
> Who trabbel so many mile!
> Do you bring me gold an' silver
> To save me body from de eart'?

Fader say,

> No, no, Sarey!
> I came to see you hung,
> An' now you mus' be hung, girl,
> You' body is boun' to de eart'.

An' she say, "Still, gentlemen, save me five an' twenty minute
mo'!" Mudder is coming.

> Mudder! mudder!
> Coming trabbling so many mile,
> Do you bring me gold an' silver
> To save me body from de eart'?

Mudder replied same as de fader,

> No, no, Sarey!
> I came to see you hung,
> An' hung you mus' be hung,
> You' body is boun' to de eart'.

An say, "Gentlemen, save me five an' twenty minute mo'!"
An' look far away off yonder, an' saw a bright light, sparkling
light, brillian' light. So ev'rybody dat was waiting to see her
hung get frightened, t'ink dey was doing wrong to her. So
all moving off to de way whe' de brightness is coming direct
to de gallows. So all move an' leave de princess alone on de
gallows stage.

So she mek her escape, pull de rope as how it was fixed to

her an' move herself to a safe place beyon' de light dat is coming.
An' she sing,

> Ye do come, me only husban',
> Trabbel so many mile!
> Do you bring me gold an' silver
> To save me body from de eart'?

No answer. Repeat twice. An' de power of de chariot an' de
great light come up to de gallows, cut it down, mash it up.
Great heap, mountain of gold and silver and all great pieces of
precious stones, diamonds an' rubies an' all precious t'ing! Der
was no end of it. And tek her up. She was help in by her
husban' an' save!

Dat's why when people marry, dey drive so rapidly home,
horse jump an' mek big! An' pour out money like mountains.
Dat's why de king an' queen an' princess so rich now.

✪◇ D ◇✪

1   As I went down to the old depot
    To see the train roll by,
    I thought I saw my dear old girl
    Hang her head and cry.

2   The night was dark and stormy;
    It sure did look like rain.
    Not a friend in the whole wide world,
    And no one knew my name.

3   No one knew my name, poor boy,
    No one knew my name;
    Not a friend in the whole wide world,
    And no one knew my name.

4   "Go away, Mr. Judge, go away, Mr. Judge,
    Just wait a little while.
    I think I saw my dear old girl
    Walk for miles and miles.

5   "Dear girl, have you brought me silver?
    Dear girl, have you brought me gold?

Have you walked these long, long miles
To see me hanged upon the hangman's pole?"

6 "Dear boy, I've brought you silver,
Dear boy, I've brought you gold;
I have not walked these long, long miles
To see you hanged upon the hangman's pole."

7 She took me from the scaffold;
She untied my hands;
The tears ran down the poor girl's cheeks:
"I love this highway man."

Captain Wedderburn's Courtship (46)

Usually it is a clever maiden who frustrates the devil or wins
a courtly husband by her skill at answering riddles; here the
man does the answering, and triumphs. The riddles themselves
are ancient, occurring in "Riddles Wisely Expounded" (see p.
3) and other of the oldest ballads. Though known in Scotland,
Maine, and Northeast Canada, the ballad is comparatively rare in
modern tradition. However, a song that uses one set of these
riddles, a lyric called "I gave my love a cherry" (B), enjoys wide
popularity in the Southern mountains.

Texts: A, Kinloch MSS., I, 83; B, Henry, p. 141.

❦❖ A ❖❦

1 The Lord of Rosslyn's daughter gaed through the wud her
lane,
And there she met Captain Wedderburn, a servant to the
king.
He said unto his livery-man, "Were't na agen the law,
I wad tak her to my ain bed, and lay her at the wa'."

2 "I'm walking here my lane," she says, "amang my father's
trees;

her lane, herself alone.

And ye may lat me walk my lane, kind sir, now gin ye
    please.
The supper-bell it will be rung, and I'll be missed awa;
Sae I'll na lie in your bed, at neither stock nor wa'."

3 He said, "My pretty lady, I pray lend me your hand,
    And ye'll hae drums and trumpets always at your command;
    And fifty men to guard ye wi', that weel their swords can
        draw;
    Sae we'll baith lie in ae bed, and ye'll lie at the wa'."

4 "Haud awa frae me, kind sir, I pray let go my hand;
    The supper-bell it will be rung, nae langer maun I stand.
    My father he'll na supper tak, gif I be miss'd awa;
    Sae I'll na lie in your bed, at neither stock nor wa'."

5 "O my name is Captain Wedderburn, my name I'll ne'er
        deny,
    And I command ten thousand men, upo yon mountains
        high.
    Tho your father and his men were here, of them I'd stand
        na awe,
    But should tak ye to my ain bed, and lay ye neist the wa'."

6 Then he lap aff his milk-white steed, and set the lady on,
    And a' the way he walkd on foot, he held her by the hand;
    He held her by the middle jimp, for fear that she should fa';
    Saying, "I'll tak ye to my ain bed, and lay thee at the wa'."

7 He took her to his quartering-house, his landlady looked
        ben,
    Saying, "Monie a pretty ladie in Edinbruch I've seen;
    But sic [a] pretty ladie is not into it a':
    Gae, mak for her a fine down-bed, and lay her at the wa'."

8 "O haud awa frae me, kind sir, I pray ye lat me be,
    For I'll na lie in your bed till I get dishes three;
    Dishes three maun be dressd for me, gif I should eat them a',
    Before I lie in your bed, at either stock or wa'.

9 " 'Tis I maun hae to my supper a chicken without a bane;
    And I maun hae to my supper a cherry without a stane;

gin, if.   *stock,* side on which one enters an alcove bed.   *jimp,* slender.   *ben,* within.

And I maun hae to my supper a bird without a gaw,
Before I lie in your bed, at either stock or wa'."

10 "Whan the chicken's in the shell, I am sure it has na bane;
And whan the cherry's in the bloom, I wat it has na stane;
The dove she is a genty bird, she flees without a gaw;
Sae we'll baith lie in ae bed, and ye'll be at the wa'."

11 "O haud awa frae me, kind sir, I pray ye give me owre.
For I'll na lie in your bed, till I get presents four;
Presents four ye maun gie me, and that is twa and twa,
Before I lie in your bed, at either stock or wa'.

12 " 'Tis I maun hae some winter fruit that in December grew;
And I maun hae a silk mantil that waft gaed never through;
A sparrow's horn, a priest unborn, this nicht to join us twa,
Before I lie in your bed, at either stock or wa'."

13 "My father has some winter fruit that in December grew;
My mither has a silk mantil the waft gaed never through;
A sparrow's horn ye soon may find, there's ane on every
    claw,
And twa upo the gab o it, and ye shall get them a'.

14 "The priest he stands without the yett, just ready to come
    in;
Nae man can say he e'er was born, nae man without he sin;
He was haill cut frae his mither's side, and frae the same
    let fa';
Sae we'll baith lie in ae bed, and ye'se lie at the wa'."

15 "O haud awa frae me, kind sir, I pray don't me perplex,
For I'll na lie in your bed till ye answer questions six:
Questions six ye maun answer me, and that is four and twa,
Before I lie in your bed, at either stock or wa'.

16 "O what is greener than the gress, what's higher than thae
    trees?
O what is worse than women's wish, what's deeper than
    the seas?

gaw, gall. *genty,* gentle. *waft,* weft. *gab,* mouth. *yett,* gate.

What bird craws first, what tree buds first, what first does
   on them fa'?
Before I lie in your bed, at either stock or wa'."

17 "Death is greener than the gress, heaven higher than thae
        trees;
    The devil's waur than women's wish, hell's deeper than the
        seas;
    The cock craws first, the cedar buds first, dew first on them
        does fa';
    Sae we'll baith lie in ae bed, and ye's lie at the wa'."

18 Little did this lady think, that morning whan she raise,
    That this was for to be the last o a' her maiden days.
    But there's na into the king's realm to be found a blither
        twa,
    And now she's Mrs. Wedderburn, and she lies at the wa'.

✿◇ **B** ◇✿

1 I gave my love a cherry without a stone;
   I gave my love a chicken without a bone;
   I gave my love a ring without an end;
   I gave my love a baby with no crying.

2 How can there be a cherry without a stone?
   How can there be a chicken without a bone?
   How can there be a ring without an end?
   How can there be a baby with no crying?

3 A cherry, when it's blooming, it has no stone;
   A chicken, when it's pipping, it has no bone;
   A ring, when it's rolling, it has no end;
   A baby, when it's sleeping, has no crying.

The Bailiff's Daughter of Islington (105)

No less than twenty ballads of returned lovers follow the plot
pattern of "The Bailiff's Daughter of Islington." In such pieces
the appearance of the returning merchant, knight, sailor, soldier,

or of the girl left behind is seldom enough to effect recognition; some token must be shown or confession made. Invariably one lover tests the other by watching his or her reaction to the news of his or her death or defection.

The ballad has been a popular favorite in England since 1600. Text: Percy, *Reliques*, III, 133. Tune: Rimbault, p. 100.

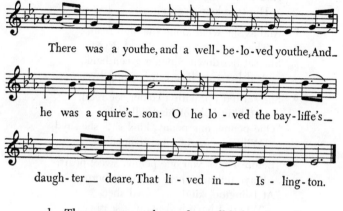

There was a youthe, and a well-be-lo-ved youthe, And he was a squire's son: O he lo-ved the bay-liffe's daugh-ter deare, That li-ved in Is-ling-ton.

1 There was a youthe, and a well-beloved youthe,
        And he was a squire's son:
   He loved the bayliffe's daughter deare,
        That lived in Islington.

2 Yet she was coye and would not believe
        That he did love her soe,
   Noe nor at any time would she
        Any countenance to him showe.

3 But when his friendes did understand
        His fond and foolish minde,
   They sent him up to faire London
        An apprentice for to binde.

4 And he had been seven long yeares,
        And never his love could see:
   "Many a teare have I shed for her sake,
        When she little thought of mee."

5   Then all the maids of Islington
       Went forth to sport and playe,
  All but the bayliffe's daughter deare;
       She secretly stole awaye.

6   She pulled off her gowne of greene,
       And put on ragged attire,
  And to faire London she would go
       Her true love to enquire.

7   And as she went along the high road,
       The weather being hot and drye,
  She sat her downe upon a green bank,
       And her true love came riding bye.

8   She started up, with a colour soe redd,
       Catching hold of his bridle-reine;
  "One penny, one penny, kind sir," she sayd,
       "Will ease me of much paine."

9   "Before I give you one penny, sweet-heart,
       Praye tell me where you were borne."
  "At Islington, kind sir," sayd shee,
       "Where I have had many a scorne."

10 "I prythee, sweet-heart, then tell to mee,
       O tell me, whether you knowe
  The bayliffe's daughter of Islington."
       "She is dead, sir, long agoe."

11 "If she be dead, then take my horse,
       My saddle and bridle also;
  For I will into some farr countrye,
       Where noe man shall me knowe."

12 "O staye, O staye, thou goodlye youthe,
       She standeth by thy side;
  She is here alive, she is not dead,
       And readye to be thy bride."

13 "O farewell griefe, and welcome joye,
       Ten thousand times therefore;
  For nowe I have founde mine owne true love,
       Whom I thought I should never see more."

John of Hazelgreen (293)

Having the narrator a participant in the song is a little awkward, but the device occurs in many sentimental ballads of reunited lovers. Though the ballad as it stands seems refined and smooth enough, even suspiciously so, Scott put an even higher polish on the theme in his "Jock of Hazeldean." Scott's poem and the folk version are interestingly confounded in a Virginia and a New Brunswick text (see *Bulletin* 3:9 and references there).

Elizabeth Cochrane's MS., about 1730, at Harvard (p. 126) furnishes the oldest text.

1 Into a sweet May morning,
       As the sun clearly shone,
   I heard a propper damsell
       Making a heavy moan;
   Making a heavy moan,
       I marvelled what she meant,
   And it was for a gentleman,
       Sir John of Hasillgreen.

2 "What aileth thee now, bony maid,
       To mourn so sore into the tide?
   O happy were the man," he sayes,
       "That had thee to his bride,
   To ly down by his side;
       Then he were not to[o] mean;"
   But still she let the tears down fall
       For pleasant Hasilgreen.

3 "Oh what for a man is Hasillgreen?
       Sweet heart, pray tell to me."
   "He is a propper gentleman,
       Dwels in the South Countrie;
   With shoulders broad and arms long,
       And comely to be seen;

His hairs are like the threeds of gold,
    My pleasant Hasilgreen."

4   "Now Hasilgreen is married,
        Let all this talking be."
    "If Hasilgreen be married,
        This day then woe to me;
    For I may sigh and sob no more,
        But close my weeping e'en,
    And hold my peace and cry no more,
        But dy for Hasilgreen."

5   "Will you let Hasilgreen alone,
        And go along with me?
    I'll marry you on my eldest son,
        Make you a gay lady."
    "Make me a gay lady?" she sayes,
        "I am a maid too mean;
    I'll rather stay at home," she cries,
        "And dy for Hasilgreen."

6   He takes this pretty maid him behind
        And fast he spurred the horse,
    And they're away to Bigger toun,
        Then in to Biggar Cross.
    Their lodging was far sought,
        And so was it foreseen;
    But still she let the tears doun fall
        For pleasant Hasillgreen.

7   He's ta'en this pretty maid by the hand,
        And he is doun the toun;
    He bought for her a pettycoat,
        Yea, and a trailing goun;
    A silken kell fitt for her head,
        Laid o'er with silver sheen;
    But still she let the tears doun fall
        For pleasant Hasilgreen.

8   He's ta'en this bony mey him behind,
        And he is to the Place,

e'en, eyes.   *kell,* net cap.   *mey,* maid.

Where there was mirth and merryness,
  And ladyes fair of face;
And ladyes fair of face,
  Right seemly to be seen,
But still she let the tears doun fall
  For pleasant Hasilgreen.

9 Young Hasilgreen ran hastilie
     To welcome his father dear;
   He's ta'en that pretty maid in his arms,
     And kist off her falling tear:
   "O bony mey, now for thy sake
     I would be rent and ri'en;
   I would give all my father's land
     To have thee in Hasilgreen."

10 "O hold your tongue now, son," he says,
      "Let no more talking be;
    This maid has come right far from home
      This day to visit thee.
    This day should been your wedding-day,
      It shall be thy bridall-e'en,
    And thou's get all thy father's lands,
      And dwell in Hasillgreen."

Polly Oliver's Rambles

One of the more endearing creations of the broadside muse
is the resourceful maiden who disguises herself as a soldier or
sailor and, undiscovered for a time, follows her lover to war.
The situation in which Polly Oliver and other maiden warriors
find themselves is always good for a couple of titillating stanzas
that come perilously close to indecency. The present text of
"Polly Oliver's Rambles," a ballad sung as early as 1740, is
taken from a provincial English broadside of about 1840;
Kidson, *Traditional Tunes,* p. 116, supplies the music.

ri'en riven, torn.

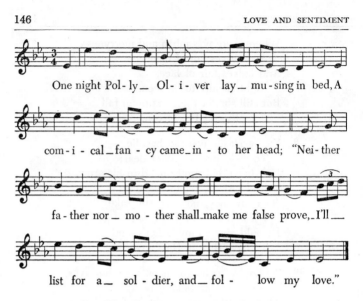

One night Pol- ly— Ol- i- ver lay— mu-sing in bed, A

com-i - cal—fan - cy came—in - to her head; "Nei-ther

fa - ther nor— mo - ther shall—make me false prove,—I'll—

list for a— sol - dier, and— fol - low my love."

1   One night Polly Oliver lay musing in bed,
    A comical fancy came into her head;
    "Neither father nor mother shall make me false prove,
    I'll 'list for a soldier and follow my love."

2   Early next morning this fair maid arose,
    She dressed herself in a suit of men's clothes,
    Coat, waistcoat and breeches, and sword by her side,
    On her father's black gelding like a dragoon she did ride.

3   She rode till she came to fair London town,
    She dismounted her horse at the sign of the crown;
    The first that came to her was a man from above,
    The next that came down was Polly Oliver's true love.

4   "Good evening, good evening, kind captain," said she;
    "Here's a letter from your true love Polly Oliver," said she;
    He opened the letter and a guinea was found,
    For him and his companions to drink her health round.

5   Supper being ended, she held down her head
    And called for a candle to light her to bed;
    The captain made this reply, "I have a bed at my ease,
    You may lie with me, countryman, if you please."

6   "To lie with a captain is a dangerous thing,
    I'm a new enlisted soldier to fight for my king;
    To fight for my king by sea and by land,
    Since you are my captain, I'll be at your command."

7   Early next morning this fair maid arose,
    And dressed herself in her own suit of clothes,
    And downstairs she came from her chamber above,
    Saying, "Here is Polly Oliver, your own true love."

8   He at first was surprised, but laughed at the fun,
    And then they were married and all things were done;
    "If I had laid with you the first night, the fault had been
      mine,
    I hope to please you better, love, for now is the time."

v : PASTOURELLES

If a medieval French *trouvère* or minstrel catered to a courtly audience, he would be sure to have in his repertoire a number of pastourelles—short poems describing love encounters between a gallant and a shepherdess in the fields or woods, his proposals, her demurrers, his subsequent success or failure. The knight was usually the winner of these aristocratic sex duels, but when the folk took over the form—as in the following ballads—the story had a different ending. In later centuries, the knight of the early ballads becomes a dragoon, still later, a foot soldier; his modern descendant thrives in the traveling-salesman-and-the-farmer's-daughter jokes told in men's clubrooms.

The Broomfield Hill (43)

The maiden of the ballad remains a maiden by casting a spell over her lover with soporific broom blossoms, a potent ingredient in witches' brews. This version, from Scott's *Minstrelsy*, III, 271 (1803), interprets the girl's strewing of the blossoms to be merely a sign that she has kept the appointment; other versions are more definite about the magical properties of broom—"And aye the thicker that you do strew," the witch assures the girl, "the sounder he will sleep" (Child, I, 395).

1   There was a knight and a lady bright,
       Had a true tryste at the broom;
     The ane gaed early in the morning,
       The other in the afternoon.

2   And ay she sat in her mother's bower door,
       And ay she made her mane:
     "O whether should I gang to the Broomfield Hill,
       Or should I stay at hame?"

148

3 "For if I gang to the Broomfield Hill,
    My maidenhead is gone;
  And if I chance to stay at hame,
    My love will ca' me mansworn."

4 Up then spake a witch-woman,
    Ay from the room aboon:
  "O ye may gang to the Broomfield Hill,
    And yet come maiden hame.

5 "For when ye gang to the Broomfield Hill,
    Ye'll find your love asleep,
  With a silver belt about his head,
    And a broom-cow at his feet.

6 "Take ye the blossom of the broom,
    The blossom it smells sweet,
  And strew it at your true-love's head,
    And likewise at his feet.

7 "Take ye the rings off your fingers,
    Put them on his right hand,
  To let him know, when he doth awake,
    His love was at his command."

8 She pu'd the broom flower on Hive Hill,
    And strewd on's white hals-bane,
  And that was to be wittering true
    That maiden she had gane.

9 "O where were ye, my milk-white steed,
    That I hae coft sae dear,
  That wadna watch and waken me,
    When there was maiden here?"

10 "I stamped wi' my foot, master,
    And gard my bridle ring,
  But na kin thing wald waken ye,
    Till she was past and gane."

11 "And wae betide ye, my gay goss-hawk,
    That I did love sae dear,

mansworn, perjured. *broom-cow*, broom branch. *hals-bane*, neck.
wittering, token. *coft*, bought. *gard*, made.

That wadna watch and waken me
    When there was maiden here."

12 "I clapped wi' my wings, master,
        And aye my bells I rang,
    And aye cry'd, Waken, waken, master,
        Before the ladye gang."

13 "But haste and haste, my gude white steed,
        To come the maiden till,
    Or a' the birds of gude green wood
        Of your flesh shall have their fill."

14 "Ye need na burst your gude white steed
        Wi' racing o'er the howm;
    Nae bird flies faster through the wood,
        Than she fled through the broom."

The Knight and the Shepherd's Daughter (110)

The journey to court is reminiscent of "Child Waters": the story itself belongs to the class of Chaucer's "Wife of Bath's Tale," though without the magic or philosophizing. A noble-born knight, here the queen's brother, seduces a shepherd's daughter. She follows him to court, where he—a most unwilling husband—is awarded to her by the king. After the wedding, the shepherdess turns out to be a princess. In the older tales, the ugly hag whom the knight is forced to marry because of an ill-considered promise is disenchanted into a beautiful woman.

The ballad is still sung in England and has even been reported in America. Our text is from the Kinloch MSS., V, 255.

1 There was a shepherd's dochter
       Kept sheep upon yon hill,
   And by cam a gay braw gentleman,
       And wad hae had his will.

howm, riverbank.
braw, brave, fine.

2 He took her by the milk-white hand,
       And laid her on the ground,
   And whan he got his will o her
       He lift her up again.

3 "O syne ye've got your will o me,
       Your will o me ye've taen,
   'Tis all I ask o you, kind sir,
       Is to tell to me your name."

4 "Sometimes they call me Jack," he said,
       "Sometimes they call me John,
   But whan I am in the king's court,
       My name is Wilfu Will."

5 Then he loup on his milk-white steed,
       And straught away he rade,
   And she did kilt her petticoats,
       And after him she gaed.

6 He never was sae kind as say,
       O lassie, will ye ride?
   Nor ever had she the courage to say,
       O laddie, will ye bide!

7 Until they cam to a wan water,
       Which was called Clyde,
   And then he turned about his horse,
       Said, Lassie, will ye ride?

8 "I learned it in my father's hall,
       I learned it for my weel,
   That whan I come to deep water,
       I can swim as it were an eel.

9 "I learned it in my mother's bower,
       I learned it for my better,
   That whan I come to broad water,
       I can swim like any otter."

10 He plunged his steed into the ford,
       And straught way thro he rade,

kilt, tuck up.

And she set in her lilly feet,
  And thro the water wade.

11   And whan she cam to the king's court,
       She tirled on the pin,
     And wha sae ready's the king himsel
       To let the fair maid in?

12   "What is your will wi me, fair maid?
       What is your will wi me?"
     "There is a man into your court
       This day has robbed me."

13   "O has he taen your gold," he said,
       "Or has he taen your fee?
     Or has he stown your maidenhead,
       The flower of your bodye?"

14   "He has na taen my gold, kind sir,
       Nor as little has he taen my fee,
     But he has taen my maidenhead,
       The flower of my bodye."

15   "O gif he be a married man,
       High hangit shall he be,
     But gif he be a bachelor,
       His body I'll grant thee."

16   "Sometimes they call him Jack," she said,
       "Sometimes they call him John,
     But whan he's in the king's court,
       His name is Sweet William."

17   "There's not a William in a' my court,
       Never a one but three,
     And one of them is the Queen's brother;
       I wad laugh gif it war he."

18   The king called on his merry men,
       By thirty and by three;
     Sweet Willie, wha used to be foremost man,
       Was the hindmost a' but three.

tirled . . . , rattled at latchpin.

19 O he cam cripple, and he cam blind,
    Cam twa-fald oer a tree:
"O be he cripple, or be he blind,
    This very same man is he."

20 "O whether will ye marry the bonny may,
    Or hang on the gallows-tree?"
"O I will rather marry the bonny may,
    Afore that I do die."

21 But he took out a purse of gold,
    Weel locked in a glove:
"O tak ye that, my bonny may,
    And seek anither love."

22 "O I will hae none o your gold," she says,
    "Nor as little ony of your fee,
But I will hae your ain body,
    The king has granted me."

23 O he took out a purse of gold,
    A purse of gold and store;
"O tak ye that, fair may," he said,
    "Frae me ye'll neer get mair."

24 "O haud your tongue, young man," she says,
    "And I pray you let me be;
For I will hae your ain body,
    The king has granted me."

25 He mounted her on a bonny bay horse,
    Himsel on the silver grey;
He drew his bonnet out oer his een,
    He whipt and rade away.

26 O whan they cam to yon nettle bush,
    The nettles they war spread:
"O an my mither war but here," she says,
    "These nettles she wad sned."

27 "O an I had drank the wan water
    Whan I did drink the wine,

twa-fald, doubled up. *tree,* cane. *may,* maid. *een,* eyes. *an,* if only. *sned,* cut.

That eer a shepherd's dochter
Should hae been a love o mine!"

28 "O may be I'm a shepherd's dochter,
     And may be I am nane;
     But you might hae ridden on your ways,
     And hae let me alane."

29 O whan they cam unto yon mill,
     She heard the mill clap:

          .   .   .   .   .

               .   .   .   .   .

30 "Clap on, clap on, thou bonny mill,
     Weel may thou, I say,
     For mony a time thou's filled my pock
     Wi baith oat-meal and grey."

31 "O an I had drank the wan water
     Whan I did drink the wine,
     That eer a shepherd's dochter
     Should hae been a love o mine!"

32 "O may be I'm a shepherd's dochter,
     And may be I am nane;
     But you might hae ridden on your ways,
     And hae let me alane.

33 "But yet I think a fitter match
     Could scarcely gang thegither
     Than the King of France's auld dochter
     And the Queen of Scotland's brither."

The Baffled Knight (112)

One of the *Pills to Purge Melancholy* (V, 112, 1719), this
song describes how a country girl once frustrated an overly
ardent lover. A cluster of such "escape" pieces was assembled

auld, eldest.

in a lengthy seventeen-century broadside which Percy pruned and printed in his *Reliques* (III, 238).

1 There was a knight, and he was young,
  A riding along the way, sir,
 And there he met a lady fair,
  Among the cocks of hay, sir.

2 Quoth he, "Shall you and I, lady,
  Among the grass lye down a?
 And I will have a special care
  Of rumpling of your gown a."

3 "If you will go along with me
  Unto my father's hall, sir,
 You shall enjoy my maidenhead,
  And my estate and all, sir."

4 So he mounted her on a milk-white steed,
  Himself upon another,
 And then they rid upon the road,
  Like sister and like brother.

5 And when she came to her father's house,
  Which was moated round about, sir,
 She stepped streight within the gate,
  And shut this young knight out, sir.

6 "Here is a purse of gold," she said,
  "Take it for your pains, sir;
 And I will send my father's man
  To go home with you again, sir.

7 "And if you meet a lady fair,
  As you go thro the next town, sir,
 You must not fear the dew of the grass,
  Nor the rumpling of her gown, sir.

8 "And if you meet a lady gay,
  As you go by the hill, sir,
 If you will not when you may,
  You shall not when you will, sir."

VI: DOMESTIC TRAGEDIES

Edward (13)

Text A, the version of "Edward" published in Percy's *Reliques* (1765; I, 53), may well be the best known of the older ballads among sophisticated readers. A Scottish judge contributed the copy; presumably Percy himself was responsible for the fake-antique spelling—"quhy" for "why," "ze" for "ye"—which is here eliminated. Entirely developed through dialogue, the ballad manages to generate enormous dramatic tension. As a result, there is no more powerful climax in any ballad than the surprise revelation of the mother's guilt in the last lines of "Edward." Some scholars suspect the folk had literary assistance here (see *SFLQ*, IV, 1, 159).

The "Edward" story has proved too "strong" for the American folk: a brother or a brother-in-law, not the sufferer's father, is the victim in American versions, and the mother has no share in the crime. But according to Archer Taylor's full-scale study *Edward and Sven i Rosengard* (1931), the American ballads may be nearer the original form of the story since a brother was also the victim in the lost English or Scottish version from which the Scandinavian ballads descended. In A, Edward intends to go into exile. Another Scottish version (Motherwell MS., p. 139; Child, I, 169) has him setting his foot in a "bottomless boat," thus suggesting that in an ancient form of the story Edward submitted himself to exposure in an open boat, a medieval punishment for fratricide.

Text B from North Carolina (Brown, II, 42) represents the American tradition.

❀◇ A ◇❀

1   "Why dois your brand sae drap wi' bluid,
               Edward, Edward?
   Why dois your brand sae drip wi' bluid?
      And why sae sad gang yee, O?"

brand, sword.

"O, I hae killed my hauke sae guid,
          Mither, mither,
O, I hae killed my hauke sae guid,
     And I had nae mair bot hee, O."

2   "Your haukis bluid was nevir sae reid,
               Edward, Edward,
     Your haukis bluid was nevir sae reid,
        My deir son I tell thee, O."
     "O, I hae killed my reid-roan steid,
               Mither, mither,
     O, I hae killed my reid-roan steid,
        That erst was sae fair and frie, O."

3   "Your steid was auld, and ye hae gat mair,
               Edward, Edward,
     Your steid was auld, and ye hae gat mair,
        Sum other dule ye drie, O."
     "O, I hae killed my fadir deir,
               Mither, mither,
     O, I hae killed my fadir deir,
        Alas, and wae is mee, O!"

4   "And whatten penance wul ye drie for that,
               Edward, Edward?
     And whatten penance wul ye drie for that?
        My deir son, now tell me, O."
     "Ile set my feit in yonder boat,
               Mither, mither,
     Ile set my feit in yonder boat,
        And Ile fare ovir the sea, O."

5   "And what wul ye doe wi' your towirs and your ha',
               Edward, Edward,
     And what wul ye doe wi' your towirs and your ha',
        That were sae fair to see, O?"
     "Ile let thame stand tul they doun fa',
               Mither, mither,
     Ile let thame stand tul they doun fa',
        For here nevir mair maun I bee, O."

dule, grief. *drie,* endure.

6   "And what wul ye leive to your bairns and your wife,
            Edward, Edward?
    And what wul ye leive to your bairns and your wife,
        When ye gang ovir the sea, O?"
    "The warldis room, late them beg thrae life,
            Mither, mither,
    The warldis room, late them beg thrae life,
        For thame nevir mair wul I see, O."

7   "And what wul ye leive to your ain mither deir,
            Edward, Edward?
    And what wul ye leive to your ain mither deir?
        My deir son, now tell me, O."
    "The curse of hell frae me sall ye beir,
            Mither, mither,
    The curse of hell frae me sall ye beir,
        Sic counseils ye gave to me, O."

❁❖ B ❖❁

1   "How comes that blood all over your shirt?
    My son, come tell it to me."
    "It's the blood of my little guinea pig—
    O mother, please let me be.
    It's the blood of my little guinea pig—
    O mother, please let me be."

2   "Your guinea pig's blood is not so red.
    My son, come tell it to me."
    "It's the blood of my little hunting dog
    That played in the field for me . . ."

3   "Your dog lies yonder, O my son,
    And this it could not be."
    "It is the blood of my old roan horse
    That pulled the plow for me . . ."

4   "How comes that blood all over your shirt?
    My son, you must tell to me."
    "It's the blood of my little brother Bill
    Who I killed in the field today . . ."

warldis room, space of the world.

5   "And what will you do when your father comes home?
    My son, come tell it to me."
    "I'll put my feet in the bottom of a boat
    I'll put my feet in the bottom of a boat
    And sail across the sea.
    And sail across the sea."

Lizie Wan (51)

The borrowings from "Edward" are obvious. Moreover, the
poetic way of saying "never" in the final stanza also characterizes
several American "Edward" ballads. Scandinavian analogues of
that ballad also employ an ingenious variety of circumlocutions
for "never."
Text: Herd MSS. I, 151; II, 78.

1   Lizie Wan sits at her father's bower door,
        Weeping and making a mane,
    And by there came her father dear:
        "What ails thee, Lizie Wan?"

2   "I ail, and I ail, dear father," she said,
        "And I'll tell you a reason for why;
    There is a child between my twa sides,
        Between my dear billy and I."

3   Now Lizie Wan sits at her father's bower door,
        Sighing and making a mane,
    And by there came her brother dear:
        "What ails thee, Lizie Wan?"

4   "I ail, and I ail, dear brither," she said,
        "And I'll tell you a reason for why;
    There is a child between my twa sides,
        Between you, dear billy, and I."

5   "And hast thou tald father and mother o that?
        And hast thou tald sae o me?"

billy, friend, brother.

And he has drawn his gude braid sword,
  That hang down by his knee.

6 And he has cutted aff Lizie Wan's head,
     And her fair body in three,
   And he's awa to his mother's bower,
     And sair aghast was he.

7 "What ails thee, what ails thee, Geordy Wan?
     What ails thee sae fast to rin?
   For I see by thy ill colour
     Some fallow's deed thou hast done."

8 "Some fallow's deed I have done, mother,
     And I pray you pardon me;
   For I've cutted aff my greyhound's head;
     He wadna rin for me."

9 "Thy greyhound's bluid was never sae red,
     O my son Geordy Wan!
   For I see by thy ill colour
     Some fallow's deed thou hast done."

10 "Some fallow's deed I hae done, mother,
      And I pray you pardon me;
    For I hae cutted aff Lizie Wan's head
      And her fair body in three."

11 "O what wilt thou do when thy father comes hame,
      O my son Geordy Wan?"
    "I'll set my foot in a bottomless boat,
      And swim to the sea-ground."

12 "And when will thou come hame again,
      O my son Geordy Wan?"
    "The sun and the moon shall dance on the green
      That night when I come hame."

fallow's, felon's.

The Twa Sisters (10)

Scandinavian analogues make it clear that the core of this cruel tale is the supernatural revelation of the murderer by the musical instrument pieced from the girl's corpse. Our Scottish version, B, handles this feature of the story with admirable subtlety and poetry; the same passage in A, which is English, is carried to excess and teeters on the brink of the ludicrous. Scores of American texts of this ballad have been printed to date, but in only one (Brown, II, 34) is the murderer discovered miraculously. The others, most of which stem from the late English version represented here by C, cut out the supernatural detection altogether.

Scholars have been greatly interested in the various refrains used in "The Two Sisters" (see *JFS*, 8:242). Obviously the refrains have no direct bearing on the narrative, but are simply stray phrases that happen to suit the musical flourishes. The recital of cities is common to Scottish versions, though the ballad in Scott's *Minstrelsy* has "Binnorie, Binnorie . . . / By the bonny mill-dams of Binnorie." The usual American refrain is that of D, except that the more common wording runs "I'll be true to my love, if my love will be true to me."

Texts: A, *Wit Restor'd*, 1658, p. 51; B, Jamieson's Brown MS., p. 39; C, *Notes and Queries*, 1 ser., VI, 102 (1852), from Lancashire; D, Davis, p. 96, from Virginia. The tune (Davis, p. 555) is meant to accompany a different Virginia text, but can easily be adapted to C or D.

❧◇ A ◇❧

1 There were two sisters, they went playing,
      With a hie downe downe a downe-a
   To see their father's ships come sailing in.
      With a hy downe downe a downe-o

2 And when they came unto the sea-brym,
   The elder did push the younger in.

3   "O sister, O sister, take me by the gowne,
    And drawe me up upon the dry ground."

4   "O sister, O sister, that may not bee,
    Till salt and oatmeale grow both of a tree."

5   Somtymes she sanke, somtymes she swam,
    Until she came unto the mil[l]-dam.

6   The miller runne hastily downe the cliffe,
    And up he betook her withouten her life.

7   What did he doe with her brest-bone?
    He made him a violl to play thereupon.

8   What did he doe with her fingers so small?
    He made him peggs to his violl withall.

9   What did he doe with her nose-ridge?
    Unto his violl he made him a bridge.

10 What did he doe with her veynes so blew?
    He made him strings to his violl thereto.

11 What did he doe with her eyes so bright?
    Upon his violl he played at first sight.

12 What did he doe with her tongue so rough?
    Unto the violl it spake enough.

13 What did he doe with her two shinnes?
    Unto the violl they danc'd Moll Syms.

14 Then bespake the treble string,
    "O yonder is my father the king."

15 Then bespake the second string,
    "O yonder sitts my mother the queen."

16 And then bespake the strings all three,
    "O yonder is my sister that drowned mee."

17 "Now pay the miller for his payne,
    And let him bee gone in the divel's name."

❧◇ B ◇❧

1   There was twa sisters in a bow'r,
        Edinburgh, Edinburgh
    There was twa sisters in a bow'r,
        Stirling for ay
    There was twa sisters in a bow'r,
    There came a knight to be their wooer.
        Bonny Saint Johnston stands upon Tay

2   He courted the eldest wi' glove an ring,
    But he lov'd the youngest above a' thing.

3   He courted the eldest wi' brotch an knife,
    But lov'd the youngest as his life.

4   The eldest she was vexed sair,
    An' much envi'd her sister fair.

5   Into her bow'r she could not rest,
    Wi' grief an' spite she almos' brast.

6   Upon a morning fair an' clear,
    She cried upon her sister dear:

7   "O sister, come to yon sea stran',
    An' see our father's ships come to lan'."

8   She's ta'en her by the milk-white han',
    An' led her down to yon sea stran'.

9   The younges' stood upon a stane,
    The eldest came an' threw her in.

10 She tooke her by the middle sma',
    An' dashed her bonny back to the jaw.

11 "O sister, sister, tak' my han',
    An I'se mack you heir to a' my lan'.

12 "O sister, sister, tak' my middle,
    An' ye's get my goud and my gouden girdle.

jaw, wave.

13   "O sister, sister, save my life,
      An' I swear I'se never be nae man's wife."

14   "Foul fa' the han' that I should tacke,
      It twin'd me an my wardles make.

15   "Your cherry cheeks an' yallow hair
      Gars me gae maiden for evermair."

16   Sometimes she sank, an' sometimes she swam,
      Till she came down yon bonny mill-dam.

17   O out it came the miller's son,
      An' saw the fair maid swimmin' in.

18   "O father, father, draw your dam,
      Here's either a mermaid or a swan."

19   The miller quickly drew the dam,
      An' there he found a drown'd woman.

20   You cou'dna see her yallow hair
      For gold and pearle that were so rare.

21   You cou'dna see her middle sma'
      For gouden girdle that was sae braw.

22   You cou'dna see her fingers white,
      For gouden rings that was sae gryte.

23   An' by there came a harper fine,
      That harped to the king at dine.

24   When he did look that lady upon,
      He sigh'd and made a heavy moan.

25   He's ta'en three locks o' her yallow hair,
      An' wi' them strung his harp sae fair.

26   The first tune he did play and sing,
      Was, "Farewell to my father the king."

27   The nextin tune that he play'd syne,
      Was, "Farewell to my mother the queen."

wardles make, earthly mate. *gar,* make. *braw,* splendid. *syne,*
then.

28 The lasten tune that he play'd then,
Was, "Wae to my sister, fair Ellen."

❀◇ C ◇❀

1 There was a king of the north countree,
Bow down, bow down, bow down
There was a king of the north countree,
And he had daughters one, two, three.
I'll be true to my love, and my love'll be true to me.

2 To the eldest he gave a beaver hat,
And the youngest she thought much of that.

3 To the youngest he gave a gay gold chain,
And the eldest she thought much of the same.

4 These sisters were walking on the bryn,
And the elder pushed the younger in.

5 "Oh sister, oh sister, oh lend me your hand,
And I will give you both houses and land."

6 "I'll neither give you my hand nor glove,
Unless you give me your true love."

7 Away she sank, away she swam,
Until she came to a miller's dam.

8 The miller and daughter stood at the door,
And watched her floating down the shore.

9 "Oh father, oh father, I see a white swan,
Or else it is a fair woman."

10 The miller he took up his long crook,
And the maiden up from the stream he took.

11 "I'll give to thee this gay gold chain,
If you'll take me back to my father again."

12 The miller he took the gay gold chain,
And he pushed her into the water again.

13 The miller was hanged on his high gate
   For drowning our poor sister Kate.

14 The cat's behind the buttery shelf,
   If you want any more, you may sing it yourself.

There lived an old Lord by the north-ern sea;

Bow down, There lived an old Lord by the

north-ern sea, The boughs they bend _ to me, ___ There

lived an old Lord by the north-ern sea, And

he had daugh-ters one, two, three. That will be true,

True to my love, love, and my love will be true to me. _

❀◇ D ◇❀

1 There was an old man in the North Countrie,
   Bow down, bow down.
   There was an old man in the North Countrie,
   And he had daughters, one, two, three.
   Love will be true, true to my love,
   Love will be true to you.

2   There was a young man came courting there,
     And he did choose the youngest fair.

3   He gave to the youngest a gay gold ring,
     And to the oldest not a single thing.

4   He gave to the youngest a beaver hat,
     And the oldest she thought hard of that.

5   "Sister, O sister, let's walk the sea shore,
     To see the ships come sailing o'er."

6   They were walking along on yonder sea-brim
     When the oldest shoved the youngest in.

7   "O sister, O sister, hand me your hand,
     And you may have my house and land.

8   "O sister, O sister, hand me your glove,
     And you may have my own true love."

9   "I'll neither hand you hand nor glove,
     For all I want is your true love."

10   So down she sank and away she swam
     Until she reached the old mill dam.

11   The miller threw out his old grab-hook
     And pulled the fair maiden out of the brook.

12   "O miller, O miller, here's three gold rings,
     If you'll take me to my father's again."

13   He up with her fingers and off with her rings
     And threw her back in the brook again.

14   The miller was hung at his mill gate
     For drowning of my sister Kate.

Sheath and Knife (16)

Incestuous passion, a not uncommon ballad theme, is regarded
by the folk as a reprehensible crime that must be horribly

expiated, yet the offenders are dealt with sympathetically.
Even the ballad sinner who confesses (Child, II, 16) that he
has had two children by his mother and five by a sister is
miraculously saved by the Blessed Virgin. Sheath and knife in
this ballad (from Motherwell's MS., p. 286) seem to have no
more esoteric function than to symbolize a mother with an
unborn child. The refrain lines are highly atmospheric, a trip
to the broom suggesting sexual dalliance.

1   It is talked the warld all over,
    The brume blooms bonnie and says it is fair
  That the king's dochter gaes wi' child to her brither.
    And we'll never gang doun to the brume onie mair

2   He's ta'en his sister doun to her father's deer park,
  Wi' his yew-tree bow and arrows fast slung to his back.

3   "Now when that ye hear me gi'e a loud cry,
  Shoot frae thy bow an arrow and there let me lye.

4   "And when that ye see I am lying dead,
  Then ye'll put me in a grave, wi' a turf at my head."

5   Now when he heard her gi'e a loud cry,
  His silver arrow frae his bow he suddenly let fly.
    Now they'll never, etc.

6   He has made a grave that was lang and was deep,
  And he has buried his sister, wi' her babie at her feet.
    And they'll never, etc.

7   And when he came to his father's court hall,
  There was music and minstrels and dancing and all.
    But they'll never, etc.

8   "O Willie, O Willie, what makes thee in pain?"
  "I have lost a sheath and knife that I'll never see again."
    For we'll never, etc.

9   "There is ships o' your father's sailing on the sea
  That will bring as good a sheath and a knife unto thee."

10 "There is ships o' my father's sailing on the sea,
  But sic a sheath and a knife they can never bring to me."
    Now we'll never, etc.

The Twa Brothers (49)

Accidentally while wrestling (A) or purposefully in a fit of
passion (B), one brother fatally wounds another. In a series of
dying requests, the survivor is charged to dissemble the news
to their parents, but to let the dying lad's sweetheart know
the truth. Several Scottish versions incorporate passages from
"Edward," and the ghost's warning in B is reminiscent of
"Sweet William's Ghost."

This ballad has disappeared from British tradition; it is rela-
tively common, however, in America, where most texts are
garbled replicas of Scottish B. Numerous hints in the new-
world texts have been interpreted to mean that the quarrel between the brothers arose from rivalry over the sweetheart, and
there is even some reason to think that before recorded tradition
the girl was the brothers' sister! (see *Bulletin,* 5:6). One also
suspects that once upon a time the brothers were not little
schoolboys but grown men, for as the ballad now stands, the
youngsters are not old enough for serious romantic attach-
ments. The ages were gradually reduced to make the quarrel
over the sister appear free of sexual passion. When the sister
was supplanted by a permissible sweetheart, maturity should
have been, but was not, restored to the principals.

Texts: A, Sharpe's *Ballad Book,* p. 56; B, Motherwell's MS.,
p. 259.

❧ A ☙

1   There were twa brethren in the north,
      They went to the school thegither;
   The one unto the other said,
      "Will you try a warsle afore?"

2   They warsled up, they warsled down,
      Till Sir John fell to the ground,
   And there was a knife in Sir Willie's pouch,
      Gied him a deadlie wound.

3   "Oh brither dear, take me on your back,
        Carry me to yon burn clear,
    And wash the blood from off my wound,
        And it will bleed nae mair."

4   He took him up upon his back,
        Carried him to yon burn clear,
    And wash'd the blood from off his wound,
        But aye it bled the mair.

5   "Oh brither dear, take me on your back,
        Carry me to yon kirkyard,
    And dig a grave baith wide and deep,
        And lay my body there."

6   He's ta'en him up upon his back,
        Carried him to yon kirkyard,
    And dug a grave baith deep and wide,
        And laid his body there.

7   "But what will I say to my father dear,
        Gin he chance to say, Willie, whar's John?"
    "Oh say that he's to England gone,
        To buy him a cask of wine."

8   "And what will I say to my mother dear,
        Gin she chance to say, Willie, whar's John?"
    "Oh say that he's to England gone,
        To buy her a new silk gown."

9   "And what will I say to my sister dear,
        Gin she chance to say, Willie, whar's John?"
    "Oh say that he's to England gone,
        To buy her a wedding ring."

10 "But what will I say to her you lo'e dear,
        Gin she cry, Why tarries my John?"
    "Oh tell her I lie in Kirk-land fair,
        And home again will never come."

burn, brook.   *gin,* if.

❧❍ B ❍❧

1   There was two little boys going to the school,
       And twa little boys they be,
     They met three brothers playing at the ba',
       And ladies dansing hey.

2   "It's whether will ye play at the ba', brither,
       Or else throw at the stone?"
     "I am too little, I am too young,
       O brother let me alone."

3   He pulled out a little penknife,
       That was baith sharp and sma,
     He gave his brother a deadly wound
       That was deep, long and sair.

4   He took the holland sark off his back,
       He tore it frae breast to gare,
     He laid it to the bloody wound,
       That still bled mair and mair.

5   "It's take me on your back, brother," he says,
       "And carry me to yon kirkyard,
     And make me there a very fine grave,
       That will be long and large.

6   "Lay my bible at my head," he says,
       "My chaunter at my feet,
     My bow and arrows by my side,
       And soundly I will sleep.

7   "When you go home, brother," he says,
       "My father will ask for me;
     You may tell him I am in Saussif town,
       Learning my lessons free.

8   "When you go home, brother," he says,
       "My mother will ask for me;

sark, shirt, tunic. *gare*, gore, place where tunic widens, knee.

You may tell her I am in Sausaf town,
    And I'll come home merrily.

9   "When you go home, brother," he says,
        "Lady Margaret will ask for me;
    You may tell her I'm dead and in grave laid,
        And buried in Sausaff toun."

10 She put the small pipes to her mouth,
        And she harped both far and near,
    Till she harped the small birds off the briers.
        And her true love out of the grave.

11 "What's this? what's this, Lady Margaret?" he says,
        "What's this you want of me?"
    "One sweet kiss of your ruby lips,
        That's all I want of thee."

12 "My lips they are so bitter," he says,
        "My breath it is so strong,
    If you get one kiss of my ruby lips,
        Your days will not be long."

The Bonny Hind (50)

The unique version of this poignant tragedy was taken down
from the recitation of a Scottish milkmaid in 1771. Analogous
incidents of accidental incest occur in Icelandic and Finnish
folk poetry. The "bonny hind" may be merely a covert symbol
for the sister, but it is more likely that the brother uses the
term because he believes her soul has been transformed into
a doe.

Text: Herd MSS., II, 65.

1   O may she comes and may she goes,
        Down by yon gardens green,
    And there she spied a gallant squire
        As squire had ever been.

may, maiden, virgin.

2 And may she comes, and may she goes,
    Down by yon hollin tree,
And there she spied a brisk young squire,
    And a brisk young squire was he.

3 "Give me your green manteel, fair maid,
    Give me your maidenhead;
Gif ye winna gie me your green manteel,
    Gi' me your maidenhead."

4 He has taen her by the milk-white hand,
    And softly laid her down,
And when he's lifted her up again
    Given her a silver kaim.

5 "Perhaps there may be bairns, kind sir,
    Perhaps there may be nane;
But if you be a courtier,
    You'll tell to me your name."

6 "I am nae courtier, fair maid,
    But new come frae the sea;
I am nae courtier, fair maid,
    But when I courteth thee.

7 "They call me Jack when I'm abroad,
    Sometimes they call me John;
But when I'm in my father's bower
    Jock Randal is my name."

8 "Ye lee, ye lee, ye bonny lad,
    Sae loud's I hear ye lee!
Ffor I'm Lord Randal's yae daughter,
    He has nae mair nor me."

9 "Ye lee, ye lee, ye bonny may,
    Sae loud's I hear ye lee!
For I'm Lord Randal's yae yae son,
    Just now come oer the sea."

10 She's putten her hand down by her spare,
    And out she's taen a knife,

hollin, holly.   *kaim,* comb.   *yae,* only.   *spare,* opening in gown.

And she has putn 't in her heart's bluid,
    And taen away her life.

11 And he's taen up his bonny sister,
        With the big tear in his een,
    And he has buried his bonny sister
        Amang the hollins green.

12 And syne he's hyed him oer the dale,
        His father dear to see:
    "Sing O and O for my bonny hind,
        Beneath yon hollin tree!"

13 "What needs you care for your bonny hyn?
        For it you needna care;
    There's aught score hyns in yonder park,
        And five score hyns to spare.

14 "Four score of them are siller-shod,
        Of thae ye may get three;"
    "But O and O for my bonny hyn,
        Beneath yon hollin tree!"

15 "What needs you care for your bonny hyn?
        For it you need na care;
    Take you the best, gi' me the warst,
        Since plenty is to spare."

16 "I care na for your hyns, my lord,
        I care na for your fee;
    But O and O for my bonny hyn,
        Beneath the hollin tree!"

17 "O were ye at your sister's bower,
        Your sister fair to see,
    Ye'll think na mair o your bonny hyn
        Beneath the hollin tree."

een, eyes.

The Cruel Brother (11)

Possibly this ballad suppresses an incest theme: the cruel brother may not be so much jealous of his family prerogative as he is simply jealous. But whatever the theme, the ballad is remarkable for its suspenseful passages of incremental repetition (stanzas 9-10, 14-15, 21-26), the bride's stoical suffering, the expressive testament. Because the brother's crime seems motiveless by modern standards, the ballad survives only weakly in British and American tradition.

Text: A. F. Tytler's Brown MS., p. 31, with additions from Jamieson, I, 66—see Child, I, 145.

1   There was three ladies play'd at the ba',
      With a hey ho and a lillie gay
    There came a knight and play'd oer them a'.
      As the primrose spreads so sweetly

2   The eldest was baith tall and fair,
    But the youngest was beyond compare.

3   The midmost had a graceful mien,
    But the youngest look'd like beautie's queen.

4   The knight bow'd low to a' the three,
    But to the youngest he bent his knee.

5   The ladie turned her head aside,
    The knight he woo'd her to be his bride.

6   The ladie blush'd a rosy red,
    And sayd, "Sir knight, I'm too young to wed."

7   "O ladie fair, give me your hand,
    And I'll make you ladie of a' my land."

8   "Sir knight, ere ye my favor win,
    You maun get consent frae a' my kin."

9   He's got consent frae her parents dear,
    And likewise frae her sisters fair.

10   He's got consent frae her kin each one,
      But forgot to spiek to her brother John.

11   Now, when the wedding day was come,
      The knight would take his bonny bride home.

12   And many a lord and many a knight
      Came to behold that ladie bright.

13   And there was nae man that did her see,
      But wish'd himself bridegroom to be.

14   Her father dear led her down the stair,
      And her sisters twain they kiss'd her there.

15   Her mother dear led her thro the closs,
      And her brother John set her on her horse.

16   She lean'd her o'er the saddle-bow,
      To give him a kiss ere she did go.

17   He has ta'en a knife, baith lang and sharp,
      And stabb'd that bonny bride to the heart.

18   She had no' ridden half thro the town,
      Until her heart's blude stain'd her gown.

19   "Ride softly on," says the best young man,
      "For I think our bonny bride looks pale and wan."

20   "O lead me gently up yon hill,
      And I'll there sit down and make my will."

21   "O what will you leave to your father dear?"
      "The silver-shod steed that brought me here."

22   ["What will you leave to your mother dear?"
      "My velvet pall and my silken gear."

23   "What will you leave to your sister Anne?"
      "My silken scarf and my gowden fan."]

24   "What will you leave to your sister Grace?"
      "My bloody cloaths to wash and dress."

closs, close, yard.

25 "What will you leave to your brother John?"
"The gallows-tree to hang him on."

26 "What will you leave to your brother John's wife?"
"The wilderness to end her life."

27 This ladie fair in her grave was laid,
And many a mass was o'er her said.

28 But it would have made your heart right sair,
To see the bridegroom rive his haire.

rive, tear.

VII: TABLOID CRIME

Lord Randal (12)

"L'Avvelenato" ("The Poisoned Man"), which is the Italian counterpart of "Lord Randal," was cited over three hundred years ago, and since poison is a highly unusual weapon in British balladry, it may be that the ballad was transplanted to Scotland and England from Italy. Scott's text in the *Minstrelsy* (III, 292), our A, sets out the dialogue pattern that has remained marvelously constant throughout the mass of variants collected. His version, unfortunately, is defective in not giving the will of the dying huntsman, but the representative American text (B) collected in Missouri (Belden, p. 26) supplies this feature. The bequests vary widely in America as in Britain, especially that for the true-love, who, ironically, proves false. Both old- and new-world versions bequeath "Hell's fire and brimstone . . . to scorch her bones brown" (Cox, p. 26), while a South Carolina Lord Randal (Smith, p. 102) asserts passionately,

> "I will her a keg of powder
> To blow her sky high!"

The victim bears many different names: Laird Rowland (Scotland), Reynolds, Tyranty (New England), Duranty, Durango (Oklahoma). He becomes a Johnny Randolph in Virginia and a McDonald in South Carolina and elsewhere. The title is generally dropped in America.

❀◈ A ◈❀

1   "O where hae ye been, Lord Randal, my son?
    O where hae ye been, my handsome young man?"
"I hae been to the wild wood; mother, make my bed soon,
    For I'm weary wi' hunting, and fain wald lie down."

2   "Where gat ye your dinner, Lord Randal, my son?
    Where gat ye your dinner, my handsome young man?"

178

"I din'd wi' my true-love; mother, make my bed soon,
For I'm weary wi' hunting, and fain wald lie down."

3 "What gat ye to your dinner, Lord Randal, my son?
What gat ye to your dinner, my handsome young man?"
"I gat eels boil'd in broo; mother, make my bed soon,
For I'm weary wi' hunting, and fain wald lie down."

4 "What became of your bloodhounds, Lord Randal, my son?
What became of your bloodhounds, my handsome young
man?"
"O they swell'd and they died; mother, make my bed soon,
For I'm weary wi' hunting, and fain wald lie down."

5 "O I fear ye are poisoned, Lord Randal, my son!
O I fear ye are poisoned, my handsome young man!"
"O yes! I am poison'd; mother, make my bed soon,
For I'm sick at the heart, and fain wald lie down."

❦◇ **B** ◇❦

1 "Oh, where have you been, Lord Randal, my son?
Oh, where have you been, my handsome young man?"
"Oh, I've been to the wildwood; mother, make my bed
soon,
I'm weary of hunting and I fain would lie down."

2 "And whom did you meet there, Lord Randal, my son?"
"Oh, I met with my true love; mother, make my bed
soon . . ."

3 "What got you for supper, Lord Randal, my son?"
"I got eels boiled in broth; mother, make my bed soon . . ."

4 "And who got your leavings, Lord Randal, my son?"
"I gave them to my dogs; mother, make my bed soon . . ."

5 "And what did your dogs do, Lord Randal, my son?"
"Oh, they stretched out and died; mother, make my bed
soon . . ."

6 "Oh, I fear you are poisoned, Lord Randal, my son."
"Oh, yes, I am poisoned; mother, make my bed soon . . ."

broo, broth.

7 "What will you leave your mother, Lord Randal, my son?"
   "My house and my lands; mother, make my bed soon . . ."

8 "What will you leave your sister, Lord Randal, my son?"
   "My gold and my silver; mother, make my bed soon . . ."

9 "What will you leave your brother, Lord Randal, my son?"
   "My horse and my saddle; mother, make my bed soon . . ."

10 "What will you leave your true-love, Lord Randal, my son?"
   "A halter to hang her; mother, make my bed soon,
   For I'm sick at my heart and I want to lie down."

❧◊ C ◊❧

Text C, "The Croodlin' Dow," from Motherwell's MS., p.
238, represents several versions of "Lord Randal" in which a
child replaces the handsome young man. Scott conjectures that
these versions are merely adaptations for the nursery, the
inevitable wicked stepmother of fairy tales intruding as vil-
lainess. The appearance of both stepmother and mother in
the ballad seemed to Grundtvig and Child a hopeless incon-
sistency. But Barry (p. 71) argues interestingly that in "The
Croodlin' Dow" we have the only trace in English balladry of
"the spirit of a dead mother returning to comfort a child abused
by a cruel stepmother." Rationalizing generations of singers
have transformed the ghost into the living woman, thus eradi-
cating the supernatural at the expense of consistency. There
are both Scottish and American versions where the problem of
the two mothers has been solved by making a witch-grand-
mother the poisoner.

1 "Oh whare hae ye been a' day, my bonnie wee croodlin
      dow?
   Oh whare hae ye been a' day, my bonnie wee croodlin
      dow?"
   "I've been at my step-mother's; oh mak my bed, mammie,
      now!
   I've been at my step-mother's; oh mak my bed, mammie,
      now!"

croodlin, cooing.   *dow,* dove.

2 "Oh what did ye get at your step-mother's, my bonnie wee
    croodlin dow?" [*Twice*]
  "I gat a wee wee fishie; oh mak my bed, mammie, now!"
    [*Twice*]

3 "Oh whare gat she the wee fishie, my bonnie wee croodlin
    dow?"
  "In a dub before the door; oh mak my bed, mammie, now!"

4 "What did ye wi the wee fishie, my bonnie wee croodlin
    dow?"
  "I boild it in a wee pannie; oh make my bed, mammy,
    now!"

5 "Wha gied ye the banes o the fishie till, my bonnie wee
    croodlin dow?"
  "I gied them till a wee doggie; oh mak my bed, mammie,
    now!"

6 "Oh whare is the little wee doggie, my bonnie wee croodlin
    dow?
  Oh whare is the little wee doggie, my bonnie wee croodlin
    dow?"
  "It shot out its fit and died, and sae maun I do too;
  Oh mak my bed, mammy, now, now, oh mak my bed,
    mammy, now!"

The Cruel Mother (20)

Though the murdered twins are bound hand and foot so that
they will not walk abroad as ghosts, they accost their mother
in the substantial, full-fleshed form taken by ballad revenants.
In other versions, British and American, the bonnie babies not
only predict hell for their mother but spell out her penance, too
(Child, I, 225):

> "Seven years a fish in the sea,
> And seven years a bird in the tree,

dub, tub. *fit,* feet. *maun,* must.

Seven years to ring a bell,
And seven years porter in hell."

Text: Motherwell, *Minstrelsy,* p. 161a.

1 She leaned her back unto a thorn,
      Three, three, and three by three
   And there she has her two babes born.
      Three, three, and thirty-three

2 She took frae 'bout her ribbon-belt,
   And there she bound them hand and foot.

3 She has ta'en out her wee penknife,
   And there she ended baith their life.

4 She has howked a hole baith deep and wide,
   She has put them in baith side by side.

5 She has covered them o'er wi' a marble stane,
   Thinking she would gang maiden hame.

6 As she was walking by her father's castle wa',
   She saw twa pretty babes playing at the ba'.

7 "O bonnie babes! gin ye were mine,
   I would dress you up in satin fine!

8 "O I would dress you in the silk,
   And wash you ay in morning milk!"

9 "O cruel mother! we were thine,
   And thou made us to wear the twine.

10 "O cursed mother! heaven's high,
    And that's where thou will neer win nigh.

11 "O cursed mother! hell is deep,
    And there thou'll enter step by step."

howk, dig. *gin,* if. *win,* make one's way.

Mary Hamilton (173)

The search for the historical Mary Hamilton has proved tantalizing but elusive. There was a circle of ladies-in-waiting to Mary, Queen of Scots, popularly called "the four Maries," but a Mary Hamilton was not among them. Her crime and punishment, however, parallel a scandal of Mary's reign involving a French attendant who was executed for murdering her newborn child. Not Darnley, "the hichest Stewart of a'," but the queen's apothecary, the highest steward, was the Frenchwoman's accomplice in love and crime. This was in 1563.

In 1719 a beautiful Scottish maid-of-honor at Peter the Great's court named Mary Hamilton was beheaded for infanticide. Other circumstances in the Russian case beside the name tally with the ballad: the girl, for one thing, refused to wear sober clothes to the scaffold. Also, her lover was a high-born courtier. One would be tempted to consider the ballad an outgrowth of the Russian tragedy of 1719 if it were not for the troublesome fact that some form of the ballad seems to have circulated in Scotland before 1719. This older form was probably a ballad in which the Frenchwoman's crime was foisted upon one of the four Maries. Perhaps such a connection arose because of the common use of "mary" in Scotland for servant maid. There is in fact a version of "Mary Hamilton" (see Child, IV, 509) in which the girl is simply "Marie" and her lover is a "pottinger," the court apothecary of the criminal records. Apparently the news from St. Petersburg and the real Mary Hamilton's jaunty demeanor caught the Scottish imagination and the old ballad was revamped to suit a new "heroine."

C. K. Sharpe's *Ballad Book*, 1823, p. 18, furnishes the present text. A late version of the ballad, composed simply of the scaffold speech, is printed with the "goodnight" ballads (p. 219). The authentic tune preserved by Greig, p. 109, suits either ballad.

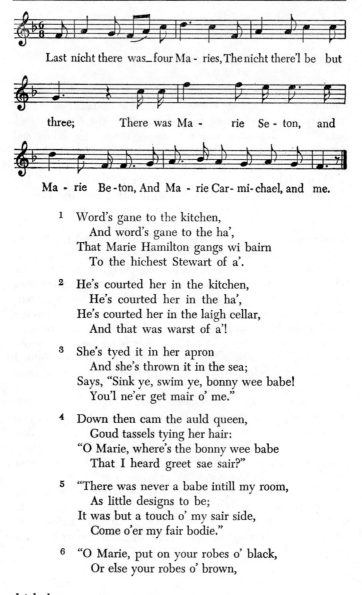

Last nicht there was—four Ma - ries, The nicht there'l be but
three;   There was Ma -   rie Se - ton, and
Ma - rie Be - ton, And Ma - rie Car - mi- chael, and me.

1   Word's gane to the kitchen,
        And word's gane to the ha',
    That Marie Hamilton gangs wi bairn
        To the hichest Stewart of a'.

2   He's courted her in the kitchen,
        He's courted her in the ha',
    He's courted her in the laigh cellar,
        And that was warst of a'!

3   She's tyed it in her apron
        And she's thrown it in the sea;
    Says, "Sink ye, swim ye, bonny wee babe!
        You'l ne'er get mair o' me."

4   Down then cam the auld queen,
        Goud tassels tying her hair:
    "O Marie, where's the bonny wee babe
        That I heard greet sae sair?"

5   "There was never a babe intill my room,
        As little designs to be;
    It was but a touch o' my sair side,
        Come o'er my fair bodie."

6   "O Marie, put on your robes o' black,
        Or else your robes o' brown,

laigh, low. *greet,* weep.

For ye maun gang wi' me the night,
    To see fair Edinbro' town."

7 "I winna put on my robes o' black,
    Nor yet my robes o' brown;
  But I'll put on my robes o' white,
    To shine through Edinbro' town."

8 When she gaed up the Cannogate,
    She laugh'd loud laughters three;
  But whan she cam down the Cannogate
    The tear blinded her ee.

9 When she gaed up the Parliament stair,
    The heel cam aff her shee;
  And lang or she cam down again
    She was condemned to dee.

10 When she cam down the Cannogate,
    The Cannogate sae free,
  Many a ladie look'd o'er her window,
    Weeping for this ladie.

11 "Ye need nae weep for me," she says,
    "Ye need nae weep for me;
  For had I not slain mine own sweet babe,
    This death I wadna dee.

12 "Bring me a bottle of wine," she says,
    "The best that e'er ye hae,
  That I may drink to my weil-wishers,
    And they may drink to me.

13 "Here's a health to the jolly sailors,
    That sail upon the main;
  Let them never let on to my father and mother
    But what I'm coming hame.

14 "Here's a health to the jolly sailors,
    That sail upon the sea;
  Let them never let on to my father and mother
    That I cam here to dee.

15 "Oh, little did my mother think,
    The day she cradled me,

What lands I was to travel through,
What death I was to dee.

16   "Oh, little did my father think,
       The day he held up me,
     What lands I was to travel through,
       What death I was to dee.

17   "Last night I wash'd the queen's feet,
       And gently laid her down;
     And a' the thanks I've gotten the nicht
       To be hang'd in Edinbro' town!

18   "Last nicht there was four Maries,
       The nicht there'l be but three;
     There was Marie Seton, and Marie Beton,
       And Marie Carmichael, and me."

Little Musgrave and the Lady Barnard (81)

Balladry has its share of unfaithful wives, informers, and
inopportunely returning husbands, and can turn out as sordid
a tale as any scandal sheet—witness "Little Musgrave." A
stanza from the ballad is quoted in Beaumont and Fletcher's
Knight of the Burning Pestle, V, 3 (1611), but the oldest English copy preserved, our text, dates from 1658. The numerous
later English and Scottish versions disagree only in details, but
key details. Our text has Musgrave startled from sleep by Lord
Barnard's horn; in a Pepys broadside it is a friend in Barnard's
troop that sounds the unheeded warning:

> But one of the men, that Mousgrove did love,
> And respected his friendship most deare,
> To give him knowledge Lord Barnet was neere,
> Did winde his bugle most cleere.

Several versions have Musgrave, upon discovery, cravenly curse
the lady in his despair. The butchery of Lady Barnard is usually less cruel than in the ballad printed here, though more than
one old-world text pictures her as far gone in pregnancy—
with gory results:

"I'm not sae wae for my lady,
For she lies cauld and dead;
But I'm right wae for my young son,
Lies sprawling in her blood."

Though known among recent Scottish immigrants to Canada,
the ballad has not been reported from Britain in this century.
The abundant American versions are, as a rule, more circum-
stantial about Lord Barnard's absence—he is visiting King
Henry in London—and no American Musgrave (Matty Grove)
is so low as to put the blame upon Lady Barnard (Banner,
Arnold, Daniel). For a discussion of the American tradition,
both as to story and music, see Barry, pp. 150-94.

Text: *Wit Restor'd*, 1658, p. 174.

1   As it fell one holy-day—
        Hay downe—
     As many be in the yeare,
     When young men and maids together did goe,
        Their mattins and masses to heare,

2   Little Musgrave came to the church-dore;
        The priest was at private masse;
     But he had more minde of the faire women
        Then he had of our lady['s] grace

3   The one of them was clad in green,
        Another was clad in pall,
     And then came in Lord Barnard's wife,
        The fairest amonst them all.

4   She cast an eye on Little Musgrave,
        As bright as the summer sun;
     And then bethought this Little Musgrave,
        This lady's heart have I woonn.

5   Quoth she, "I have loved thee, Little Musgrave,
        Full long and many a day;"
     "So have I loved you, fair lady,
        Yet never a word durst I say."

6   "I have a bower at Buckelsfordbery,
     Full daintyly it is [d]eight;
  If thou wilt wend thither, thou Little Musgrave,
     Thou's lig in mine armes all night."

7   Quoth he, "I thank yee, faire lady,
     This kindness thou showest to me;
  But whether it be to my weal or woe,
     This night I will lig with thee."

8   With that he heard, a little tynë page,
     By his ladye's coach as he ran:
  "All though I am my ladye's foot-page,
     Yet I am Lord Barnard's man.

9   "My lord Barnard shall knowe of this,
     Whether I sink or swim;"
  And ever where the bridges were broake
     He laid him downe to swimme.

10   "A sleepe or wake, thou Lord Barnard,
     As thou art a man of life,
  For Little Musgrave is at Bucklesfordbery,
     A bed with thy own wedded wife."

11   "If this be true, thou little tinny page,
     This thing thou tellest to me,
  Then all the land in Bucklesfordbery,
     I freely will give to thee.

12   "But if it be a ly, thou little tinny page,
     This thing thou tellest to me,
  On the hyest tree in Bucklesfordbery
     Then hanged shalt thou be."

13   He called up his merry men all:
     "Come saddle me my steed;
  This night must I to Bucklesfordbery,
     For I never had greater need."

14   And some of them whistld, and some of them sung,
     And some these words did say,

deight, furnished.   *tynë,* tiny.

And ever when my lord Barnard's horn blew,
"Away, Musgrave, away!"

15 "Methinks I hear the thresel-cock,
Methinks I hear the jaye;
Methinks I hear my lord Barnard,
And I would I were away."

16 "Lye still, lye still, thou Little Musgrave,
And huggell me from the cold;
'Tis nothing but a shephard's boy,
A driving his sheep to the fold.

17 "Is not thy hawke upon a perch?
Thy steed eats oats and hay;
And thou a fair lady in thine arms,
And wouldst thou bee away?"

18 With that my lord Barnard came to the dore,
And lit a stone upon;
He plucked out three silver keys,
And he opened the dores each one.

19 He lifted up the coverlett,
He lifted up the sheet:
"How now, how now, thou Littell Musgrave,
Doest thou find my lady sweet?"

20 "I find her sweet," quoth Little Musgrave,
"The more 'tis to my paine;
I would gladly give three hundred pounds
That I were on yonder plaine."

21 "Arise, arise, thou Littell Musgrave,
And put they clothës on;
It shall nere be said in my country
I have killed a naked man.

22 "I have two swords in one scabberd,
Full deere they cost my purse;
And thou shalt have the best of them,
And I will have the worse."

thresel-cock, thrush.   *huggell,* hug and huddle.

23   The first stroke that Little Musgrave stroke,
         He hurt Lord Barnard sore;
      The next stroke that Lord Barnard stroke,
         Little Musgrave nere struck more.

24   With that bespake this faire lady,
         In bed whereas she lay:
      "Although thou'rt dead, thou Little Musgrave,
         Yet I for thee will pray.

25   "And wish well to thy soule will I,
         So long as I have life;
      So will I not for thee, Barnard,
         Although I am thy wedded wife."

26   He cut her paps from off her brest;
         Great pitty it was to see
      That some drops of this ladie's heart's blood
         Ran trickling down her knee.

27   "Woe worth you, woe worth, my mery men all
         You were not borne for my good;
      Why did you not offer to stay my hand,
         When you see me wax so wood?

28   "For I have slaine the bravest sir knight
         That ever rode on a steed;
      So have I done the fairest lady
         That ever did woman's deed.

29   "A grave, a grave," Lord Barnard cryd,
         "To put these lovers in;
      But lay my lady on the upper hand,
         For she came of the better kin."

Young Hunting (68)

Gone completely from Scottish tradition, in which it originated, "Young Hunting" survives surprisingly in America,
though most of the forty or so American texts are variants of a

wax wood, go mad.

single version, and that a debased form of the story. The
detection of the body by floating a candle fixed in cork over
the water and watching for the spot where the flame burns
brighter is a belief unknown to the American folk and, therefore, disappears from the new-world story. Rather it is the
bird (the new host of the murdered man's soul?) that points
out the body. The bird also fixes the guilt upon the murderess.
The medieval ordeal by fire which concludes our text (Herd
MSS., I, 182) is too barbarous a scene for modern taste and
falls away. In another Scottish version, the guilty person is
detected by the fact that ". . . as the traitor she came near
[the body], His wounds they gushit out" (Child, II, 146). The
single graceful detail in the standard American version is that
the young sportsman receives his wound as he bends from his
horse to kiss his mistress a final good-by.

1   "O lady, rock never your young son young
         One hour longer for me,
     For I have a sweetheart in Garlick's Wells
         I love thrice better than [thee].

2   "The very sols of my love's feet
         Is whiter then thy face:"
     "But nevertheless na, Young Hunting,
         Ye'l stay wi me all night."

3   She has birl'd in him Young Hunting
         The good ale and the beer,
     Till he was as fou drunken
         As any wild-wood steer.

4   She has birl'd in him Young Hunting
         The good ale and the wine,
     Till he was as fou drunken
         As any wild-wood swine.

5   Up she has tain him Young Hunting,
         And she has had him to her bed,

         .   .   .   .   .

              .   .   .   .   .

birl in, pour drink into.   *fou,* full.

6   And she has minded her on a little penknife,
        That hangs low down by her gare,
    And she has gin him Young Hunting
        A deep wound and a sare.

7   Out an spake the bonny bird,
        That flew abon her head:
    "Lady, keep well thy green clothing
        Fra that good lord's blood."

8   "O better I'le keep my green clothing
        Fra that good lord's blood
    Nor thou can keep thy flattering toung,
        That flatters in thy head.

9   "Light down, light down, my bonny bird,
        Light down upon my hand,

     .   .   .   .

         .   .   .

10 "O siller, O siller shall be thy hire,
        An goud shall be thy fee,
    An every month into the year
        Thy cage shall changed be."

11 "I winna light down, I shanna light down,
        I winna light on thy hand;
    For soon, soon wad ye do to me
        As ye done to Young Hunting."

12 She has booted an spir'd him Young Hunting
        [As] he had been gan to ride,
    A hunting-horn about his neck,
        An the sharp sourd by his side.

13 And she has had him to yon wan water,
        For a' man calls it Clyde,

     .   .   .   .   .

         .   .   .

14 The deepest pot intill it all
        She has puten Young Hunting in;

gare, gore, place where dress widens, knee.   *spir,* spur.

A green turff upon his breast,
  To hold that good lord down.

15 It fell once upon a day
     The king was going to ride,
   And he sent for him Young Hunting,
     To ride on his right side.

16 She has turn'd her right and round about,
     She sware now by the corn,
   "I saw na thy son, Young Hunting,
     Sen yesterday at morn."

17 She has turn'd her right and round about,
     She swear now by the moon,
   "I saw na thy son, Young Hunting,
     Sen yesterday at noon.

18 "It fears me sair in Clyde Water
     That he is drownd therein:"
   O thay ha sent for the king's duckers,
     To duck for Young Hunting.

19 They ducked in at the tae water-bank,
     Thay ducked out at the tither:
   "We'll duck no more for Young Hunting,
     All tho he wear our brother."

20 Out an spake the bonny bird,
     That flew abon their heads,

     .   .   .   .   .

        .   .   .   .   .

21 "O he's na drownd in Clyde Water,
     He is slain and put therein;
   The lady that lives in yon castil
     Slew him and put him in.

22 "Leave aff your ducking on the day,
     And duck upon the night;
   Whear ever that sakeless knight lys slain,
     The candels will shine bright."

ducker, diver. *tae . . . tither*, the one . . . the other. *sakeless*,
innocent.

23   Thay left off their ducking o' the day,
       And ducked upon the night,
     And where that sakeless knight lay slain,
       The candles shone full bright.

24   The deepest pot intill it a'
       Thay got Young Hunting in;
     A green turff upon his breast,
       To hold that good lord down.

25   O thay ha sent aff men to the wood
       To hew down baith thorn an fern,
     That they might get a great bonefire
       To burn that lady in.
     "Put na the wyte on me," she says,
       "It was [my] may Catheren."

26   Whan thay had tane her may Catheren,
       In the bonefire set her in;
     It wad na take upon her cheeks,
       Nor take upon her chin,
     Nor yet upon her yallow hair,
       To healle the deadly sin.

27   Out they hae tain her may Catheren,
       And they hay put that lady in;
     O it took upon her cheek, her cheek,
       An it took upon her chin,
     An it took on her fair body,
       She burnt like hoky-gren.

Childe Maurice (Gill Morice) (83)

The Greek dramatists would have relished the plot of "Childe Maurice." They might even have approved of the order of events, for the poet Gray found the ballad a complete drama, one in which "Aristotle's best rules are observed." As it happens, the Scottish politician John Home shaped the ballad into

may, maid   *hoky-gren,* coals of green timber (*hollins grene*[?], green holly).

the highly successful tragedy of *Douglas* (1756), and Scotsmen, though only Scotsmen, thought *Douglas* superior to anything of Shakespeare's.

The ballad has barely survived into modern tradition. The text from the Motherwell MS., p. 480, printed below is one of the clearest versions and preserves in stanza 16 a classic illustration of ballad irony.

1   Gill Morice stood in stable-door,
      With red gold shined his weed;
   A bonnie boy him behind,
      Dressing a milk-white steed.

2   "Woe's me for you, maister,
      Your name it waxes wide;
   It is not for your rich, rich robes,
      Nor for your meikle pride,
   But all is for yon lord's ladie,
      She lives on Ithan side."

3   "Here's to thee, my bonnie wee boy,
      That I pay meat and fee;
   You will run on to Ithan side
      An errand unto me."

4   "If ye gar me that errand run,
      Sae sair against my will,
   I'll make a vow, and keep it true,
      I'll do your errand ill."

5   "I fear nae ill of thee, boy,
      I fear nae ill of thee;
   I fearna ill of my bonnie boy,
      My sister's son are ye.

6   "Ye'll tak here this green manteel,
      It's lined with the frieze;
   Ye'll bid her come to gude green-wood,
      To talk with Gill Morice.

7   "Ye'll tak here this sark o silk,
      Her ain hand sewed the sleeve;

gar, make. *sark,* shirt.

Ye'll bid her come to gude green-wood,
And ask not Burnard's leave."

8   When he gade to Ithan side
They were hailing at the ba,
And four and twenty gay ladyes
They lookd ower castle wa.

9   "God mak you safe, you ladies all,
God mak you safe and sure;
But Burnard's lady amang you all,
My errand is to her.

10 "Ye'll tak here his green manteel,
It's a' lined wi the frieze;
Ye're bidden come to gude green-wood
And speak to Gill Morice.

11 "Ye'll tak here this sark of silk,
Your ain hand sewed the sleeve;
Ye're bidden come to gude green-wood,
And ask not Burnard's leave."

12 Up it stood the little nurice,
She winked with her ee:
"Welcome, welcome, bonnie boy,
With luve-tidings to me."

13 "Ye lie, ye lie, ye false nurice,
Sae loud's I hear ye lie;
It's to the lady of the house,
I'm sure ye are not shee."

14 Then out and spoke him bold Burnard,
Behind the door stood he:
"I'll go unto gude green-wood,
And see what he may be.

15 "Come, bring to me the gowns of silk,
Your petticoats so small,
And I'll go on to gude green-wood,
I'll try with him a fall."

16   Gill Morice stood in gude green-wood,
        He whistled and he sang:
     "I think I see the woman come
        That I have loved lang."

17   "What now, what now, ye Gill Morice,
        What now, and how do ye?
     How lang hae ye my lady luved?
        This day come tell to me."

18   "First when I your lady loved,
        In green-wood amang the thyme,
     I wot she was my first fair love
        Or ever she was thine.

19   "First when I your lady loved,
        In green-wood amang the flouirs,
     I wot she was my first fair love,
        Or ever she was yours."

20   He's taen out a lang, lang brand
        That he was used to wear,
     And he's taen aff Gill Morice head,
        And put it on a spear:
     The soberest boy in a' the court
        Gill Morice head did bear.

21   He's put it in a braid basin,
        And brocht it in the ha,
     And laid it in his lady's lap;
        Said, "Lady, tak a ba!"

22   "Play ye, play ye, my lady," he said,
        "Play ye frae ha to bower;
     Play ye wi Gill Morice head,
        He was your paramour."

23   "He was not my paramour,
        He was my son indeed;
     I got him in my mother's bower,
        And in my maiden-weed.

brand, sword.

24 "I got him in my mother's bower,
       Wi meikle sin and shame;
    I brocht him up in good green-wood,
       Got mony a shower o rain.

25 "But I will kiss his bluidy head,
       And I will clap his chin;
    I'll make a vow, and keep it true,
       I'll never kiss man again.

26 "Oftimes I by his cradle sat,
       And fond to see him sleep;
    But I may walk about his grave,
       The saut tears for to weep."

27 "Bring cods, bring cods to my ladye,
       Her heart is full of wae;"
    "None of your cods, Burnet," she says,
       "But lay me on the strae."

28 "Pox on you, my lady fair,
       That wudna telled it me;
    If I had known he was your son,
       He had not been slain by me;
    And for ae penny ye wud hae gien
       I wud hae gien him three."

29 "Keep weel your land, Burnet," she said,
       "Your land and white monie;
    There's land eneuch in Norroway
       Lies heirless I wot the day."

30 The one was killed in the mornin air,
       His mother died at een,
    And or the mornin bells was rung
       The threesome were a' gane.

cods, pillows.   *eneuch,* enough.

Lamkin (93)

The name, or nickname, of the ruthless mason may once have had great significance in the ballad, since the point is driven home (stanzas 8-11) that Lamkin is annoyed by it. Was he then, until his final rage, a "lambkin," a timid man easily taken advantage of? If so, the continued use of the term adds an ironical touch to the story. But unfortunately for this theory, in many of the better versions Lord Wearie warns his lady to lock up the house against Lamkin's malice. More probably, "Lamkin," the Flemish diminutive of Lambert, was a taunting name for a Fleming, many of whom were employed on medieval Scottish and English buildings (see *JFDS*, 1:7). Lamkin's great care to save Lady Wearie's blood in a silver basin reminds us of "Sir Hugh." Here the purpose, however, is perhaps not to use the blood as a curative or in magical rites, but rather to keep aristocratic blood from seeping away into the floor, an indignity punished by the soul carried in the blood. The receptacle for such blood must traditionally be silver—compare "Cock Robin": "Who caught his blood?" / "I," said the fish, / "In my little silver dish, / I caught his blood."

The ballad has been sparsely reported in recent years from England, Scotland, Newfoundland, New England, the South, and the Middle West. The motive for the gruesome crime remains the same, except for a corrupt Virginia version (Davis, p. 357) which implies an extinct love affair between Lamkin and Lady Wearie.

Text: Jamieson, I, 176.

1   It's Lamkin was a mason good as ever built wi' stane;
    He built Lord Wearie's castle, but payment got he nane.

2   "O pay me, Lord Wearie, come, pay me my fee:"
    "I canna pay you, Lamkin, for I maun gang o'er the sea."

3   "O pay me now, Lord Wearie, come, pay me out o' hand:"
    "I canna pay you, Lamkin, unless I sell my land."

4   "O gin ye winna pay me, I here sall mak a vow,
       Before that ye come hame again, ye sall ha'e cause to rue."

5   Lord Wearie's got a bonny ship, to sail the saut sea faem;
       Bade his lady weel the castle keep, ay till he should come
          hame.

6   But the nourice was a fause limmer as e'er hung on a tree;
       She laid a plot wi' Lamkin, whan her lord was o'er the sea.

7   She laid a plot wi' Lamkin, when the servants were awa',
       Loot him in at a little shot-window, and brought him to the
          ha'.

8   "O where's a' the men o' this house, that ca' me Lamkin?"
       "They're at the barn-well thrashing; 'twill be lang ere they
          come in."

9   "And whare's the women o' this house, that ca' me Lamkin?"
       "They're at the far well washing; 'twill be night or they
          come hame."

10   "And whare's the bairns o' this house, that ca' me Lamkin?"
       "They're at the school reading; 'twill be night or they come
          hame."

11   "O whare's the lady o' this house, that ca's me Lamkin?"
       "She's up in her bower sewing, but we soon can bring her
          down."

12   Then Lamkin's tane a sharp knife, that hang down by his
          gaire,
       And he has gi'en the bonny babe a deep wound and a sair.

13   Then Lamkin he rocked, and the fause nourice sang,
       Till frae ilka bore o' the cradle the red blood out sprang.

14   Then out it spak the lady, as she stood on the stair:
       "What ails my bairn, nourice, that he's greeting sae sair?

15   "O still my bairn, nourice, O still him wi' the pap!"
       "He winna still, lady, for this nor for that."

gin, if. *nourice,* nurse. *limmer,* bitch. *gaire,* gore, where gown
widens, knee. *greeting,* weeping.

16 "O still my bairn, nourice, O still him wi' the wand!"
   "He winna still, lady, for a' his father's land."

17 "O still my bairn, nourice, O still him wi' the bell!"
   "He winna still, lady, till ye come down yoursel."

18 O the firsten step she steppit, she steppit on a stane;
   But the neisten step she steppit, she met him Lamkin.

19 "O mercy, mercy, Lamkin, ha'e mercy upon me!
   Though you've ta'en my young son's life, ye may let mysel
     be."

20 "O sall I kill her, nourice, or sall I let her be?"
   "O kill her, kill her, Lamkin, for she ne'er was good to me."

21 "O scour the bason, nourice, and mak it fair and clean,
   For to keep this lady's heart's blood, for she's come o' noble
     kin."

22 "There need nae bason, Lamkin, lat it run through the floor;
   What better is the heart's blood o' the rich than o' the
     poor?"

23 But ere three months were at an end, Lord Wearie came
     again;
   But dowie, dowie was his heart when first he came hame.

24 "O wha's blood is this," he says, "that lies in the chamer?"
   "It is your lady's heart's blood; 'tis as clear as the lamer."

25 "And wha's blood is this," he says, "that lies in my ha'?"
   "It is your young son's heart's blood; 'tis the clearest ava."

26 O sweetly sang the black-bird that sat upon the tree;
   But sairer grat Lamkin, when he was condemnd to die.

27 And bonny sang the mavis, out o' the thorny brake;
   But sairer grat the nourice, when she was tied to the stake.

neisten, next. *dowie,* sad. *lamer,* amber. *ava,* of all. *grat,* wept.

Naomi Wise (Poor Omie Wise)

When "Naomi Wise" is accompanied by its melancholy tune, especially if a folk fiddle scrapes out the music, the effect is haunting. Perhaps the strength of the tune explains the distribution throughout the South of this pedestrian ballad about a murder that occurred in Randolph County, North Carolina, in 1808. Discovering he had a chance to win a local heiress, Jonathan Lewis determined to rid himself of orphaned Naomi Wise, whom he had gotten with child and promised to marry. The ballad describes the murder accurately. Lewis escaped before conviction. When brought back for trial many years later, he was acquitted because of lack of witnesses.

The text below, recorded from North Carolina tradition in 1874, is the oldest copy of the ballad (Brown, II, 692). The tune is transcribed from Victor 21625 (1927).

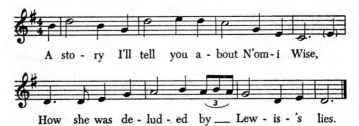

A sto - ry I'll tell you a - bout N'om-i Wise,

How she was de - lud - ed by __ Lew - is - 's lies.

1   Come all good people, I'd have you draw near,
    A sorrowful story you quickly shall hear;
    A story I'll tell you about N'omi Wise,
    How she was deluded by Lewis's lies.

2   He promised to marry and use me quite well;
    But conduct contrary I sadly must tell,
    He promised to meet me at Adams's spring;
    He promised me marriage and many fine things.

3   Still nothing he gave, but yet flattered the case.
    He says, "We'll be married and have no disgrace,

Come get up behind me, we'll go up to town.
And there we'll be married, in union be bound."

4   I got up behind him and straightway did go
To the bank of Deep river where the water did flow;
He says, "Now Naomi, I'll tell you my mind,
I intend here to drown you and leave you behind."

5   "O pity your infant and spare me my life;
Let me go rejected and be not your wife;"
"No pity, no pity," this monster did cry;
"In Deep river's bottom your body shall lie."

6   The wretch then did choke her, as we understand,
And threw her in the river below the milldam;
Be it murder or treason, O! what a great crime,
To drown poor Naomi and leave her behind.

7   Naomi was missing they all did well know,
And hunting for her to the river did go;
And there found her floating on the water so deep,
Which caused all the people to sigh and to weep.

8   The neighbors were sent for to see the great sight,
While she lay floating all that long night;
So early next morning the inquest was held;
The jury correctly the murder did tell.

The Jealous Lover

Collectors agree that "The Jealous Lover" is by all odds the most widely known of the native American ballads. It cannot be connected with any actual crime; no author is known. Barry (*American Speech,* III, 441-47) argues that the American ballad is a free adaptation from an English murder broadside. The intrusion into Southern texts of certain stanzas from a cloyingly sentimental English song of T. H. Bayly's titled "She Never Blamed Him" has been demonstrated by Belden (p. 324). The Bayly song was written in the 1820s and enjoyed enormous popularity during the Civil War.

Jealousy is supposedly the lover's motive, but this is another instance of folk prudery. From the mention of setting a wedding day and from comparison with franker English broadside relatives of the ballad, it becomes clear that Florilla has been "gotten into trouble"—compare "The Wexford Girl." The hearers' sympathy for the victim might be jeopardized if it were known that she had been a bad girl.

Text: *JAF*, 22:370; New Hampshire, 1908.

1   Down by yon weeping willow,
    Where flowers so sweetly bloom,
    There sleeps the fair Florilla,
    So silent in her tomb.

2   She died not broken-hearted,
    Nor sickness e'er befell,
    But in one moment parted
    From all she loved so well.

3   One night the moon shone brightly,
    And gentle zephyrs blew,
    Up to her cottage lightly
    Her treacherous lover drew.

4   He says, "Come let us wander,
    In those dark woods we'll stray,
    And there we'll sit and ponder
    Upon our wedding-day."

5   "Those woods look dark and dreary,
    I am afraid to stray,
    Of wandering I am weary,
    So I'll retrace my way."

6   "Those woods, those gently zephyrs,
    Your feet no more will roam,
    So bid adieu forever
    To parents, friends, and home."

7   Down on her knees before him
    She begged for her life,
    When deep into her bosom
    He plunged that hateful knife.

8   "O William! I'll forgive you,"
    Was her last dying breath,
    Her pulses ceased their motion,
    Her eyes were closed in death.

9   Down by yon weeping willow,
    Where flowers so sweetly bloom,
    There sleeps that fair Florilla,
    So silent in her tomb.

Fuller and Warren

Amasa Fuller strode into the Lawrenceburg, Indiana, office
of Palmer Warren one January day in 1820 and put a bullet
through Warren's left breast. "I have been ridding the world of
a vile serpent! I glory in the dead!" the contemporary newspapers
report him to have boasted. Warren had won away the affections
of the young lady to whom Fuller was engaged. Both young
men were admired in Lawrenceburg, and Fuller naturally is
extolled in the ballad; not a good word has ever been uttered
for the "fickle-minded maid." At Fuller's hanging, according to
our version, the rope broke and the doctors had to take over.
No such thing happened.

Though sung in New England—the present text is from Maine
(*Bulletin*, 9:14)—the ballad was especially popular in the South-
west and was once a bunkhouse favorite of the cowboys.

1   Ye sons of Columbia, attention now I pray,
    To a sad story I'm going to tell;
    It happened of late in Indiana state,
    To a hero that none could excel.

2   He was handsome in deportment, comeleye and fair,
    A brave hero as ever was known;
    But I'm sorry to say, instead of his wedding day,
    Poor Fuller lies silent in his tomb.

3   Like Samson he courted the choicest of the fair,
    And intended to make her his wife;

But like Delilah fair, she did his heart ensnare,
And she robbed him of his honor and his life.

4 He gave to her a gold ring, the token of true love,
And supposed it was the image of a dove;
To get married in speed, they mutually agreed,
And swore it by the powers above.

5 When Fuller came to hear he was deprived of his dear
Whom he promised by the powers he would wed,
With a heart full of woe unto Warren he did go,
And smiling unto Warren he says:

6 "Young man, you know you've injured me to gratify your
cause,
By reporting I had left a prudent wife;
Now acknowledge that you've wronged me, or I will break
the law,
Or, Warren, I'll deprive you of your life."

7 "Young man," he replies, "your request must be denied,
For my heart unto your darling it is bound;
And, further, I can say, this is our wedding day,
In spite of all the heroes in the town!"

8 Young Fuller in a passion of love and anger flew,
And Minnie began for to cry;
But with one fatal shot, he killed Warren on the spot,
And smiling says, "I'm ready now to die."

9 Young Fuller was condemned by the honorable board
Of Lawrence[burg to die]
That enormous death, to hang above the earth,
Like [Haman] on the gallows so high.

10 Now the time was drawing nigh when young Fuller he
must die;
With a smile he bid the world all adieu;
Like an angel he did stand, for he was a handsome man,
On his breast he wore a ribbon of blue.

11 The smiling gods of love looking down from above,
When the rope it broke asunder as we stand;

Two doctors for the pay committed murder, we may say,
When they hung him by the main strength of hand.

12 Come all you young married men that's got a prudent wife,
Be loving, be honest and be kind;
You may look through Judges, Genesis, Samuel, Kings and
Jews,
And the truth of my story you will find,

13 That marriage is a lottery, and few that wins the prize
That's pleasing to the heart and the eye;
But those that never marry is said to be the wise,—
Now, ladies and gentlemen,—good-bye!

Jim Fisk

The fatal shooting of "Jubilee Jim" Fisk, "Jay Gould's fellow
bandit in Wall Street, in the Grand Central Hotel, New York
City, on the sixth of January, 1872, by Edward Stokes, his rival
for the affections of actress Josie Mansfield, aroused a great deal
of excitement—not only because the actors in the drama had
already been before the public a good deal, Fisk being popularly
known as 'Prince of Erie,' member of the Tweed ring, and
corrupter of New York officials, but also because Fisk had made
himself popular among the rabble by his ostentatious liberality,
having among other things sent a trainload of provisions to Chicago after the disastrous fire there a few months before" (Belden). The socially conscious broadside poet feared Stokes would
not be convicted because of his social position and wealth; actually he was penniless. Stokes served four years in the New York
State Prison.

Broadside copies of the Fisk ballad recommended that it be
sung to the tune of the homiletic song "Never Go Back on the
Poor" from which the ballad was adapted. Only New England
and the Midwest report traditional copies of the ballad. A
Missouri text is here reproduced from Belden, p. 415.

1 If you will listen a while I will sing you a song
Of this glorious land of the free,

The difference I will show 'twixt the rich and the poor
In a trial by jury, you see;

2   If you have plenty of cash you can hold up your head
And walk from your own prison door;
But they will hang you up high if you have neither friend or
     gold,
Let the rich go, but hang up the poor.
In a trial of murder we have now,
And the rich ones get off slow but sure;
With their thousands to buy both the jury and the judge
You can bet they'll go back on the poor.

3   Let me speak of a man who is dead in his grave,
As good a man as ever was born.
Jim Fisk he was called, and his money he gave
To outcast, the poor and forlorn.
If a man was in trouble Jim Fisk would help him along
To drive the grim wolf from his door;
He strove to do right, though he might of done wrong,
But never went back on the poor.

4   Jim Fisk was a man who wore his heart in his sleeve;
No matter what people may say,
He done all his deeds, both the good and the bad,
In the broad open light of the day.
With his grand six-in-hand on the beach of Long Branch
He cut a big dash, to be sure;
But Chicago's great fire showed the world that Jim Fisk
With his wealth still remembered the poor.

5   When the telegram came of the homeless that night,
They were starving to death, slow but sure,
With his lightning express nobly minded Jim Fisk
Flew to feed all the hungry and poor.

6   Now what do you think of this trial of Stokes,
Who murdered this friend of the poor?
If such men get free is anyone safe
To step outside their own door?
Is there one law for rich, is there one law for the poor?
It seems so, at least so they say.

If they hang up the poor why oughtn't the rich
To be hung up the very same way?

7 Now don't show any favor to friend or to foe,
To prince or to beggar at your door,
But the millionaire you must hang up also;
But never go back on the poor.

Pearl Bryan

Pearl Bryan, the daughter of a wealthy Greencastle, Indiana, farmer, was murdered by Scott Jackson and Alonso Walling, Cincinnati dental college students, in January 1896. Jackson was the father of Pearl's unborn child. The decapitated body was discovered a few days after the murder, and in March 1897 the men were executed. The girl's head was never found.

Indiana and West Virginia versions of "The Jealous Lover" (See p. 203) have been printed that replace Florilla with Pearl Bryan and name Scott Jackson as the jealous lover. These pieces are not to be confused with the wholly independent ballad of "Pearl Bryan."

Text: Brewster, p. 283, from Indiana.

1 Young girls, if you'll listen,
  A story I'll relate
That happened near Fort Thomas
  In the old Kentucky state.

2 On January the thirty-first
  The dreadful deed was done
By Jackson and by Walling;
  How cold Pearl's blood did run!

3 But little did her parents think
  When she left her happy home,
Their darling girl just in her youth
  Would never more return.

4 How sad it would have been to them
  To have heard Pearl's lonely voice

At midnight in that lonely spot
    Where those two boys rejoiced!

5   And little did Pearl Bryan think
        When she left her home that day,
    The grip she carried in her hand
        Would hide her head away.

6   She thought it was her lover's hand
        She could trust both night and day,
    Although it was her lover's hand
        That took her life away.

7   The driver in the seat is all
        Who tells of Pearl's sad fate,
    Of poor Pearl Bryan away from home
        In the old Kentucky state.

8   Of her aged parents we all know well
        What a fortune they would give
    If Pearl could but to them return,
        Her natural life to live.

9   In came Pearl Bryan's sister,
        And falling to her knees,
    Begging to Scott Jackson,
        "My sister's head, O please!"

10 Scott Jackson he set stubborn;
        Not a word would he proclaim.
    "I'll meet my sister in heaven,
        Where I'll find her missing head."

11 In came Walling's mother,
        Pleading for her son,

            .   .   .   .   .

            .   .   .   .   .

12 "Don't take my son, my only son;
        From him I cannot part.
    O please don't take him to prison;
        It would break my poor old heart!"

13   The jury gave a verdict,
      And to their feet they sprung:
      "For the crime these boys committed
      They surely must be hung."

Frankie and Albert (Frankie and Johnny)

The "Frankie and Johnny" ballad dramatized on Broadway
and in motion pictures and sung everywhere by college students
and nightclub entertainers is a vaudeville version of the folk
ballad "Frankie and Albert." The stage song, concocted about
1911 by the team of Frank and Bert Leighton, burlesques the
tough Negro atmosphere and encourages the hearers to smile at
Frankie's possessive passion.

The folk ballad itself seems to have grown out of a sordid
shooting that occurred in 1899 in the Negro low-life district of
St. Louis. Allen Britt, a handsome Negro of eighteen, noted,
incidentally, as a "fancy dresser," was living with a young
mulatto woman, Frankie Baker, at 212 Targee (later Johnson)
Street. About 2:30 Sunday morning, October 15, Allen staggered
home drunk and was drawn by his mistress into a violent argument about another woman he was seeing. According to Frankie's
story, Allen attacked her with a knife. She, in self-defense, fired
a single shot into him. The other woman in the affair was a Miss
Alice Pryor, a name which explains the Nellie Bly, Alice Blye,
Alice Frye in the ballad (see *Missouri Historical Review*,
36:75-77).

A few folklorists refuse to accept the Britt-Baker shooting as
the basis of "Frankie and Albert" because of reports that the
ballad was in existence before 1899 (see Randolph, II, 126). In
all likelihood, the pre-1899 ballad, if there was one, dealt with
the murder of an unfaithful man at the hands of his mistress or
wife. At the time the underworld was excited over Britt's slaying, someone—perhaps the Negro pianist Bill Dooley, who is
credited with a dirge on the subject—adapted the older ballad
to fit the new circumstances. Frankie's search through barrooms
and bawdy houses for the man who was doing her wrong may
well have been a feature of the lost ballad, for nothing of the

sort happened in the Britt-Baker affair. This would not be the
first ballad to be remade to accommodate a sensational repetition
of its plot in real life (compare notes to "Mary Hamilton"
[p. 183] and "Pearl Bryan" [p. 209]). Barry conjectures (*Bulletin,* 10:24) that "Frankie and Albert" commemorates the slaying of Charles Silver by his wife Frankie at Toe River, North
Carolina, in 1831, but the "Frankie Silver" ballads recorded
(Brown, II, 699, and references) could not by any process of
adaptation have become "Frankie and Albert."

Though deeply influenced by Negro taste and rhythms,
"Frankie and Albert" may not necessarily be Negro in origin. The
ballad's concentration, gapped narrative structure (each stanza
is a separate scene), and bold simplicity of language is in the
tradition of old-country ballads and bears comparison with the
best of them.

Texts: A, Tennessee, 1928 (*JAF,* 42:287); B, Sandburg,
American Songbag, 1927, p. 79.

❀◇ A ◇❀

1   Frankie was a good girl
     As everybody knows.
     She paid a hundred dollar bill
     For a suit of Albert's clothes,
     Just because she loved him [so].

2   Frankie went down to the bar-room;
     She called for a bottle of beer;
     She whispered to the bartender:
     Has Albert he been here?
     He is my man and he won't come home."

3   "I am not a-going to tell you no story;
     I am not a-going to tell you no lie;
     He left here about an hour ago
     With a girl called Alice Fry;
     He is your man and he won't come home."

4   Frankie went to the house
     As hard as she could run;
     And under her apron

Concealed a smokeless gun;
"He is my man but he won't come home."

5   Frankie went to the pool-room,
And knocked on the pool-room door,
And there she saw the man she loved
Standing in the middle of the floor;
"You are my man and you will come home."

6   Albert ran around the table
And fell down on his knees.
He hollowed out to Frankie:
"Don't kill me, if you please;
I'm your man and I have done you wrong."

7   Frankie stepped out in the back yard;
She heard a bull-dog bark;
"That must be the man I love slipping out in the dark.
If it is, I am a-going to lay him low;
He is my man, but he done me wrong."

8   Frankie went down to the river.
She looked from bank to bank:
"Do all you can for a gambling man,
But yet you will get no thanks;
For a gambling man won't treat you right."

9   Frankie reached down in her pocket,
And pulled that forty-four out,
And shot little Albert through that suit of clothes
People been a-talking about;
"He's my man but he won't be long."

10   "Turn me over, Frankie,
Turn me over slow,
Turn me on my right side;
My heart will overflow;
I'm your man and I have done you wrong."

11   Frankie looked down on Broadway
As far as she could see—
Two little children just a-crying and singing
"Nearer, My God, to Thee"—
Seems so sad little Albert is dead.

12   They took little Frankie to the courthouse;
     They sat her in a big arm chair;
     She was listening for the judge to say:
     "We will give her ninety-nine year—
     She killed her man in the first degree."

13   But the judge, he said to the jury:
     "Jury, I [can] see
     [Why] she shot the man she loved—
     I think she ought to go free:
     For a gambling man won't treat you right."

14   Frankie walked out on the scaffold
     As brave as she could be:
     "When I shot the man I loved,
     I murdered in the first degree;
     He is my man and I loved him so."

15   Now little Albert is buried
     And Frankie is by his side—
     Had it cut on the head and foot tomb-stones,
     "The gambler and his bride,"
     The gambling man and his bride.

                         ❦◇ B ◇❦

1   Frankie and Johnny were lovers, O lordy how they could
          love.
     Swore to be true to each other, true as the stars above;
     He was her man but he done her wrong, so wrong.

2   Johnny's mother told him, and she was mighty wise,
     Don't spend Frankie's money on that parlor Ann Eliz;
     You're Frankie's man, and you're doin' her wrong, so wrong.

3   Frankie and Johnny went walking, Johnny in his bran' new
          suit,
     "O good Lawd," says Frankie, "Don't my Johnny look
          cute?"
     He was her man but he done her wrong, so wrong.

4   Frankie went down to the corner, to buy a glass of beer;
    She says to the fat bartender, "Has my lovinest man been
        here?
    He was my man but he's done me wrong, so wrong."

5   Frankie went down to the pawn shop, she bought herself a
        little forty-four
    She aimed it at the ceiling, shot a big hole in the floor;
    "Where is my man, he's doin' me wrong, so wrong?"

6   Frankie went back to the hotel, she didn't go there for fun,
    'Cause under her long red kimono she toted a forty-four
        gun.
    He was her man but he done her wrong, so wrong.

7   Frankie went down to the hotel, looked in the window so
        high,
    There she saw her lovin' Johnny a-lovin' up Alice Bly;
    He was her man but he done her wrong, so wrong.

8   Frankie went down to the hotel, she rang that hotel bell,
    "Stand back all of you floozies or I'll blow you all to hell,
    I want my man, he's doin' me wrong, so wrong."

9   Frankie threw back her kimono, she took out her forty-four.
    Root-a-toot-toot, three times she shot, right through that
        hardwood floor,
    She shot her man, 'cause he done her wrong, so wrong.

10 Johnny grabbed off his Stetson, "O good Lawd, Frankie,
        don't shoot."
    But Frankie put her finger on the trigger, and the gun went
        root-a-toot-toot,
    He was her man but she shot him down.

11 Johnny saw Frankie a comin', down the backstairs he did
        scoot;
    Frankie had the little gun out, let him have it rooty-de-toot;
    For he was her man, but she shot him down.

12 Johnny he mounted the staircase, cried, "O Frankie don't
        shoot!"

Three times she pulled the forty-four gun a rooty-toot-toot-
toot-toot,
She nailed the man what threw her down.

13 "Roll me over easy, roll me over slow,
Roll me over easy, boys, 'cause my wounds they hurt me so,
But I was her man, and I done her wrong, so wrong."

14 "Oh my baby, kiss me once before I go.
Turn me over on my right side, doctor, where de bullet hurt
me so.
I was her man but I done her wrong, so wrong."

15 Johnny he was a gambler, he gambled for the gain.
The very last words he ever said were, "High-low Jack and
the game."
He was her man but he done her wrong, so wrong.

16 Bring out your long black coffin, bring out your funeral
clo'es;
Bring back Johnny's mother; to the churchyard Johnny goes.
He was her man but he done her wrong, so wrong.

17 Frankie went to his coffin, she looked down on his face.
She said, "O Lawd, have mercy on me, I wish I could take
his place,
He was my man, and I done him wrong, so wrong."

18 Oh bring on your rubber-tired hearses, bring on your rubber-tired hacks,
They're takin' Johnny to the buryin' groun' an' they won't
bring a bit of him back;
He was her man but he done her wrong, so wrong.

19 Frankie stood on the corner to watch the funeral go by;
"Bring back my poor dead Johnny to me," to the under-
taker she did say,
"He was my man, but he done me wrong, so wrong."

20 Frankie heard a rumbling away down in the ground,
Maybe it was little Johnny where she had shot him down.
He was her man and she done him wrong, so wrong.

21 Frankie went to Mrs. Halcomb, she fell down on her knees,
   She said, "Mrs. Halcomb, forgive me, forgive me, if you
      please,
   For I've killed my man what done me wrong, so wrong."

22 "Forgive you, Frankie darling, forgive you I never can.
   Forgive you, Frankie darling, for killing your only man,
   Oh he was your man tho' he done you wrong, so wrong."

23 Frankie said to the warden, "What are they goin' to do?"
   The warden he said to Frankie, "It's the electric chair for
      you,
   You shot your man tho' he done you wrong, so wrong."

24 The sheriff came around in the morning, said it was all for
      the best,
   He said her lover Johnny was nothin' but a doggone pest.
   He was her man but he done her wrong, so wrong.

25 The judge said to the jury, "It's as plain as plain can be;
   This woman shot her lover, it's murder in the second degree,
   He was her man tho' he done her wrong, so wrong."

26 Now it was not murder in the second degree, and was not
      murder in the third,
   The woman simply dropped her man, like a hunter drops a
      bird.
   He was her man but he done her wrong, so wrong.

27 "Oh bring a thousand policemen, bring 'em around today,
   Oh lock me in that dungeon, and throw the keys away,
   I shot my man, 'cause he done me wrong, so wrong."

28 "Yes, put me in that dungeon, oh put me in that cell,
   Put me where the northeast wind blows from the southeast
      corner of Hell.
   I shot my man, 'cause he done me wrong, so wrong."

29 Frankie mounted to the scaffold as calm as a girl can be,
   And turning her eyes to heaven, she said, "Good Lord, I
      am coming to Thee.
   He was my man, but he done me wrong, so wrong."

VIII: CRIMINALS' GOODNIGHTS

Until very recent times, executions were great public spectacles in the larger British cities. The curiosity of the populace, however, was seldom satisfied with merely watching the victim on the scaffold; of intenser interest was his anguish during his final hours, particularly his edifying repentance. Broadside printers catered to this morbid taste with a species of ballads usually called "goodnights" though also known as "gibbeting songs," "execution ballads," or "sorrowful lamentations." The speaker in such pieces—they are invariably first person—purports to be the criminal himself, but they were almost always the products of hack writers. Probably the disguise was more a convention than a deception, since the writer often gave himself away completely by following the experiences of the executed man beyond his final gasp. And because the criminal taking leave of the world was full of contrition and warned his hearers against imitating his disastrous course, good folk no less than ghouls approved of goodnights.

Among the oldest preserved ballad of this kind is "A sorrowful Sonet made by Mr. George Mannyngton . . . an houre before he suffered" at Cambridge in 1576 (printed in Clement Robinson's *A Handful of Pleasant Delights,* 1584).

> I waile in wo, I plunge in pain
> With sorrowing sobs, I do complain

are the opening lines. Mannington goes on to lament his "doleful doom," recalls the "frowning" judge's sentence, comments how little his parents and friends expected that he would come to such a sordid end. The piece concludes with a pious "farewell in Jesus Christ." Many of the devices in this "sorrowful Sonet" were re-echoed thousands of times in the next three hundred years of goodnights. The Mannington ballad is untypical, however, in not dwelling on the gory details of the crime. It is to other sources one must go to find out what Mannington's fault was—he had struck off the head of a horse at a single blow!

The popularity of the goodnight broadsides continued well into the Victorian period. Two famous executions of the 1840s were commemorated with goodnights which sold two and a half million copies each. One would think that the newspapers would have cut into the broadsheet sales, but as a vendor reported to Henry Mayhew (*London Labour and London Poor,* 1851, p. 223), the ballad peddlers had the advantage of the newspapers,

> for we gets it printed several days afore it comes off, and goes and stands with it right under the drop, and many's the penny I've turned away when I've been asked for an account of the whole business *before* it had happened.

Broadside goodnights have often been taken up into folk tradition and numerous folk pieces have been created on their model.

Mary Hamilton's Last Goodnight (compare 173)

The old Scottish ballad of "Mary Hamilton" tells the pathetic story of an unwed lady-in-waiting to Mary, Queen of Scots, who murdered the child she had borne as the result of an amorous intrigue with a courtier—in some versions the seducer is Lord Darnley, the queen's husband. She was sentenced to hang for her crime. Several American versions of "Mary Hamilton" hardly even allude to the seduction or murder, probably out of prudery, but perhaps simply to gain sympathy for the heroine, and reduce the ballad to the touching lament which the condemned woman makes on the scaffold. This form of "Mary Hamilton" furnishes us with a folk parallel for the broadside goodnight.

The present text was recorded in New Brunswick, Canada, in 1928 (Barry, p. 258). For the tune, see page 184.

1   Yestre'en the queen had four Maries
       This nicht she'll hae but three;
    There was Mary Beaton, an' Mary Seaton,
       An' Mary Carmichael an' me.

2   Last nicht I dressed Queen Mary,
      An' pit on her braw silken goon,
     An' a' the thanks I've gat this nicht
      Is tae be hanged in Edinboro toon.

3   O little did my mither ken,
     The day she cradled me,
  The land I was tae travel in,
     The death I was tae dee.

4   O happy, happy, is the maid,
     That's born o' beauty free;
  O it was my rosy dimplin' cheeks,
     That's been the deil tae me!

5   They've tied a hanky roon ma een,
     An' they'll no let me see tae dee;
  An' they've pit on a robe o' black
     Tae hang on the gallows tree.

6   Yestre'en the queen had four Maries,
     This nicht she'll hae but three;
  There was Mary Beaton, an' Mary Seaton,
     An' Mary Carmichael an' me.

Botany Bay

As capital punishment became rarer, the criminal of the goodnight ballad took leave of the world in a different sense. He was on the point of being transported to Australia or, in America, of going off to serve a long prison term. This popular broadside, originally written about 1800 but constantly reprinted by the London ballad presses in the nineteenth century, has all the standard goodnight traits: the admonition to other youths to shun bad company, the sentencing, the aged parents broken by their son's wild career, the girl left behind. Missing, however, are particulars as to the roving blade's misconduct, which leads one to suspect that the ballad was the work of a hack moralist with no specific criminal in mind.

braw, splendid. *een*, eyes.

The penal colony at Botany Bay near Sydney was established in 1788.

1   Come all you men of learning,
    And a warning take by me,
    I would have you quit night walking,
    And shun bad company.
    I would have you quit night walking,
    Or else you'll rue the day,
    You'll rue your transportation, lads,
    When you're bound for Botany Bay.

2   I was brought up in London town
    And a place I know full well,
    Brought up by honest parents
    For the truth to you I'll tell.
    Brought up by honest parents,
    And rear'd most tenderly,
    Till I became a roving blade,
    Which proved my destiny.

3   My character soon taken was,
    And I was sent to jail,
    My friends they tried to clear me,
    But nothing could prevail.
    At the Old Bailey Sessions,
    The Judge to me did say,
    "The Jury's found you guilty, lad,
    So you must go to Botany Bay."

4   To see my aged father dear,
    As he stood near the bar,
    Likewise my tender mother,
    Her old grey locks to tear;
    In tearing of her old grey locks,
    These words to me did say,
    "O, Son! O, Son! what have you done,
    That you're going to Botany Bay?"

5   It was on the twenty eighth of May,
    From England we did steer,

And, all things being safe on board,
We sail'd down the river, clear.
And every ship that we pass'd by,
We heard the sailors say,
"There goes a ship of clever hands,
And they're bound for Botany Bay."

6   There is a girl in Manchester,
A girl I know full well,
And if ever I get my liberty,
Along with her I'll dwell.
O, then I mean to marry her,
And no more to go astray;
I'll shun all evil company,
Bid adieu to Botany Bay.

The Boston Burglar

This close American adaptation of "Botany Bay" has been
collected in places as far apart as Wyoming and North Carolina,
Nova Scotia and Texas. In many variants a sentence of twenty-
one years, the conventional ballad term, is specified. The North
Carolina text printed here (from Brown, II, 554) agrees with
many another recording in implying a long train ride between the
Boston courthouse and the state penitentiary at Charlestown,
when actually the distance could only be a matter of a few city
blocks.

1   I was born in the town of Boston,
A town you all know well,
Raised up by honest parents—
The truth to you I will tell—
Raised up by honest parents,
Raised up most tenderly,
Until I became a sporting man
At the age of twenty-three.

2   My character was taken
And I was sent to jail.

The people tried, but all in vain,
To keep me out on [bail].
The juror found me guilty,
The clerk he wrote it down,
The judge he passed the sentence
To send me to Charlestown.

3   They put me on the east-bound train
One cold December day,
And every station I would pass
This is what they would say:
"There goes the Boston burglar;
His arms in chains are bound.
'Tis for some crime or other
They have sent him to Charlestown."

4   There was my aged father
A-standing at the bar,
Likewise my dear old mother
A-tearing down her hair.
She was tearing down her old gray locks
And trembling, as she said,
"My son, my son, what have you done
To be taken to Charlestown?"

5   There lives a girl in Boston,
A girl that I loved well.
If ever I gain my liberty
It's with that girl I'll dwell.
If ever I gain my liberty
There are two things I'll shun:
That being a night street walker
And drinking of the rum.

Sam Hall

The mawkish pathos of the goodnights and their repentant
"heroes" are made fun of in the ballad of defiantly unregenerate
Sam Hall. The basis of the burlesque is a serious execution

ballad marking the hanging in 1701 of Jack Hall, a chimney sweep, for burglary.

> O, my name it is Jack Hall, chimney sweep, chimney sweep,
> O, my name it is Jack Hall, chimney sweep.
> O, my name it is Jack Hall,
> And I've robbed both great and small,
> And my neck shall pay for all, when I die, when I die.

C. W. Ross, an English comic minstrel, composed the original "Sam Hall" and sang it with great success in London music halls of the 1850s. The song also enjoyed considerable popularity among cowboys and Western frontiersmen in late nineteenth-century America. Versions differ in the strength of Sam's curses; ours is a printable one sung by Bill Bender on a Stinson LP.

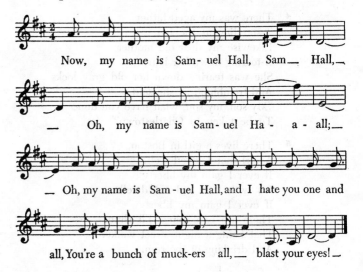

1   Now, my name is Samuel Hall, Sam Hall,
     Oh, my name is Samuel Ha-a-all;
     Oh, my name is Samuel Hall, and I hate you one and all,
     You're a bunch of muckers all, blast your eyes!

2   Now, I killed a man they said, so they said,
     Oh, I killed a man they said, yes they said;

I killed a man they said, and I left him layin' dead,
'Cause I bashed his bloody head, blast his eyes!

3 Now, they put me in the quad, in the quad,
   Oh, they put me in the qua-a-ad;
   Oh, they put me in the quad, and they left me there, by God,
   Fastened to a chain and rod, blast their eyes!

4 Now, the preacher he did come, he did come,
   Oh, the preacher he did come, he did come;
   Oh, the preacher he did come, and he looked so doggone glum
   As he talked of Kingdom Come, blast his eyes!

5 And the sheriff he come too, he come too,
   Oh, the sheriff he come too, he come too;
   Oh, the sheriff he come too, with his yellow boys and blue,
   Sayin', "Sam, I'll see you through, blast your eyes!"

6 Oh, it's up the rope, I go, up I go,
   It's up the rope I go, up I go;
   Oh, it's up the rope I go, while you critters down below
   Are sayin', "Sam, I told you so"—blast your eyes!

7 Oh, it's a swingin' I must go, I must go,
   It's a swingin' I must go-o-o;
   It's a swingin' I must go, just because she loved him so,
   Just because she loved him so, blast her eyes!

8 I must hang until I'm dead, dead, dead,
   I must hang until I'm de-e-ad;
   I must hang until I'm dead, 'cause I killed a man, they said,
   And I left him layin' dead, blast his eyes!

The Wexford Girl

Known more commonly as "The Oxford Girl" or "The Cruel Miller," sometimes as "The Lexington Girl," the folk versions of this ballad retain much of the gory circumstance of the sensational journalistic goodnights. The ultimate ancestor of "The

Wexford Girl" is an English broadside of about 1700, "The
Berkshire Tragedy; or, The Wittam Miller" (see *Roxburghe
Ballads,* VII, ii, 629), a condensed version of which, "The Lexing-
ton Miller," vended in Boston around 1810, is preserved in the
Harvard College broadside collection.

American and Canadian singers prudishly leave the motive of
the crime to be deduced; the English broadside is explicit. After
filling in his early history, his birth in Oxford, his being appren-
ticed to a miller at Wittenham, the young murderer confesses:

> By chance upon an Oxford Lass I cast a wanton eye,
> And promis'd I would marry her, if she would with me lie.

> But to the world I do declare, with sorrow, grief, and woe,
> This folly brought us in a snare, and wrought our overthrow;
> For the Damsel came to me, and said—"By you I am with
>   child:

> I hope, dear *John,* you'll marry me, for you have me defil'd."

The girl's mother persuades John to marry her daughter; the
devil persuades him to take her life. Calling for his fiancée one
evening on the pretext of fixing a wedding day,

> . . . I deluded her again into a private place
> Then took a stick out of the hedge and struck her in the face.

As in the American ballads, the girl begs mercy but is dispatched
nonetheless.

> And then I took her by the hair, to cover this foul sin,
> And dragged her to the river side and threw her body in.

Nosebleed is the excuse the murderer in the English broadside
gives his servant at the mill to explain away his bloody clothes;
the request for a candle and the flames of hell are also in the
original. Unlike the American folk versions, however, the English
broadside describes the search for the body and the trial of the
miller at great length. He eventually admitted his guilt:

> The worst of deaths I do deserve, my crime it is so bad.

And concluding the balled is the expected admonition:

> Young men, take warning by my fall, all filthy lust defy,
> By giving way to wickedness, alas! this day I die.

Our text was recorded in Nova Scotia (Mackenzie, p. 293).

1   It was in the town of Waterford,
      Where I was bred and born.
   It was in the city of Baltimore
      That I owned a flowered farm.

2   I courted manys a Wexford girl
      With dark and rolling eyes.
   I asked her for to marry me,
      And "Yes," was her reply.

3   I went up to her father's house
      About eight o'clock one night;
   I asked her for to take a walk,
      Our wedding day to appoint.

4   We walked along quite easily
      Till I came to level ground.
   I broke a stake out of the fence,
      And I beat this fair maid down.

5   Down on her bended knee she fell;
      In mercy did she cry,
   "O Willie dear, don't murder me,
      For I'm not prepared to die!"

6   He heeded not the words she said,
      But he beat her all the more,
   Till all the ground for yards around
      Was in a bloody gore.

7   I went up to my mother's house
      About twelve o'clock that night;
   My mother she'd been sitting up,
      She took an awful fright.

8   "O son, dear son, what have you done?
      What bled your hands and clothes?"
   The answer that I made to her
      Was, "Bleeding of the nose."

9   I asked her for a candle
      To light my way to bed,

Likewise a handkerchief to wrap
    Around my aching head.

10   I tied it and twisted it,
    But no comfort could I find;
The flames of Hell shone round me,
    And my true love not far behind.

11   It was in about three weeks after,
    This fair maid she was found
A floating down the river
    That leads to Wexford town.

12   And all that saw her said she was
    A beauteous handsome bride,
That she was fit for any lord, duke, or king,
    Or any squire's bride.

13   I was taken on suspicion,
    And placed in Wexford gaol,
Where there was none to pity me,
    Or none to go my bail.

14   Come all ye royal true lovers,
    A warning take by me,
And never treat your own true love
    To any cruelty.

15   For if you do you'll rue like me
    Until the day you die;
You'll hang like me, a murderer,
    All on the gallows high.

Tom Dooley

Reporters from as far as New York flocked to Iredell County, North Carolina, in 1867 and again in 1868 to see Thomas C. Dula stand trial for the murder of a discarded sweetheart, Laura Foster. Rumor then and legend now have it that Tom was assisted by a newer mistress, one Ann Melton, whom he gal-

lantly shielded through two trials and absolved in a last-hour
confession. Dula's motive, the state alleged, was revenge: the
murdered woman had communicated a venereal disease to Dula
and, through him, to Miss Melton. Though Dula's Confederate
war record was constantly kept before the juries, he was found
guilty at both trials and executed on May 1, 1868.

A long, tedious murder ballad, still sung in North Carolina, was
composed about the case (see Brown, II, 707), but more poetic
is the North Carolina lament (Henry, p. 325) printed here. Local
legend credits this and similar pieces to Dula himself, though
none of the newspaper accounts mentions either the song or
Dula's playing a banjo.

1   Oh, bow your head, Tom Dooley;
    Oh, bow your head and cry;
    You have killed poor Laury Foster
    And you know you're bound to die.

2   You have killed poor Laury Foster;
    You know you have done wrong;
    You have killed poor Laury Foster,
    Your true love in your arms.

3   I take my banjo this evening;
    I pick it on my knee;
    This time tomorrow evening
    It will be of no use to me.

4   This day and one more;
    Oh, where do you reckon I'll be?
    This day and one more,
    And I'll be in eternity.

5   I had my trial at Wilkesboro;
    Oh, what do you reckon they done?
    They bound me over to Statesville
    And there where I'll be hung.

6   The limb being oak
    And the rope being strong—
    Oh, bow your head, Tom Dooley,
    For you know you are bound to hang

7   O pappy, O pappy,
    What shall I do?
    I have lost all my money,
    And killed poor Laury too.

8   O mammy, O mammy,
    Oh, don't you weep, nor cry;
    I have killed poor Laury Foster
    And you know I am bound to die.

9   Oh, what my mammy told me
    Is about to come to pass:
    That drinking and the women
    Would be my ruin at last.

Charles Guiteau

On July 2, 1881, two shots were fired into the back of President Garfield as he walked through the waiting room of the Baltimore and Potomac depot in Washington. The president lingered for seventy-nine days, succumbing finally on September 19. The assassin, a megalomaniac politician named Charles Julius Guiteau, had been disappointed at not getting the consulship he expected as the reward for a speech written during Garfield's campaign. Guiteau pleaded insanity at his noisily sensational trial, but was found guilty and hanged in the early afternoon of June 30, 1882. The ugly revelations of political jobbery made during Guiteau's trial are credited by the historian Charles Beard with having prompted the creation of the Civil Service Commission.

Guiteau's goodnight is based on a New York broadside, "The Lamentation of James Rodgers," a murderer executed on November 12, 1858. The opening stanzas of the Rodgers ballad and its conclusion demonstrate the resemblances:

Come all you tender Christians, I hope you will draw near,
And likewise pay attention to those few lines I have here.
For the murder of Mr. Swanton I am condemned to die,
On the twelfth day of November upon the gallows high.

My name is James Rodgers—the same I ne'er deny,
Which leaves my aged parents in sorrow for to cry,
It's little ever they thought, all in my youth and bloom,
I came into New York for to meet my fatal doom. . . .

Let each wild and vicious youth a warning take by me,
To be ruled by their parents, and shun bad company.

A popular goodnight of the 1870s, "My Name It Is John T. Williams," also borrowed lines and motives from the Rodgers piece. Writers unfamiliar with the goodnight conventions have suggested that Guiteau himself wrote the ballad bearing his name. It happens that Guiteau did write verses in prison, but they were more religiose and belligerent than the ballad that keeps his notoriety alive. No broadside copy of "Charles Guiteau" survives, though such a sheet may well have been the ancestor of the versions collected from oral tradition in the South and Midwest.

Text: South Dakota tradition, Pound, p. 146.

1   Come all you tender Christians, wherever you may be,
    And likewise pay attention to these few lines from me.
    For the murder of James A. Garfield I am condemned to die
    On the thirtieth day of June upon the scaffold high.

> *My name is Charles Guiteau,*
> *My name I'll ne'er deny.*
> *I leave my aged parents*
> *In sorrow for to die.*
> *But little did they think,*
> *While in my youthful bloom,*
> *I'd be taken to the scaffold*
> *To meet my earthly doom.*

2   'Twas down at the station I tried to make my escape,
    But Providence being against me, there proved to be no
        show.
    They took me off to prison while in my youthful bloom
    To be taken to the scaffold to meet my earthly doom.

3   I tried to [play off] insane but found it ne'er would do,
    The people were all against me, to escape there was no
        clue.

Judge Cox, he read my sentence, his clerk he wrote it down,
I'd be taken to the scaffold to meet my earthly doom.

4   My sister came to see me, to bid a last farewell.
She threw her arm around me and wept most bitterly.
She says, "My darling brother, this day you must cruelly die
For the murder of James A. Garfield upon the scaffold
high."

The Gambler

This haunting goodnight, strongly colored by the Negro blues
style of repetition, resolving lines, and bobs, was collected in
Missouri in 1917 (Belden, p. 472).

1   My father was a gambler, he learnt me how to play,
        [Twice]
    Saying, "Son, don't go a-begging when you hold the ace
        and tray,
    When you hold the ace and tray."

    Hang me, O hang me, and I'll be dead and gone, [Twice]
    I wouldn't mind the hangin', it's bein' gone so long,
    It's layin' in the grave so long.
    [Repeat after each stanza]

2   They took me down to old Fort Smith as sick as I could be,
        [Twice]
    They handed me a letter saying, "Son, come home to me,"
    Saying, "Son, come home to me."

3   My father and my mother and my little sister makes three,
        [Twice]
    They all came up to the gallows to see the last of me,
    To see the last of me.

4   They put the rope around my neck and drew me very high,
        [Twice]
    And the words I heard 'em sayin' was "It won't be long till
        he'll die,
    It won't be long till he'll die."

IX: BALLADS
OF THE SCOTTISH BORDER

During the sixteenth and much of the seventeenth century the border country between England and Scotland was a lawless place where the writ of neither the Scottish nor the English king "ran." Not even the great feudal families of the district—the Percies, Nevilles, Douglases—could keep order. Practical power was in the hands of robber clans settled in the valleys of the Esk and Lid in Scotland and the Tyne and Rede in England and along the courses of the Teviot, Tweed, Yarrow, and Ettrick. Raiding the prosperous villages of Northumberland and Cumberland, the clansmen ran off cattle, captured persons to be held for ransom, looted generally. From some settlements a regular tribute was exacted. (The word "blackmail," then meaning "protection money," originated on the border in this period.) In the robber valleys themselves lingered an archaic tribal society. The clan chief commanded a band of unswervingly loyal henchmen. High standards of honor and a rigid code of comradeship prevailed. Feuds between rival clans were prosecuted with fanatic vindictiveness and led often to incredible atrocities. This primitive way of life, with its exhilarating hazards and heroic atmosphere, was fertile ground for ballads, and the border ballads have won the lawless moss-troopers the reputation of being "untaught natural poets," as the historian Trevelyan puts it, "able to express in words of power the inexorable fate of man and woman, and pity for the cruelties they nevertheless constantly inflicted on one another."

Johnie Cock (114)

The English version (A), with its tense concentration, its flashing scenes and abrupt transition, manages magically to achieve tight continuity without the help of connectives or artful arranging. The ballad is also remarkable for its strange mixture of ancient and modern, primitive belief and sophisticated artifacts.

Johnie drinks the deer's blood, implying that he believes one
can in this way absorb the strength and virtue of the animal.
The pre-Reformation palmer knows eighteenth-century American
leather when he sees it, and the man who wears the American
leather seems from his imaginative instancing of the wolf to
attribute human feelings to animals—or perhaps the wolf is his
totem animal. To the "bows of yew" imported from London
Johnie speaks animistically as though they were living and intel-
ligent. A line later his fingers are given an independent will.
Finally, the page who springs up from nowhere to take back the
sad news is Johnie's sister's son—among some primitive peoples
the closest kin. In the Scottish ballad (B) the news is carried by
a speaking bird.

Texts: A, Miss Fisher of Carlisle to Percy, 1780—Harvard
Percy Papers; B, Scott, *Minstrelsy*, I, 59 (1802).

❦❖ A ❖❦

1   Johny he has risen up i' the morn,
         Calls for water to wash his hands;
     But little knew he that his bloody hounds
         Were bound in iron bands, bands,
         Were bound in iron bands.

2   Johny's mother has gotten word o' that,
         And care-bed she has tane:
     "O Johny, for my benison,
         I beg you'l stay at hame;
     For the wine so red, and the well baken bread,
         My Johny shall want nane.

3   "There are seven forsters at Pickeram Side,
         At Pickeram where they dwell,
     And for a drop of thy heart's bluid
         They wad ride the fords of hell."

4   Johny he's gotten word of that,
         And he's turn'd wondrous keen;

care-bed, sickbed.   *tane,* taken.   *forsters,* forest rangers.

He's put off the red scarlett,
  And he's put on the Lincoln green.

5 With a sheaf of arrows by his side,
  And a bent bow in his hand,
He's mounted on a prancing steed,
  And he has ridden fast o'er the strand.

6 He's up i' Braidhouplee, and down i' Bradyslee,
  And under a buss o broom,
And there he found a good dun deer,
  Feeding in a buss of ling.

7 Johny shot, and the dun deer lap,
  And she lap wondrous wide,
Until they came to the wan water,
  And he stem'd her of her pride.

8 He 'as ta'en out the little pen-knife,
  'Twas full three quarters long,
And he has ta'en out of that dun deer
  The liver bot and the tongue.

9 They eat of the flesh, and they drank of the blood,
  And the blood it was so sweet,
Which caused Johny and his bloody hounds
  To fall in a deep sleep.

10 By then came an old palmer,
  And an ill death may he die!
For he's away to Pickram Side,
  As fast as he can drie.

11 "What news, what news?" says the Seven Forsters,
  "What news have ye brought to me?"
"I have noe news," the palmer said,
  "But what I saw with my eye.

12 "High up i' Bradyslee, low down i' Bradisslee,
  And under a buss of scroggs,

buss, bush. *ling,* heath, furze. *lap,* leaped. *drie,* be able. *scroggs,*
stunted trees.

O there I spied a well-wight man,
   Sleeping among his dogs.

13 "His coat it was of light Lincolm,
       And his breeches of the same,
    His shoes of the American leather,
       And gold buckles tying them."

14 Up bespake the Seven Forsters,
       Up bespake they ane and a':
    O that is Johny o' Cockley's Well,
       And near him we will draw.

15 O the first y stroke that they gae him,
       They struck him off by the knee;
    Then up bespake his sister's son:
       "O the next'll gar him die!"

16 "O some they count ye well-wight men,
       But I do count ye nane;
    For you might well ha' waken'd me,
       And ask'd gin I wad be ta'en.

17 "The wildest wolf in aw this wood
       Wad not ha' done so by me;
    She'd ha' wet her foot i'th wan water,
       And sprinkled it o'er my brae,
    And if that wad not ha' waken'd me,
       She wad ha' gone and let me be.

18 "O bows of yew, if ye be true,
       In London where ye were bought,
    Fingers five, get up belive,
       Manhuid shall fail me nought."

19 He has kill'd the Seven Forsters,
       He has kill'd them all but ane,
    And that wan scarce to Pickeram Side,
       To carry the bode-words hame.

20 "Is there never a boy in a' this wood
       That will tell what I can say;

well-wight, sturdy. *y,* single. *gar,* make. *gin,* if. *brae,* brow.
belive, soon. *wan,* achieved. *bode-words,* messages.

That will go to Cockley's Well,
　Tell my mither to fetch me away?"

21　There was a boy into that wood,
　　That carried the tidings away,
　And many ae was the well-wight man
　　At the fetching o' Johny away.

❧◇ B ◇❧

1　Johnie rose up in a May morning,
　　Called for water to wash his hands—
　"Gar loose to me the gude graie dogs,
　　That are bound wi' iron bands."

2　When Johnie's mother gat word o' that,
　　Her hands for dule she wrang—
　"O Johnie, for my bennison,
　　To the greenwood dinna gang!

3　"Eneugh ye hae o' the gude wheat-bread,
　　And eneugh o' the blude-red wine,
　And therefore for nae vennison, Johnie,
　　I pray ye, stir frae hame."

4　But Johnie's buskt up his gude bend bow,
　　His arrows, ane by ane,
　And he has gane to Durrisdeer,
　　To hunt the dun deer down.

5　As he came down by Merriemass,
　　And in by the benty line,
　There has he espied a deer lying,
　　Aneath a bush of ling.

6　Johnie he shot, and the dun deer lap,
　　And he wounded her on the side,
　But atween the water and the brae,
　　His hounds they laid her pride.

ae, one.　*gar,* make.　*dule,* sorrow.　*busk,* make ready.　*benty,* bent grass.　*ling,* heath, furze.　*lap,* leaped.　*brae,* riverbank.

7   And Johnie has bryttled the deer sae weel
         That he's had out her liver and lungs,
     And wi' these he has feasted his bludey hounds
         As if they had been earl's sons.

8   They eat sae much o' the vennison,
         And drank sae much o' the blude,
     That Johnie and a' his bludey hounds
         Fell asleep as they had been dead.

9   And by there came a silly auld carle,
         An ill death mote he die!
     For he's awa to Hislinton,
         Where the Seven Foresters did lie.

10   "What news, what news, ye gray-headed carle?
         What news bring ye to me?"
     "I bring nae news," said the gray-headed carle,
         "Save what these eyes did see.

11   "As I came down by Merriemass,
         And down amang the scroggs,
     The bonniest childe that I ever saw
         Lay sleeping amang his dogs.

12   "The shirt that was upon his back
         Was o' the holland fine;
     The doublet which was over that
         Was o' the Lincome twine.

13   "The buttons that were on his sleeve
         Were o' the gowd sae gude;
     The gude graie hounds he lay amang,
         Their mouths were dyed wi' blude."

14   Then out and spak the first forester,
         The heid man ower them a':
     If this be Johnie o' Breadislee,
         Nae nearer will we draw.

15   But up and spak the sixth forester,
         His sister's son was he:

bryttle, cut up. *carle,* peasant. *mote,* may. *scroggs,* stunted trees.
childe. fellow.

If this be Johnie o' Breadislee,
    We soon shall gar him die.

16   The first flight of arrows the foresters shot,
    They wounded him on the knee;
  And out and spak the seventh forester,
    The next will gar him die.

17   Johnie's set his back against an aik,
    His fute against a stane,
  And he has slain the Seven Foresters,
    He has slain them a' but ane.

18   He has broke three ribs in that ane's side,
    But and his collar bane;
  He's laid him twa-fald ower his steed,
    Bade him carry the tidings hame.

19   "O is there na a bonnie bird
    Can sing as I can say,
  Could flee away to my mother's bower,
    And tell to fetch Johnie away?"

20   The starling flew to his mother's window-stane,
    It whistled and it sang,
  And aye the ower-word o' the tune
    Was, "Johnie tarries lang!"

21   They made a rod o' the hazel-bush,
    Another o' the slae-thorn tree,
  And mony, mony were the men
    At fetching o'er Johnie.

22   Then out and spake his auld mother,
    And fast her teirs did fa';
  Ye wad nae be warn'd, my son Johnie,
    Frae the hunting to bide awa.

23   "Aft hae I brought to Breadislee
    The less gear and the mair,
  But I neer brought to Breadislee
    What grieved my heart sae sair.

aik, oak. *ower-word,* refrain. *slae-thorn,* blackthorn. *gear,* spoil.

24   "But wae betyde that silly auld carle,
         An ill death shall he die;
      For the highest tree on Merriemass
         Shall be his morning's fee."

25   Now Johnie's gude bend bow is broke,
         And his gude graie dogs are slain,
      And his bodie lies dead in Durrisdeer,
         And his hunting it is done.

Johnie Armstrong (169)

From Gilnockie, his seat in Eskdale, John Armstrong, brother
of the clan chief Lord Mangerton, led destructive forays on both
sides of the border, but principally against the English. His raids
were naturally a great embarrassment to the Scottish king, who
had to admit to the protesting English commissioners that Armstrong was outside his control. To remedy the situation, James V
took an army into the Debatable Land in the summer of 1530.
Probably through treachery of some sort, as the ballads imply,
Armstrong and his resplendent band were seized by the king and
hanged—at Carlenrig chapel, according to tradition.

Curiously enough, John Armstrong, the scourge of the English
when alive, is celebrated as a hero in English ballads. Text A,
from *Wit Restor'd*, 1658, p. 30, is one example. Here Armstrong
becomes a Westmorland man, the victim of Scottish treachery.
B, from Ramsay's *Evergreen*, 1724, II, 190, follows historical
fact and tradition more closely; at least the national enmities are
correctly placed.

❦◇ A ◇❦

1   There dwelt a man in faire Westmerland,
        Ionnë Armestrong men did him call,
     He had nither lands nor rents coming in,
        Yet he kept eight score men in his hall.

2   He had horse and harness for them all,
        Goodly steeds were all milk-white;

O the golden bands an about their necks,
    And their weapons, they were all alike.

3 Newes then was brought unto the king
    That there was sicke a won as hee,
That livëd [l]yke a bold out-law,
    And robbëd all the north country.

4 The king he writt an a letter then,
    A letter which was large and long;
He signëd it with his owne hand,
    And he promised to doe him no wrong.

5 When this letter came Ionnë untill,
    His heart it was as blythe as birds on the tree:
"Never was I sent for before any king,
    My father, my grandfather, nor none but mee.

6 "And if wee goe the king before,
    I would we went most orderly;
Every man of you shall have his scarlet cloak,
    Laced with silver laces three.

7 "Every one of you shall have his velvett coat,
    Laced with silver lace so white;
O the golden bands an about your necks,
    Black hatts, white feathers, all alyke."

8 By the morrow morninge at ten of the clock,
    Towards Edenburough gon was hee,
And with him all his eight score men;
    Good lord, it was a goodly sight for to see!

9 When Ionnë came befower the king,
    He fell downe on his knee;
"O pardon, my soveraine leige," he said,
    "O pardon my eight score men and mee!"

10 "Thou shalt have no pardon, thou traytor strong,
    For thy eight score men nor thee;
For to-morrow morning by ten of the clock,
    Both thou and them shall hang on the gallow-tree."

sicke a won, such a one

11   But Ionnë lookd over his left shoulder,
      Good Lord, what a grievous look looked hee!
    Saying, "Asking grace of a graceles face—
      Why there is none for you nor me."

12   But Ionnë had a bright sword by his side,
      And it was made of the mettle so free,
    That had not the king stept his foot aside,
      He had smitten his head from his faire boddë.

13   Saying, "Fight on, my merry men all,
      And see that none of you be taine;
    For rather then men shall say we were hanged,
      Let them report how we were slaine."

14   Then, God wott, faire Eddenburrough rose,
      And so besett poore Ionnë rounde,
    That fowerscore and tenn of Ionnës best men
      Lay gasping all upon the ground.

15   Then like a mad man Ionnë laid about,
      And like a mad man then fought hee,
    Until a falce Scot came Ionnë behinde,
      And runn him through the faire boddee.

16   Saying, "Fight on, my merry men all,
      And see that none of you be taine;
    For I will stand by and bleed but awhile,
      And then will I come and fight againe."

17   Newes then was brought to young Ionnë Armstrong,
      As he stood by his nurse's knee,
    Who vowed if ere he lived for to be a man,
      O' the treacherous Scots revengd hee'd be.

❈◇ **B** ◇❈

1   Sum speiks of lords, sum speiks of lairds,
      And siclyke men of hie degrie;
    Of a gentleman I sing a sang,
      Sumtyme calld Laird of Gilnockie.

siclyke, such-like.

2   The king he wrytes a luving letter,
      With his ain hand sae tenderly:
    And he hath sent it to Johny A[r]mstrang,
      To cum and speik with him speidily.

3   The Eliots and Armstrangs did convene,
      They were a gallant company:
    "We 'ill ryde and meit our lawful king,
      And bring him safe to Gilnockie.

4   "Make kinnen and capon ready, then,
      And venison in great plenty;
    We 'ill welcome hame our royal king;
      I hope he 'ill dyne at Gilnockie!"

5   They ran their horse on the Langum howm,
      And brake their speirs with mekle main;
    The ladys lukit frae their loft-windows,
      "God bring our men weil back again!"

6   When Johny came before the king,
      With all his men sae brave to see,
    The king he movit his bonnet to him;
      He weind he was a king as well as he.

7   "May I find grace, my sovereign liege,
      Grace for my loyal men and me;
    For my name it is only Johny Armstrang,
      And subject of yours, my liege," said he.

8   "Away, away, thou traytor, strang!
      Out of my sicht thou mayst sune be!
    I grantit nevir a traytor's lyfe,
      And now I'll not begin with thee."

9   "Grant me my lyfe, my liege, my king,
      And a bony gift I will give to thee;
    Full four and twenty milk-whyt steids,
      Were a' foald in a yeir to me.

10 "I'll gie thee all these milk-whyt steids,
      That prance and nicher at a speir,

kinnen, rabbit. *howm,* riverbank. *weind,* thought. *nicher,* neigh.

With as mekle gude Inglis gilt
   As four of their braid backs dow beir."

11 "Away, away, thou traytor strang!
      Out o' my sight thou mayst sune be!
   I grantit nevir a traytor's lyfe,
      And now I'll not begin with thee."

12 "Grant me my lyfe, my liege, my king,
      And a bony gift I'll gie to thee;
   Gude four and twenty ganging mills,
      That gang throw a' the yeir to me.

13 "These four and twenty mills complete
      Sall gang for thee throw all the yeir,
   And as mekle of gude reid wheit
      As all their happers dow to bear."

14 "Away, away, thou traytor, strang!
      Out of my sight thou mayst sune be!
   I grantit nevir a traytor's lyfe,
      And now I'll not begin with thee."

15 "Grant me my lyfe, my liege, my king,
      And a great gift I'll gie to thee;
   Bauld four and twenty sisters'-sons,
      Sall for the fecht, tho all sould flee."

16 "Away, away, thou traytor, strang!
      Out of my sight thou mayst sune be!
   I grantit nevir a traytor's lyfe,
      And now I'll not begin with thee."

17 "Grant me my lyfe, my liege, my king,
      And a brave gift I'll gie to thee;
   All betwene heir and Newcastle town
      Sall pay thair yeirly rent to thee."

18 "Away, away, thou traytor, strang!
      Out of my sight thou mayst sune be!
   I grantit nevir a traytor's lyfe,
      And now I'll not begin with thee."

mekle, much. *dow,* be able. *happers,* hoppers.

19   "Ye lied, ye lied, now, king," he says,
    "Althocht a king and prince ye be,
For I luid naithing in all my lyfe,
    I dare well say it, but honesty;

20   "But a fat horse, and a fair woman,
    Twa bony dogs to kill a deir:
But Ingland suld haif found me meil and malt,
    Gif I had livd this hundred yeir!

21   "Scho suld haif found me meil and malt,
    And beif and mutton in all plentie;
But neir a Scots wyfe could haif said
    That eir I skaithd her a pure flie.

22   "To seik het water beneth cauld yce,
    Surely it is a great folie;
I haif asked grace at a graceless face,
    But there is nane for my men and me.

23   "But had I kend, or I came frae hame,
    How thou unkynd wadst bene to me,
I wad haif kept the border-syde,
    In spyte of all thy force and thee.

24   "Wist England's king that I was tane,
    O gin a blyth man wald he be!
For anes I slew his sister's son,
    And on his breist-bane brak a tree."

25   John wore a girdle about his middle,
    Imbroiderd owre with burning gold,
Bespangled with the same mettle,
    Maist beautiful was to behold.

26   Ther hang nine targats at Johnys hat,
    And ilk an worth three hundred pound:
"What wants that knave that a king suld haif,
    But the sword of honour and the crown!

27   "O whair gat thou these targats, Johnie,
    That blink sae brawly abune thy brie?"

luid, loved.   *skaith,* harm.   *gin,* if.   *targat,* tassel.   *brie,* brow.

"I gat them in the field fechting,
  Wher, cruel king, thou durst not be.

28 "Had I my horse, and my harness gude,
      And ryding as I wont to be,
    It sould haif bene tald this hundred yeir
      The meiting of my king and me.

29 "God be withee, Kirsty, my brither,
      Lang live thou Laird of Mangertoun!
    Lang mayst thou live on the border-syde
      Or thou se thy brither ryde up and doun.

30 "And God be withee, Kirsty, my son,
      Whair thou sits on thy nurses knee!
    But and thou live this hundred yeir,
      Thy fathers better thoult never be.

31 "Farweil, my bonny Gilnock-Hall,
      Whair on Esk-syde thou standest stout!
    Gif I had lived but seven yeirs mair,
      I wald haif gilt thee round about."

32 John murdred was at Carlinrigg,
      And all his galant companie:
    But Scotland's heart was never sae wae,
      To see sae mony brave men die.

33 Because they savd their country deir
      Frae Englishmen; nane were sae bauld,
    Whyle Johnie livd on the border-syde,
      Nane of them durst cum neir his hald.

Jock o' the Side (187)

Jock o' the Side (Side is a place in Liddesdale), nephew to
the Lord Mangerton of the ballad, was a famous thief and raider
of the 1560s. His rescuer, Hobie Noble, we learn from his own
ballad,

hald, stronghold.

    . . . was an English man
And born into Bewcastle dale,
But his misdeeds they were sae great,
They banish'd him to Liddesdale. (Child, IV, 2)

In our ballad, however, he appears as a bastard brother of Jock.
Much the Miller, the timorous member of the party, has no con-
nection except the nominal one with Robin Hood's lieutenant.
   Text: Percy Folio MS., II, 203.

1   Peeter a Whi[t]feild he hath slaine,
     And John a Side, he is tane,
   And John is bound both hand and foote,
     And to the New-castle he is gone.

2   But tydings came to the Sybill o the Side,
     By the water-side as shee rann;
   Shee tooke her kirtle by the hem,
     And fast shee runn to Mangerton.

3   .   .   .   .   .   .
   The lord was sett downe at his meate;
     When these tydings shee did him tell,
     Never a morsell might he eate.

4   But lords the[y] wrunge their fingars white,
     Ladyes did pull themselves by the haire,
   Crying, "Alas and weladay!
     For John o the Side wee shall never see more.

5   "But wee'le goe sell our droves of kine,
     And after them our oxen sell,
   And after them our troopes of sheepe,
     But wee will loose him out of the New Castell."

6   But then bespake him Hobby Noble,
     And spoke these words wonderous hye;
   Sayes, "Give me five men to my selfe,
     And I'le feitch John o the Side to thee."

7   "Yea, thou'st have five, Hobby Noble,
     Of the best that are in this countrye;

I'le give thee five thousand, Hobby Noble,
　　That walke in Tyvidale trulye."

8　"Nay, I'le have but five," saies Hobby Noble,
　　"That shall walke away with mee;
Wee will ryde like noe men of warr;
　　But like poore badgers wee wilbe."

9　They stuffet up all their bags with straw,
　　And their steeds barefoot must bee;
"Come on, my brethren," sayes Hobby Noble,
　　"Come on your wayes, and goe with mee."

10　And when they came to Culerton ford,
　　The water was up, they cold it not goe;
And then they were ware of a good old man,
　　How his boy and hee were at the plowe.

11　"But stand you still," says Hobby Noble,
　　"Stand you still heere at this shore,
And I will ryde to yonder old man,
　　And see w[h]ere the gate it lyes ore.

12　"But Christ you save, father!" quoth hee,
　　"Crist both you save and see!
Where is the way over this fford?
　　For Christ's sake tell itt mee!"

13　"But I have dwelled heere three score yeere,
　　Soe have I done three score and three;
I never sawe man nor horsse goe ore,
　　Except itt were a horse of tree."

14　"But fare thou well, thou good old man!
　　The devill in hell I leave with thee,
Noe better comfort heere this night,
　　Thow gives my brethren heere and me."

15　But when he came to his brether againe,
　　And told this tydings full of woe,
And then they found a well good gate
　　They might ryde ore by two and two.

badgers, peddlers.　*gate,* path.　*horse of tree,* footbridge? boat?

16 And when they were come over the fforde,
   All safe gotten att the last,
   "Thankes be to God!" sayes Hobby Nobble,
   "The worst of our peril is past."

17 And then they came into Howbrame wood,
   And there then they found a tree,
   And cutt itt downe then by the roote;
   The lenght was thirty ffoote and three.

18 And four of them did take the planke,
   As light as it had beene a fflee,
   And carryed itt to the New Castle,
   Where as John a Side did lye.

19 And some did climbe up by the walls,
   And some did climbe up by the tree,
   Untill they came upp to the top of the castle,
   Where John made his moane trulye.

20 He sayd, "God be with thee, Sybill o the Side!
   My owne mother thou art," quoth hee;
   "If thou knew this night I were here,
   A woe woman then woldest thou bee.

21 "And fare you well, Lord Mangerton!
   And ever I say God be with thee!
   For if you knew this night I were heere,
   You wold sell your land for to loose mee.

22 "And fare thou well, Much, Miller's sonne!
   Much, Millar's sonne, I say;
   Thou has beene better att merke midnight
   Than ever thou was att noone o the day.

23 "And fare thou well, my good Lord Clough!
   Thou art thy ffather's sonne and heire;
   Thou never saw him in all thy liffe
   But with him durst thou breake a speare.

24 "Wee are brothers' childer nine or ten,
   And sisters' children ten or eleven.

merke, mirky.

We never came to the feild to fight,
　　But the worst of us was counted a man."

25　But then bespake him Hoby Noble,
　　And spake these words unto him;
　　Saies, "Sleepest thou, wakest thou, John o the Side,
　　Or art thou this castle within?"

26　"But who is there," quoth John o the Side,
　　"That knowes my name soe right and free?"
　　"I am a bastard-brother of thine;
　　This night I am comen for to loose thee."

27　"Now nay, now nay," quoth John o the Side;
　　"Itt ffeares me sore that will not bee;
　　Ffor a pecke of gold and silver," John sayd,
　　"In faith this night will not loose mee."

28　But then bespake him Hobby Noble,
　　And till his brother thus sayd hee;
　　Sayes, "Four shall take this matter in hand,
　　And two shall tent our geldings ffree."

29　Four did breake one dore without,
　　Then John brake five himsell;
　　But when they came to the iron dore,
　　It smote twelve upon the bell.

30　"Itt ffeares me sore," sayd Much, the Miller,
　　"That heere taken wee all shalbee;"
　　"But goe away, bretheren," sayd John a Side,
　　"For ever alas! this will not bee."

31　"But ffye upon thee!" sayd Hobby Noble;
　　"Much, the Miller, fye upon thee!
　　It sore feares me," said Hobby Noble,
　　"Man that thou wilt never bee."

32　But then he had Fflanders files two or three,
　　And hee fyled that iron dore,
　　And tooke John out of the New Castle,
　　And sayd, "Looke thou never come heere more!"

tent, tend.

33 When he had him fforth of the New Castle,
        "Away with me, John, thou shalt ryde:"
    But ever alas! itt cold not bee;
        For John cold neither sitt nor stryde.

34 But then he had sheets two or three,
        And bound John's boults fast to his ffeete,
    And sett him on a well good steede,
        Himselfe on another by him seete.

35 Then Hobby Noble smiled and loug[h]e,
        And spoke these words in mickle pryde:
    "Thou sitts soe finely on thy geldinge
        That, John, thou rydes like a bryde."

36 And when they came thorrow Howbrame towne,
        John's horsse there stumbled at a stone;
    "Out and alas!" cryed Much, the Miller,
        "John, thou'le make us all be tane."

37 "But fye upon thee!" saies Hobby Noble,
        "Much, the Millar, fye on thee!
    I know full well," sayes Hobby Noble,
        "Man that thou wilt never bee."

38 And when the[y] came into Howbrame wood,
        He had Fflanders files two or three
    To file John's bolts beside his ffeete,
        That hee might ryde more easilye.

39 Sayes, "John, now leape over a steede!"
        And John then hee lope over five:
    "I know well," sayes Hobby Noble,
        "John, thy ffellow is not alive."

40 Then he brought him home to Mangerton;
        The lord then he was att his meate;
    But when John o the Side he there did see,
        For faine hee cold noe more eate.

41 He sayes, "Blest be thou, Hobby Noble,
        That ever thou wast man borne!
    Thou hast feitched us home good John oth Side
        That was now cleane ffrom us gone."

mickle, much.

Hobie Noble (189)

Enticed by Sim Armstrong of the Mains to make a foray into England, Hobie is betrayed by Sim into the hands of his feud enemy the English land sergeant, whose brother, Peter of Whitfield, Noble had killed a short while before. Hobie was hanged at Carlisle; Sim, according to a dubious tradition, met the same fate a few months later.

Text: George Caw, *Poetical Museum*, 1784, p. 193.

1   Foul fa the breast first treason bred in!
       That Liddisdale may safely say;
    For in it there was baith meat and drink,
       And corn unto our geldings gay.
          Fala la diddle, etc.

2   We were stout-hearted men and true,
       As England it did often say;
    But now we may turn our backs and fly,
       Since brave Noble is seld away.

3   Now Hobie he was an English man,
       And born into Bewcastle dale,
    But his misdeeds they were sae great,
       They banish'd him to Liddisdale.

4   At Kershope-foot the tryst was set,
       Kershope of the lily lee;
    And there was traitour Sim o' the Mains,
       With him a private companie.

5   Then Hobie was graith'd his body weel,
       I wat it was wi' baith good iron and steel;
    And he has pull'd out his fringed grey,
       And there, brave Noble, he rade him weel.

6   Then Hobie is down the water gane,
       Een as fast as he may drie;

graith, armor.

Tho they should ha' brusten and broken their hearts,
    Frae that tryst Noble he would not be.

7   "Weel may ye be, my feiries five!
    An daye, what is your wills wi' me?"
  Then they cryd a' wi' ae consent,
    "Thou'rt welcome here, brave Noble, to me.

8   "Wilt thou with us in England ride?
    And thy safe-warrand we will be,
  If we get a horse worth a hundred punds,
    Upon his back that thou shalt be."

9   "I dare not with you into England ride,
    The land-sargeant has me at feid;
  I know not what evil may betide
    For Peter of Whitfield his brother's dead.

10 "And Anton Shiel, he loves not me,
    For I gat twa drifts of his sheep;
  The great Earl of Whitfield loves me not,
    For nae gear frae me he e'er cou'd keep.

11 "But will ye stay till the day gae down,
    Until the night come o'er the grund,
  And I'll be a guide worth ony twa
    That may in Liddisdale be fund.

12 "Tho dark the night as pick and tar,
    I'll guide ye o'er yon hills fu' hie,
  And bring ye a' in safety back,
    If you'll be true and follow me."

13 He's guided them o'er moss and muir,
    O'er hill and houp, and mony ae down,
  Til they came to the Foulbogshiel,
    And there brave Noble he lighted down.

14 Then word is gane to the land-sargeant,
    In Askirton where that he lay:
  "The deer that ye hae hunted lang
    Is seen into the Waste this day."

feirie, comrade.   *feid*, feud.   *drift*, drove.   *houp*, hollow.

15   "Then Hobie Noble is that deer;
         I wat he carries the style fu' hie!
      Aft has he beat your slough-hounds back,
         And set yourselves at little ee.

16   "Gar warn the bows of Hartlie-burn,
         See they shaft their arrows on the wa'!
      Warn Willeva and Spear Edom,
         And see the morn they meet me a'.

17   "Gar meet me on the Rodrie-haugh,
         And see it be by break o' day;
      And we will on to Conscowthart Green,
         For there, I think, w'll get our prey."

18   Then Hobie Noble has dream'd a dream,
         In the Foulbogshiel where that he lay;
      He thought his horse was neath him shot,
         And he himself got hard away.

19   The cocks could crow, and the day could dawn,
         And I wat so even down fell the rain;
      If Hobie had no wakend at that time,
         In the Foulbogshiel he had been tane or slain.

20   "Get up, get up, my feiries five—
         For I wat here makes a fu' ill day—
      And the warst clock of this companie
         I hope shall cross the Waste this day."

21   Now Hobie thought the gates were clear,
         But, ever alas! it was not sae;
      They were beset wi' cruel men and keen,
         That away brave Noble could not gae.

22   "Yet follow me, my feiries five,
         And see of me ye keep good ray,
      And the worst clock of this companie
         I hope shall cross the Waste this day."

23   There was heaps of men now Hobie before,
         And other heaps was him behind,

slough-hounds, sleuth-, blood-hounds. *ee,* awe. *gar,* do. *clock*
limper. *gate,* road. *ray,* track.

That had he been as wight as Wallace was
    Away brave Noble he could not win.

24   Then Hobie he has but a laddies sword,
    But he did more than a laddies deed;
In the midst of Conscouthart Green,
    He brake it o'er Jers a Wigham's head.

25   Now they have tane brave Hobie Noble,
    Wi' his ain bowstring they band him sae;
And I wat his heart was neer sae sair
    As when his ain five band him on the brae.

26   They have tane him [on] for West Carlisle;
    They askd him if he knew the way;
Whateer he thought, yet little he said;
    He knew the way as well as they.

27   They hae tane him up the Ricker-gate;
    The wives they cast their windows wide,
And ilka wife to anither can say,
    That's the man loos'd Jock o' the Side!

28   "Fy on ye, women! why ca' ye me man?
    For it's nae man that I'm us'd like;
I'm but like a forfoughen hound,
    Has been fighting in a dirty syke."

29   Then they hae tane him up thro Carlisle town,
    And set him by the chimney-fire;
They gave brave Noble a wheat loaf to eat,
    And that was little his desire.

30   Then they gave him a wheat loaf to eat
    And after that a can o beer;
Then they cried a' wi' ae consent,
    Eat, brave Noble, and make good cheer!

31   "Confess my lord's horse, Hobie," they say,
    "And the morn in Carlisle thou's no die;"
"How shall I confess them?" Hobie says,
    "For I never saw them with mine eye."

win, get.   *brae,* hillside.   *forfoughen,* fought out.   *syke,* ditch.

32   Then Hobie has sworn a fu' great aith,
          By the day that he was gotten or born,
      He never had onything o' my lord's
          That either eat him grass or corn.

33   "Now fare thee weel, sweet Mangerton!
          For I think again I'll neer thee see;
      I wad betray nae lad alive,
          For a' the goud in Christentie.

34   "And fare thee well now, Liddisdale,
          Baith the hie land and the law!
      Keep ye weel frae traitor Mains!
          For goud and gear he'll sell ye a'.

35   "I'd rather be ca'd Hobie Noble,
          In Carlisle, where he suffers for his faut,
      Before I were ca'd traitor Mains,
          That eats and drinks of meal and maut."

Captain Car (Edom o' Gordon) (178)

The assassination of the Regent Murray in 1570 opened another period of conflict between Catholics and Protestants,
queen's party and king's party, in Scotland. Adam Gordon,
brother of the Earl of Huntly, who was a partisan of Mary,
Queen of Scots (Mary was then a prisoner in England), fought
two engagements in Aberdeenshire in the autumn of 1571 with
the Protestant family of Forbes and their adherents. Both battles
were victories for Gordon and in both he showed remarkable
kindness to the prisoners. But Gordon's good record was immediately besmirched by an incident that occurred during the same
campaign. One of his officers, Captain Ker (Car, Carr), who had
been sent out to harry the Forbes' territory, lay siege to the small
castle of Towie in November 1571. Lady Forbes stubbornly refused to surrender, whereupon Ker, acting perhaps on instructions from Gordon, set fire to the place. The lady, her children,
and some twenty servants and retainers suffocated or were
burned to death. Even by the tough standards of the sixteenth

century the burning was considered a vile atrocity, and Gordon and Ker never outlived their ill fame.

Text A from Cotton Vespasian MS. A xxv, No. 67, about 1580 (Child, III, 430), has a Lady Hamilton as heroine; B, from a copy obtained by Sir David Dalrymple and printed in 1755 (Child, III, 433), has a Lady Rhodes. Both introduce a traitor to "kindle the fire in." Greig, p. 110, reports the ballad's being sung in Aberdeenshire in this century.

❧ A ❧

1 It befell at Martynmas,
       When wether waxed colde,
   Captain Care said to his men,
       We must go take a holde.

   Syck, sike, and to-towe sike,
       And sike, and like to die;
   The sikest nighte that euer I abode,
       God lord haue mercy on me!

2 "Haille, master, and wether you will,
       And wether ye like it best;"
   "To the castle of Crecrynbroghe,
       And there we will take our reste."

3 "I knowe wher is a gay castle,
       Is builded of lyme and stone;
   Within their is a gay ladie,
       Her lord is riden and gone."

4 The ladie she lend on her castle-walle,
       She loked vpp and downe;
   There was she ware of an host of men,
       Come riding to the towne.

5 "Se yow, my meri men all,
       And se yow what I see?
   Yonder I see an host of men,
       I muse who they bee."

---

holde, lodging.   *to-towe*, too, too.

6   She thought he had ben her wed lord,
          As he comd riding home;
     Then was it traitur Captain Care
          The lord of Ester-towne.

7   They wer no soner at supper sett,
          Then after said the grace,
     Or Captaine Care and all his men
          Wer lighte aboute the place.

8   "Gyue ouer thi howsse, thou lady gay,
          And I will make the a bande;
     To-nighte thou shall ly within my armes,
          To-morrowe thou shall ere my lande."

9   Then bespacke the eldest sonne,
          That was both whitt and redde:
     "O mother dere, geue ouer your howsse,
          Or elles we shalbe deade."

10   "I will not geue ouer my hous," she saithe,
          "Not for feare of my lyffe;
     It shalbe talked throughout the land,
          The slaughter of a wyffe.

11   "Fetch me my pestilett,
          And charge me my gonne,
     That I may shott at yonder bloddy-butcher,
          The lord of Ester-towne."

12   Styfly vpon her wall she stode,
          And lett the pellettes flee;
     But then she myst the blody bucher,
          And she slew other three.

13   "[I will] not geue ouer my hous," she saithe,
          "Neither for lord nor lowne;
     Nor yet for traitour Captain Care,
          The lord of Ester-towne.

14   "I desire of Captain Care,
          And all his bloddye band,

lighte, alighted.   *ere,* heir, inherit.   *lowne,* low-born.

That he would saue my eldest sonne,
 The eare of all my lande."

15 "Lap him in a shete," he sayth,
 "And let him down to me,
And I shall take him in my armes,
 His waran shall I be."

16 The captayne sayd unto him selfe:
 Wyth sped, before the rest,
He cut his tongue out of his head,
 His hart out of his brest.

17 He lapt them in a handkerchef,
 And knet it of knotes three,
And cast them ouer the castell-wall,
 At that gay ladye.

18 "Fye vpon the, Captain Care,
 And all thy bloddy band!
For thou hast slayne my eldest sonne,
 The ayre of all my land."

19 Then bespake the youngest sonne,
 That sat on the nurse's knee,
Sayth, "Mother gay, geue ouer your house;
 It smoldereth me."

20 "I woud geue my gold," she saith,
 "And so I wolde my ffee,
For a blaste of the westryn wind,
 To dryue the smoke from thee.

21 "Fy vpon the, John Hamleton,
 That euer I paid the hyre!
For thou hast broken my castel-wall,
 And kyndled in the ffyre."

22 The lady gate to her close parler,
 The fire fell aboute her head;
She toke up her children thre,
 Seth, "Babes, we are all dead."

waran, security. *gate*, went. *close parler*, strong-room?

23   Then bespake the hye steward,
        That is of hye degree;
    Saith, "Ladie gay, you are in close,
        Wether ye fighte or flee."

24   Lord Hamleton dremd in his dream,
        In Caruall where he laye,
    His halle were all of fyre,
        His ladie slayne or daye.

25   "Busk and bowne, my mery men all,
        Even and go ye with me;
    For I dremd that my haal was on fyre,
        My lady slayne or day."

26   He buskt him and bownd hym,
        And like a worthi knighte;
    And when he saw his hall burning,
        His harte was no dele lighte.

27   He sett a trumpett till his mouth,
        He blew as it plesd his grace;
    Twenty score of Hamlentons
        Was light aboute the place.

28   "Had I knowne as much yesternighte
        As I do to-daye,
    Captain Care and all his men
        Should not haue gone so quite.

29   "Fye vpon the, Captain Care,
        And all thy blody bande!
    Thou haste slayne my lady gay,
        More wurth then all thy lande.

30   "If thou had ought eny ill will," he saith,
        "Thou shoulde haue taken my lyffe,
    And haue saved my children thre,
        All and my louesome wyffe."

daye, dead. *busk and bowne,* make ready. *no dele,* not the least.
quite, requited.

❧❖ B ❖❧

1 It fell about the Martinmas,
   When the wind blew schrile and cauld,
Said Edom o Gordon to his men,
   "We maun draw to a hald.

2 "And what an a hald sall we draw to,
   My merry men and me?
We will gae to the house of the Rhodes,
   To see that fair lady."

3 She had nae sooner busket hersell,
   Nor putten on her gown,
Till Edom o Gordon and his men
   Were round about the town.

4 They had nae sooner sitten down,
   Nor sooner said the grace,
Till Edom o Gordon and his men
   Were closed about the place.

5 The lady ran up to her tower-head,
   As fast as she could drie,
To see if by her fair speeches
   She could with him agree.

6 As soon as he saw the lady fair,
   And hir yates all locked fast,
He fell into a rage of wrath,
   And his heart was aghast.

7 "Cum down to me, ye lady fair,
   Cum down to me; let's see;
This night ye's ly by my ain side,
   The morn my bride sall be."

8 "I winnae cum down, ye fals Gordon,
   I winnae cum down to thee;
I winnae forsake my ane dear lord,
   That is sae far frae me."

hald, hold, stronghold. *busk*, make ready. *drie*, be able.

9   "Gi' up your house, ye fair lady,
        Gi' up your house to me,
     Or I will burn yoursel therein,
        Bot and your babies three."

10 "I winnae gie up, you fals Gordon,
        To nae sik traitor as thee,
     Tho you should burn mysel therein,
        Bot and my babies three."

11 "Set fire to the house," quoth fals Gordon,
        "Sin better may nae bee;
     And I will burn hersel therein,
        Bot and her babies three."

12 "And ein wae worth ye, Jock my man!
        I paid ye weil your fee;
     Why pow ye out my ground-wa-stane,
        Lets in the reek to me?

13 "And ein wae worth ye, Jock my man!
        For I paid you weil your hire;
     Why pow ye out my ground-wa-stane,
        To me lets in the fire?"

14 "Ye paid me weil my hire, lady,
        Ye paid me weil my fee,
     But now I'm Edom o Gordon's man,
        Maun either do or die."

15 O then bespake her youngest son,
        Sat on the nurse's knee,
     "Dear mother, gi'e owre your house," he says,
        "For the reek it worries me."

16 "I winnae gi'e up my house, my dear,
        To nae sik traitor as he;
     Cum weil, cum wae, my jewels fair,
        Ye maun tak share wi me."

sik, such. *ein wae worth ye,* may an equal woe befall you. *pow,*
pull. *ground-wa-stane,* foundation stone.

17 O then bespake her dochter dear,
      She was baith jimp and sma;
    "O row me in a pair o shiets,
      And tow me owre the wa."

18 They rowd her in a pair of shiets,
      And towd her owre the wa,
    But on the point of Edom's speir
      She gat a deadly fa.

19 O bonny, bonny was hir mouth,
      And chirry were her cheiks,
    And clear, clear was hir yellow hair,
      Where on the reid bluid dreips!

20 Then wi his speir he turnd hir owr;
      O gin hir face was wan!
    He said, "You are the first that eer
      I wist alive again."

21 He turnd hir owr and owr again;
      O gin hir skin was whyte!
    He said, "I might ha spard thy life
      To been some man's delyte."

22 "Busk and boon, my merry men all,
      For ill dooms I do guess;
    I cannae luik in that bonny face,
      As it lyes on the grass."

23 "Them luiks to freits, my master deir,
      Then freits will follow them;
    Let it neir be said brave Edom o Gordon
      Was daunted with a dame."

24 O then he spied hir ain dear lord,
      As he came owr the lee;
    He saw his castle in a fire,
      As far as he could see.

---

jimp, slender. *tow,* let down by rope. *gin,* how. *wist,* wished.
boon, make ready. *doom,* judgment, punishment. *them luiks to
freits,* those who trust in omens.

25   "Put on, put on, my mighty men,
         As fast as ye can drie!
     For he that's hindmost of my men
         Sall neir get guid o me."

26   And some they raid, and some they ran,
         Fu fast out-owr the plain,
     But lang, lang eer he coud get up
         They were a' deid and slain.

27   But mony were the mudie men
         Lay gasping on the grien;
     For o fifty men that Edom brought out
         There were but five ged heme.

28   And mony were the mudie men
         Lay gasping on the grien,
     And mony were the fair ladys
         Lay lemanless at heme.

29   And round and round the waes he went,
         Their ashes for to view;
     At last into the flames he flew,
         And bad the world adieu.

The Bonny Earl of Murray (181)

Hearing rumors that the Earl of Murray was implicated in
some of his cousin Bothwell's rebellious activities, James VI of
Scotland issued a commission to the Earl of Huntly to apprehend
Murray. Just a few weeks before, Murray had been enticed south
by royal promises and lay at his mother Lady Doune's castle of
Donibristle on the Fife shore. There on February 7, 1592, Huntly
surrounded Murray and his handful of retainers. The house was
set afire. Murray burst through a cordon of Huntly's men and,
since it was dark, he might have hidden among the shore crags
and so escaped, but "he was discovered by the tip of his head-
piece, which had taken fire before he left the house, and unmerci-

out-owr, over. *mudie*, bold. *grien*, green. *ged*, went. *lemanless*,
loverless. *waes*, walls.

fully slain" (Spottiswood). The ballad implies that the king was jealous of the queen's admiration for the handsome and popular nobleman and wished him dead; certainly if James only wanted to have the earl taken in charge, it was unwise of him to send Huntly, Murray's bitterest enemy, to arrest him. Popular resentment over Murray's death, of which the ballad itself is one reflection, ran so high that the king had to remove the court to Glasgow.

The oldest text of the ballad, here printed from Ramsay's *Tea-Table Miscellany*, 1750, p. 356, imitates the ancient Celtic dirges for the dead, the coronachs.

1   Ye Highlands, and ye Lawlands,
        Oh where have you been?
     They have slain the Earl of Murray,
        And they layd him on the green.

2   "Now wae be to thee, Huntly!
        And wherefore did you sae?
     I bade you bring him wi' you,
        But forbade you him to slay."

3   He was a braw gallant,
        And he rid at the ring;
     And the bonny Earl of Murray,
        Oh he might have been a king!

4   He was a braw gallant,
        And he play'd at the ba';
     And the bonny Earl of Murray
        Was the flower among them a'.

5   He was a braw gallant,
        And he play'd at the glove;
     And the bonny Earl of Murray,
        Oh he was the Queen's love!

6   Oh lang will his lady
        Look o'er the castle Down,
     Eer she see the Earl of Murray
        Come sounding thro the town!

braw, brave, fine.

Willie Macintosh (183)

William Macintosh and the men of his clan thought to avenge
the Earl of Murray (see previous ballad) by harrying Huntly's
lands. But Huntly and a small band caught up with the ma-
rauders at a hill called Stapliegate and badly defeated the Mac-
intoshes. The ballad confuses Willie Macintosh with an earlier
clan chief of the same name who had destroyed Auchindown
castle some forty years before.

Text: *The Thistle of Scotland*, 1823, p. 106.

1   "Turn, Willie Macintosh,
       Turn, I bid you;
    Gin ye burn Auchindown,
       Huntly will head you."

2   "Head me or hang me,
       That canna fley me;
    I'll burn Auchendown
       Ere the life lea' me."

3   Coming down Deeside,
       In a clear morning,
    Auchindown was in flame,
       Ere the cock-crawing.

4   But coming o'er Cairn[gorm],
       And looking down, man,
    I saw Willie Macintosh
       Burn Auchindown, man.

5   "Bonny Willie Macintosh,
       Whare left ye your men?"
    "I left them in the Stapler,
       But they'll never come hame."

6   "Bonny Willie Macintosh,
       Whare now is your men?"

gin, if.   *head*, behead.   *fley*, frighten.

"I left them in the Stapler,
Sleeping in their sheen."

Fire of Frendraught (196)

After great effort the Marquis of Huntly had managed to patch up the feud between Crichton of Frendraught and young Rothiemay, whose father Frendraught had killed when the elder Rothiemay resisted arrest (see stanza 11). Another family at odds with Frendraught, the Leslies, were lying in wait for him to leave Huntly's castle. To insure his guest's safe passage home, Huntly sent his son Lord John Gordon (Viscount Melgum) and young Rothiemay as escorts. At Frendraught, the young men were induced by the lady of the castle to stay till morning—a fatal decision, as it turned out, for the tower in which the young men and their servants were sleeping suddenly burst into flames during the night (October 8-9, 1630). The guests could neither descend the burning timber stairs nor break through the bars on the windows. Frendraught's lady is accused by the ballad of having set the fire, but Frendraught had so much to lose—the friendship of Huntly as well as house, papers, and treasure—that it would have made Rothiemay's death too expensive. The fire was probably either accidental or set by the Leslies. Sophia Hay, daughter of the Earl of Errol, was the Viscountess Melgum, as in the ballad.

Text: Motherwell, *Minstrelsy*, p. 167.

1   The eighteenth of October,
        A dismal tale to hear
    How good Lord John and Rothiemay
        Was both burnt in the fire.

2   When steeds was saddled and well bridled,
        And ready for to ride,
    Then out it came her false Frendraught,
        Inviting them to bide.

sheen, shoes.

3   Said, "Stay this night untill we sup,
         The morn untill we dine;
      'Twill be a token of good 'greement
         'Twixt your good lord and mine."

4   "We'll turn again," said good Lord John—
         "But no," said Rothiemay—
      "My steed's trapan'd, my bridle's broken,
         I fear the day I'm fey."

5   When mass was sung, and bells was rung,
         And all men bound for bed,
      Then good Lord John and Rothiemay
         In one chamber was laid.

6   They had not long cast off their cloaths,
         And were but now asleep,
      When the weary smoke began to rise,
         Likewise the scorching heat.

7   "O waken, waken, Rothiemay!
         O waken, brother dear!
      And turn you to our Saviour,
         There is strong treason here."

8   When they were dressed in their cloaths,
         And ready for to boun,
      The doors and windows was all secur'd,
         The roof-tree burning down.

9   He did him to the wire-window,
         As fast as he could gang;
      Says, "Wae to the hands put in the stancheons!
         For out we'll never win."

10   When he stood at the wire-window,
         Most doleful to be seen,
      He did espy her, Lady Frendraught,
         Who stood upon the green.

11   Cried, "Mercy, mercy, Lady Frendraught!
         Will ye not sink with sin?

trapan, injure treacherously. *fey,* marked by fate. *boun,* go.
stancheon, iron bar.

For first your husband killed my father,
    And now you burn his son."

12 O then out spoke her Lady Frendraught,
    And loudly did she cry—
"It were great pity for good Lord John,
    But none for Rothiemay;
But the keys are casten in the deep draw-well,
    Ye cannot get away."

13 While he stood in this dreadful plight,
    Most piteous to be seen,
There called out his servant Gordon,
    As he had frantic been:

14 "O loup, O loup, my dear master!
    O loup and come to me!
I'll catch you in my arms two,
    One foot I will not flee.

15 "O loup, O loup, my dear master!
    O loup and come away!
I'll catch you in my arms two,
    But Rothiemay may lie."

16 "The fish shall never swim in the flood,
    Nor corn grow through the clay,
Nor the fiercest fire that ever was kindled
    Twin me and Rothiemay.

17 "But I cannot loup, I cannot come,
    I cannot win to thee;
My head's fast in the wire-window,
    My feet burning from me.

18 "My eyes are seething in my head,
    My flesh roasting also,
My bowels are boiling with my blood;
    Is not that a woeful woe?

19 "Take here the rings from my white fingers,
    That are so long and small,

loup, leap.   *twin,* part.

And give them to my lady fair,
    Where she sits in her hall.

20 "So I cannot loup, I cannot come,
    I cannot loup to thee;
My earthly part is all consumed,
    My spirit but speaks to thee."

21 Wringing her hands, tearing her hair,
    His lady she was seen,
And thus addressed his servant Gordon,
    Where he stood on the green.

22 "O wae be to you, George Gordon!
    An ill death may you die!
So safe and sound as you stand there,
    And my lord bereaved from me."

23 "I bad him loup, I bad him come,
    I bad him loup to me;
I'd catch him in my arms two,
    A foot I should not flee.

24 "He threw me the rings from his white fingers,
    Which were so long and small,
To give to you, his lady fair,
    Where you sat in your hall."

25 Sophia Hay, Sophia Hay,
    O bonny Sophia was her name—
Her waiting maid put on her cloaths,
    But I wat she tore them off again.

26 And aft she cried, "Ohon! alas! alas!
    A sair heart's ill to win;
I wan a sair heart when I married him,
    And the day it's well return'd again."

I wat, I know; indeed.   *ohon,* Gaelic cry of lament.

Katharine Jaffray (221)

Scott's "Lochinvar" retells this tale of an abducted bride in a rather more dashing style. In some versions of the ballad, Katharine resists her cavalier abductor; in others it is she who has arranged the affair. Both versions here are Scottish: A is from the Herd MSS. (Child, IV, 219); B, recorded about 1850 (Greig, 160), is furnished with a tune.

❧ A ☙

1 There livd a lass in yonder dale,
    And doun in yonder glen, O.
  And Kathrine Jaffray was her name,
    Well known by many men, O.

2 Out came the Laird of Lauderdale,
    Out frae the South Countrie,
  All for to court this pretty maid,
    Her bridegroom for to be.

3 He has teld her father and mither baith,
    And a' the rest o her kin,
  And has teld the lass hersell,
    And her consent has win.

4 Then came the Laird of Lochinton,
    Out frae the English border,
  All for to court this pretty maid,
    Well mounted in good order.

5 He's teld her father and mither baith,
    As I hear sindry say,
  But he has nae teld the lass her sell,
    Till on her wedding day.

6 When day was set, and friends were met,
    And married to be,

Lord Lauderdale came to the place,
  The bridal for to see.

7 "O are you come for sport, young man,
     Or are you come for play?
   Or are you come for a sight o our bride,
     Just on her wedding day?"

8 "I'm nouther come for sport," he says,
     "Nor am I come for play;
   But if I had one sight o your bride,
     I'll mount and ride away."

9 There was a glass of the red wine
     Filld up them atween,
   And ay she drank to Lauderdale,
     Wha her true-love had been.

10 Then he took her by the milk-white hand,
      And by the grass-green sleeve,
    And he mounted her high behind him there,
      At the bridegroom he askt nae leive.

11 Then the blude run down by the Cowden Banks,
      And down by Cowden Braes,
    And ay she gard the trumpet sound,
      "O this is foul, foul play!"

12 Now a' ye that in England are,
      Or are in England born,
    Come nere to Scotland to court a lass,
      Or else ye'l get the scorn.

13 They haik ye up and settle ye by,
      Till on your wedding day,
    And gie ye frogs instead o fish,
      And play ye foul, foul play.

gar, make. *haik ye up,* keep you in suspense. *settle ye by,* set
you aside.

❦◇ B ◇❦

Loch - na - gar cam— frae the west In -
to the low coun - trie, An' he's coor- ted Kath'- rine
Jaf - fray, An' stole her heart a - way.

1 Lochnagar cam frae the west
   Into the low countrie,
An' he's coorted Kath'rine Jaffray,
   An' stole her heart away.

2 Hame he cam, ane Amosdale,
   Cam fae the north countrie,
An' he has gained her father's heart,
   But an' her mother's tee.

3 A bridal day it then was set,
   An' the bridal day cam on,
An' who appeared among the guests
   But Lochnagar himsel?

4 A glass was filled o good red wine,
   Weel drunk between them twa:
Said he, "I'll drink wi you, bridegroom,
   An' syne boun me awa.

5 "A few words wi your bridesmaiden
   I hope you'll grant me then:

fae, from. *tee,* too. *syne,* then. *boun,* betake oneself.

I'm sure before her wedding day
  I would have gotten ten."

6   Out spoke then the first groomsman,
    An' an angry man was he,
  Says, "I will keep my bonnie bride
    Until the sun gae tee;

7   "Until the sun gae tee," he said,
    "Until the sun gae tee,
  An' deliver her ower to her bridegroom,
    Which is my duty to dee."

8   But he's taen her by the middle jimp,
    An' never stoppit to ca',
  He's taen her by the milk-white han'
    An' led her through the ha'.

9   He leaned him ower his saiddle-bow,
    An' kissed her cheek an' chin,
  An' then he wissed them a' good nicht,
    An' hoised her on ahin.

10   He drew a trumpet fae his breist,
    An' blew baith loud an' shrill;
  A hunner o well-airmed men
    Cam Lochnagar until.

11   A hunner o weel-airmed men,
    Wi milk-white steeds an' grey,
  A hunner o weel-airmed men
    Upon his wedding day.

12   Horsemen rode, an' bridesmen ran,
    An' ladies in full speed,
  But you wadna hae seen his yellow locks
    For the dust o his horse' feet.

13   She turned in the saiddle-bow,
    Addressed her late bridegroom,
  Says, "The compliments I got fae you,
    I'll return them back again."

jimp, slender.   *hoised*, hoisted.   *ahin*, behind.

14 So Katharine Jaffray was marriet at morn,
  An' she was marriet at noon;
She was twice marriet in ae day,
  Ere she keest aff her goon.

x: HISTORICAL BALLADS

Chevy Chase
(The Hunting of the Cheviot) (162)

Sir Philip Sydney confesses that "I never heard the old song of *Percy* and *Douglas* that I found not my heart moved more than with a trumpet"; Ben Jonson is supposed to have said that he would rather have been the author of "Chevy Chase" than of all his works; Addison analyzed this "favorite ballad of the common people" in two *Spectator* papers (Nos. 70 and 74), comparing it favorably with the classical epics. The ballad on which these praises were lavished deals obliquely with the Battle of Otterburn, fought August 19, 1388, in which a small force of Scotsmen under the Earl of Douglas, which was pulling back home after pillaging in England, was fallen upon by Henry Percy, Earl of Northumberland. Though Douglas was killed, the English lost the engagement, suffering disastrous casualties and the ignominy of Percy's capture.

Two minstrel ballads, both much older than the ballad printed here, celebrate the same event. The older, found in a manuscript of about 1550 (Child, III, 295), tells the story with reasonable accuracy; the other (Bodleian MS. Ashmole 48, about 1555; Child, III, 307) follows local legend and partisan traditions rather than the chronicles and warps history badly in order to glorify the English, especially the House of Percy. Our ballad, a modernization of the Bodleian text, was widely reprinted on broadsides up through the eighteenth century.

"Chevy Chase" is traditionally sung to one or the other of the following tunes.

Air: "In Peascod Time"

Air: "Flying Fame"

1   God prosper long our noble king,
      Our liffes and saftyes all!
  A woefull hunting once there did
      In Cheuy Chase befall.

2   To driue the deere with hound and horne
      Erle Pearcy took the way:
  The child may rue that is vnborne
      The hunting of that day!

3   The stout Erle of Northumberland
      A vow to God did make
  His pleasure in the Scottish woods
      Three sommers days to take,

4   The cheefest harts in Cheuy C[h]ase
      To kill and beare away:
  These tydings to Erle Douglas came
      In Scottland where he lay.

5 Who sent Erle Pearcy present word
   He wold prevent his sport;
   The English erle, not fearing that,
   Did to the woods resort,

6 With fifteen hundred bowmen bold,
   All chosen men of might,
   Who knew ffull well in time of neede
   To ayme their shafts arright.

7 The gallant greyhound[s] swiftly ran
   To chase the fallow deere;
   On Munday they began to hunt,
   Ere daylight did appeare.

8 And long before high noone the[y] had
   A hundred fat buckes slaine;
   Then hauing dined, the drouyers went
   To rouze the deare againe.

9 The bowmen mustered on the hills,
   Well able to endure;
   Theire backsids all with speciall care
   That day were guarded sure.

10 The hounds ran swiftly through the woods
   The nimble deere to take,
   That with their cryes the hills and dales
   An eccho shrill did make.

11 Lord Pearcy to the querry went
   To view the tender deere;
   Quoth he, "Erle Douglas promised once
   This day to meete me here;

12 "But if I thought he wold not come,
   Noe longer wold I stay."
   With that a braue younge gentlman
   Thus to the erle did say:

13 "Loe, yonder doth Erle Douglas come,
   Hys men in armour bright;
   Full twenty hundred Scottish speres
   All marching in our sight.

14   "All men of pleasant Tiuydale,
        Fast by the riuer Tweede:"
     "O ceaze your sportts!" Erle Pearcy said,
        "And take your bowes with speede.

15   "And now with me, my countrymen,
        Your courage forth advance!
     For there was neuer champion yett,
        In Scottland nor in Ffrance,

16   "That euer did on horsbacke come,
        [But], if my hap it were,
     I durst encounter man for man,
        With him to breake a spere."

17   Erle Douglas on his milk-white steede,
        Most like a baron bold,
     Rode formost of his company,
        Whose armor shone like gold.

18   "Shew me," sayd hee, "whose men you bee
        That hunt so boldly heere,
     That without my consent doe chase
        And kill my fallow deere."

19   The first man that did answer make
        Was noble Pearcy hee,
     Who sayd, "Wee list not to declare
        Nor shew whose men wee bee;

20   "Yett wee will spend our deerest blood
        Thy cheefest harts to slay."
     Then Douglas swore a solempne oathe,
        And thus in rage did say:

21   "Ere thus I will outbraued bee,
        One of vs tow shall dye;
     I know thee well, an erle thou art;
        Lord Pearcy, soe am I.

22   "But trust me, Pearcye, pittye it were,
        And great offence, to kill

hap, chance.

Then any of these our guiltlesse men,
    For they haue done none ill.

23   "Let thou and I the battell trye,
     And set our men aside:"
   "Accurst bee [he!]" Erle Pearcye sayd,
     "By whome it is denyed."

24   Then stept a gallant squire forth—
     Witherington was his name—
   Who said, "I wold not haue it told
     To Henery our king, for shame,

25   "That ere my captaine fought on foote,
     And I stand looking on.
   You bee two Erles," quoth Witheringhton,
     "And I a squier alone;

26   "I'le doe the best that doe I may,
     While I haue power to stand;
   While I haue power to weeld my sword,
     I'le fight with hart and hand."

27   Our English archers bent their bowes;
     Their harts were good and trew;
   Att the first flight of arrowes sent,
     Full foure score Scotts the[y] slew.

28   To driue the deere with hound and horne,
     Dauglas bade on the bent;
   Two captaines moued with mickle might,
     Their speres to shiuers went.

29   They closed full fast on euery side,
     Noe slackness there was found,
   But many a gallant gentleman
     Lay gasping on the ground.

30   O Christ! it was great greeue to see
     How eche man chose his spere,
   And how the blood out of their brests
     Did gush like water cleare.

31   At last these two stout erles did meet,
     Like captaines of great might;
  Like lyons woode they layd on lode;
     The[y] made a cruell fight.

32   The[y] fought vntill they both did sweat,
     With swords of tempered steele,
  Till blood downe their cheekes like raine
     The trickling downe did feele.

33   "O yeeld thee, Pearcye!" Douglas sayd,
     "And in faith I will thee bringe
  Where thou shall high advanced bee
     By James our Scottish king.

34   "Thy ransome I will freely giue,
     And this report of thee,
  Thou art the most couragious knight
     [That ever I did see.]"

35   "Noe, Douglas!" quoth Erle Percy then,
     "Thy profer I doe scorne;
  I will not yeelde to any Scott
     That euer yett was borne!"

36   With that there came an arrow keene,
     Out of an English bow,
  Which stroke Erle Douglas on the brest
     A deepe and deadlye blow.

37   Who neuer sayd more words than these:
     "Fight on, my merry men all!
  For why, my life is att [an] end,
     Lord Pearcy sees my fall."

38   Then leauing liffe, Erle Pearcy tooke
     The dead man by the hand;
  Who said, "Erle Dowglas, for thy life,
     Wold I had lost my hand;

39   "O Christ! my verry hart doth bleed
     For sorrow for thy sake,

woode, mad.

For sure, a more redoubted knight
    Mischance could neuer take."

40 A knight amongst the Scotts there was
    Which saw Erle Douglas dye,
Who streight in hart did vow revenge
    Vpon the Lord Pearcye.

41 Sir Hugh Mountgomerye was he called,
    Who, with a spere full bright,
Well mounted on a gallant steed,
    Ran feircly through the fight,

42 And past the English archers all,
    Without all dread or feare,
And through Erle Percyes body then
    He thrust his hatfull spere.

43 With such a vehement force and might
    His body he did gore,
The staff ran through the other side
    A large cloth yard and more.

44 Thus did both those nobles dye,
    Whose courage none cold staine;
An English archer then perceiued
    The noble erle was slaine.

45 He had [a] good bow in his hand,
    Made of a trusty tree;
An arrow of a cloth yard long
    To the hard head haled hee.

46 Against Sir Hugh Mountgomerye
    His shaft full right he sett;
The grey goose winge that was there-on
    In his harts bloode was wett.

47 This fight from breake of day did last
    Till setting of the sun,
For when the rung the euening-bell
    The battele scarse was done.

hale, set.

48 With stout Erle Percy there was slaine
    Sir John of Egerton,
Sir Robert Harcliffe and Sir William,
    Sir James, that bold barron.

49 And with Sir George and Sir James,
    Both knights of good account,
Good Sir Raphe Rebbye there was slaine,
    Whose prowesse did surmount.

50 For Witherington needs must I wayle
    As one in dolefull dumpes,
For when his leggs were smitten of,
    He fought vpon his stumpes.

51 And with Erle Dowglas there was slaine
    Sir Hugh Mountgomerye,
And Sir Charles Morrell, that from feelde
    One foote wold neuer flee;

52 Sir Roger Heuer of Harcliffe tow,
    His sisters sonne was hee;
Sir David Lambwell, well esteemed,
    But saved he cold not bee.

53 And the Lord Maxwell, in like case,
    With Douglas he did dye;
Of twenty hundred Scottish speeres,
    Scarce fifty-fiue did flye.

54 Of fifteen hundred Englishmen
    Went home but fifty-three;
The rest in Cheuy Chase were slaine,
    Vnder the greenwoode tree.

55 Next day did many widdowes come
    Their husbands to bewayle;
They washt their wounds in brinish teares,
    But all wold not prevayle.

56 Theyr bodyes, bathed in purple blood,
    The[y] bore with them away;
They kist them dead a thousand times
    Ere the[y] were cladd in clay.

57   The newes was brought to Eddenborrow,
       Where Scottlands king did rayne,
   That braue Erle Douglas soddainlye
       Was with an arrow slaine.

58   "O heauy newes!" King James can say;
       "Scottland may wittenesse bee
   I haue not any captaine more
       Of such account as hee."

59   Like tydings to King Henery came,
       Within as short a space,
   That Pearcy of Northumberland
       Was slaine in Cheuy Chase.

60   "Now God be with him!" said our king,
       "Sith it will noe better bee;
   I trust I haue within my realme
       Fiue hundred as good as hee.

61   "Yett shall not Scotts nor Scotland say
       But I will vengeance take,
   And be revenged on them all
       For braue Erle Percyes sake."

62   This vow the king did well performe
       After on Humble-downe;
   In one day fifty knights were slayne,
       With lords of great renowne.

63   And of the rest of small account,
       Did many hundreds dye:
   Thus endeth the hunting in Cheuy Chase,
       Made by the Erle Pearcye.

64   God saue our king, and blesse this land
       With plentye, ioy, and peace,
   And grant hencforth that foule debate
       Twixt noble men may ceaze!

The Death of Queen Jane (170)

Jane Seymour, Henry VIII's third queen, died twelve days after the birth of Prince Edward in 1537. The ballad is historically incorrect in having the prince delivered by a Caesarian operation, but the existence of the ballad is itself of historical value since it is an index to the queen's popularity among the common people. The Scottish version printed here (from Kinloch, p. 116) takes greater interest in the funeral pomp than does any other version.

1   Queen Jeanie, Queen Jeanie, travel'd six weeks and more,
     Till women and midwives had quite gi'en her o'er:
     "O if ye were women as women should be,
     Ye would send for a doctor, a doctor to me."

2   The doctor was called for and set by her bedside:
     "What aileth thee, my ladie, thine eyes seem so red?"
     "O doctor, O doctor, will ye do this for me,
     To rip up my two sides, and save my babie?"

3   "Queen Jeanie, Queen Jeanie, that's the thing I'll ne'er do,
     To rip up your two sides to save your babie:"
     Queen Jeanie, Queen Jeanie, travel'd six weeks and more,
     Till midwives and doctors had quite gi'en her o'er.

4   "O if ye were doctors as doctors should be,
     Ye would send for King Henry, King Henry to me:"
     King Henry was called for, and sat by her bedside,
     "What aileth thee, Jeanie? what aileth my bride?"

5   "King Henry, King Henry, will ye do this for me,
     To rip up my two sides, and save my babie?"
     "Queen Jeanie, Queen Jeanie, that's what I'll never do,
     To rip up your two sides to save your babie."

6   But with sighing and sobbing she's fallen in a swoon
     Her side it was ript up, and her babie was found;

travel, be in labor.

At his bonie babie's christ'ning there was meikle joy and
    mirth,
But bonnie Queen Jeanie lies cold in the earth.

7   Six and six coaches, and six and six more,
    And royal King Henry went mourning before;
    O two and two gentlemen carried her away,
    But royal King Henry went weeping away.

8   O black were their stockings, and black were their bands
    And black were the weapons they held in their hands;
    O black were their mufflers, and black were their shoes,
    And black were the cheverons they drew on their luves.

9   They mourned in the kitchen, and they mourn'd in the ha',
    But royal King Henry mourn'd langest of a':
    Farewell to fair England, farewell for ever more!
    For the fair flower of England will never shine more.

Lilliburlero

One of the most effective pieces of propaganda ever concocted,
"Lilliburlero" is credited with having "contributed not a little"
to driving James II out of his three "brave, war-like kingdoms"
during the revolution of 1688. "Never had so slight a thing so
great an effect," wrote Burnet, a contemporary historian.

James, a Catholic, had made Talbot, a "furious Papist" newly
created Earl of Tyrconnel, his deputy in Ireland. The English
Protestants foresaw oppression for their co-religionists in Ireland
and feared the "Papists" might even take over the British Army,
in which until then they were excluded by law from holding
commissions. The song pretends to be a dialogue between two
Irishmen, congratulating each other on the triumph over the
English and the Protestants. The Marquis of Wharton was the
author. Irish Catholics are said to have used "Lilliburlero bullen
a-la" as a watchword in their massacre of Protestants in 1641. Its
revival here as the refrain was an ingenious stroke.

meikle, much.   *chevron*, glove.   *luve*, palm.

Text from Percy's *Reliques,* I, 359. The tune—Purcell's tidying of an old Irish air—rather than the words were thought by Hume to account for the enormous popularity of "Lilliburlero." The traditional set is printed here from Chappell, *Popular Music,* II, 572.

1   Ho! broder Teague, dost hear de decree?
    Lilli burlero, bullen a-la.
    Dat we shall have a new deputie,
    Lilli burlero burlen a-la.
    Lero lero, lilli burlero, lero lero, bullen a-la,
    Lero *lero, lilli burlero, lero lero, bullen a-la.*

2   Ho! by shaint Tyburn, it is de Talbote:
     And he will cut de Englishmen's troate.

3   Dough by my shoul de English do praat,
     De law's on dare side, and Creish knows what.

4   But if dispence do come from de pope,
     We'll hang Magna Charta, and dem in a rope.

5   For de good Talbot is made a lord,
     And with brave lads is coming aboard:

6   Who all in France have taken a sware,
     Dat dey will have no protestant heir.

7   Ara! but why does he stay behind?
     Ho! by my shoul 'tis a protestant wind.

8   But see de Tyrconnel is now come ashore,
     And we shall have commissions gillore.

9   And he dat will not go to de mass,
     Shall be turn out, and look like an ass.

10   Now, now de hereticks will go down,
     By Chrish and shaint Patrick, de nation's our own.

11   Dare was an old prophesy found in a bog,
     "Ireland shall be rul'd by an ass, and a dog."

12   And now dis prophesy is come to pass,
     For Talbot's de dog, and James is de ass.

Brave Wolfe

A Colonial ballad-writer probably composed this pedestrian dirge soon after the news of Wolfe's death on the Plains of Abraham was received in Boston (September 1759). Songsters continually reprinted the ballad up to about 1850; since then it has been traditional in Canada, New England, and as far south as West Virginia (Combs, p. 176). The early stanzas dealing with Wolfe's courtship, a passage told awkwardly in the first

person, bears little relation to the main events of the ballad. It is
true, however, that Wolfe became engaged before coming out
to America. The parley with Montcalm is fiction.

Text: Shoemaker, p. 108, which is word for word the copy in
The Forget-Me-Not Songster, 1843, p. 133.

1 Cheer up, my young men all; let nothing fright you.
   Though oft objections rise, let it delight you.
   Let not your fancy move whene'er it comes to trial;
   Nor let your courage fail at the first denial.

2 I sat down by my love, thinking that I wooed her;
   I sat down by my love, but sure not to delude her.
   But when I go to speak, my tongue it doth so quiver,
   I dare not speak my mind whenever I am with her.

3 Love, here's a ring of gold; 'tis long that I have kept it.
   My dear, now for my sake, I pray you to accept it.
   When you the posy read, pray, think upon the giver;
   My dear, remember me, or I'm undone forever.

4 Then Wolfe he took his leave of his most lovely jewel;
   Although it seemed to be to him an act most cruel.
   Although it's for a space I'm forced to leave my love,
   My dear, where'er I rove, I'll ne'er forget my dove.

5 So then this valiant youth embarked on the ocean
   To free America from faction's dire commotion.
   He landed at Quebec, being all brave and hearty;
   The city to attack with his most gallant party.

6 Then Wolfe drew up his men in rank and file so pretty.
   On Abraham's lofty heights, before this noble city.
   A distance from the town the noble French did meet them
   In double numbers there, resolved for to beat them.

(A Parley—Wolfe and Montcalm Together)

7 Montcalm and this brave youth, together they are walking;
   So well they do agree, like brothers they are talking.
   Then each one to his post, as they do now retire,
   Or then their numberous hosts began their dreadful fire.

8   Then instant from his horse fell this noble hero.
     May we lament his loss in words of deepest sorrow.

9   The French are seen to break, their columns are all flying;
     Then Wolfe he seems to wake, though in the act of dying.
     And lifted up his head (the drums did sound and rattle),
     And to his army said: "I pray, how goes the battle?"

10   His aide-de-camp replied: "Brave gen'ral, 'tis in our favor.
     Quebec and all her pride, 'tis nothing now can save her.
     She falls into our hands, with all her wealth and treasure."
     "Oh, then," brave Wolfe replied, "I quit the world with
          pleasure."

Paul Jones

Of the many broadside ballads that celebrated Paul Jones'
intrepid duel with the forty-four-gun *Serapis* off Flamborough
Head, Yorkshire, on September 23, 1779, one at least, thanks to
frequent reprinting in songsters, was taken up into tradition. Our
North Carolina text (Brown, II, 524) agrees with several songsters in omitting the refrain "Hurrah, our country forever, hurrah!" found at the end of each stanza in the broadside and in
other traditional texts. The final line alludes to the strange behavior of Captain Landais of the *Alliance,* who poured three or
four broadsides in the *Richard* by mistake, but otherwise ignored
Jones' order to join battle. Captain Richard Pearson (not Pierce)
was the British commander.

1   A forty-gun frigate from Baltimore came,
     Her guns mounted forty, and *Richard* by name,
     Went cruising the channel of old England,
     With a noble commander, Paul Jones was the man.

2   We had not sailed long before we did spy
     A large forty-four and a twenty close by,
     All these warlike vessels full laden with store;
     Our captain pursued them on the bold York shore.

3   At the hour of twelve Pierce came alongside
    With a large speaking trumpet: "Whence came you?" he
        cried.
    "Quick give me an answer, I've hailed you before,
    Or at this moment a broadside I'll pour."

4   We fought them five glasses, five glasses so hot,
    Till sixty bright seamen lay dead on the spot,
    Full seventy wounded lay bleeding in gore.
    How fierce our loud cannons on the *Richard* did roar.

5   Our gunner got frightened, to Paul Jones he came.
    "Our ship she is sinking, likewise in a flame."
    Paul Jones he smiled in the height of his pride,
    Saying, "This day I'll conquer or sink alongside."

6   Here's health to those widows who shortly must weep,
    For the loss of their husbands who sunk in the deep.
    Here's a health to those young girls who shortly must
        mourn
    For the loss of their sweethearts that's overboard thrown.

7   Here's a health to Paul Jones with sword in hand—
    He was foremost in action, in giving command.
    Here's a health to Paul Jones and all his crew—
    If we hadn't a French Captain, boys, what could we do!

The Constitution *and the* Guerrière

The engagement between the *Constitution,* under Captain
Isaac Hull, and the *Guerrière,* under Captain Richard Dacres,
was fought on August 19, 1812, off the coast of Nova Scotia.
Though the ships were of equal armament, Hull succeeded in
reducing the *Guerrière* to a wreck in twenty-five minutes, with a
loss of seventy-eight British sailors killed and wounded. The
Americans lost fourteen men (see Neeser, p. 95). As the rollick-
ing meter might suggest, the ballad was based on an old drinking
song—"A Drop of Brandy, O!" It was a staple of nineteenth-century songsters, particularly patriotic ones, and in the Civil War

was parodied in the Union "Yankee Boys So Hardy, O!" "The *Chesapeake* and the *Shannon*" is a contemporary British "mock" of "The *Constitution* and the *Guerrière*."

Text: *The Forecastle Songster*, 1852, p. 29, which differs with the text in Colcord, p. 130, in only two phrases.

1   It ofttimes has been told
     That British seamen bold,
     Could flog the tars of France so neat and handy, O!
     But they never found their match,
     Till the Yankees did them catch,
     Oh, the Yankee boys, for fighting, are the dandy, O!

2   The *Guerrière*, a frigate bold,
     On the foaming ocean rolled,
     Commanded by proud Dacres, the grandee, O!
     With a choice of British crew,
     As a rammer ever drew,
     They could flog the French, two to one so handy, O!

3   When this frigate bore in view,
     Says proud Dacres to his crew,
     "Come, clear the ship for action and be handy, O!
     To the weather gage, boys, get her,"
     And to make his men fight better,
     Gave them to drink, gunpowder mixed with brandy, O!

4   Then, Dacres loudly cries,
     "Make this Yankee ship your prize,
     You can in thirty minutes, neat and handy, O!
     Thirty five's enough I'm sure,
     And if you'll do it in a score,
     I'll treat you to a double share of brandy, O!"

5   The British shot flew hot,
     Which the Yankees answered not,
     Till they got within the distance they call handy, O!
     "Now," says Hull unto his crew,
     "Boys, let's see what we can do,
     If we take this boasting Briton we're the dandy, O!"

6 The first broadside we pour'd,
Carried her mainmast by the board,
Which made this lofty frigate look abandon'd, O!
Then Dacres shook his head,
And to his officers he said,
"Lord, I didn't think these Yankees were so handy, O!"

7 Our second told so well,
That their fore and mizen fell,
Which dous'd the royal ensign so handy, O!
"By George," says he, "we're done,"
And then fired a lee gun,
While the Yankees struck up Yankee doodle dandy, O!

8 Then Dacres came on board
To deliver up his sword,
Loth was he to part with it, it was so handy, O!
"Oh, keep your sword," says Hull,
"For it only makes you dull,
So cheer up, come, let us have a little brandy, O!"

9 Come, fill your glasses full,
And we'll drink to Captain Hull,
And so merrily we'll push about the brandy, O!
John Bull may toast his fill
Let the world say what it will,
But the Yankee boys for fighting are the dandy, O!

The Chesapeake and the Shannon

On June 1, 1813, the *Guerrière* was avenged when the British frigate *Shannon* pounced upon the *Chesapeake* off Boston Lighthouse and silenced the American guns in less than fifteen minutes. The battered *Shannon* towed her prize to Halifax, Nova Scotia. British sailors mocked the boastful American ballad on the taking of the *Guerrière* by remodeling it to fit the more recent British victory. Numerous English collections print folk versions. Text and tune: Mackenzie, p. 208, from Nova Scotia. Tune known also as "The Landlady of France" or "A Drop of Brandy, O!"

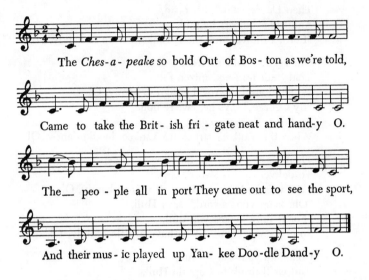

The *Ches-a-peake* so bold Out of Bos-ton as we're told,

Came to take the Brit-ish fri-gate neat and hand-y   O.

The__ peo-ple all in port They came out to see the sport,

And their mus-ic played up Yan-kee Doo-dle Dand-y   O.

1   The *Chesapeake* so bold
     Out of Boston as we're told,
     Came to take the British frigate neat and handy O.
     The people all in port
     They came out to see the sport,
     And their music played up Yankee Doodle Dandy O.

2   Before this action it begun
     The Yankees made much fun
     Saying, "We'll tow her up to Boston neat and handy O;
     And after that we'll dine,
     Treat our sweethearts all with wine,
     And we'll dance a jig of Yankee Doodle Dandy O."

3   Our British frigate's name
     All for the purpose came
     In so cooling Yankee's courage neat and handy O,
     Was the *Shannon*, Captain Brookes,

And his crew all hearts of oaks,
And in fighting they were allowed to be the dandy O.

4   The action scarce begun
When they flinchéd from their guns,
They thought they had worked us neat and handy O;
But Brookes he wove his sword,
Saying, "Come, my boys, we'll board,
And we'll stop this playing up Yankee Doodle Dandy O."

5   When Britons heard this word
They all sprang on board;
They hauled down the Yankee's ensign neat and handy O.
Notwithstanding all their brags
The British raised their flags
On the Yankee's mizzen-peak was quite the dandy O.

6   Brookes and all his crew
In courage stout and true
They worked the Yankee frigate neat and handy O.
O may they ever prove
In fighting or in love
That the bold British tars will be the dandy O!

The Last Fierce Charge

Of the spate of cloyingly pathetic ballads that came out of the
Civil War, this is one of the few to last in oral memory. Most
singers specify Fredericksburg or Gettysburg as the scene. The
present text (Eddy, p. 304), with its spare structure and plain
phrasing, differs widely from the usual version, which tends to be
self-consciously literary.

1   'Twas just before the last fierce charge
Two soldiers drew their rein,
With parting words and shaking of the hands,
For they ne'er might meet again.

2   One had blue eyes and curly hair,
Eighteen but a month ago,

While down his cheeks the tears did flow;
  He was only a boy, you know.

3   The other was tall, dark, stern, and proud,
      His hopes in this world were dim,
    For he only thought the more of her
      Who was all this world to him.

4   This dark, tall man was the first to speak,
      Saying, "Charlie, my hour has come;
    Will you promise a little trouble to take
      For me when I am gone?"

5   "If you write home before you go,
      Will you do as much for me?
    I've a mother at home must hear the news,
      Oh, tell her tenderly."

6   Just then the order came for the charge,
      A moment hand touched hand,
    Aye answered aye, and on they ran,
      That brave devoted band.

7   They rode till they came to the crest of the hill,
      Where the rebels with shot and shell
    Poured volleys of death in those toiling ranks,
      And those two soldiers fell.

8   Now who will write to the blue-eyed girl
      What her dying lover said?
    And who will tell the mother at home
      That her only son is dead?

xi: ACCIDENTS
AND DISASTERS

Sir Patrick Spens (Spence) (58)

Percy's "Sir Patrick Spence" in the *Reliques* (I, 72; text A),
"given from two MS. copies transmitted from Scotland," may well
be the finest thing in Scottish balladry. Though the ballad's ex-
cellence hardly needs demonstrating, one cannot resist calling
attention to the powerfully swift transition in stanza 3, the irony
which charges the contrast between the Scottish lords' fastidious-
ness in keeping their cork heels dry and later their hats floating
about on the sea, or the effective repetition of the poignant
stanzas about the waiting ladies.

The chronicles fail to mention Sir Patrick Spens, though his
mission seems to have been the high matter of transporting a
Scottish princess to Norway or a Norwegian princess to Scotland.
A daughter of Alexander III was married to Eric, King of Norway, in 1281. The courtiers who accompanied the new queen to
Norway in August of that year were drowned on the return
voyage. Text B (from Jamieson, I, 57) fits these circumstances
tightly. Scott's *Minstrelsy* has Sir Patrick's commission read:

> "To Noroway, to Noroway,
> To Noroway o'er the faem;
> The king's daughter of Noroway,
> 'Tis thou maun bring her hame . . ."

which might refer to Margaret of Norway, shipwrecked off the
Scottish coast in 1290. No convincing historical parallel has been
found for a shipwreck in the early leagues of an outbound voyage, the situation in text A.

Rimbault, p. 47, supplies the fine tune that goes with Percy's
version.

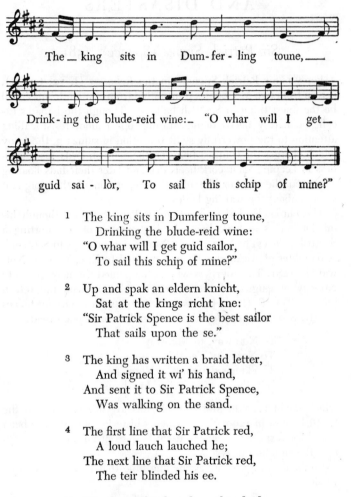

The — king   sits   in   Dum-fer - ling   toune, —

Drink - ing the blude-reid wine:— "O whar   will I   get—

guid sai - lòr,   To   sail   this   schip   of mine?"

1   The king sits in Dumferling toune,
    Drinking the blude-reid wine:
  "O whar will I get guid sailor,
    To sail this schip of mine?"

2   Up and spak an eldern knicht,
    Sat at the kings richt kne:
  "Sir Patrick Spence is the best sailor
    That sails upon the se."

3   The king has written a braid letter,
    And signed it wi' his hand,
  And sent it to Sir Patrick Spence,
    Was walking on the sand.

4   The first line that Sir Patrick red,
    A loud lauch lauched he;
  The next line that Sir Patrick red,
    The teir blinded his ee.

5   "O wha is this has done this deid,
    This ill deid don to me,

braid, broad, official?

To send me out this time o' the yeir,
    To sail upon the se?!

6 "Mak hast, mak hast, my mirry men all,
    Our guid schip sails the morne:"
  "O say na sae, my master deir,
    For I feir a deadlie storme.

7 "Late late yestreen I saw the new moone,
    Wi' the auld moone in hir arme,
  And I feir, I feir, my deir master,
    That we will cum to harme."

8 O our Scots nobles were richt laith
    To weet their cork-heild schoone;
  Bot lang owre a' the play wer playd,
    Thair hats they swam aboone.

9 O lang, lang, may their ladies sit,
    Wi' thair fans into their hand,
  Or eir they se Sir Patrick Spence
    Cum sailing to the land.

10 O lang, lang, may the ladies stand,
    Wi' thair gold kems in their hair,
  Waiting for their ain deir lords,
    For they'll se thame na mair.

11 Have owre, have owre to Aberdour,
    It's fiftie fadom deip,
  And thair lies guid Sir Patrick Spence,
    Wi' the Scots lords at his feit.

❂◇ B ◇❂

1 The king sits in Dunfermlin town,
    Sae merrily drinkin' the wine:
  "Whare will I get a mariner,
    Will sail this ship o' mine?"

2 Then up bespak a bonny boy,
    Sat just at the king's knee:

"Sir Patrick Spence is the best sea-man,
  That e'er set foot on sea."

3 The king has written a braid letter,
     Seal'd it wi' his ain hand;
   He has sent word to Sir Patrick,
     To come at his command.

4 "O wha is this, or wha is that,
     Has tald the king o' me?
   For I was never a good seaman,
     Nor ever intend to be."

5 They mounted sail on Munenday morn,
     Wi' a' the haste they may,
   And they hae landed in Norraway,
     Upon the Wednesday.

6 They hadna been a month, a month
     In Norraway but three,
   Till lads o Norraway began to say,
     "Ye spend a' our white monie.

7 "Ye spend a' our good kingis goud,
     But and our queenis fee:"
   "Ye lie, ye lie, ye liars loud,
     Sae weel's I hear you lie.

8 "For I brought as much white money
     As will gain my men and me;
   I brought half a fou o' good red goud
     Out o'er the sea with me.

9 "Be't wind or weet, be't snaw or sleet,
     Our ships maun sail the morn:"
   "O ever alack! my master dear,
     I fear a deadly storm.

10 "I saw the new moon late yestreen,
      Wi' the auld moon in her arm;
    And if we gang to sea, master,
      I fear we'll suffer harm."

braid, broad, official? *white monie*, silver.   *fou*, two-bushel measure.

11   They hadna sailed a league on sea,
      A league but barely ane,
    Till anchors brak, and tap-masts lap;
      There came a deadly storm.

12   "Whare will I get a bonny boy
      Will tak thir sails in hand,
    That will gang up to the tap-mast,
      See an he ken dry land?"

13   Laith, laith were our good Scots lords
      To weet their leathern shoon;
    But or the morn at fair day-light,
      Their hats were wat aboon.

14   Mony was the feather bed,
      That flotter'd on the faem,
    And mony was the good Scots lord
      Gaed awa that ne'er cam hame,
    And mony was the fatherless bairn
      That lay at hame greetin.

15   It's forty miles to Aberdeen,
      And fifty fathoms deep;
    And there lyes a' our good Scots lord,
      Wi' Sir Patrick at their feet.

16   The ladies crack't their fingers white,
      The maidens tore their hair,
    A' for the sake o' their true loves,
      For them they ne'er saw mair.

17   Lang, lang may our ladies stand,
      Wi' their fans in their hand,
    Ere they see Sir Patrick and his men
      Come sailing to the land.

lap, leaped.   *flotter,* bobble.   *greet* weep.

Bessy Bell and Mary Gray (201)

Thinking to escape the plague which was raging in Perth in 1645, Bessy Bell and Mary Gray built themselves a hut in an out-of-the-way place some eight miles from the city and retired to it, but to no avail. An English nursery rhyme mentions the two Scottish gentlewomen as cozy housekeepers; the plague, however, is forgotten.

Text: C. K. Sharpe, *Ballad Book*, p. 62.

1   O Bessie Bell and Mary Gray,
    They war twa bonnie lasses;
    They bigget a bower on yon burn brae,
    And theekit it o'er wi' rashes.
    They theekit it o'er wi' rashes green,
    They theekit it o'er wi' heather;
    But the pest cam frae the burrows-town,
    And slew them baith thegither.

2   They thought to lye in Methven kirk yard,
    Amang their noble kin;
    But they maun lye in Stronach haugh,
    To biek forenent the sin.
    And Bessy Bell and Mary Gray,
    They war twa bonnie lasses;
    They bigget a bower on yon burn brae,
    And theekit it o'er wi' rashes.

Springfield Mountain

According to a contemporary record, Timothy Myrick of Springfield Mountain, now Wilbraham, Massachusetts, was "bit

bigget, built. *burn brae,* brookside hill. *theek,* thatch. *burrows-town,* corporate town; thus, large town. *biek,* bask. *forenent,* in, in face of. *sin,* sun.

by a Ratel Snake one August the 7th 1761, and Dyed within about two or three ours, he being twenty two years . . . old and vary near the point of marridge." From this accident has sprung what is probably the oldest ballad in American folk tradition.

Phillips Barry, who exhaustively studied a full complement of "Springfield Mountain" texts assembled from all over the country (*Bulletin,* Nos. 7-12), distinguished four types: two serious groups, in one of which Myrick is the victim's name, in the other, Curtis; and two comic groups, one calling the victim's betrothed Sally, the other, Molly. Each of the four types shows numerous variations besides the difference in names. The serious versions seem to have developed from a broadside elegy written shortly after Myrick's death, though Barry overcautiously dates the source ballad about 1830. Stage comedians of the 1830s and 40s whose stock in trade was "taking off" rustic Yankees—performers like George Spear, "Yankee" Hill, and Judson Hutchinson—are probably responsible for the humorous versions; definitely they popularized the Molly type. As sung on the stage, the final words of lines were prolonged inanely and intoned with a stage-Yankee nasal twang. Some tasteless double meanings as well as exaggeratedly bumpkinish dialogue were also introduced. Strangely enough, these mocking songs were taken back by the folk and have almost succeeded in driving out the serious versions.

The four texts given here represent Barry's four types. The tune, the vulgate air commonly sung with all four types, derives ultimately from a fourteenth-century plain chant.

✥❖ A ❖✥

[The Myrick type; recorded April 30, 1849, at Wilbraham (*Bulletin,* 7:5).]

> 1   On Springfield Mountain there did dwell
> a likely youth 'twas known full well
> Left't Merrick's only Son
> A likely youth near twenty one

> 2   One Friday Morning he did go
> down to the Meadow for to mow

Hee mowed around and he did feel
a poisoning Serpent at his heel

3   When he received this deadly wound
he dropped his Scythe upon the ground
and straight for Home was his intent
calling aloud Still as he went

4   'twas all around his voice was heard
but unto him no friend appeared
they thought he did Some workman call
but Timothy alone must fall

5   At length his careful Father went
to Seek his Son in discontent
and there his only Son he found
Dead as a Stone lay on the ground

6   'twas the Seventh of August year 61
this fatal accident was done
may this a warning be to all
to be prepared when God shall call

7   Who knows but that his blessed feet
are treading the Celestial Street
the brightest Angels bowing round
Jehovah and his golden crown.

❦◇ B ◇❦

[The Curtis type; from *Harper's Magazine* 59 (1879), p. 798
(*Bulletin* 8:6).]

1   On Springfield Mountain there did dwell
A likely youth and known full well—
A likely youth of twenty one,
Leftenant Curts's only son—
    Only son, only son, only son—
    Leftenant Curts's only son.

2   One Monday morning he did go
Down to the meadow for to mow.
He mowed all day. At last he feels

A pison sarpent bite his heels.
Bite his heels, bite his heels, bite his heels—
A pison sarpent bite his heels.

3   He laid his scythe upon the ground—
He laid it down and looked around
To see if nobody he couldn't espy
To carry him home that he might die. . . .

4   He looked around, but looked in vain—
No one was there to ease his pain;
So he made up his mind his time had come,
And laid his head on a cold stun. . . .

5   So this young man gave up the ghost,
And forth to Abraham's bosom did post
Out of the meadow he came to mow,
With nobody by to see him go. . . .

❀◆ C ◆❀

[The Sally type; Vermont, July, 1933 (*Bulletin,* 10:6).]

1   On Springfield Mountain there did dwell,
A lovely youth I knew full well;
Ri tuga nuga nay, ru tuga nuga nay,
Ri tuga nuga nuga nuga, na di O.

2   He took his scythe and off did go,
Down in the meadow for to mow.

3   And as he mowed across the field,
A poisonous serpent bit him on the heel.

4   They bore him to his Sally dear,
Which made him feel so deuced queer.

5   "Why, Johnny dear, why did you go
Down to the meadow for to mow?"

6   "Why, Sally dear, and didn't you know,
'Twas Daddy's grass and it had to be mowed?"

7   At last he died, gave up the ghost,
    To Moses' bosom he did post.

8   Now young and old, a warning take,
    And shun the bite of a rattlesnake.

❀❖ **D** ❖❀

[The Molly type; "The Pesky Sarpent," copyright 1840 by George
Spear (*Bulletin*, 11:13).]

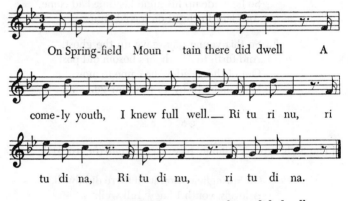

On Spring-field Moun - tain there did dwell   A
come-ly youth,   I knew full well.__ Ri tu ri nu,   ri
tu di na,   Ri tu di nu,   ri tu di na.

1   On Springfield Mountain there did dwell
    A comely youth I knew full well.
    Ri tu ri nu, ri tu di na,
    Ri tu di nu, ri tu di na.

2   One Monday morning he did go
    Down in the meadow for to mow.

3   He scarce had mow-ed half the field,
    When a PESKY SARPENT bit his heel.

4   He took his scythe and with a blow
    He laid the pesky Sarpent low.

5   He took the Sarpent in his hand,
    And straightway went to Molly Bland.

6   Oh Molly, Molly, here you see
     The Pesky Sarpent what bit me.

7   Now Molly had a ruby lip
     With which the pizen she did sip.

8   But Molly had a rotten tooth,
     Which the Pizen struck and kill'd 'em both.

9   The neighbors found that they were dead,
     So laid them both upon one bed.

10   And all their friends both far and near
     Did cry and howl they were so dear.

11   Now all you maids a warning take,
     From Molly Bland and Tommy Blake.

12   And mind when you're in love, don't pass
     Too near to patches of high grass.

The Avondale Mine Disaster

Penny broadsides similar in style to this ballad fluttered in the wake of both minor and major mine disasters. Only a few, however, were taken up into tradition. One of the few is "The Avondale Mine Disaster," a version of which has been collected as far afield as Newfoundland. The ballad follows the facts accurately except for the date—it should be September 6. Avondale is near Wilkes-Barre, Pennsylvania.

Text: Shoemaker, p. 212.

1   Good Christians all, both great and small, I pray you lend
     an ear,
    And listen with attention while the truth I do declare;
    When you hear this lamentation, it will cause you to all turn
     pale—
    All about the suffocation in the mines of Avondale.

2   On the sixteenth day of September, in eighteen sixty-nine,
    Those miners all, they got a call to go work in the mines;

But little did they think of death would gloom their vale
Before they would return again from the mines of Avondale.

3   The women, and the children, too, their hearts were filled
        with joy
    To see their men go work again, and likewise every boy;
    But a dismal sight, in broad daylight, which made them
        soon turn pale,
    When they saw the breakers burning in the mines of Avon-
        dale.

4   From here and there and everywhere they gathered in a
        crowd,
    Some tearing off their clothes and hair, and crying out aloud;
    "Get out our husbands and our sons, for death is going to
        steal
    Their lives away, without delay, in the mines of Avondale!"

5   But all in vain! there was no hope one single soul to save;
    There was no second outlet to this ignominious cave.
    No pen can write the awful fright, and horror did prevail
    Among those dying victims in the mines of Avondale.

6   A consultation then took place; some were asked to volunteer
    For to go down in this dismal shaft to seek their comrades
        dear.
    Two Welshmen brave, without dismay and courage without
        fail,
    Went down the shafts without delay, in the mines of Avon-
        dale.

7   When at the bottom they arrived, and thought to make
        their way,
    One of them died for the want of air, while the other in great
        dismay—
    He gave a sign to lift him up, to tell the fearful tale,
    That all were lost forever in the mines of Avondale.

8   A second effort then took place, to send down some fresh air.
    The next men that went down again, they took of them great
        care.

They traversed then the chambers, and this time did not fail
In finding their dead bodies in the mines of Avondale.

9   Sixty-seven was the number that in one heap were found.
They seemed to be awaiting their sad fate underground.
They found a father with his son clasped in his arms so frail;
There were heart-rending scenes in the mines of Avondale.

10 Now to conclude and make an end, the number to pen
        down,
One hundred and ten of brave, stout men were smothered
        underground.
There in their grave 'till their last day; their widows weep
        and wail,
And oft-rent cries may rend the skies all around through
        Avondale.

Casey Jones

John Luther Jones, nicknamed "Casey" because he was brought
up in Cayce, Kentucky, was killed early in the morning of April
30, 1900, just north of Vaughan, Mississippi, when the Illinois
Central "Cannonball," which he was driving, plowed into the
caboose and rear cars of a freight train. The cars were protruding
onto the main line from a siding. Casey ordered his fireman to
jump a few minutes before the collision; he himself remained at
the throttle, or brakes, of his famous Engine 382.

The thirty-six-year-old engineer would have been forgotten if
it had not been for the hero-worship of a Negro engine wiper in
the roundhouse at Canton, Mississippi, the southern terminus of
Casey's run. Wallis or Wallace or "Wash" Saunders or Sanders—
the name of Casey's admirer is variously recorded—made up a
song about the wreck which, according to the recollection of
other workmen in the Canton railroad shops, was fashioned from
stanzas in current Negro railroad songs. Two vaudeville performers, T. L. Seibert and E. W. Newton, heard Saunders' ballad
and revamped it into a song in a somewhat lighter vein. This
version, copyrighted in 1909, is the "Casey Jones" most generally
sung today. Another vaudeville team, Bert and Frank Leighton,
are probably responsible for the next most popular version of the

ballad, our text B, a ballad distinguished by its praise of rail-roading and its authentic railroad lingo. The Leightons had a brother who was an engineer on Casey's road.

Though Saunders' original "Casey Jones" is now beyond re-covery, its contents can be deduced from Negro versions recorded 1908-30 and from fragments of related railroad songs. A group of such fragments has been assembled here as texts C to G and are separately accredited. The Negro ballad of "Joseph Mica" is also involved in the "Casey Jones" complex. The Negro con-ception of Casey Jones makes him out to be a ladies' man of notorious sexual powers. Probably it was a racy suggestion in Saunders' piece that inspired Siebert to add the lines, ascribed in the song to Mrs. Casey, "Go to bed, children, and hush your cryin', / 'Cause you got another papa on the Salt Lake Line."

For further details about Casey Jones, his wreck, and his ballad, see *Railroad Man's Magazine,* November 1910, May 1918; *Erie Railroad Magazine,* April 1932; F. H. Hubbard, *Railroad Ave-nue,* 1945, pp. 5-23.

Texts: A, sheet-music version, copyright 1909; B, Hubbard, p. 18; C to G, credits with texts.

☙◊ A ◊❧

1   Come, all you rounders, if you want to hear
A story 'bout a brave engineer.
Casey Jones was the rounder's name
On a six-eight wheeler, boys, he won his fame.
The caller called Casey at a half past four,
Kissed his wife at the station door,
Mounted to the cabin with his orders in his hand
And he took his farewell trip to the promised land:
    Casey Jones, mounted to the cabin,
    Casey Jones, with his orders in his hand,
    Casey Jones, mounted to the cabin,
    And he took his farewell trip to the promised land.

2   "Put in your water and shovel in your coal,
Put your head out the window, watch them drivers roll,
I'll run her till she leaves the rail

six-eight wheeler, six truck and eight drive wheels; actually Casey's engine was a ten-wheeler.

'Cause I'm eight hours late with the western mail."
He looked at his watch and his watch was slow,
He looked at the water and the water was low,
He turned to the fireman and then he said,
"We're goin' to reach Frisco but we'll all be dead:"
Casey Jones, goin' to reach Frisco,
Casey Jones, but we'll all be dead,
Casey Jones, goin' to reach Frisco,
"We're goin' to reach Frisco, but we'll all be dead."

3 Casey pulled up that Reno Hill,
He tooted for the crossing with an awful shrill,
The switchman knew by the engine's moan
That the man at the throttle was Casey Jones.
He pulled up within two miles of the place
Number Four stared him right in the face,
He turned to the fireman, said, "Boy, you better jump,
'Cause there's two locomotives that's a-goin' to bump:"
Casey Jones, two locomotives,
Casey Jones, that's a-goin' to bump,
Casey Jones, two locomotives,
"There's two locomotives that's a-goin' to bump."

4 Casey said just before he died,
"There's two more roads that I'd like to ride."
The fireman said what could they be?
"The Southern Pacific and the Santa Fe."
Mrs. Casey sat on her bed a-sighin',
Just received a message that Casey was dyin'.
Said, "Go to bed, children, and hush your cryin',
'Cause you got another papa on the Salt Lake Line:"
Mrs. Casey Jones, got another papa,
Mrs. Casey Jones, on that Salt Lake Line,
Mrs. Casey Jones, got another papa,
"And you've got another papa on the Salt Lake Line."

❧◊ B ◊❧

1 Come all you rounders, I want you to hear
The story told of a brave engineer.
Old Casey Jones was the rounder's name;

On a six-eight wheeler he won his fame.
Caller called Casey at half-past four;
He kissed his wife at the station door,
Climbed into the cab with his order in his hand,
Says, "This is my trip to the Promised Land."

2   Through the South Memphis yards on the fly,
He heard his fireboy say, "You got a white eye."
And all the switchmen knew by the engine's moans
That the man at the throttle was Casey Jones.
It had been raining some five or six weeks;
The railroad track looked like the bed of a creek.
They loaded him down to a thirty-mile gait
And threw the southbound mail about eight hours late.

3   Fireman hollered: "Casey, you're going too fast.
You run the block-board the last station we passed."
Casey says: "Yes, but I think we'll make it through,
For she's steaming better than ever I knew."
Says Casey: "Fireman, don't you fret.
Keep knocking at that firebox; don't you give up yet,
For I'm going to run her till she leaves the rail
Or make it on time with the southbound mail."

4   Around the curve and over the hump,
Two locomotives were bound to bump.
Fireman hollered: "Casey, she's just ahead!
We might jump and make it, but we'll be dead!"
Around the curve he spied a train,
Reversing his engine caused bells to ring.
Fireman jumped off, but Casey stayed on.
He's a good engineer, but he's dead and gone.

5   Poor Casey Jones, he was all right.
He stuck to his duty both day and night.
They loved to hear the whistle and the ring of Number 3,
And he came into Memphis on the old I. C.
Headaches and backaches and all kinds of pain
Are not apart from a railroad train.

six-eight wheeler, six truck and eight drive wheels; actually Casey's
engine was a ten-wheeler. *white eye,* clear signal.

Tales that are earnest, noble and grand
Are all in the life of a railroad man.

❧❖ C ❖❧

[Stanzas said to have been sung by Wallis Sanders. From *American Ballads and Songs*, John A. and Alan Lomax, 1934, p. 38.]

1   On a Sunday mornin' it begins to rain,
    'Round the curve spied a passenger train,
    Under de cab lay po' Casey Jones,
    He's a good engineer, but he's dead an' gone,
    Dead an' gone, dead an' gone,
    Kase he's been on de cholly so long.

2   Casey Jones was a good engineer,
    Tol' his fireman not to have no fear,
    All I want's a lil water an' coal,
    Peep out de cab an' see de drivers roll,
    Oh, see de drivers roll, see de drivers roll,
    Peep out de cab an' see de drivers roll.

3   On a Sunday mornin' it begins to rain,
    'Round de curve come a passenger train,
    Tol' his fireman he'd better jump,
    Kase dose two locomotives is boun' to bump,
    [Boun' to bump, boun' to bump,
    Kase dose two locomotives is boun' to bump.

❧❖ D ❖❧

[From Mississippi, 1908—*JAF*, 26:165.]

1   Casey Jones was a brave engineer;
    Casey looked at the fireman, and the fireman said,
    "What do you care?
    If I keep your boilers red and hot,
    We'll make it to Canton by four o'clock."
      Casey Jones was a brave engineer,
      He died with the throttle in his right hand.
on de cholly, on the bum.

2 All the way by the last board he passed,
   Thirty-five minutes late with the [U.] S. mail.
   Casey Jones said to his fireman,
   "We'll make it to Canton, or leave the rail:
   We are thirty-five minutes late with the [U.] S. mail."

3 Just as he got in a mile of the place,
   He spied number Thirty-five right in his face.
   Said to the fireman, "You'd better jump!
   For these locomotives are bound to bump."

4 When Casey's family heard of his death,
   Casey's daughter fell on her knees,
   "Mamma! mamma! how can it be,
   Papa got killed on the old I. C?"

5 "Hush your mouth, don't draw a breath;
   We'll draw a pension from Casey's death!"

❀◇ E ◇❀

[From Mississippi, 1909—*JAF*, 26:167.]

   Casey Jones was long and tall;
   He pulled the throttle on the cannon-ball;
   Pulled the whistle and gave a squall;
   Said, "I'm going to ride the scoundrel to Niagra Fall."

❀◇ F ◇❀

[From Mississippi, before 1910—*JAF*, 24:352.]

1 Casey Jones was engineer,
   Told his fireman not to fear.
   All he wanted was a boiler hot,
   Run in Canton 'bout four o'clock.

2 One Sunday mornin' it was drizzlin' rain,
   Looked down road an' saw a train.
   Fireman says: "Let's make a jump;
   Two locomotives an' dey bound to bump."

3   Casey Jones, I know him well,
    Told de fireman to ring de bell.
    Fireman jump an' say "Good-bye,
    Casey Jones, you're bound to die."

4   Went on down to de depot track,
    Beggin' my honey to take me back,
    She turn 'roun' some two or three times:
    "Take you back when you learn to grind."

5   Womens in Kansas, all dressed in red,
    Got de news dat Casey was dead.
    De womens in Jackson, all dressed in black,
    Said, in fact, he was a cracker-jack.

["The verse about 'begging his honey' is intended to
give the scene after the wreck, when the fireman, who
did not stay on the engine with Casey, was out of a
job."]

❀◊ G ◊❀

["Kassie Jones," as sung by Furry Lewis on Victor 21664
(1928). Many lines are unintelligible, others are clichés from
songs about "natu'al-bohn eas'men"—pimps. Stanza 7 has
a double meaning. Bessie Smith, the famous blues singer,
elaborated stanza 8 into a sensuous song entitled "J. C. Holmes
Blues."]

1   I woke up this mornin' 'bout four o'clock.
    Mr. Kassie tol' the fireman get his boiler hot.
    Put on your water, put on your coal,
    Put your head out de window, see my drivers roll,
                    See my drivers roll.
    Put your head out de window, see my drivers roll.

2   Lord, some people said Mr. Kassie couldn't run;
    Let me tell you what Mr. Kassie done:
    He left Memphis was a quarter to nine,
    Got into Newport News it was dinnah time,
                    It was dinnah time.
    Got into Newport News it was dinnah time.

*　　*　　*

4 Lord, people said to Kassie, "You runnin' over time.
You got another loser with the 109."
Kassie said, "It ain't in mind
I run any closer 'less I make my time."

5 Said to all the passengers, "Better keep yourself hid,
I'm not going to shake you like Cheney did."

6 Mr. Kassie run his engine into a mile of the place.
No. 4 stabbed him in the face.
The sheriff told Kassie, "Well, you must leave town."
Free to my soul, I'm Alabama bound.

7 Mrs. Kassie said she dreamt a dream
The night she borrowed the sewin' machine.
The needle got broke, she could not sew.
She loved Mr. Kassie 'cause she tol' me so.

8 There was a woman named Miss Alice Fry
Says, "I'm going to ride with Mr. Kassie 'fore I die.
I ain't good-lookin', but I takes my time.
I'm a ramblin' woman with a ramblin' mind . . ."

9 Kassie looked at his water, water was low.
Looked at his watch, watch was slow.
On the road again.
Natu'al-bohn eas'man on the road again.

*　　*　　*

11 Mr. Kassie said before he died,
One more road that he wanted to ride.
People tell Kassie, "Which road?" Said he:
"Southern Pacific and Sankta Fe."

12 This mornin' I heard someone was dyin'.
Mrs. Kassie's children on the doorstep cryin'.
"Mama, mama, I can't keep from cryin'
Papa got killed on the Southern Line.
On the Southern Line.
Papa got killed on the Southern Line."

13   "Mama, mama, how can it be?
     Killed my father in the first degree."
     "Children, children, won't you hold your breath,
     You'll draw another pension from your father's death."
                    On the road again.
     I'm a natu'al-bohn eas'man on the road again.

14   Tuesday mornin' it looked like rain;
     Aroun' the curve came a passenger train.
     Under the bar lay Kassie Jones,
     Good engineer but he's dead and gone.
                    Dead and gone.
                    On the road again . . .

Joseph Mica

No engineer of this name is known.

All three stanzas of this ballad are found in the songs about
Casey Jones. The mention of Jim Jones in stanza 2 is arresting, for
a lost ballad about a certain Jimmie Jones seems to have been the
core of Saunders' "Casey Jones." Casey left Memphis an hour and
a half behind time on his fatal run; he told his fireman he would
make up the time if the boiler was kept hot; he was due at
Canton at four o'clock. The correspondences with stanza 3, however, may be coincidental.

Text: *JAF*, 24:352.

1   Joseph Mica was good engineer,
    Tole his fireman not to fear.
    All he want is water'n coal,
    Poke his head out, see drivers roll.

2   Early one mornin' look like rain,
    'Round de curve come passenger train.
    On powers lie ole Jim Jones,
    Good ole engineer, but daid an' gone.

3   Left Atlanta hour behin',
    Tole his fireman to make up the time.
    All he want is boiler hot,
    Run in there 'bout four o'clock.

The Wreck of the Old 97

The "Old 97" was the Southern Railroad's fast mail between Washington and Atlanta. Engineer Joseph A. Broady had the run between Monroe, Virginia, and Spencer, North Carolina. On Sunday afternoon, September 27, 1903, while running at excessive speed down Stillhouse Trestle, which skirted White Oak Mountain north of Danville, Virginia, the train plunged from the track. The engine landed a hundred feet from the spot the flanges had let go of the rails. Engineer, conductor, firemen, and seven mail clerks were found mangled in the wreckage.

Songs about the wreck had been circulating locally around Spencer and in Virginia for twenty years before one of them suddenly came into prominence when Vernon Dalhart made a recording of it for Victor in 1924. Dalhart's rendition sold five million copies. From 1930-1939, Victor was involved in protracted litigation with one of the many persons who claimed to have written the song. Though the case worked up to the Supreme Court twice, no legal author has yet been established. Dalhart's version resembles our text from North Carolina (Brown, II, 516), with these exceptions: The engineer is called "Pete," not "Steve." Actually Broady's nickname was Steve, an allusion to the daredevil Steve Broadie, then famous for his jump from the Brooklyn Bridge. The association with the daredevil explains "Steve Brooklyn" in our text. Dalhart wrongly gives Broady's destination as Center, and instead of Broady's having "lost his air-brakes," Dalhart says Broady "lost his average," a meaningless phrase at this point. There can be little doubt that the North Carolina version belongs with the pre-Dalhart songs.

In meter and tune, "The Wreck of the Old 97," as the lawyers' briefs noted, is based on Henry C. Work's "The Ship That Never Returned," a tearfully sentimental song of the 1860s. More accurately, the ballad is based not on Work's song but on a parody of it, "The Lover That Never Returned" (see Brown, II, 508), because this parody has the same final stanza as "The Wreck of the Old 97," a stanza which is completely out of place in the railroad song, but suits a ballad of parted lovers neatly.

1   They gave him his orders at Monroe, Virginia,
    Saying, "Steve, you're away behind time.
    This is not Thirty-eight, but it's old Ninety-seven,
    You must put her in Spencer on time.

2   Steve Brooklyn said to his black greasy fireman:
    "Just shovel in a little more coal,
    And when we cross that White Oak Mountain
    You can watch old Ninety-seven roll."

3   It's a mighty rough road from Lynchburg to Danville
    And a line on a three-mile grade.
    It was on this grade that he lost his air-brakes
    And you see what a jump he made.

4   He was going down grade making ninety miles an hour,
    When his whistle began to scream.
    He was found in the wreck with his hand on the throttle,
    And was scalded to death by the steam.

5   Come all you young ladies, you must take warning.
    From this time now and on;
    Never speak harsh words to a loving husband,
    For he may leave you and never return.

The Ballet of the Boll Weevil

Mr. Boll Weevil, deadliest of all cotton pests, emigrated from
Mexico to Texas about 1898. Within a few years his depredations
had demoralized the cotton states. The plantation Negro, who has
always had a great gift for personifying animals and insects,
dramatizes the calamity in a naïve little dialogue. In it one can
often detect the singers' perverse sympathy with the boll weevil,
who persists and multiplies despite the white man's efforts to
eradicate him. Many Negro singers have gone so far as to identify
themselves with the insect in his quest for a home, as shown by
the common concluding stanza (*JAF*, 28:15):

> "If anybody axes you who wuz it writ dis song,
> Tell 'em it wuz a dark-skinned nigger

With a pair of blue duckins on
A-lookin' fur a home,
Jes' a-lookin' fur a home.

Texts: A, Mississippi (Hudson, p. 199); B, Texas, one of the
Negro Folk Songs as Sung by Lead Belly, ed. John A. and Alan
Lomax, 1936, p. 184.

❀◇ A ◇❀

1 First time I saw little Weevil he was on the western plain,
Next time I saw him he was riding a Memphis train.
   He was seeking him a home, a happy home.

2 Next time I saw him he was settin' on a cotton square.
The next time I saw him he had his family there.
   He was seeking him a home, a happy home.

3 Next time I saw him he was runnin' a spinnin' wheel;
The next time I saw him he was ridin' in an automobile.
   He was seeking him a home, a happy home.

4 Mr. Merchant said to the farmer, "Well what do you think
         of that?
If you'll get rid of little Weevil, I'll give you a Stetson hat."
   He's seeking him a home, a happy home.

5 Mr. Farmer took little Weevil and put him in paris green.
"Thank you, Mr. Farmer; it's the best I ever seen.
   I'm going to have a home, a happy home."

6 Then he took little Weevil, put him in a block of ice.
"Thank you, Mr. Farmer; it is so cool and nice.
   I'm going to have a home, a happy home."

7 Mr. Farmer then got angry and sent him up in a balloon.
"Good-by, Mr. Farmer; I'll see you again next June.
   I'll be seeking me a home, a happy home."

8 Little Weevil took Mr. Farmer, throwed him in the sand,
Put on Mr. Farmer's overcoat, stood up like a natural man.
   "I'm going to have a home, a happy home."

9 Little Weevil said to the sharp-shooter, "Better get up on
         your feet.

Look down across the Delta at the cotton we'll have to reap.
We've got us a home, a happy home."

10 Mr. Merchant said to the farmer, "I can not see your route.
Got a mortgage on old Beck and Kate; just as well be taking
   them out.
And bring them home, and bring them home."

11 "Come on, old woman, and we will travel out West.
The weevils et up everything we've got but your old cotton
   dress.
And it's full of holes, it's full of holes."

❀◇ B ◇❀

Talk— a-bout de lates',— De la-tes' of— this song,

Dese de-vil-ish boll wee-vils, Dey gon-na

rob— you of a home,— Dey look-in' for a

home, Dey look-in' for a home.___

I'll have a home,— I'll have a home,—

I'll have a home,— I'll have— a home.—

1   Talk about de lates', de lates' of this song,
    Dese devilish boll weevils, dey gonna rob you of a home—
    Dey lookin' for a home, dey lookin' for a home.

2   The first time I seed him, he was settin' on de square,
    The nex' time I seed him, he was spreadin' ev'ywhere—
    He was lookin' for a home, he was lookin' for a home.

3   Farmer taken the boll weevil, put him in de san',
    Boll weevil said to de farmer, "Dis is treatin' me like a
        man—
    I have a home, I have a home."

4   Farmer taken the boll weevil, put him in de ice,
    Boll weevil said to de farmer, "This is treatin' me mighty
        nice—
    I'll have a home, I'll have a home."

5   The farmer an' his ol' lady went out 'cross de fiel'.
    The farmer said to de ol' lady: "I found a lotta meat an'
        meal—
    I'll have a home . . ." [Four times]

6   Ol' lady said to de ol' man: "I'm tryin' my level bes',
    To keep dese devilish boll weevils outa my ol' cotton dress—
    It's full of holes . . ." [Four times]

7   Farmer said to de ol' lady: "What do you think of that?
    I got some devilish boll weevils in my ol' Stetson hat—
    It's full of holes . . ." [Four times]

8   Farmer tol' de merchant, "I didn't make but one bale,
    Before I let you have that one, I'll suffer an' die in jail—
    I'll have a home, I'll have a home,
    I'll have a home, I'll have a home."

The Titanic

The White Star liner *Titanic* sank with a loss of 1513 lives the
night of April 14-15, 1912. Southern balladeers immediately
clapped the news into broadsides, one of them dated April 13!
(see Brown, II, 662). Text A (White, p. 347) probably goes back
to just such a tinted broadsheet, vended regularly in Negro
districts before World War I for five cents. It has been reported
from tradition in places as far apart as Alabama, Michigan, and
Texas. The first of the fragments of a Negro song collected here
as text B was reported from Mississippi in 1909 and taunts a
steamboat captain for neglect of duty; the second adapts this
rhyme to the *Titanic* (White, 348).

❦ A ❦

1   It was on one Monday morning just about one o'clock
When that great *Titanic* began to reel and rock;
People began to scream and cry,
Saying, "Lord, am I going to die?"
   It was sad when that great ship went down,
   It was sad when that great ship went down,
   Husbands and wives and little children lost their lives,
   It was sad when that great ship went down.

2   When that ship left England it was making for the shore,
The rich had declared that they would not ride with the
     poor,
So they put the poor below,
They were the first to go.

3   While they were building they said what they would do,
We will build a ship that water can't go through;
But God with power in hand
Showed the world that it could not stand.

4   Those people on that ship were a long ways from home,
With friends all around they didn't know that the time had
     come;

Death came riding by,
Sixteen hundred had to die.

5   While Paul was sailing his men around,
    God told him that not a man should drown;
    If you trust me and obey,
    I will save you all to-day.

6   You know it must have been awful with those people on the
        sea,
    They say that they were singing, "Nearer My God to Thee."
    While some were homeward bound,
    Sixteen hundred had to drown.

❀◊ B ◊❀

O where were you when the steamer went down, Captain?
    [*Three times*]
I was with my honey in the heart of town.

❀   ❀   ❀

Oh! where was you when de old *Titanic* went down?
    [*Three times*]
I was on de back of er mule singing "Alabama Bound."

XII: OUTLAWS, PIRATES, BADMEN, AND HEROES

ROBIN HOOD

"Rymes of Robyn Hood" are mentioned as common commodities in the long, didactic poem *Piers Plowman* of 1377, and in the next century several chroniclers, both Scottish and English, also allude to the popularity of the ballads about Robin Hood and his merry men. None of the early chroniclers has anything to say about the outlaw as a historical person, but their silence has been more than made up for by the antiquaries who have since gone into the question. German scholars would have Robin a debased manifestation of the god Woden, or at least a Teutonic woodsprite. In *Ivanhoe*, Scott casts Robin Hood (his Locksley) as the leader of Saxon guerrillas still holding out against the Norman regime. Diligent searches in ancient manorial rolls and court records have unearthed a number of Robin Hoods of the 1100s, 1200s, and 1300s, several of them plausible prospects for the outlaw who relieved feudal oppression by robbing high churchmen and noblemen, but the biography of such a man, even if it could be reconstructed, would be pale stuff beside the exploits of the legendary character.

The crime that sent Robin into outlawry we never learn. Once in the greenwood, he gathers his trusty band and passes the time in archery contests, interrupting the sport now and then to rob a passing churchman of his fat revenues or to chase the king's deer. For though Robin protests he is the king's most loyal subject, his respect does not extend to the game laws or to the king's officers, one of whom, the Sheriff of Nottingham, is his chief enemy. Similarly, monks and bishops are Robin's victims even though he is profoundly religious, especially in his devotion to the Virgin. In the later ballads he is somewhat more humorous and prankish than he is in the medieval pieces, but even the earliest ballads make him out to be a genial soul for all his brawling and slaughtering, and his courteous manner as a robber has made him the model for all courtly highwaymen since his day. The main recipients of his loot were the peasants who lived on the fringe of

Barnesdale in Yorkshire and Sherwood Forest, Robin's favorite haunts; and they in turn, whatever the risk, would hide the outlaw and his band from pursuers. In the earliest state of the legend, Robin Hood's intimates were the giant Little John and the diminutive Much. Will Scathelock or Scarlet and Will Stately or Stutly are latecomers; even later are Friar Tuck and Maid Marian.

Stylistically the Robin Hood ballads are in a class by themselves. The older ballads like "Robin Hood and the Monk," though based on traditional song, seem to have been composed and recited not by folk singers but by professional minstrels, mostly minstrels catering to the yeomanry, the small independent landowners. Too ambitious and lengthy for folk compositions, the ballads often develop two strands of narrative concurrently, the narrator shuttling back and forth between them. In folk ballads the setting is unimportant; the Robin Hood pieces dwell lovingly on the forest scenery and the atmosphere thus created is essential to their charm. And everywhere the minstrel intrudes into the story. Several of the ballads open with his request for attention. He announces his subject—no surprises here. Every once in a while, especially when the minstrel is becoming fabulous—or needs a line of padding—he will protest his truthfulness: "For sooth, as I yow say," "Sertenly withouten layn." When he moves from one scene to another, the reciter is careful to warn the hearers of the fact:

> Let us leave talking of Little John,
>   For hee is bound fast to a tree,
> And talke of Guy and Robin Hood,
>   In the green woode where they bee.

He concludes conventionally with a pious wish for the audience:

> God that is euer a crowned kyng,
>   Bryng vs all to his blisse!

When the minstrels passed from the scene, Robin Hood was taken up by the broadside poets. Most of the Robin Hood ballads since 1600 are their work. Because national heroes are not exportable, English Robin Hood is little sung about in Scotland, Ireland, or America; for that matter, surprisingly few Robin Hood ballads have survived even in English tradition. Those which have, like the American and Scottish folk examples, are clearly only one or two removes from some mediocre broadside print, for tradition has worked very slight changes upon them.

Robin Hood and the Monk (119)

Despite the danger, pious Robin feels compelled to hear Mass in Nottingham. Along the way he has a quarrel with his sole companion, Little John, who returns to the forest. A monk in the church recognizes Robin and slips out to inform the sheriff. Robin makes a heroic stand when set upon, but he is captured. Somehow the sad news reaches the merry men. Little John and Much chance upon the monk, who is carrying letters about the outlaw's capture to the king. The outlaws murder the monk and his page and take over the mission. Their news is generously rewarded by the king, who sends back letters under the privy seal ordering that Robin be brought to him. Arriving in Nottingham, the false messengers are feted by the sheriff. When the sheriff goes off drunk to bed, Little John kills the porter and frees Robin Hood. While Robin Hood and his lieutenant are renewing their pledges of friendship at a forest banquet, the sheriff cringes in anticipation of the king's rage. The king, however, is more amused than angry at Little John's trick.

Preserved in a MS. of about 1450, "Robin Hood and the Monk" is perhaps the best rounded of the early Robin Hood ballads, showing consummate narrative skill in spite of two or three damaged passages. The reconciliation of Little John and Robin toward the end neatly balances the quarrel episode near the beginning, while the epilogue at the king's court has the effect of tucking in all the loose ends. Especially fine is the scene that ends in the monk's death. There is well-managed irony in Little John's conversation with the porter on the walls and good sense in the reasons that Little John gives to the king and later to the sheriff for the monk's disappearance. The music and purposive alliteration in the early stanzas are the more obvious of the many subtle metrical and rhetorical effects to be found in the poem.

The present text is based upon W. W. Skeat's transcript of

MS. Ff. 5/48 in the Cambridge University Library, with many emendations adopted from Child, III, 97. It is obviously minstrel work.

Hints for easier reading:
"v" and "u" are interchanged.
the, the (article), thee, that.
hem, them.
her, their.
hit, it.
can, did (e.g., *can say,* did say).

1   In somer, when the shawes be sheyne,
         And leves be large and long,
     Hit is full mery in feyre foreste
         To here the foulys song:

2   To se the dere draw to the dale,
         And leve the hilles hee,
     And shadow hem in the levës grene,
         Vnder the grene-wode tre.

3   Hit befel on Whitsontide,
         Erly in a May morning,
     The son vp feyre can shyne,
         And the birddis mery can syng.

4   "This is a mery mornyng," seid Litull John,
         "Be hym that dyed on tre;
     A more mery man then I am one
         Lyves not in Cristiantë.

5   "Pluk vp thi hert, my dere mayster,"
         Litull John can sey,
     "And thynk hit is a full fayre tyme
         In a mornyng of May."

6   "Ye[a], on thyng greves me," seid Robyn,
         "And does my hert mych woo;

shaw, wood, thicket.   *sheyne,* beautiful.   *foulys,* birds.   *hee,* high.
on tre, on the cross.

That I may not no solem day
  To mas nor matyns goo.

7 "Hit is a fourtnet and more," seid he,
  "Syn I my sauyour see;
To-day wil I to Notyngham," seid Robyn,
  "With the myght of mylde Marye."

8 Than spake Moche, the mylner sun,
  Euer more wel hym betyde!
"Take twelue of thi wyght yemen,
  Well weppynd, be thi side.
Such on wolde thi selfe slon,
  That twelue dar not abyde."

9 "Of all my mery men," seid Robyn,
  "Be my feith I wil non haue,
But Litull John shall beyre my bow,
  Til that me list to drawe."

10 "Thou shall beyre thin own," seid Litull Jon,
  "Maister, and I wyl beyre myne,
And we well shete a peny," seid Litull Jon,
  "Vnder the grene-wode lyne."

11 "I wil not shete a peny," seyd Robyn Hode,
  "In feith, Litull John, with the,
But euer for on as thou shetis," seide Robyn,
  "In feith I holde the thre."

12 Thus shet thei forth, these yemen too,
  Bothe at buske and brome,
Til Litull John wan of his maister
  Fiue shillings to hose and shone.

13 A ferly strife fel them betwene,
  As they went bi the way;
Litull John seid he had won fiue shillings,
  And Robyn Hode seid schortly nay.

---

mylner, miller. *wyght,* sturdy. *slon,* slay. *me list,* I choose. *lyne,* linden. *holde,* wager. *buske,* brush. *brome,* broom. *shone,* shoes. *ferly,* unusual.

14   With that Robyn Hode lyed Litul Jon,
     And smote hym with his hande;
  Litul Jon waxed wroth therwith,
     And pulled out his bright bronde.

15   "Were thou not my maister," sed Litull John,
     "Thou shuldis by hit ful sore;
  Get the a man wher thou w[ilt],
     For thou getis me no more."

16   Then Robyn goes to Notyngham,
     Hym selfe mornyng allone,
  And Litull John to mery Scherwode,
     The pathes he knew ilkone.

17   Whan Robyn came to Notyngham,
     Sertenly withouten layn,
  He prayed to God and myld Mary
     To bryng hym out saue agayn.

18   He gos in to Seynt Mary chirch,
     And kneled down before the rode;
  Alle that euer were the church within
     Beheld wel Robyn Hode.

19   Beside hym stod a gret-hedid munke,
     I pray to God woo he be!
  Fful sone he knew gode Robyn,
     As sone as he hym se.

20   Out at the durre he ran,
     Fful sone and anon;
  Alle the yatis of Notyngham
     He made to be sparred euerychon.

21   "Rise vp," he seid, "thou prowde schereff,
     Buske the and make the bowne;
  I haue spyed the kynggis felon,
     Ffor sothe he is in this town."

---

lye, to call a liar.   *bronde*, sword.   *by*, pay for.   *ilkone*, each one.
layn, lie.   *rode*, crucifix.   *yate*, gate.   *spar*, shut.   *buske and bowne*, make ready.

22 "I haue spyed the false felon,
   As he stondis at his masse;
  Hit is long of the," seid the munke,
   "And euer he fro vs passe.

23 "This traytur name is Robyn Hode,
   Vnder the grene-wode lynde;
  He robbyt me onys of a hundred pound,
   Hit shalle neuer out of my mynde."

24 Vp then rose this prowde shereff,
   And radly made him yare;
  Many was the moder son
   To the kyrk with hym can fare.

25 In at the durres thei throly thrast,
   With staves ful gode wone;
  "Alas, alas!" seid Robyn Hode,
   "Now misse I Litull John."

26 But Robyn toke out a too-hond sworde,
   That hangit down be his kne;
  Ther as the schereff and his men stode thyckust,
   Thedurwarde wolde he.

27 Thryes thorowout them he ran then,
   For sothe as I yow sey,
  And woundyt mony a moder son,
   And twelue he slew that day.

28 His sworde vpon the schireff hed
   Sertanly he brake in too;
  "The smyth that the made," seid Robyn,
   "I pray to God wyrke hym woo!

29 "Ffor now am I weppynlesse," seid Robyn,
   "Alasse! agayn my wylle;
  But if I may fle these traytors fro,
   I wot thei wil me kyll."

---

long of the, thy fault. *lynde,* linden. *onys,* once. *radly,* quickly.
yare, ready. *throly,* strenuously. *thrast,* pressed. *wone,* number.
wot, know.

30   Robyn in to the churchë ran,
         Throout hem euerilkon,

          .   .   .   .   .

              .   .   .   .   .

[*Robin's men learn of his capture.*]

31   Sum fel in swonyng as thei were dede,
         And lay stil as any stone;
      Non of theym were in her mynde
         But only Litull Jon.

32   "Let be your rule," seid Litull Jon,
         "Ffor his luf that dyed on tre,
      Ye that shulde be dughty men;
         Het is gret shame to se.

33   "Oure maister has bene hard bystode
         And yet scapyd away;
      Pluk vp your hertis, and leve this mone,
         And harkyn what I shal say.

34   "He has seruyd Oure Lady many a day,
         And yet wil, securly;
      Therfor I trust in hir specialy
         No wyckud deth shal he dye.

35   "Therfor be glad," seid Litul John,
         "And let this mournyng be;
      And I shal be the munkis gyde,
         With the myght of mylde Mary.

36   .   .   .   .   .   .
         "We will go but we too;
      And I mete hym," seid Litul John,

              .   .   .   .   .   .

37   "Loke that ye kepe wel owre tristil-tre,
         Vnder the levys smale,

euerilkon, each one. *rule,* wailing. *bystode,* pressed. *securly,*
surely. *tristil-tre,* rendezvous tree.

And spare non of this venyson,
    That gose in thys vale."

38 Fforthe then went these yemen too,
    Litul John and Moche on fere,
And lokid on Moch emys hows,
    The hye way lay full nere.

39 Litul John stode at a wyndow in the mornyng,
    And lokid forth at a stage;
He was war wher the munke came ridyng,
    And with hym a litul page.

40 "Be my feith," seid Litul John to Moch,
    "I can the tel tithyngus gode;
I se wher the munke cumys rydyng,
    I know hym be his wyde hode."

41 They went in to the way, these yemen bothe,
    As curtes men and hende;
Thei spyrred tithyngus at the munke,
    As they hade bene his frende.

42 "Ffro whens come ye?" seid Litull Jon,
    "Tel vs tithyngus, I yow pray,
Off a false owtlay, [callid Robyn Hode,]
    Was takyn yisterday.

43 "He robbyt me and my felowes bothe
    Of twenti marke in serten;
If that false owtlay be takyn,
    Ffor sothe we wolde be fayn."

44 "So did he me," seid the munke,
    "Of a hundred pound and more;
I layde furst hande hym apon,
    Ye may thonke me therfore."

45 "I pray God thanke you," seid Litull John,
    "And we wil when we may;

emys hows, uncle's house. *at a stage,* from a high story. *tithyngus,*
tidings. *hende,* kindly. *spyrr,* ask.

We wil go with you, with your leve,
  And bryng yow on your way.

46 "Ffor Robyn Hode hase many a wilde felow,
      I tell you in certen;
    If thei wist ye rode this way,
      In feith ye shulde be slayn."

47 As thei went talking be the way,
      The munke and Litull John,
    John toke the munkis horse be the hede,
      Fful sone and anon.

48 Johne toke the munkis horse be the hed,
      Ffor sothe as I yow say;
    So did Much the litull page,
      Ffor he sulde not scape away.

49 Be the golett of the hode
      John pulled the munke down;
    John was nothyng of hym agast,
      He lete hym falle on his crown.

50 Litull John was so[re] agreyvd,
      And drew out his swerde in hye;
    This munke saw he shulde be ded,
      Lowd mercy can he crye.

51 "He was my maister," seid Litull John,
      "That thou hase browght in bale;
    Shalle thou neuer cum at our kyng,
      Ffor to telle hym tale."

52 John smote of the munkis hed,
      No longer wolde he dwell;
    So did Moch the litull page,
      Ffor ferd lest he wolde tell.

53 Ther thei beryed hem bothe,
      In nouther mosse nor lyng,
    And Litull John and Much infere
      Bare the letturs to oure kyng.

golett, gullet. *agast,* alarmed. *hye,* haste. *lyng,* grass. *infere,*
together.

54 . . . . .

  He knelid down vpon his kne:
  "God yow saue, my lege lorde,
   Ihesus yow saue and se!

55 "God yow saue, my lege kyng!"
  To speke John was full bolde;
  He gaf hym the letturs in his hond,
   The kyng did hit vnfold.

56 The kyng red the letturs anon,
  And seid, "So mot I the,
  Ther was neuer yoman in mery Inglond
   I longut so sore to se.

57 "Wher is the munke that these shuld haue brouyt?"
  Oure kyng can say:
  "Be my trouth," seid Litull John,
   "He dyed after the way."

58 The kyng gaf Moch and Litul Jon
  Twenti pound in sertan,
  And made theim yemen of the crown,
   And bade theim go agayn.

59 He gaf John the seel in hand,
  The sheref for to bere,
  To bryng Robyn hym to,
   And no man do hym dere.

60 John toke his leve at oure kyng,
  The sothe as I yow say;
  The next way to Notyngham
   To take, he yede the way.

61 Whan John came to Notyngham
  The yatis were sparred ychon;
  John callid vp the porter,
   He answerid sone anon.

62 "What is the cause," seid Litul Jon,
  "Thou sparris the yates so fast?"

so mot I the, so may I thrive. *dere,* harm. *next,* nearest. *yede,*
went. *yatis,* gates. *spar.* shut.

"Because of Robyn Hode," seid [the] porter,
    "In depe prison is cast.

63 "John and Moch and Wyll Scathlok,
    Ffor sothe as I yow say,
Thei slew oure men vpon our wallis,
    And sawten vs euery day."

64 Litull John spyrred after the schereff,
    And sone he hym fonde;
He oppyned the kyngus priue seell,
    And gaf hym in his honde.

65 Whan the scheref saw the kyngus seell,
    He did of his hode anon;
"Where is the munke that bare the letturs?"
    He seid to Litull John.

66 "He is so fayn of hym," seid Litul John,
    "Ffor sothe as I yow say,
He has made hym abot of Westmynster,
    A lorde of that abbay."

67 The scheref made John gode chere,
    And gaf hym wyne of the best;
At nyght thei went to her bedde,
    And euery man to his rest.

68 When the scheref was on slepe,
    Dronken of wyne and ale,
Litul John and Moch for sothe,
    Toke the way vnto the jale.

69 Litul John callid vp the jayler,
    And bade hym rise anon;
He seyd Robyn Hode had brokyn prison,
    And out of hit was gon.

70 The porter rose anon sertan,
    As sone as he herd John calle;
Litul John was redy with a swerd,
    And bare hym to the walle.

sawten, assault. *did of,* doffed.

71 "Now wil I be porter," seid Litul John,
        "And take the keyes in honde:"
    He toke the way to Robyn Hode,
        And sone he hym unbonde.

72 He gaf hym a gode swerd in his hond,
        His hed [ther]with for to kepe,
    And ther as the walle was lowyst
        Anon down can thei lepe.

73 Be that the cok began to crow,
        The day began to spryng;
    The scheref fond the jaylier ded,
        The comyn bell made he ryng.

74 He made a crye thoroout al the tow[n],
        Wheder he be yoman or knave,
    That cowthe bryng hym Robyn Hode,
        His warison he shuld haue.

75 "Ffor I dar neuer," said the scheref,
        "Cum before oure kyng;
    Ffor if I do, I wot serten
        Ffor sothe he wil me heng."

76 The scheref made to seke Notyngham,
        Bothe be strete and stye,
    And Robyn was in mery Scherwode,
        As light as lef on lynde.

77 Then bespake gode Litull John,
        To Robyn Hode can he say,
    "I haue done the a gode turne for an euyll,
        Quyte the whan thou may.

78 "I haue done the a gode turne," seid Litull John,
        "Ffor sothe as I yow say;
    I haue brought the vnder grene-wode lyne;
        Ffare wel, and haue gode day."

79 "Nay, be my trouth," seid Robyn Hode,
        "So shall hit neuer be;

cowthe, could.   *warison,* reward.   *quyte,* repay.

I make the maister," seid Robyn Hode,
   "Off alle my men and me."

80 "Nay, be my trouth," seid Litull John,
    "So shalle hit neuer be;
  But lat me be a felow," seid Litull John,
    "No noder kepe I be."

81 Thus John gate Robyn Hod out of prison,
    Sertan withoutyn layn;
  Whan his men saw hym hol and sounde,
    Ffor sothe they were full fayne.

82 They filled in wyne and made hem glad,
    Vnder the levys smale,
  And yete pastes of venyson,
    That gode was with ale.

83 Than worde came to oure kyng
    How Robyn Hode was gon,
  And how the scheref of Notyngham
    Durst neuer loke hym vpon.

84 Then bespake oure cumly kyng,
    In an angur hye:
  "Litull John hase begyled the schereff,
    In faith so hase he me.

85 "Litul John has begyled vs bothe,
    And that full wel I se;
  Or ellis the schereff of Notyngham
    Hye hongust shulde he be.

86 "I made hem yemen of the crowne,
    And gaf hem fee with my hond;
  I gaf hem grith," seid oure knyg,
    "Thorowout all mery Inglond.

87 "I gaf theym grith," then seid oure kyng;
    "I say, so mot I the,
  Ffor sothe soch a yemen as he is on
    In all Inglond ar not thre.

kepe, care. *yete,* ate. *grith,* pardon.

88   "He is trew to his maister," seid our kyng;
        "I sey, be swete Seynt John,
    He louys better Robyn Hode
        Then he dose vs ychon.

89   "Robyn Hode is euer bond to hym,
        Bothe in strete and stalle;
    Speke no more of this matter," seid oure kyng,
        "But John has begyled vs alle."

90   Thus endys the talkyng of the munke
        And Robyn Hode i-wysse;
    God, that is euer a crowned kyng,
        Bryng vs all to his blisse!

Robin Hood and Little John (125)

No less than a dozen of the Robin Hood ballads are based on
the formula "Robin Hood meets a stranger; the stranger fights
Robin and beats him; Robin calls 'Hold,' summons his men,
invites the stranger to join his band." Admirers may find it an-
noying to have Robin Hood continually being defeated in these
encounters, but perhaps the generous hero is merely flattering
a man whom he has already sized up as a likely prospect. The
present text was learned from Kentucky tradition (*American
Speech*, II, 75), but it follows the eighteenth-century English
broadside copies closely, though briefer and with a few corrup-
tions and a few improvements. Note the internal rhyme in the
third line of each stanza.

1   When Robin Hood was about eighteen years old
        He chancéd to meet Little John,
    A jolly brisk blade just fit for his trade
        For he was a sturdy young man.

2   Altho he was little his limbs they were large,
        His stature was seven feet high.

i-wysse, to be sure.

Wherever he came, he soon quickened his name
And presently caused them to fly.

3 One day these two met on a long narrow bridge,
And neither of them would give way,
When Robin stepped up to the stranger and said,
"I'll show you brave Nottingham play."

4 "You speak like a coward," the stranger he said,
"As there with your long-bow you stand;
I vow and protest you may shoot at my breast
While I have but a staff in my hand."

5 "The name of a coward," said Robin, "I scorn,
And so my long-bow I lay by
And then for your sake a staff I will take
The strength of your manhood to try."

6 Then Robin he stepped out into a grove
And pulled up a staff of green oak,
And this being done straight back he did come,
And thus to the stranger he spoke:

7 "Behold thou my staff, it is lusty and tough,
On this long narrow bridge let us play;
Then he who falls in, the other shall win
The battle and then we'll away."

8 Then Robin hit the stranger a crack on the crown
That caused the blood to appear
And thus so enraged they more closely engaged
And laid on the blows most severe.

9 The stranger gave Robin a crack on the crown
That was a most terrible stroke,
The very next blow laid Robin below
And tumbled him into the brook.

10 "Oh where are you now?" the stranger he cried;
With a hearty laugh in reply,
"Oh, faith, in the flood," quoth bold Robin Hood,
"And floating away with the tide."

11   Then Robin he waded all out of the deep
         And pulled himself up by a thorn,
      Then just at the last he blew a loud blast
         So merrily on his bugle horn.

12   The hills they did echo, the valley did ring
         Which caused his gay men to appear,
      All dressed in green most fair to be seen
         Straight up to the master they steer.

13   "What aileth thee, master?" quoth William Stutely,
         "You seem to be wet to the skin."
      "No matter," quoth he, "This villain you see
         In fighting hath tumbled me in."

14   "We'll pluck out his eyes and duck him likewise,"
         Then seized they the stranger right there,
      "Nay, let him go free," quoth bold Robin Hood,
         "For he's a brave fellow. Forbear!

15   "Cheer up jolly blade and don't be afraid
         Of all these gay men that you see,
      There are four-score and nine and if you will be mine
         You may wear of my own liverie."

16   A brace of fat deer was quickly brought in,
         Good ale and strong liquor likewise.
      The feast was so good, all in the greenwood
         Where this jolly babe was baptised.

Robin Hood Rescuing Three Squires (140)

   The rescue of the three poaching squires by a disguised Robin
Hood is one of a score of adventures in which Robin cheats the
noose of one or more guiltless victims. Scottish and American
traditional offshoots of this broadside have been recorded, but
they are poor specimens.
   Text: *English Archer*, York, about 1790, p. 65.

1   There are twelve months in all the year,
      As I hear many men say,
    But the merriest month in all the year
      Is the merry month of May.

2   Now Robin Hood is to Nottingham gone,
      With a link a down and a day,
    And there he met a silly old woman,
      Was weeping on the way.

3   "What news? what news, thou silly old woman?
      What news hast thou for me?"
    Said she, "There's three squires in Nottingham town
      To-day is condemned to die."

4   "O have they parishes burnt?" he said,
      "Or have they ministers slain?
    Or have they robbed any virgin,
      Or with other men's wives have lain?"

5   "They have no parishes burnt, good sir,
      Nor yet have ministers slain,
    Nor have they robbed any virgin,
      Nor with other men's wives have lain."

6   "O what have they done?" said bold Robin Hood,
      "I pray thee tell to me:"
    "It's for slaying of the king's fallow deer,
      Bearing their long bows with thee."

7   "Dost thou not mind, old woman," he said,
      "Since thou made me sup and dine?
    By the truth of my body," quoth bold Robin Hood,
      "You could not tell it in better time."

8   Now Robin Hood is to Nottingham gone,
      With a link a down and a day,
    And there he met with a silly old palmer,
      Was walking along the highway.

9   "What news? what news, thou silly old man?
      What news, I do thee pray?"
    Said he, "Three squires in Nottingham town
      Are condemned to die this day."

10   "Come change thy apparel with me, old man,
     Come change thy apparel for mine;
  Here is forty shillings in good silver,
     Go drink it in beer or wine."

11   'O thine apparel is good," he said,
     "And mine is ragged and torn;
  Whereever you go, whereever you ride,
     Laugh ne'er an old man to scorn."

12   "Come change thy apparel with me, old churl,
     Come change thy apparel with mine;
  Here are twenty pieces of good broad gold,
     Go feast thy brethren with wine."

13   Then he put on the old man's hat,
     It stood full high on the crown:
  "The first bold bargain that I come at,
     It shall make thee come down."

14   Then he put on the old man's cloak,
     Was patch'd black, blew, and red;
  He thought no shame all the day long
     To wear the bags of bread.

15   Then he put on the old man's breeks,
     Was patch'd from ballup to side;
  "By the truth of my body," bold Robin can say,
     "This man lov'd little pride."

16   Then he put on the old man's hose,
     Were patch'd from knee to wrist;
  "By the truth of my body," said bold Robin Hood,
     "I'd laugh if I had any list."

17   Then he put on the old man's shoes,
     Were patch'd both beneath and aboon;
  Then Robin Hood swore a solemn oath,
     "It's good habit that makes a man."

18   Now Robin Hood is to Nottingham gone,
     With a link a down and a down,

breeks, breeches.   *ballup,* front, fly.   *list,* desire.

And there he met with the proud sheriff,
    Was walking along the town.

19 "O save, O save, O sheriff," he said,
    "O save, and you may see!
  And what will you give to a silly old man
    To-day will your hangman be?"

20 "Some suits, some suits," the sheriff he said,
    "Some suits I'll give to thee;
  Some suits, some suits, and pence thirteen
    To-day's a hangman's fee."

21 Then Robin he turns him round about,
    And jumps from stock to stone;
  "By the truth of my body," the sheriff he said,
    "That's well jumpt, thou nimble old man."

22 "I was ne'er a hangman in all my life,
    Nor yet intends to trade;
  But curst be he," said bold Robin,
    "That first a hangman was made.

23 "I've a bag for meal, and a bag for malt,
    And a bag for barley and corn;
  A bag for bread, and a bag for beef,
    And a bag for my little small horn.

24 "I have a horn in my pocket,
    I got it from Robin Hood,
  And still when I set it to my mouth,
    For thee it blows little good."

25 "O wind thy horn, thou proud fellow,
    Of thee I have no doubt;
  I wish that thou give such a blast
    Till both thy eyes fall out."

26 The first loud blast that he did blow,
    He blew both loud and shrill;
  A hundred and fifty of Robin Hood's men
    Came riding over the hill.

27 The next loud blast that he did give,
   He blew both loud and amain,
   And quickly sixty of Robin Hood's men
   Came shining over the plain.

28 "O who are you," the sheriff he said,
   "Come tripping over the lee?"
   "They're my attendants," brave Robin did say,
   "They'll pay a visit to thee."

29 They took the gallows from the slack,
   They set it in the glen,
   They hang'd the proud sheriff on that,
   Releas'd their own three men.

Robin Hood's Death (120)

Feverish and overcome by sickness, Robin Hood hastens to Kirklees Priory to be bled by his cousin, an inmate of the place. The nun (or prioress) has arranged with the villainous Sir Roger of Doncaster to do away with her kinsman if he should ever come into her power. She does not let the opportunity pass her by. Our version of the ballad (*English Archer*, Paisley, 1786, via Child, III, 106) concludes with the fake epitaph supposed to have been set over Robin's grave, but since Ritson, it has been customary to ignore this addition.

1 When Robin Hood and Little John
   Down a down a down a down
   Went oer yon bank of broom,
      Said Robin Hood bold to Little John,
      "We have shot for many a pound.
      Hey, etc.

2 "But I am not able to shoot one shot more,
      My broad arrows will not flee;
   But I have a cousin lives down below,
      Please God, she will bleed me."

slack, low ground.

3 Now Robin he is to fair Kirkly gone,
  As fast as he can win;
 But before he came there, as we do hear,
  He was taken very ill.

4 And when he came to fair Kirkly Hall,
  He knock'd all at the ring,
 But none was so ready as his cousin herself
  For to let bold Robin in.

5 "Will you please to sit down, cousin Robin," she said,
  "And drink some beer with me?"
 "No, I will neither eat nor drink,
  Till I am blooded by thee."

6 "Well, I have a room, cousin Robin," she said,
  "Which you did never see,
 And if you please to walk therein,
  You blooded by me shall be."

7 She took him by the lily-white hand,
  And led him to a private room,
 And there she blooded bold Robin Hood,
  While one drop of blood would run down.

8 She blooded him in a vein of the arm,
  And locked him up in the room;
 Then did he bleed all the live-long day,
  Until the next day at noon.

9 He then bethought him of a casement there,
  Thinking for to get down;
 But was so weak he could not leap,
  He could not get him down.

10 He then bethought him of his bugle-horn,
  Which hung low down to his knee;
 He set his horn unto his mouth,
  And blew out weak blasts three.

11 Then Little John, when hearing him,
  As he sat under a tree,

win, travel.

"I fear my master is now near dead,
    He blows so wearily."

12 Then Little John to fair Kirkly is gone,
    As fast as he can dree;
  But when he came to Kirkly Hall,
    He broke locks two or three:

13 Until he came bold Robin to see,
    Then he fell on his knee;
  "A boon, a boon," cries Little John,
    "Master, I beg of thee."

14 "What is that boon," said Robin Hood,
    "Little John, [thou] begs of me?"
  "It is to burn fair Kirkly Hall,
    And all their nunnery."

15 "Now nay, now nay," quoth Robin Hood,
    "That boon I'll not grant thee;
  I never hurt woman in all my life,
    Nor men in woman's company.

16 "I never hurt fair maid in all my time,
    Nor at mine end shall it be;
  But give me my bent bow in my hand,
    And a broad arrow I'll let flee;
  And where this arrow is taken up,
    There shall my grave digged be.

17 "Lay me a green sod under my head,
    And another at my feet;
  And lay my bent bow by my side,
    Which was my music sweet;
  And make my grave of gravel and green,
    Which is most right and meet.

18 "Let me have length and breadth enough,
    With a green sod under my head;
  That they may say, when I am dead
    Here lies bold Robin Hood."

dree, be able.

Sir Andrew Barton (167)

Barton's father had been robbed of a fine ship and cargo by Portuguese men-of-war, to revenge which he and his brothers were licensed by the Scottish king in 1506 to make reprisals. Apparently the Bartons soon lapsed from retaliation into indiscriminate piracy. And they were not only harassing Portuguese shipping but stopping English merchantmen as well.

At this point the ballad begins. On the complaint of English merchants, Henry the Eighth dispatches Lord Charles Howard (actually Sir Thomas and Sir Edward Howard) to hunt down the Scotsman. The admiral, after three days at sea, overtakes a merchant ship commanded by a certain Henry Hunt. Just the day before, Hunt had been Andrew Barton's prisoner. Hunt volunteers to retrace his course and lead the way to Barton. He describes the pirate's ordnance, advising Howard to concentrate first on sinking the pinnace which accompanies Barton's ship. But most important, he emphasizes, the Scottish sailors must not be allowed to go aloft to the topcastle. For there on the high stage of the mast Barton has a magazine of beams, mysterious weapons which give him the fire power of twenty ships. The minstrel seems to have no clear idea what the beams were. As best we can make out, they were butts of wood impregnated with inflammable substance. These were set afire and hurled into the enemy ships.

The attempt to launch the beams turns out to be the crucial incident in the engagement that ensues. Barton's sailors mounting to the topcastle are brought down by the English archers. At last Barton himself attempts the climb in full armor, but he is first wounded under the shoulder-piece and next under the collar. Falling to the deck, he makes a speech to inspirit his men that is among the most heroic utterances in all poetry. The clemency of King Henry was as the ballad represents it.

"Sir Andrew Barton" has long been extinct in tradition, unless one accepts Barry's argument (pp. 253 ff.) that some texts of "Henry Martin" are truncated versions of the older ballad. The present text is from the Percy Folio MS., III, 399.

1 As itt beffell in m[i]dsummer-time,
    When burds singe sweetlye on euery tree,
Our noble king, King Henery the Eighth,
    Ouer the riuer of Thames past hee.

2 Hee was no sooner ouer the riuer,
    Downe in a fforrest to take the ayre,
But eighty merchants of London cittye
    Came kneeling before King Henery there:

3 "O yee are welcome, rich merchants,
    [Good saylers, welcome unto me!"]
They swore by the rood the[y] were saylers good,
    But rich merchants they cold not bee.

4 "To Ffrance nor Fflanders dare we nott passe,
    Nor Burdeaux voyage wee dare not ffare,
And all ffor a ffalse robber that lyes on the seas,
    And robb[s] vs of our merchants ware."

5 King Henery was stout, and he turned him about,
    And swore by the Lord that was mickle of might,
"I thought he had not beene in the world throughout
    That durst haue wrought England such vnright."

6 But euer they sighed, and said, alas!
    Vnto King Harry this answere againe:
"He is a proud Scott that will robb vs all
    If wee were twenty shipps and hee but one."

7 The king looket ouer his left shoulder,
    Amongst his lords and barrons soe ffree:
"Haue I neuer lord in all my realme
    Will ffeitch yond traitor vnto mee?"

8 "Yes, that dare I!" sayes my lord Chareles Howard,
    Neere to the king wheras hee did stand;
"If that Your Grace will giue me leaue,
    My selfe wilbe the only man."

9 "Thou shalt haue six hundred men," saith our king,
    "And chuse them out of my realme soe ffree;

rood, cross.   *mickle,* great.

Besids marriners and boyes,
   To guide the great shipp on the sea."

10 "Ile goe speake with Sir Andrew," sais Charles, my lord
    Haward;
   "Vpon the sea, if hee be there;
I will bring him and his shipp to shore,
   Or before my prince I will neuer come neere."

11 The ffirst of all my lord did call,
   A noble gunner hee was one;
This man was three score yeeres and ten,
   And Peeter Simon was his name.

12 "Peeter," sais hee, "I must sayle the sea,
   To seeke out an enemye; God be my speed
Before all others I haue chosen thee;
   Of a hundred guners thoust be my head."

13 "My lord," sais hee, "if you haue chosen mee
   Of a hundred gunners to be the head,
Hange me att your maine-mast tree
   If I misse my marke past three pence bread."

14 The next of all my lord he did call,
   A noble bowman hee was one;
In Yorekeshire was this gentleman borne,
   And William Horsley was his name.

15 "Horsley," sayes hee, "I must sayle to the sea,
   To seeke out an enemye; God be my speede!
Before all others I haue chosen thee;
   Of a hundred bowemen thoust be my head."

16 "My lord," sais hee, "if you haue chosen mee
   Of a hundred bowemen to be the head,
Hang me att your mainemast-tree
   If I misse my marke past twelue pence bread."

17 With pikes, and gunnes, and bowemen bold,
   This noble Howard is gone to the sea

thoust, thou shalt.   *bread,* breadth.

On the day before midsummer-euen,
 And out att Thames mouth sayled they.

18 They had not sayled dayes three
  Vpon their iourney they tooke in hand,
 But there they mett with a noble shipp,
  And stoutely made itt both stay and stand.

19 "Thou must tell me thy name," sais Charles, my lord
   Haward,
  "Or who thou art, or ffrom whence thou came,
 Yea, and where thy dwelling is,
  To whom and where thy shipp does belong."

20 "My name," says hee, "is Henery Hunt,
  With a pure hart and a penitent mind;
 I and my shipp they doe belong
  Vnto the New-castle that stands vpon Tine."

21 "Now thou must tell me, Harry Hunt,
  As thou hast sayled by day and by night,
 Hast thou not heard of a stout robber?
  Men calls him Sir Andrew Bartton, Knight."

22 But euer he sighed, and sayd, "Alas!
  Ffull well, my lord, I know that wight;
 He robd me of my merchants ware,
  And I was his prisoner but yesternight.

23 "As I was sayling vppon the sea,
  And [a] Burdeaux voyage as I did ffare,
 He clasped me to his archborde,
  And robd me of all my merchantsware.

24 "And I am a man both poore and bare,
  And euery man will haue his owne of me,
 And I am bound towards London to ffare,
  To complaine to my prince Henerye."

25 "That shall not need," sais my lord Haward;
  "If thou canst lett me this robber see,

archborde, stern.

Ffor euery peny he hath taken thee ffroe,
    Thou shalt be rewarded a shilling," quoth hee.

26 "Now God fforefend," sais Henery Hunt,
    "My lord, you shold worke soe ffarr amisse!
God keepe you out of that traitors hands!
    For you wott ffull litle what a man hee is.

27 "Hee is brasse within, and steele without,
    And bea[m]es hee beares in his topcastle stronge;
His shipp hath ordinance cleane round about;
    Besids, my lord, hee is verry well mand.

28 "He hath a pinnace, is deerlye dight,
    Saint Andrews crosse, that is his guide;
His pinnace beares nine score men and more,
    Besids fifteen cannons on euery side.

29 "If you were twenty shippes, and he but one,
    Either in archbord or in hall,
He would ouercome you euerye one,
    And if his bea[m]es they doe downe ffall."

30 "This is cold comfort," sais my Lord Haward,
    "To wellcome a stranger thus to the sea;
I'le bring him and his shipp to shore,
    Or else into Scottland hee shall carrye mee."

31 "Then you must gett a noble gunner, my lord,
    That can sett well with his eye,
And sinke his pinnace into the sea,
    And soone then ouercome will hee bee.

32 "And when that you haue done this,
    If you chance Sir Andrew for to bord,
Lett no man to his topcastle goe;
    And I will giue you a glasse, my lord.

33 "And then you need to ffeare no Scott,
    Whether you sayle by day or by night;
And to-morrow, by seuen of the clocke,
    You shall meete with Sir Andrew Bartton, **Knight**.

wot, know.   *deerlye dight,* richly fitted out.   *hall,* hull?

34 "I was his prisoner but yesternight,
　　And he hath taken mee sworne," quoth hee;
"I trust my L[ord] God will me fforgiue
　　And if that oath then broken bee.

35 "You must lend me six peeces, my lord," quoth hee,
　　"Into my shipp, to sayle the sea,
And to-morrow, by nine of the clocke,
　　Your Honour againe then will I see."

36 And the hache-bord where Sir Andrew lay
　　Is hached with gold deerlye dight:
"Now by my ffaith," sais Charles, my lord Haward,
　　"Then yonder Scott is a worthye wight!

37 "Take in your ancyents and your standards,
　　Yea that no man shall them see,
And put me fforth a white willow wand,
　　As merchants vse to sayle the sea."

38 But they stirred neither top nor mast,
　　But Sir Andrew they passed by:
"Whatt English are yonder," said Sir Andrew,
　　"That can so litle curtesye?

39 "I haue beene admirall ouer the sea
　　More then these yeeres three;
There is neuer an English dog, nor Portingall,
　　Can passe this way without leaue of mee.

40 "But now yonder pedlers, they are past,
　　Which is no litle greffe to me:
Ffeich them backe," sayes Sir Andrew Bartton,
　　"They shall all hang att my maine-mast tree."

41 With that the pinnace itt shott of,
　　That my Lord Haward might itt well ken;
Itt stroke downe my lords fforemast,
　　And killed fourteen of my lord his men.

42 "Come hither, Simon!" sayes my lord Haward,
　　"Looke that thy words be true thou sayd;

nache-bord, stern. *ancyent,* ensign.

I'le hang thee att my maine-mast tree
 If thou misse thy marke past twelue pence bread."

43 Simon was old, but his hart itt was bold;
  Hee tooke downe a peece, and layd itt ffull lowe;
 He put in chaine yeards nine,
  Besids other great shott lesse and more.

44 With that hee lett his gun-shott goe;
  Soe well hee settled itt with his eye,
 The ffirst sight that Sir Andrew sawe,
  Hee see his pinnace sunke in the sea.

45 When hee saw his pinnace sunke,
  Lord! in his hart hee was not well:
 "Cutt my ropes! itt is time to be gon!
  I'le goe ffeitch yond pedlers backe my selfe!"

46 When my lord Haward saw Sir Andrew loose,
  Lord! in his hart that hee was ffaine:
 "Strike on your drummes! spread out your ancyents!
  Sound out your trumpetts! sound out amaine!"

47 "Ffight on, my men!" sais Sir Andrew Bartton;
  "Weate, howsoeuer this geere will sway,
 Itt is my lord Adm[i]rall of England
  Is come to seeke mee on the sea."

48 Simon had a sonne; with shott of a gunn—
  Well Sir Andrew might itt ken—
 He shott itt in att a priuye place,
  And killed sixty more of Sir Andrews men.

49 Harry Hunt came in att the other syde,
  And att Sir Andrew hee shott then;
 He droue downe his fformast-tree,
  And killed eighty more of Sir Andrews men.

50 "I haue done a good turne," sayes Harry Hunt;
  "Sir Andrew is not our kings ffriend;
 He hoped to haue vndone me yesternight,
  But I hope I haue quitt him well in the end."

Weate for *I wot?* I know?

51   "Euer alas!" sayd Sir Andrew Barton,
      "What shold a man either thinke or say?
    Yonder ffalse theeffe is my strongest enemye,
      Who was my prisoner but yesterday.

52   "Come hither to me, thou Gourden good,
      And be thou readye att my call,
    And I will giue thee three hundred pound
      If thou wilt lett my beames down ffall."

53   With that hee swarued the maine-mast tree,
      Soe did he itt with might and maine;
    Horseley, with a bearing arrow,
      Stroke the Gourden through the braine.

54   And he ffell into the haches againe,
      And sore of this wound that he did bleed;
    Then word went throug[h] Sir Andrews men,
      That the Gourden hee was dead.

55   "Come hither to me, James Hambliton,
      Thou are my sisters sonne, I haue no more;
    I will giue [thee] six hundred pound
      If thou will lett my beames downe ffall."

56   With that hee swarued the maine-mast tree,
      Soe did hee itt with might and maine:
    Horseley, with another broad arrow,
      Strake the yeaman through the braine.

57   That hee ffell downe to the haches againe;
      Sore of his wound that hee did bleed;
    Couetousness getts no gaine,
      Itt is verry true, as the Welchman sayd.

58   But when hee saw his sisters sonne slaine,
      Lord! in his heart hee was not well:
    "Goe ffeitch me downe my armour of pro[offe],
      Ffor I will to the topcastle my-selfe.

59   "Goe ffeitch me downe my armour of prooffe,
      For itt is guilded with gold soe cleere;

swarue, climb.   *haches,* deck.

God be with my brother, John of Bartton!
    Amongst the Portingalls hee did itt weare."

60   But when hee had his armour of prooffe,
      And on his body hee had itt on,
    Euery man that looked att him
      Sayd, "Gunn nor arrow hee neade feare none."

61   "Come hither, Horsley!" sayes my lord Haward,
      "And looke your shaft that itt goe right;
    Shoot a good shoote in the time of need,
      And ffor thy shooting thoust be made a knight."

62   "I'le doe my best," sayes Horslay then,
      "Your Honor shall see beffore I goe;
    If I shold be hanged att your mainemast,
      I haue in my shipp but arrowes tow."

63   But att Sir Andrew hee shott then;
      Hee made sure to hitt his marke;
    Vnder the spole of his right arme
      Hee smote Sir Andrew quite throw the hart.

64   Yett ffrom the tree hee wold not start,
      But hee clinged to itt with might and maine;
    Vnder the coller then of his jacke,
      He stroke Sir Andrew thorrow the braine.

65   "Ffight on my men," sayes Sir Andrew Bartton,
      "I am hurt, but I am not slaine;
    I'le lay mee downe and bleed a-while,
      And then I'le rise and ffight againe.

66   "Ffight on my men," sayes Sir Andrew Bartton,
      "These English doggs they bite soe lowe;
    Ffight on ffor Scottland and Saint Andrew
      Till you heare my whistle blowe!"

67   But when the cold not heare his whistle blow,
      Sayes Harry Hunt, "I'le lay my head
    You may bord yonder noble shipp, my lord,
      For I know Sir Andrew hee is dead."

spole, shoulder.   *jacke,* coat of mail.

68   With that they borded this noble shipp,
       Soe did they itt with might and maine;
    The ffound eighteen score Scotts aliue,
       Besids the rest were maimed and slaine.

69   My lord Haward tooke a sword in his hand,
       And smote off Sir Andrews head;
    The Scotts stood by did weepe and mourne,
       But neuer a word durst speake or say.

70   He caused his body to be taken downe,
       And ouer the hatch-bord cast into the sea,
    And about his middle three hundred crownes:
       "Whersoeuer thou lands, itt will bury thee."

71   With his head they sayled into England againe,
       With right good will, and fforce and main,
    And the day beffore Newyeeres euen
       Into Thames mouth they came againe.

72   My lord Haward wrote to King Heneryes grace,
       With all the newes hee cold him bring:
    "Such a Newyeeres gifft I haue brought to your Gr[ace]
       As neuer did subiect to any king.

73   "Ffor merchandyes and manhood,
       The like is nott to be ffound;
    The sight of these wold doe you good,
       Ffor you haue not the like in your English ground."

74   But when hee heard tell that they were come,
       Full royally hee welcomed them home;
    Sir Andrews shipp was the kings Newyeeres guifft;
       A brauer shipp you neuer saw none.

75   Now hath our king Sir Andrews shipp,
       Besett with pearles and precyous stones;
    Now hath England two shipps of warr,
       Two shipps of warr, before but one.

76   "Who holpe to this?" sayes King Henerye,
       "That I may reward him ffor his paine:"

holpe, helped.

"Harry Hunt, and Peeter Simon,
   William Horseleay, and I the same."

77   "Harry Hunt shall haue his whistle and chaine,
      And all his jewells, whatsoeuer they bee,
  And other rich giffts that I will not name,
      For his good service he hath done mee.

78   "Horslay, right thoust be a knight,
      Lands and liuings thou shalt haue store;
  Howard shalbe erle of Nottingham,
      And soe was neuer Haward before.

79   "Now, Peeter Simon, thou art old;
      I will maintaine thee and thy sonne;
  Thou shalt haue fiue hundred pound all in gold
      Ffor the good service that thou hast done."

80   Then King Henerye shiffted his roome;
      In came the Queene and ladyes bright;
  Other arrands they had none
      But to see Sir Andrew Bartton, Knight.

81   But when they see his deadly fface,
      His eyes were hollow in his head;
  "I wold giue a hundred pound," sais King Henerye,
      "The man were aliue as hee is dead!

82   "Yett ffor the manfull part that hee hath playd,
      Both heere and beyond the sea,
  His men shall haue halfe a crowne a day
      To bring them to my brother, King Jamye."

Henry Martyn (250)

So closely related are "Sir Andrew Barton" and "Henry
Martyn" that some scholars consider them the same song. Our
text A (Belden, p. 88), a typical American version, reads like
a hurried summary of the infinitely more vivid and detailed "Sir
Andrew Barton." The perfunctory tone that pervades the piece
suggests that broadside prints played some role in its trans-

mission. According to Barry (pp. 256-57), the Captain Charles Stewart who supplants Lord Charles Howard was an American naval hero (1778-1869). Text B (Sharp, *One Hundred English Folksongs*, No. 1, with tune), the characteristic English form of the ballad, could easily be a prologue to "Sir Andrew Barton."

✵◇ A ◇✵

1 Three brothers in old Scotland did dwell,
  Three loving brothers were they;
  They all cast lots to see which of them
  Should go robbing around the salt sea.

2 The lot fell on to Andy Bardan,
  The youngest of the three,
  For to maintain the other two
  A-robbing around the salt sea.

3 He had not sailed very many long nights
  Before a ship he did spy;
  It sailed far off, it sailed far off,
  And then it came sailing close by.

4 "Who's there, who's there?" said Andy Bardan,
  "Who's there that sails so nigh?"
  "We are the rich merchants from old England,
  If no offense, let us pass by."

5 "Oh no! oh no!" said Andy Bardan,
  "Oh no, that never can be!
  Your ship and your cargo we'll have, my boys,
  And your bodies sink in the salt sea."

6 The news came unto king Henry
  (For it was him they crowned)
  His ship and his cargo both were lost
  And all his merry men drowned.

7 "Go build a ship both wide and deep
  And build it safe and secure,
  And if Andy Bardan you do not bring in
  Your lives shall no longer endure."

8   They had not sailed very many long nights
Before a ship they did spy;
It sailed far off, it sailed far off,
And then it came sailing close by.

9   "Who's there? Who's there?" said Captain Charles Stewart,
"Who's there that sails so nigh?"
"We are the bold robbers from old Scotland;
If no offense, let us pass by."

10   "Oh no! oh no!" said Captain Charles Stewart,
"Oh no! that never can be;
Your ship and your cargo we'll have, my boys,
And your bodies sink in the salt sea."

11   "Peel on! peel on!" said Andy Bardan,
And loud the cannon did roar;
And Captain Charles Stewart took Andy Bardan,
He took him to fair England's shore.

12   "What now, what now?" said Andy Bardan,
"What now my fate it will be!
The gallows is ready for Andy Bardan,
The bold robber around the salt sea.

13   "Go dig my grave both wide and deep,
And dig it close to the sea;
And tell my brothers as they pass by
I've done robbing around the salt sea."

❧ B ❧

There were three broth-ers in mer-ry Scot-land, In

mer-ry Scot-land there were three, And they did cast

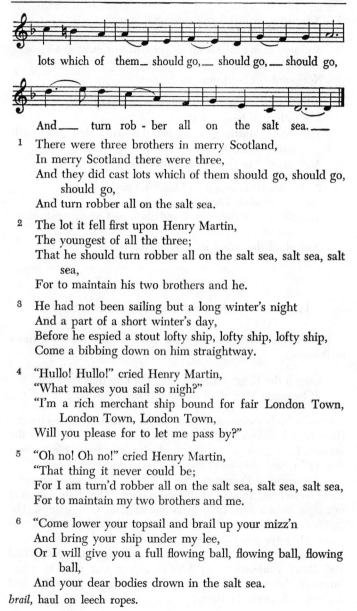

lots which of them— should go,— should go, — should go,

And— turn rob - ber all on the salt sea.—

1   There were three brothers in merry Scotland,
    In merry Scotland there were three,
    And they did cast lots which of them should go, should go,
        should go,
    And turn robber all on the salt sea.

2   The lot it fell first upon Henry Martin,
    The youngest of all the three;
    That he should turn robber all on the salt sea, salt sea, salt
        sea,
    For to maintain his two brothers and he.

3   He had not been sailing but a long winter's night
    And a part of a short winter's day,
    Before he espied a stout lofty ship, lofty ship, lofty ship,
    Come a bibbing down on him straightway.

4   "Hullo! Hullo!" cried Henry Martin,
    "What makes you sail so nigh?"
    "I'm a rich merchant ship bound for fair London Town,
        London Town, London Town,
    Will you please for to let me pass by?"

5   "Oh no! Oh no!" cried Henry Martin,
    "That thing it never could be;
    For I am turn'd robber all on the salt sea, salt sea, salt sea,
    For to maintain my two brothers and me.

6   "Come lower your topsail and brail up your mizz'n
    And bring your ship under my lee,
    Or I will give you a full flowing ball, flowing ball, flowing
        ball,
    And your dear bodies drown in the salt sea.

brail, haul on leech ropes.

7   "Oh no! we won't lower our lofty topsail,
      Nor bow ourselves under your lee,
      And you shan't take from us our rich merchant goods, mer-
          chant goods, merchant goods,
      Nor point our bold guns to the sea."

8   With broadside and broadside and at it they went
      For fully two hours or three,
      Till Henry Martin gave to her the death shot, the death
          shot, the death shot,
      And straight to the bottom went she.

9   Bad news, bad news to old England came,
      Bad news to fair London Town,
      There's been a rich vessel and she's cast away, cast away,
          cast away,
      And all of the merry men drown'd.

Captain Ward and the Rainbow (287)

The taunting words of Captain Ward as the *Rainbow* turns to flee—

"Go tell the King of England, go tell him thus from me,
   If he reigns king of all the land, I will reign king at sea"

—remain fairly constant in all versions, whatever other changes there may be. Also fixed is the cliché, "If you are brass on the outside, I am good steel within," which comes from "Sir Andrew Barton," whose ship was "brass within and steel without."

A fisherman of Feversham, Kent, John Ward commandeered a royal vessel in 1604 and turned pirate. The *Rainbow* sent out against him may have been one of Drake's old ships. The incident here recounted must have occurred about 1607, because Mountjoy, last of the admirals that the king says would have taken Ward if they had been living, died in 1606. Child and Barry conjecture that Ward's career was over in 1609; however, he was still reported as preying on Venetian and Maltese commerce in 1615.

Our text is from the *Forecastle Songster*, 1852, p. 226. Traditional copies in both England and America show only minor differences with the broadside and songster copies (compare Barry, p. 351).

1 Come all ye jolly sailors bold,
  That live by tuck of drum;
 I'll tell you of a rank robber
  Now on the seas is come.

2 His name is called Captain Ward,
  As you the truth shall hear;
 For there's not been such a robber
  This hundred and fifty years.

3 He wrote a letter to our king,
  On the fifth of January,
 To see if he would take him in,
  And all his company.

4 To see if he would accept of him
  And all his jolly sailors bold;
 And for a ransom he would give
  Two thousand pounds in gold.

5 "First he beguiled the wild Turks,
  And then the king of Spain;
 Pray, how can he prove true to us,
  When he proves false to them?

6 "Oh no! oh no!" then said the king
  "For no such thing can be;
 For he has been a rank robber,
  And a robber on the sea."

7 "O then," says Captain Ward, "my boys,
  Let's put to sea again,
 And see what prizes we can find
  On the coast of France and Spain."

8 Then we espied a lofty ship
  A sailing from the west;

She was loaded with silks and satins
And cambrics of the best.

9   Then we bore up to her straightway,
    They thinking no such thing:
  We robb'd them of their merchandise,
    And bade them tell their king.

10 And when their king did hear of this,
    His heart was grieved full sore,
  To think his ships could not get past,
    As they had done before.

11 Then he caused a worthy ship
    And a worthy ship of fame;
  The Rainbow she was called,
    And the Rainbow was her name.

12 He rigged her and freighted her,
    And sent her to the sea,
  With five hundred bold mariners
    To bear her company.

13 They sailed east, they sailed west,
    But nothing could espy,
  Until they came to the very spot
    Where Captain Ward did lie.

14 "Who is the owner of this ship?"
    The Rainbow then did cry
  "Here I am," says Captain Ward,
    "Let no man me deny."

15 "What brought you here? you cowardly dog
    You ugly, wanton thief!
  What makes you lie at anchor
    And keep our king in grief?"

16 "You lie, you lie," says Captain Ward
    "As ever I heard you lie;
  I never robb'd an Englishman,
    An Englishman but three.

17 "As for the worthy Scotchmen,
        I love them as my own;
    My chief delight is for to pull
        The French and Spaniards down."

18 "Why, curse thee, so bold a robber!
        We'll soon humble your pride:"
    With that the gallant Rainbow,
        She shot out of her side

19 Full fifty good brass cannons,
        Well charged on every side;
    And then they fired their great guns,
        And gave Ward a broadside.

20 "Fire on, fire on," says Captain Ward,
        "I value you not a pin;
    If you are brass on the outside,
        I am good steel within."

21 They fought from eight o'clock in the morn
        Till eight o'clock at night.
    At length the gallant Rainbow
        Began to take her flight.

22 "Go home, go home!" says Captain Ward,
        "And tell your king from me,
    If he reigns king upon dry land,
        I will reign king at sea."

23 With that the gallant Rainbow,
        She shot and shot in vain;
    And left the rover's company,
        And home returned again.

24 "Tell our royal king of England
        His ship is return'd again;
    For Captain Ward he is too strong,
        He never will be taken."

25 "O shame! O shame!" said the king,
        "For no such thing can be;
    For I have lost two thousand pounds,
        Besides lost jewels three.

26   "The first was brave Lord Clifford,
          Great Earl of Cumberland;
      The second was brave Lord Mountjoy,
          As you shall understand;

27   "The third was brave Lord Essex,
          From field would never flee;
      Who would have gone unto the sea,
          And brought proud Ward to me."

Captain Kidd

At the Old Bailey, London, on May 9, 1701, Captain William Kidd—the ballads always call him Robert—was sentenced to die for murder and piracy; two weeks later he was marched out to Execution Dock, Wapping, and hanged in chains between the high- and low-tide marks. In that two weeks there circulated in London a broadside "goodnight" moralizing on Kidd's fate that since has become traditional in America, being reported from Florida and Michigan, Mississippi and Massachusetts. The original broadside is in the Earl of Crawford's collection; later broadside and songbook texts are registered in Mackenzie, pp. 278-79.

A Scotsman, Kidd received through the sponsorship of Robert Livingston of New York a royal commission to suppress piracy in the Indian Ocean. He sailed from New York in 1696 on the *Adventure Galley* and put into Boston on his return in 1699. In the meanwhile he had himself fallen into piracy—under duress from his crew, he protested—and was held in Boston and shortly bound over to the Admiralty in London. The William Moore so prominent in the ballad was a gunner aboard the *Adventure Galley*. Kidd claimed he had been forced to kill Moore in order to stamp out a mutiny led by the gunner.

Linscott, p. 131, furnishes our text, a somewhat condensed version but containing all the vital stanzas. A typical goodnight, "Captain Kidd" has the same metrical pattern as the goodnight parody "Sam Hall" (see p. 223).

1   Oh! my name was Robert Kidd, as I sailed, as I sailed,
    Oh, my name was Robert Kidd, as I sailed.
    My name was Robert Kidd, God's laws I did forbid,
    And most wickedly I did, as I sailed, as I sailed,
    And most wickedly I did, as I sailed.

2   Oh! my parents taught me well, as I sailed, as I sailed,
    My parents taught me well, to shun the gates of hell,
    But against them I rebelled, as I sailed, as I sailed . . .

3   I murdered William Moore, as I sailed, as I sailed,
    I murdered William Moore and left him in his gore,
    Not many leagues from shore, as I sailed, as I sailed . . .

4   And being cruel still, as I sailed, as I sailed,
    And being cruel still, my gunner I did kill,
    And his precious blood did spill, as I sailed, as I sailed . . .

5   My mate was sick and died, as I sailed, as I sailed,
    My mate was sick and died, which me much terrified.
    He called me to his bedside, as I sailed, as I sailed . . .

6   And unto me did say, "See me die, see me die,"
    And unto me did say, "Take warning now by me,
    There comes a reckoning day, you must die, you must
        die . . ."

7   I steered from sound to sound, as a sailed, as I sailed,
    I steered from sound to sound, and many ships I found,
    And most of them I burned, as I sailed, as I sailed . . .

8   I spied three ships from France, as I sailed, as I sailed,
    I spied three ships from France, to them I did advance,
    And took them all by chance, as I sailed, as I sailed . . .

9   I spied three ships from Spain, as I sailed, as I sailed,
    I spied three ships from Spain, I fired on them amain,
    Till most of them were slain, as I sailed, as I sailed . . .

10 I'd ninety bars of gold, as I sailed, as I sailed,
    I'd ninety bars of gold, and dollars manifold,
    With riches uncontrolled, as I sailed, as I sailed . . .

11   Then fourteen ships I saw, as I sailed, as I sailed,
Then fourteen ships I saw, and brave men they were,
Ah! they were too much for me, as I sailed, as I sailed . . .

12   To Newgate I am cast, and must die, and must die,
To Newgate I am cast, with a sad and heavy heart,
To receive my just desert, I must die, I must die . . .

13   Take warning now by me, for I must die, I must die,
Take warning now by me, and shun bad company,
Lest you come to hell with me, for I must die, I must
die . . .

Dick Turpin and the Lawyer

A protracted string of artful robberies is the substance of the English "Dick Turpin" ballads. This particular adventure invariably figures in the series. Turpin plied his trade in the vicinity of York, where he was hanged April 10, 1739.

Text: Mackenzie, p. 311. The refrain is a corruption of "O rare Turpin, hero, O rare Turpin, O."

1   As Turpin was riding across the moor
There he saw a lawyer riding on before.
Turpin, riding up to him, said, "Are you not afraid
To meet Dick Turpin, that mischievous blade?"
Singing Eh ro, Turpin I ro.

2   Says Turpin to the lawyer for to be cute,
"I hid my money into my boot."
Says the lawyer to Turpin, "He can't find mine,
For I hid it in the cape of my coat behind."

3   They rode along together to the foot of the hill,
When Turpin bid the lawyer to stand still,
Saying, "The cape of your coat it must come off,
For my horse is in want of a new saddle-cloth."

4   Turpin robbed the lawyer of all his store;
He told him to go home and he would get more;

"And the very first town you do come in
You can tell them you was robbed by Dick Turpin."

My Bonny Black Bess

This version of Turpin's tribute to his faithful mare was re-corded in Montana in 1915 (Pound, p. 155). It is a far jauntier ballad than the commoner American version, derived from an uninspired English broadside of about 1840, in which Bess's heart bursts after a frantic ride from London to York. The alibi episode was first attached to the Turpin legend cycle by the English novelist Harrison Ainsworth in *Rockwood* (1834). Be-fore Ainsworth, it was told of the highwayman "Swift Nicks," who died in 1676.

1 Let the lover his mistress's beauty rehearse,
   And laud her attractions in languishing verse;
   Be it mine in rude strain but with truth to express
   The love that I bear to my Bonny Black Bess.

2 From the West was her dam, from the East was her sire;
   From the one came her swiftness, the other her fire;
   No peer of the realm better blood can possess
   Than flows in the blood of my Bonny Black Bess.

3 Look! Look! how that eyeball glows bright as a brand,
   That neck proudly arching, those nostrils expand;
   Mark that wide flowing mane, of which each silky tress
   Might adorn prouder beauties, though none like Black Bess.

4 Mark that skin sleek as velvet and dusky as night,
   With its jet undisfigured by one lock of white,
   That throat branched with veins, prompt to charge or caress,
   Now is she not beautiful, Bonny Black Bess?

5 Over highway and byway, in rough or smooth weather,
   Some thousands of miles have we journeyed together;
   Our couch the same straw, our meals the same mess,
   No couple more constant than I and Black Bess.

6 By moonlight, in darkness, by night and by day
   Her headlong career there is nothing can stay;
   She cares not for distance, she knows not distress.
   Can you show me a courser to match with Black Bess?

7 Once it happened in Cheshire, near Durham, I popped
   On a horseman alone whom I suddenly stopped;
   That I lightened his pockets you'll readily guess—
   Quick work makes Dick Turpin when mounted on Bess.

8 Now it seems the man knew me: "Dick Turpin," said he,
   "You shall swing for this job, as you live, d'ye see?"
   I laughed at his threats and his vows of redress—
   I was sure of an alibi then with Black Bess.

9 Brake, brook, meadow, and ploughed field Bess fleetly be-
      strode;
   As the crow wings his flight we selected our road.
   We arrived at Hough Green in five minutes or less,
   My neck it was saved by the speed of Black Bess.

10 Stepping carelessly forward I lounge on the green,
   Taking excellent care that by all I am seen;
   Some remarks on time's flight to the squires I address;
   But I say not a word of the flight of Black Bess.

11 I mention the hour—it is just about four,
   Play a rubber at bowls, think the danger is o'er,
   When athwart my next game like a checkmate in chess
   Comes the horseman in search of the rider of Bess.

12 What matter details? Off with triumph I came.
   He swears to the hour and the squires swear the same.
   I had robbed him at four, while at four, they profess
   I was quietly bowling—all thanks to Black Bess.

13 Then one halloo, boys, one loud cheering halloo,
   For the swiftest of coursers, the gallant, the true,
   For the sportsman inborn shall the memory bless
   Of the horse of the highwaymen, Bonny Black Bess.

Brennan on the Moor

It's of a fear - less high - way - man a

sto - ry now I'll tell: His name was Wil - lie

Bren - nan, and in Ire - land he did dwell; 'Twas

on the Lime-rick moun-tains he com-menced his wild ca -

reer, Where man - y a wealth - y gen - tle man be -

fore him shook with fear. Bren nan on the moor,

Bren - nan on the moor, Bold and yet un -

daunt - ed stood young Bren - nan on the moor.

The noted eighteenth-century highwayman, Willie Brennan, made the Kilworth mountains near Fermoy in County Cork his preserve. Like Robin Hood, Brennan shared his loot with the poor, and, again like Robin Hood, recruited his confederates from men who had beaten him at his own game. His career ended on the gallows in 1804. Irish broadsides, copied by the London ballad press, were taken up by folk singers in Ireland, England, and America (see references in Belden, p. 284). The present text and tune are from Kidson, *Traditional Tunes*, p. 124.

1   It's of a fearless highwayman a story now I'll tell:
     His name was Willie Brennan, and in Ireland he did dwell;
     'Twas on the Limerick mountains he commenced his wild
         career,
     Where many a wealthy gentleman before him shook with
         fear.
         Brennan on the moor, Brennan on the moor,
         Bold and yet undaunted stood young Brennan on the
         moor.

2   A brace of loaded pistols he carried night and day,
     He never robb'd a poor man upon the King's highway;
     But what he'd taken from the rich, like Turpin and Black
         Bess,
     He always did divide it with the widow in distress.

3   One night he robbed a packman, his name was [Pedlar]
         Bawn;
     They travelled on together, till day began to dawn;
     The pedlar seeing his money gone, likewise his watch and
         chain,
     He at once encountered Brennan and robbed him back
         again.

4   When Brennan saw the pedlar was as good a man as he,
     He took him on the highway, his companion for to be;
     The pedlar threw away his pack without any more delay,
     And proved a faithful comrade until his dying day.

5 One day upon the highway Willie he sat down,
   He met the Mayor of Cashel, a mile outside the town;
   The Mayor he knew his features, "I think, young man,"
       said he,
   "Your name is Willie Brennan, you must come along with
       me."

6 As Brennan's wife had gone to town provisions for to buy,
   When she saw her Willie, she began to weep and cry;
   He says, "Give me that tenpence;" as soon as Willie spoke,
   She handed him the blunderbuss from underneath her cloak.

7 Then with his loaded blunderbuss, the truth I will unfold,
   He made the Mayor to tremble, and robbed him of his
       gold;
   One hundred pounds was offered for his apprehension there,
   And with his horse and saddle to the mountains did re-
       pair.

8 Then Brennan being an outlaw upon the mountain high,
   Where cavalry and infantry to take him they did try,
   He laughed at them with scorn, until at length, it's said,
   By a false-hearted young man he was basely betrayed.

9 In the County of Tipperary, in a place they called Clon-
       more,
   Willie Brennan and his comrade that day did suffer sore;
   He lay among the fern which was thick upon the field,
   And nine wounds he had received before that he did yield.

10 Then Brennan and his companion knowing they were be-
       trayed,
   He with the mounted cavalry a noble battle made;
   He lost his foremost finger, which was shot off by a ball;
   So Brennan and his comrade they were taken after all.

11 So they were taken prisoners, in irons they were bound,
   And conveyed to Clonmel jail, strong walls did them sur-
       round;
   They were tried and found guilty, the judge made this
       reply,
   "For robbing on the King's highway you are both con-
       demned to die."

12   Farewell unto my wife, and to my children three,
       Likewise my aged father, he may shed tears for me,
       And to my loving mother, who tore her gray locks and
           cried,
       Saying, "I wish, Willie Brennan, in your cradle you had
           died."

The Wild Colonial Boy

Aside from the ballad, very little is known about the person
or activities of Jack Doolan (Dolan, Dowling). Our Australian
version (from A. B. Paterson's *Old Bush Songs*, 1905, p. 33)
dates his career from 1861, but others say 1836. A Michigan
lady, who learned the ballad from a lumberjack son, confused
Castlemaine, Australia, with Castlemaine, Ireland, thus giving
Doolan an Irish birthplace as well as name (Gardiner and
Chickering, p. 326). In Vermont (Flanders and Brown, p. 130)
the ballad deals with a "wild Columbian boy" named Jack
Dolden who was born in Ireland, "in a place called Casco,
Maine"! Undoubtedly Australian in origin, the ballad shows the
strong influence of the Irish broadsides of the "come-all-ye" type.

1   'Tis of a wild Colonial boy, Jack Doolan was his name,
       Of poor but honest parents he was born in Castlemaine.
       He was his father's only hope, his mother's only joy,
       And dearly did his parents love the wild Colonial boy.

       Come, all my hearties, we'll roam the mountains high,
       Together we will plunder, together we will die.
       We'll wander over valleys, and gallop over plains,
       And we'll scorn to live in slavery, bound down with iron
           chains.

2   He was scarcely sixteen years of age when he left his
           father's home,
       And through Australia's sunny clime a bushranger did roam.
       He robbed those wealthy squatters, their stock he did de-
           stroy,
       And a terror to Australia was the wild Colonial boy.

3   In sixty-one this daring youth commenced his wild career,
With a heart that knew no danger, no foeman did he fear.
He stuck up the Beechworth mail coach, and robbed Judge
    MacEvoy,
Who trembled, and gave up his gold to the wild Colonial
    boy.

4   He bade the Judge "Good morning," and told him to be-
    ware,
That he'd never rob a hearty chap that acted on the square,
And never to rob a mother of her son and only joy,
Or else you may turn outlaw, like the wild Colonial boy.

5   One day as he was riding the mountain side along,
A-listening to the little birds, their pleasant laughing song,
Three mounted troopers rode along—Kelly, Davis, and
    FitzRoy,
They thought that they would capture him—the wild
    Colonial boy.

6   "Surrender now, Jack Doolan, you see there's three to one.
Surrender now, Jack Doolan, you daring highwayman."
He drew a pistol from his belt, and shook the little toy.
"I'll fight, but not surrender," said the wild Colonial boy.

7   He fired at Trooper Kelly, and brought him to the ground,
And in return from Davis received a mortal wound.
All shattered through the jaws he lay still firing at FitzRoy,
And that's the way they captured him—the wild Colonial
    boy.

Sam Bass

A likable young cowpuncher, Sam Bass suddenly went bad
after a spree in which he embezzled the money he had received
for a herd of beeves he had driven to Kansas. In 1877 he formed
a gang that robbed a Union Pacific train at Big Springs, Ne-
braska, of $60,000 in gold; but his accomplices were indiscreet
in spending their share and all except the leader were killed or
captured. Sam returned to Texas, robbing several trains in the

Fort Worth–Dallas area before his career was cut short at Round Rock, Texas, on his twenty-seventh birthday, July 21, 1878. The Texas Rangers had released Sam's old comrade Jim Murphy on the promise that he would rejoin the outlaw and betray his movements—which Murphy did.

Text: C. J. Finger, *Frontier Ballads*, 1927, p. 65.

1   Sam Bass was born in Indiana which was his native home.
    Before he reached young manhood, the boy began to roam.
    He first came out to Texas, a cowboy for to be—
    A better hearted fellow you scarce could hope to see.

2   Sam bought him first some race stock and also the Denton
        mare.
    He matched her in all races and took her to the fair.
    He fairly coined money and spent it frank and free.
    He drank the best of whiskey wherever he might be.

3   He left where he was working one pretty summer day
    A-headin' for the Black Hills with his cattle and his pay.
    In Custer City sold the lot and then went on a spree,
    His chums they was all cowboys rough and hard as they
        could be.

4   A-ridin' back to Texas they robbed the U. P. train;
    For safety split in couples and started out again.
    The sheriff took Jo Collins who had a sack of mail
    And with his pardner landed him inside the county jail.

5   But Sam got back to Texas all right side up with care.
    And in the town of Benton he did his money share.
    The lad he was so reckless, three robberies did he do,
    The passenger and express car and U. S. mail car, too.

6   Now Sam he had four pardners, all bold and daring bad.
    There was Richardson and Jackson, Jo Collins and Old Dad.
    More daring bolder outlaws the rangers never knew,
    They dodged the Texas rangers and beat them, too.

7   Sam had another pardner called Arkansaw for short,
    But Thomas Floyd the ranger cut his career quite short.
    This Floyd stood six feet in his socks and passed for mighty
        fly.

But them that knows will tell you he's a dead beat on the
    sly.

8   Jim Murphy was arrested and then let out on bail,
He jumped the train for Terrel after breaking Tyler jail.
But old Mayor Jones stood in with Jim and it was all a stall,
A put-up job to catch poor Sam, before the coming fall.

9   Sam met his fate at Round Rock, July the twenty-first.
They dropped the boy with rifle balls and then they took
    his purse,
Poor Sam he is a dead lad, and six foot under clay.
And Jackson's in the mesquite aiming to get away.

10 Jim, he took Sam Bass' gold and didn't want to pay,
His only idea it was to give brave Sam away,
He sold out to Sam and Barnes and left their friends to
    mourn—
And Jim he'll get a scorching when Gabriel blows his horn.

11 Perhaps he's got to heaven, there's none of us can say,
My guess it is and surmise, he's gone the other way,
And if brave Sam could see him as in the place he rolls,
There'll be a lively mix-up down there among the coals.

Jesse James

Jesse James' grudge against the law was planted by an un-
just beating he received in 1863 at the hands of the federal
militia—he was being punished because an older brother was
riding with Quantrill's Confederate guerrillas. Jesse eventually
joined Quantrill's troop himself and there learned the menacing
arts that later served him so well when he turned bank and
train robber. After the Civil War, Jesse went out to California,
but returned shortly to Missouri to begin with his brother Frank
a fifteen-year run of dramatic robberies in Missouri, Kansas,
Iowa, and Minnesota. Legends about his dashing manner, his
feats of horsemanship, the favors he did for the poor, were
current even in his lifetime. All the outlaw needed to be pro-
pelled into heroic fame was death by treachery, and that con-

summation was supplied by Robert Ford, a member of Jesse's gang. At the time, Jesse was living in St. Joseph, Missouri, under the alias of Thomas Howard. Ford, attracted by the $10,000 reward on Jesse's head, shot his chief in the back—so the story runs—while Jesse stood on a stepladder righting a picture of his wife (or a framed "God Bless Our Home"). April 3, 1882, was the fatal day.

The standard version of "Jesse James" (A, from Belden, p. 402) is signed in the final stanza by Billy Gashade, an unidentified person, possibly the minstrel that set the piece afloat. Text B (Belden, p. 403), an unusual version taken down in 1916 in St. Joseph, bristles with authentic detail. For example, it is true that Jesse's mother, Mrs. Zerelda Samuel, lost her arm when Pinkerton detectives bombed the James homestead in 1875. Her youngest son, as the ballad says, was killed in the explosion. "Governor C" represents Governor Crittenden. And Ford was indeed "plunked" in a barroom brawl—in Creede, Colorado, in 1892.

✿◊ A ◊✿

1   Jesse James was a lad that killed many a man.
        He robbed the Danville train.
    But that dirty little coward that shot Mr. Howard
        Has laid poor Jesse in the grave.
    [*or*, He stole from the rich and he gave to the poor;
        He'd a hand and a heart and a brain.]

2   It was Robert Ford, that dirty little coward,
        I wonder how he does feel;
    For he ate of Jesse's bread and slept in Jesse's bed
        And laid poor Jesse in the grave.

    Poor Jesse had a wife to mourn for his life,
        His children they were brave;
    But that dirty little coward that shot Mr. Howard
        And laid poor Jesse in the grave!

3   It was his brother Frank who robbed the Gallatin bank
        And carried the money from the town.

It was at this very place they had a little chase,
    For they shot Capt. Sheets to the ground.

4   They went to the crossing not very far from here,
        And there they did the same;
    With the agent on his knees he delivered up the keys
        To the outlaws Frank and Jesse James.

5   It was on Wednesday night, the moon was shining bright,
        They robbed the Glen[dale] train.
    The people they did say, for many miles away,
        It was robbed by Frank and Jesse James.

6   It was on a Saturday night, Jesse was at home,
        Talking with his family brave.
    Robert Ford came along like a thief in the night
        And laid poor Jesse in the grave.

7   The people held their breath when they heard of Jesse's
            death
        And wondered how he ever came to die.
    It was one of the gang called little Robert Ford,
        He shot poor Jesse on the sly.

8   This song was made by Billy Gashade
        As soon as the news did arrive.
    He said there is no man with the law in his hand
        Can take Jesse James when alive.

⊛◇ B ◇⊛

1   Jesse James was one of his names,
        Another it was Howard.
    He robbed the rich of every stitch.
        You bet he was no coward.

2   His mother she was elderly,
        His father was a preacher,
    Though some do say, I can't gainsay,
        His mother was his teacher.

3   Her strong right arm it came to harm.
        Detectives blew it off, sir.

And killed her son, the youngest one.
No wonder such she'd scoff, sir.

4   My Jesse dear, your mother here
     Has taught more than she ought ter,
  For Robert Ford, I pledge my word,
     Has marked you for his slaughter.

5   For robbing trains Bob had no brains,
     Unless Jess plainly showed him.
  Our governor for peace or war
     Explained this for to goad him.

6   So Robert Ford he scratched his gourd,
     And then he said, "I'll go you,
  Give me a price that's something nice,
     And then, by gee, I'll show you!"

7   Then Governor C. he laughed with glee,
     And fixed a price to suit him,
  And Bob agreed, with ready speed,
     To find Jess James and shoot him.

8   And then he did as he was bid
     And shot Jess in the back, sir,
  Then ran away on that same day,
     For cash he did not lack, sir.

9   He did his best to live out west,
     But no one was his friend there.
  "You've killed your cousin," they went buzzin',
     However free he'd spend there.

10   And then one day, the papers say,
     Bob Ford got his rewarding:
  A cowboy drunk his heart did plunk.
     As you do you'll git according.

Stagolee (Stackerlee)

Born with a veil over his face, Stagolee "could see ghosts and raise forty-one kinds of hell," according to legend. And though a thoroughly black-hearted bully, he is nonetheless remembered as a hero because of his defiant lawlessness. The glorifying of such men by the Negro folk community perplexes the sociologists, "but when one considers the Negro has had little opportunity to develop outside of labor and hell-raising, this tendency is not surprising" (Johnson, *John Henry*, p. 142). Some writers ascribe magical properties to the "ox-blood" or "rawhide" Stetson over which Stagolee killed Billy Lyons; our version A, however, doubts the hat was a Stetson, and anyhow the hat was only an excuse. New Orleans, Memphis, and St. Louis contest the honor of being the scene of the crime, though the frequency of Market Street and Jefferson Pen in ballads and fragments gives the edge to the Missouri city.

Text A is a composite made up from versions in the R. W. Gordon collection (*New York Times Magazine*, June 5, 1927). B, a Georgia version (Odum and Johnson, *The Negro and His Songs*, p. 198), confounds Billy and bully and is thus able to spare Stagolee any blame.

❀◇ A ◇❀

1   Now what you all know about this?
    An' what you all know about that?
    They say Stack killed ole Billy Lyons
    'Bout a damned ole Stetson hat!
    Oh, poor, poor, Stackolee!

2   It was on a dark
    And cold stormy night
    That Billy Lyons and Stackolee
    They had that awful fight.
    That bad, that bad man Stackolee!

3   "Oh, Stackolee, oh, Stackolee,
Please spare my life!
For I have got two babies,
And a darling little wife!"
That bad, that bad man Stackolee!

4   "I care not for your babies
Nor your darling little wife.
You done ruint my Stetson hat
An' I'm bound to have your life!"
That bad, that bad man Stackolee!

5   It was no Stetson hat.
He didn't have a good excuse.
They say he killed ole Bily Lyons
'Cause he gave his gal abuse.
Oh poor, poor Stackolee!

6   Stacko's wench was a good girl,
She was true as steel;
She said, "I'll stand by you, Stack,
On you I'm never goin' to squeal!"
Down at the trial of Stackolee.

7   The judge put on the black cap
His voice was stern and cold
"I sentences you to be hanged
The Lord have mercy on your soul!"
That bad, that bad man Stackolee!

8   He had a rubber-tired hearse . . .
A lot of rubber-tired hacks
Took ole Stackolee to the cemetery
Never to bring him back.
Oh poor, poor Stackolee!

❁◇ B ◇❁

1   I got up one mornin' jes' 'bout four o'clock;
Stagolee an' big bully done have one finish' fight.
What 'bout? All 'bout dat rawhide Stetson hat.

2   Stagolee shot bully; bully fell down on de flo',
Bully cry out: "Dat fohty-fo' it hurts me so."
Stagolee done kill dat bully now.

3   Sent for de wagon, wagon didn't come,
Loaded down wid pistols an' all dat gatlin' gun.
Stagolee done kill dat bully now.

4   Some give a nickel, some give a dime;
I didn't give a red copper cent, 'cause he's no friend o' mine.
Stagolee done kill dat bully now.

5   Fohty dollar coffin, eighty dollar hack,
Carried po' man to cemetery but failed to bring him back,
Ev'ybody been dodgin' Stagolee.

John Henry

The masterpiece of Negro balladry has had more written about it than any other native ballad. As late as 1925, the leading Southern ballad men considered John Henry and John Hardy, the "hero" of another song cycle, the same person—the Negro steel-driver John Hardy, gambler, roué, drunkard, and murderer, who was hanged at Welch, West Virginia, in January, 1894 (Cox, pp. 175-77). Since then elaborate investigations in the field (Guy B. Johnson, *John Henry*, 1929, and Louis W. Chappell, *John Henry*, 1933) have separated the two and filled out the John Henry legend. The real-life John Henry sifted out of the mass of traditional lore seems to have been a Negro of prodigious strength, a steel-driver who worked between 1870 and 1872 on the Chesapeake and Ohio's Big Bend Tunnel just east of Hinton, West Virginia. Steel-drivers hammered drills into the rock, boring the holes into which the blasting explosive was poured. Their assistants, the shakers or turners, brought up the sharpened drills, held them in place, dislodged them from the bored holes. Steel drills were just being introduced into tunneling operations in the 1870s, and it was after winning a grueling all-day contest with one of these machines that Henry dropped dead of exhaustion.

Older than the ballad probably are the John Henry work songs, examples of which are given here as texts D, E, and F. They may well have been made up and sung by John Henry's co-workers after his death. The ballad itself developed more gradually. As in "Frankie and Albert," each stanza is a distinct scene or episode, the order and number of stanzas varying considerably. For a Negro ballad, however, the structure is remarkably formal and uniform, which suggests that the ballad was occasionally taken up into print and its form solidified in this way, though only one "John Henry" broadside, the work of a white redactor about 1900, has been discovered.

The confusion of John Henry and John Hardy was inevitable. Besides the resemblance in their names, both were Negroes, both steel-drivers, and they came to their glorious and inglorious ends respectively in nearby counties. It is obviously out of place for John Hardy, a man destined to be hanged, to predict his death in the Big Bend Tunnel; just as John Hardy's tough language seems improper in the mouth of kindly, heroic John Henry. Henry had no vicious traits, unless being a "heavy wi' women" is a vice. In fact, divine attributes are often given him. Like the Christ child in "The Cherry Tree Carol" he is an infant prophet, and in one version of "John Henry," chief among the mourning women is Mary Magdalene. Chappell stresses the importance of the sexual symbolism in the ballad, insisting that the phrases which marvel at Henry's occupational skill are also alluding to his phenomenal sexual prowess.

Text A, from Pennsylvania (Chappell, p. 120), emphasizes the contest with the steam drill, but is otherwise typical; B, from Illinois, and C, from West Virginia (Johnson, pp. 92 and 108), preserve unusual and curious features. From none of these versions, unfortunately, does one learn that John Henry's wife was Polly Ann or Julie Ann. Of the work songs, D, recorded in Lynchburg, Virginia (Scarborough, *On the Trail of Negro Folk-Songs*, p. 219), was sung to the hymn "Come, Thou Fount of Every Blessing," but with long grunts (here indicated by dashes) every half-line. E was sung by an Alabama construction gang in 1914-15 (White, p. 261); F came to Chappell (p. 99) from Jamaica, West Indies.

❧ A ☙

1   John Henry was a very small boy,
Sitting on his mammy's knee;
He picked up a hammer and a little piece of steel,
Saying, "A hammer'll be the death of me, O Lord,
A hammer'll be the death of me."

2   John Henry went up on the mountain
And he came down on the side.
The mountain was so tall and John Henry was so small
That he laid down his hammer and he cried, "O Lord,"
He laid down his hammer and he cried.

3   John Henry was a man just six feet in height,
Nearly two feet and a half across the breast.
He'd take a nine-pound hammer and hammer all day long
And never get tired and want to rest, O Lord,
And never get tired and want to rest.

4   John Henry was a steel-driving man, O Lord,
He drove all over the world.
He come to Big Bend Tunnel on the C. & O. Road
Where he beat the steam drill down, O Lord,
Where he beat the steam drill down.

5   John Henry said to the captain,
"Captain, you go to town,
Bring me back a twelve-pound hammer
And I'll beat that steam drill down, O Lord,
And I'll beat that steam drill down."

6   They placed John Henry on the right-hand side,
The steam drill on the left;
He said, "Before I let that steam drill beat me down
I'll die with my hammer in my hand, O Lord,
And send my soul to rest."

7   The white folks all got scared,
Thought Big Bend was a-fallin' in;
John Henry hollered out with a very loud shout,

"It's my hammer a-fallin' in the wind, O Lord,
It's my hammer a-fallin' in the wind."

8 John Henry said to his shaker,
"Shaker, you better pray,
For if I miss that little piece of steel
Tomorrow'll be your buryin' day, O Lord,
Tomorrow'll be your buryin' day."

9 The man that invented that steam drill
He thought he was mighty fine.
John Henry sunk the steel fourteen feet
While the steam drill only made nine, O Lord,
While the steam drill only made nine.

10 John Henry said to his loving little wife,
"I'm sick and want to go to bed.
Fix me a place to lay down, Child;
There's a roarin' in my head, O Lord,
There's a roarin' in my head."

❧◇ B ◇❧

1 Lissen to my story;
'Tis a story true;
'Bout a mighty man,—John Henry was his name,
An' John Henry was a steel-driver too—
Lawd,—Lawd,—
John Henry was a steel-driver too.

2 John Henry had a hammah;
Weighed nigh fo'ty poun';
Eb'ry time John made a strike
He seen his steel go 'bout two inches down,—
Lawd,—Lawd,—
He seen his steel go 'bout two inches down.

3 John Henry's woman, Lucy,—
Dress she wore was blue;
Eyes like stars an' teeth lak-a marble stone,
An' John Henry named his hammah "Lucy" too,—

Lawd,—Lawd,—
John Henry named his hammah "Lucy" too.

4 Lucy came to see him;
Bucket in huh han';
All th' time John Henry ate his snack,
O Lucy she'd drive steel lak-a man,—
Lawd,—Lawd,—
O Lucy she'd drive steel lak-a man.

5 John Henry's Cap'n Tommy,—
V'ginny gave him birth;
Loved John Henry like his only son,
And Cap' Tommy was the whitest man on earth,—
Lawd,—Lawd,—
Cap' Tommy was th' whitest man on earth.

6 One day Cap' Tommy told him
How he'd bet a man;
Bet John Henry'd beat a steam-drill down,
Jes' 'cause he was th' best in th' lan',—
Lawd,—Lawd,—
'Cause he was th' best in th' lan'.

7 John Henry tol' Cap' Tommy;
Lightnin' in his eye;
"Cap'n, bet yo' las' red cent on me,
Fo' I'll beat it to th' bottom or I'll die,—
Lawd,—Lawd,—
I'll beat it to th' bottom or I'll die."

8 "Co'n pone's in my stomach;
Hammah's in my han';
Haint no steam-drill on dis railroad job
Can beat 'Lucy' an' her steel-drivin' man,
Lawd,—Lawd,—
Can beat 'Lucy' an' her steel-drivin' man."

9 "Bells ring on de engines;
Runnin' down th' line;
Dinnahs done when Lucy pulls th' co'd;
But no hammah in this mountain rings like mine,—

Lawd,—Lawd,—
No hammah in this mountain rings like mine."

10   Sun shined hot an' burnin'
Wer'n't no breeze at-tall;
Sweat ran down like watah down a hill
That day John Henry let his hammah fall,—
Lawd,—Lawd,—
That day John Henry let his hammah fall.

11   John Henry kissed his hammah;
White Man turned on steam;
Li'l Bill held John Henry's trusty steel,—
'Twas th' biggest race th' worl' had ever seen,—
Lawd,—Lawd,—
Th' biggest race th' worl' had ever seen.

12   White Man tol' John Henry,—
"Niggah, dam yo' soul,
You might beat dis steam an' drill o' mine
When th' rocks in this mountain turn to gol',—
Lawd,—Lawd,—
When th' rocks in this mountain turn to gol'."

13   John Henry tol' th' white man;
Tol' him kind-a sad:
"Cap'n George I want-a be yo' fr'en;
If I beat yo' to th' bottom, don't git mad,—
Lawd,—Lawd,—
If I beat yo' to th' bottom don't git mad."

14   Cap' Tommy sees John Henry's
Steel a-bitin' in;
Cap'n slaps John Henry on th' back,
Says, "I'll give yo' fifty dollars if yo' win,—
Lawd,—Lawd,—
I'll give yo' fifty dollars if yo' win."

15   White Man saw John Henry's
Steel a-goin' down;
White Man says,—"That man's a mighty man,
But he'll weaken when th' hardes' rock is foun',—

Lawd,—Lawd,—
He'll weaken when th' hardes' rock is foun'."

16 John Henry, O John Henry,—
John Henry's hammah too;
When a woman's 'pendin' on a man
Haint no tellin' what a mighty man can do,—
Lawd,—Lawd,—
No tellin' what a mighty man can do.

17 John Henry, O, John Henry!
Blood am runnin' red!
Falls right down with his hammah to th' groun',
Says, "I've beat him to th' bottom but I'm dead,—
Lawd,—Lawd,—
I've beat him to th' bottom but I'm dead."

18 John Henry kissed his hammah;
Kissed it with a groan;
Sighed a sigh an' closed his weary eyes,
Now po' Lucy has no man to call huh own,—
Lawd,—Lawd,—
Po' Lucy has no man to call huh own.

19 Cap' Tommy came a-runnin'
To John Henry's side;
Says, "Lawd, Lawd,—O Lawdy, Lawdy, Lawd,—
He's beat it to th' bottom but he's died,—
Lawd,—Lawd,—
He's beat it to th' bottom but he's died."

20 Lucy ran to see him;
Dress she wore was blue;
Started down th' track an' she nevvah did turn back,
Sayin', "John Henry, I'll be true—true to you,—
Lawd,—Lawd,—
John Henry, I'll be true—true to you."

21 John Henry, O, John Henry!
Sing it if yo' can,—
High an' low an' ev'ry where yo' go,—
He died with his hammah in his han',—

Lawd,—Lawd,—
He died with his hammah in his han'.

22 Buddie, where'd yo' come from
To this railroad job?
If yo' wantta be a good steel-drivin' man,
Put yo' trus' in yo' hammah an' yo' God,—
Lawd,—Lawd,—
Put yo' trus' in yo' hammah an' yo' God.

❦❖ C ❖❦

1 John Henry, who was a baby
Sitting on his papa's knee.
He said, "The Big Ben Tunnel on the C. & O. Road,
It is sure to be the death of me.
It is sure to be the death of me."

O shaker, huh turner, let her go down,
O shaker, huh turner, let her go down.

2 They took John Henry from the big white house
And they put him in the tunnel for to drive,
With two nine-pound hammers hanging by his side
And the steam drill pointing to the sky, *etc.*

O shaker, huh turner, let her go down,
O shaker, huh turner, let her go down.

3 John Henry was standing on the right hand side
And the steam drill standing on the left.
He said, "Before I would let you beat me down,
I would hammer my fool self to death, *etc.*

Oh, he died with his hammer in his hand,
Oh, he died with his hammer in his hand.

4 John Henry, he had a woman,
Her name was Mary Magdalene.
She would go to the tunnel and sing for John,
Just to hear John Henry's hammer ring, *etc.*

Oh, he died with his hammer in his hand,
Oh, he died with his hammer in his hand.

5   Well, they took John Henry to the new burying ground
And they covered him up in the sand,
And I see his little woman coming down the street,
She says, "Yonder lay my steel-driving man," *etc.*

Oh, he died with his hammer in his hand,
Oh, he died with his hammer in his hand.

6   Some said he come from Kentucky,
Some said he come from Spain.
It was written on his tombstone and placed at his head,
"John Henry was an East Virginia man," *etc.*

Oh, he died with his hammer in his hand,
Oh, he died with his hammer in his hand.

❀◇ D ◇❀

1   Ef I had 'bout—fo'ty-five dollahs—
All in gol', yas—all in gol'—
I'd be rich as—ol' man Cahtah—
Wealth untol', yas—wealth untol'.

2   Dis ol' hammah—kill John Henry—
Kill him daid, yas—kill him daid—
Knock de brains out—of mah pahdner—
In his haid, yas—in his haid.

3   I'm gwine back to—South Ca'lina—
Fah away, yas—fah away—
I'm gwine see my—Esmeraldy—
I cain't stay, no—I cain't stay.

❀◇ E ◇❀

1   This old hammer killed John Henry,
But it can't kill me.
Take this hammer, take it to the Captain,
Tell him I'm gone, babe, tell him I'm gone.

2   If he asks you what wuz the matter,
Tell him you don't know, babe,
Tell him you don't know.

3   If he asks you wuz I running
    Tell him no, tell him no.

❧◊ **F** ◊❧

1   Ten pound hammer kill John Henry, [*Three times*]
    Somebody dying every day.

2   Oh me pardner, oh me pardner,
    Somebody dying every day.

3   I am sorry for me pardner,
    Somebody dying every day.

⁕4   I come wid Merican to put this tunnel through.

5   Number nine tunnel kill me pardner.

6   Number nine tunnel no will kill me.

7   Dis ole hammer it sound like diamon'.

8   Ten pound hammer will never kill me.

9   Wake up, shake up, climb up Jacob ladder.

10   Rocks and mountain hang about me.

11   If I live to see December.

12   Take this hammer to the walker.

13   Tell him I am going, buddy.

14   Going, buddy, to my country,
    Somebody dying every day.

John Hardy

This Negro "bad badman" killed a fellow miner in a crap-game dispute over twenty-five cents, for which he was hanged at Welch, West Virginia, in January 1894 (*JAF*, 32:505). The ballads about his crime and execution are constantly being confused with the ballad cycle about the semi-mythical John Henry.

In text A, from West Virginia (R. W. Gordon in *New York Times Magazine,* June 5, 1927), the opening stanza is lifted from John Henry's prophecy that the Big Bend Tunnel would be his death. The singer has tried to make sense of this intrusive stanza by having John Hardy get captured at the Big Bend Tunnel. The final stanzas in both A and B (Brown II, 564; North Carolina) refer accurately to John Hardy's remarkable conversion while in prison, his baptism, and his pious behavior on the scaffold.

☙ A ❧

1　When little John Hardy was four years old
　　He climbed on his mamma's knee
　　And said, "The Big Bend Tunnel on the B. & O. road
　　Is bound to be the death of me.
　　　　Lord, Lord!
　　Is bound to be the death of me!"

2　John grew into a man, a desperate man,
　　Carried a gun and a razor every day.
　　He killed a man in Charleston Town,
　　An' you ought ter seen John Hardy git away!
　　　　Lord, Lord!
　　You ought ter seen John Hardy git away!

3　John Hardy had a lovin' little wife
　　And children he had three,
　　But he cared no more for his wife and babes
　　Than he cared for the rocks in the sea—
　　　　Lord, Lord!
　　Than he cared for the rocks in the sea.

4　John Hardy was a standin' in the barroom door,
　　He was unconcerned in the game;
　　Up stepped a yeller gal with twenty dollars in her hand,
　　Said, "Deal John Hardy in the game!"
　　　　Lord, Lord!
　　Said, "Deal John Hardy in the game!"

5　John Hardy stepped up with the money in his hand,
　　Said, "I have money to play,

An' the one who wins this yeller gal's money
I have powder to blow him away!"
    Lord, Lord!
"I have powder to blow him away!"

6 The cards was dealt an' the money on the board,
Dave Campbell won that twenty dollar bill.
John Hardy drew his pistol, an' he took sure aim an' fired
An' he caused Dave Campbell's brains to spill—
    Lord, Lord!
He caused Dave Campbell's brains to spill!

7 John Hardy had twelve miles to go
An' six of them he ran.
He ran till he came to the river bank
Then he fell on his bosom an' he swam—
    Lord, Lord!
He fell on his bosom an' he swam.

8 John Hardy went to the Big Bend Tunnel,
    An' thought he was out of the way;
Up stepped a policeman an' took him by the arm,
Said, "John Hardy, come an' go along with me—
    Lord, Lord!
John Hardy, come an' walk along with me!"

9 John Hardy had a lovin' little wife,
An' she was dressed in blue;
She was hangin' around John Hardy's neck
Sayin', "John Hardy, I've been true to you!"
    Lord, Lord!
"John Hardy, I've been true to you!"

10 John has traveled in the East, an' he's traveled in the West
An' he's traveled this whole world round.
He has been to the river, an' he's been baptized,
An' he's standin' on his hangin' ground!
    Lord, Lord!
He's standin' on his hangin' ground!

❦◇ B ◇❦

1 John Hardy was standing in the gambling room door.
   He was not concerned in the game.
   Up stepped his little woman, threw down fifty cents,
   Says, "Count John Hardy in the game."
   Lord, Lord, says, "Count John Hardy in the game."

2 John Hardy picked up his fifty cents,
   Says, "Half of this I'll play.
   The man that wins my fifty cents,
   Shoot him down and leave him lay."
   Lord, Lord! "Shoot him down and leave him lay."

3 John Hardy lost his fifty cents;
   Was all he had in the game.
   He drew a forty-four from his side,
   Blowed out that poor negro's brains,
   Lord, Lord! blowed out that poor negro's brains.

4 John Hardy had ten miles to go,
   And half of that he run;
   He ran till he came to the broad river bank.
   He fell to his breast and swum.
   Lord, Lord! he fell to his breast and swum.

5 John Hardy was lying on the broad river bank,
   As drunk as a man could be.
   Up stepped John Gamel and another police,
   Says, "John, come go with me,
   John Hardy, come go with me."

6 They took John Hardy to have his trial.
   No one would go his bail.
   His father and mother was standing by
   When they locked John Hardy up in jail,
   Lord, Lord! when they locked John Hardy up in jail.

7 John Hardy had but one little girl;
   He kept her dressed in red.
   And when she saw her papa through the cold iron bars

Says, "Mama, I had rather see him dead."
Lord, Lord! says, "Mama, I had rather see him dead."

8   "Oh, when I die don't bury me at all,
    Put me down in a silver gum.
    Sing the songs my father used to sing,
    With a big brass horn blow on.
    Blow on! with a big brass horn blow on."

9   The last time I saw John Hardy's face
    He was standing on a scaffold high.
    The last word I heard John Hardy say
    Was "I want to go to heaven when I die."
    Lord, Lord! was "I want to go to heaven when I die."

Dupree

The various ballads about Frank Dupree illustrate the differences between Negro and white styles of folk song. Dupree, a white man from Abbeville, South Carolina, entered an Atlanta jewelry store one December day in 1921, snatched a diamond ring, and, in making his escape, killed a policeman. According to the ballads, he took a taxi to Memphis and Chicago, but could not stay away from his sweetheart or from Atlanta. Actually, he was captured in Detroit. Tried and convicted, Dupree was hanged on September 1, 1922.

Text A (Morris, p. 88) is an incomplete folk re-creation of a phonograph record popular in Georgia and Florida during the months preceding Dupree's execution. A doggerel "goodnight," it is heavily overlaid with moralizing and cheap pathos. The Negro version, B (Odum and Johnson, *Negro Workaday Songs,* p. 55), dramatizes instead of telling the story—note the heavy use of dialogue—and the criminal, far from being contrite or moralizing, modestly accepts his lawyer's praises. Sexual passion is frankly expressed in the Negro ballad. The line "Michigan water tastes like cherry wine" in stanza 3 has strayed from Jelly Roll Morton's "Michigan Water Blues," composed about 1912.

❧ A ❧

1   I want my buddies and all my friends
    To take this warning from me.
    Quit your drinking whiskey and live like men;
    Don't live like Frankie Dupree.

2   I went to Atlanta with my sweetheart fair;
    We walked into a jewelry store.
    I took a diamond while standing there,
    But I'll never take no more.

3   I took that diamond, and I left that shop;
    I walked out on the street.
    I pulled my pistol, and I shot that cop;
    I laid him dead at my feet.

4   I jumped in my flivver, and I left that town,
    To make my getaway.
    But my sweetheart she didn't come around,
    So I could not stay away.

5   And then I was captured and went to trial,
    And at last the judge did say.
    "Frank Dupree, you are just a child,
    But you have thrown your life away."

6   "Oh come here, Mama, and come here quick,
    And see the last of your son.
    You see what rambling and drinking rum
    And a sporting life has done."

❧ B ❧

1   Dupree was a bandit; he was so brave and bol';
    He stoled a diamond ring for some of Betty's jelly roll.

2   Betty tol' Dupree, "I want a diamond ring."
    Dupree tol' Betty, "I'll give you anything."

3   "Michigan water taste like cherry wine,
    The reason I know: Betty drink it all the time.

4   "I'm going away to the end of the railroad track.
Nothing but sweet Betty can bring me back."

5   Dupree tol' the lawyer, "Clear me if you can,
For I have money to back me, sure as I'm a man."

6   The lawyer tol' Dupree, "You are a very brave man,
But I think you will go to jail and hang."

7   Dupree tol' the judge, "I am not so brave and bol',
But all I wanted was Betty's jelly roll."

8   The judge tol' Dupree, "Jelly roll's gonna be your ruin."
"No, no, judge, for that is what I've done quit doin'."

9   The judge tol' Dupree, "I believe you quit too late,
Because it is already your fate."

XIII: SONGS
OF THE FORECASTLE
AND LUMBER SHANTY

The George Aloe and the Sweepstake (285)

A ballad of "The *George Aloo* and the *Swiftestake*," undoubtedly an earlier form of this song, was registered in 1611, and a character in Fletcher's play *The Two Noble Kinsmen*, printed in 1634, quotes a few stanzas from it. Thus, even though our text, the earliest extant copy, dates only from about 1670 (*Roxburghe Ballads*, VI, 408), the ballad probably originated about 1600 and described an event that occurred shortly before.

The paternal relationship of "The *George Aloe* and the *Sweepstake*" to "High Barbaree" (p. 407), emerges from even a superficial comparison of the two.

1   The George Aloe and the Sweepstake too,
    With hey, with hoe, for and a nony no
  They were two merchant-men, a sailing for Safee.
    And alongst the coast of Barbary

2   The George Aloe to anchor came,
  But the jolly Sweepstake kept on her way.

3   They had not sayled leagues two or three
  Before they spyed a [sail] upon the sea.

4   "O hail, O hail, you lusty gallants,
  From whence is your good ship, or whither is she bound?"

5   "O we are some merchant-men, sailing for Safee:"
  "And we be French rebels, a roving on the sea.

6   "O hail, O hail, you English dogs, hail!"
  "Then come aboard, you French dogs, and strike down your
      sail!"

7   "Amain, amain, you gallant Englishmen!"
  "Come, you French swades, and strike down your sails!"

amain, Fr., strike sails.   *swade*, peapod, fool.

8   They laid us aboard on the starboard side,
And they overthrew us into the sea so wide.

9   When tidings to the George Aloe came
That the jolly Sweepstakes by a Frenchman was tane,

10   "To top, to top, thou little ship-boy,
And see if this French man-of-war thou canst descry."

11   "A sail, a sail, under your lee,
Yea, and another under her bough."

12   "Weigh anchor, weigh anchor, O jolly boatswain,
We will take this Frenchman if we can."

13   We had not sailed leagues two or three
But we met the French man-of-war upon the sea.

14   "All hail, all hail, you lusty gallants,
Of whence is your fair ship, and whither is she bound?"

15   "O we are merchant-men, and bound for Safee;"
"And we are Frenchmen, roving upon the sea.

16   "Amain, amain, you English dogs!"
"Come aboard, you French rogues, and strike your sails!"

17   The first good shot the George Aloe shot,
It made the Frenchmen's hearts sore afraid.

18   The second shot the George Aloe did afford,
He struck their main-mast over the board.

19   "Have mercy, have mercy, you brave Englishmen."
"O what have you done with our brethren on shore?"
As they sayled into Barbary

20   "We laid them aboard on the starboard side,
And we threw them into the sea so wide."

21   "Such mercy as you have shewed unto them,
Even the like mercy shall you have again."

22   We laid them aboard on the larboard side,
    And we threw them into the sea so wide.

23   Lord, how it grieve[d] our hearts full sore
    To see the drowned Frenchmen [float] along the shore!

24   Now, gallant seamen all, adieu,
    With hey, with hoe, for and a nony no
    This is the last news that I can write to you.
    To England's coast from Barbary

The Greenland Whale Fishery

British whalers of the late eighteenth century were the first
to take up this ballad, but it was soon a favorite with naval and
merchant seamen as well. In the early versions the date is somewhere in the 1790s; the ship is the *Lion;* the commander a
Captain Speedicut(t). These details are lost in the American
versions, as in the excellent text recorded by Colcord, p. 151,
which is also the source of the tune.

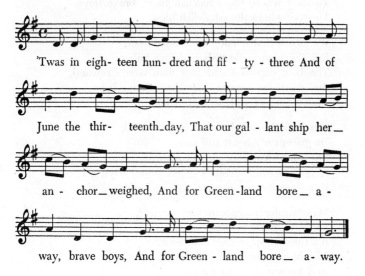

'Twas in eigh-teen hun-dred and fif-ty-three And of
June the thir-teenth day, That our gal-lant ship her
an-chor weighed, And for Green-land bore a-
way, brave boys, And for Green-land bore a-way.

1   'Twas in eighteen hundred and fifty-three
And of June the thirteenth day,
That our gallant ship her anchor weighed,
And for Greenland bore away, brave boys,
And for Greenland bore away.

2   The lookout in the crosstrees stood,
With his spyglass in his hand.
"There's a whale, there's a whale, there's a whalefish," he
    cried,
"And she blows at every span, brave boys,
And she blows at every span."

3   The captain stood on the quarter-deck,
And a fine little man was he.
"Overhaul! Overhaul! Let your davit-tackles fall,
And launch your boats for sea, brave boys,
And launch your boats for sea."

4   Now the boats were launched and the men aboard,
And the whale was in full view;
Resolv-ed was each seaman bold
To steer where the whalefish blew, brave boys,
To steer where the whalefish blew.

5   We struck that whale, the line paid out,
But she gave a flourish with her tail;
The boat capsized and four men were drowned,
And we never caught that whale, brave boys,
And we never caught that whale.

6   "To lose the whale," our captain said,
"It grieves my heart full sore;
But oh! to lose four gallant men,
It grieves me ten times more, brave boys,
It grieves me ten times more.

7   "The winter star doth now appear,
So, boys, we'll anchor weigh;
It's time to leave this cold country,
And homeward bear away, brave boys,
And homeward bear away."

8   Oh, Greenland is a dreadful place,
    A land that's never green,
    Where there's ice and snow, and the whalefishes blow,
    And the daylight's seldom seen, brave boys,
    And the daylight's seldom seen.

The Sea Captain

The perilous siren that lures mariners to their destruction has
been tamed in "The Sea Captain." Here she plays the role of
the resourceful maidens of "The Broomfield Hill" and the
pastourelles, who protect their virginity by ingenious stratagems.
The only trace of the maiden's former supernatural powers is her
ability to sing her captors to sleep.

Text: Mackenzie, p. 74.

1   It was of a sea captain that followed the sea.
    Let the winds blow high or blow low O.
  "I shall die, I shall die," the sea captain did cry,
    "If I don't get that maid on the shore O,
    If I don't get that maid on the shore."

2   This captain had jewels, this captain had gold,
    This captain had costly a ware O.
  And all he would give to this pretty fair maid,
    If she'd please take a sail from the shore O . . .

3   With great persuasions they got her on board,
    The weather being fine and clear O.
  She sang so sweet, so neat and complete,
    That she sang all the seamen to sleep O . . .

4   She took all his jewels, she took all his gold,
    She took all his costly a ware O.
  She took his broadsword to make her an oar,
    And she paddled her way to the shore O . . .

5   "O were my men mad or were my men drunk,
    Or were my men deep in despair O,

> To let her away with her beauty so gay
> To roam all alone on the shore O,
> To roam all alone on the shore?"

The Mermaid (289)

To set sail on Friday is inviting bad luck enough, but seeing a mermaid is a sure sign of disaster.

"The Mermaid" was a staple selection in old songsters and college songbooks, which explains its wide popularity. A half-dozen English counties and a dozen states report variants, not to mention Scotland, Canada, and the Maritime Provinces (see Belden, p. 101). Our text A (Chappell, *Popular Music*, p. 742) is the oldest record of the serious form of the ballad. The songbooks have set afloat a facetious Americanized version represented by our text B (from *Songs of Williams*, 1898, compared with other college collections).

❦◇ A ◇❦

1   One Friday morn when we set sail,
       Not very far from land,
    We there did espy a fair pretty maid,
       With a comb and a glass in her hand, her hand, her hand,
       With a comb and a glass in her hand.

   While the raging seas did roar,
      And the stormy winds did blow,
   While we jolly sailor-boys were up into the top,
      And the land-lubbers lying down below, below, below,
      And the land-lubbers lying down below.

2   Then up starts the captain of our gallant ship,
       And a brave young man was he:
    "I've a wife and a child in fair Bristol town,
       But a widow I fear she will be, will be, will be,
       But a widow I fear she will be.

   For the raging seas . . .

3   Then up starts the mate of our gallant ship,
     And a bold young man was he:
  "Oh! I have a wife in fair Portsmouth town,
     But a widow I fear she will be, will be, will be,
     But a widow I fear she will be.

For the raging seas . . .

4   Then up starts the cook of our gallant ship,
     And a gruff old soul was he:
  "Oh! I have a wife in fair Plymouth town,
     But a widow I fear she will be, will be, will be,
     But a widow I fear she will be.

For the raging seas . . .

5   And then up spoke the little cabin-boy,
     And a pretty little boy was he;
  "Oh! I am more griev'd for my daddy and my mammy
     Than you for your wives all three, all three, all three,
     Than you for your wives all three.

For the raging seas . . .

6   Then three times round went our gallant ship,
     And three times round went she;
  For the want of a life-boat they all went down,
     And she sank to the bottom of the sea, the sea, the sea,
     And she sank to the bottom of the sea.

For the raging seas . . .

B

'Twas Fri-day morn when we— set— sail, And we
were not far from the land, When the cap-tain— spied a
love-ly mer-maid, With a comb and a glass in her hand.
Oh, the o-cean waves may roll, And the storm-y winds may
blow, While—we poor sail-ors go skip-ping to the tops,
While the land-lub-bers lie down be-low, be-low, be-low,
While the land - lub - bers lie down be - low.

1　'Twas Friday morn when we set sail,
　　And we were not far from the land,
　　When the captain spied a lovely mermaid,
　　With a comb and a glass in her hand.

Oh, the ocean waves may roll,
And the stormy winds may blow,
While we poor sailors go skipping to the tops,

While the landlubbers lie down below, below, below,
While the landlubbers lie down below.

2 Then up spoke the captain of our gallant ship,
And a well-spoken man was he;
"I have married a wife in Salem town,
And tonight she a widow will be."

3 Then up spoke the cook of our gallant ship,
And a greasy old cook was he;
"I care more for my kettles and pans,
Than I do for the roaring of the sea."

4 Then up spoke the cabin boy of our gallant ship,
And a dirty little brat was he;
"I have friends in Boston town
That don't care a ha-penny for me."

5 Then three times around went our gallant ship,
And three times around went she;
And the third time that she went around,
She sank to the bottom of the sea.

High Barbaree

Two men-of-war are cruising along the pirate-infested coast of High Barbaree. The ballad promptly forgets one of the ships; the other engages and sinks a sea rover. Almost certainly the story once followed the same lines as "The *George Aloe* and the *Sweepstake*," a reworking of which it seems to be: the ships were separated; one was sunk by a pirate; the other avenged the loss. Two sea fights have thus been contracted into one, yet the pair of ships are retained in the initial stanza. The fighting ship's name frequently appears as *Prince of Luther*, but this is evidently a corruption of the far more plausible *Prince Rupert*, honoring the Stuart general and admiral.

Text and tune: S. B. Luce, *Naval Songs*, 1902, p. 77.

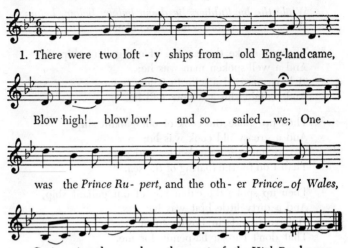

1. There were two loft - y ships from __ old Eng-land came,

Blow high! __ blow low! __ and so __ sailed __ we; One __

was the *Prince Ru - pert,* and the oth - er *Prince __ of Wales,*

Cruis - ing down a - long the coast of the High Bar - ba - ree. __

1   There were two lofty ships from old England came,
    Blow high! blow low! and so sailed we;
    One was the *Prince Rupert* and the other *Prince of Wales,*
    Cruising down along the coast of the High Barbaree.

2   "Aloft! aloft!" our jolly bos'n cries,
    "Look ahead, look astern, look a-weather and a-lee,
    Look along down the coast . . ."

3   "There's none upon the stern, there's none upon the lee,
    But there's a lofty ship to windward—she is sailing fast and
       free,
    Sailing down along the coast . . ."

4   "Oh! hail her, oh! hail her!" our gallant captain cried,
    "Are you a man-of-war or a privateer?" said he,
    "Cruising down along the coast . . ."

5   "Oh! I am no man-of-war,—no privateer," said she,
    "But I am a salt-sea pirate, a-looking for a fee!
    Cruising down along the coast . . ."

6   "If you are a jolly pirate, I'd have you come this way!
    Bring out your quarter-guns, boys; we'll show these pirates
        play,
    Sailing down along the coast . . ."

7   'Twas broadside to broadside a long time they lay,
    Until the *Prince Rupert* shot the pirate's masts away,
    Cruising down along the coast . . .

8   "Oh, quarter! oh, quarter!" these pirates did cry,
    But the quarters that we gave them—we sunk them in the
        sea,
    Cruising down along the coast of the High Barbaree.

The Golden Vanity (286)

A broadside of 1682-85, in which Sir Walter Raleigh plays the
ungrateful captain, seems to have been the ultimate ancestor of
the abundant traditional copies of this ballad found in the
British Isles and America. Sir Walter has dropped out entirely;
the English ship's name appears variously as *Merry Golden Tree,
Golden China Tree, Golden Willow Tree, Golden Merrilee*. Most
traditional versions persist in the melancholy ending in which
the cabin boy is cheated of his earned reward, but many American singers sentimentalize the conclusion, bestowing the captain's daughter, wealth, and other honors on the hero. The cabin
boy shows himself surprisingly canny in the Scottish version
printed here from W. H. Logan's *Pedlar's Pack of Ballads*, 1869,
p. 42.

1   There was a gallant ship, and a gallant ship was she,
    Eck iddle du, and the Lowlands low
    And she was called The Goulden Vanitie,
    As she sailed to the Lowlands low.

2   She had not sailed a league, a league but only three,
    When she came up with a French gallee,
    As she sailed . . .

3   Out spoke the little cabin-boy, out spoke he:
     "What will you give me if I sink that French gallee?
     As ye sail . . ."

4   Out spoke the captain, out spoke he:
     "We'll gie ye an estate in the North Countrie,
     As we sail . . ."

5   "Then row me up ticht in a black bull's skin,
     And throw me o'er deck-buird, sink I or swim,
     As ye sail . . ."

6   So they've rowed him up ticht in a black bull's skin,
     And have thrown him o'er deck-buird, sing he or s[wi]m,
     As they sail . . .

7   About, and about, and about went he,
     Until he came up with the French gallee,
     As they sailed . . .

8   Oh some were playing cards, and some were playing dice,
     When he took out an instrument, bored thirty holes at twice,
     As they sailed . . .

9   Then some they ran with cloaks, and some they ran with
        caps,
     To try if they could stap the saut-water draps,
     As they sailed . . .

10   About, and about, and about went he,
     Until he cam back to The Goulden Vanitie,
     As they sailed . . .

11   "Now throw me o'er a rope and pu' me up on buird,
     And prove unto me as guid as your word,
     As ye sail . . ."

12   "We'll no throw you o'er a rope, nor pu' you up on buird,
     Nor prove unto you as guid as our word,
     As we sail . . ."

13   Out spoke the little cabin-boy, out spoke he.
     "Then hang me, I'll sink ye as I sunk the French gallee,
     As ye sail . . ."

14 But they've thrown him o'er a rope, and have pu'd him up
        on buird,
    And have proved unto him far better than their word,
    As they sailed . . .

The Flying Cloud

To get a job in the Michigan lumber camps in the golden
days of lumbering (1870–1900) "one had to be able to sing
["The *Flying Cloud*"] through from end to end!" (Rickaby,
p. 223). Old sailors disagree as to whether the ballad was quite
this popular in the fo'c'sle.

How and when the ballad originated remains a mystery. The
Flying Cloud was Donald McKay's trimmest California clipper.
Built in 1851, she set a record that same year by plowing from
New York around Cape Horn to San Francisco in eighty-nine
days and twenty hours—a record not yet beaten. Of a much less
fortunate design, the slow *Ocean Queen* served her owners as
an immigrant boat during the 1850s. Neither was ever a slave
or pirate ship. Their names were borrowed arbitrarily to grace
a tale with which the ships had nothing to do. The events the
ballad describes must have happened, if they ever really happened, in the 1820s, when Britain, Spain, and the United States
were making a concerted drive to stamp out piracy and un-
licensed "blackbirding" in West Indian waters. While Hollahan
(the usual form of the name) was in Newgate awaiting trial,
some ballad writer may have got hold of the young Irish cooper's
story and spun it into a broadside goodnight, as an earlier writer
had done for Captain Kidd. But there is no record of a Hollahan
trial and no broadside print. Horace Beck argues mistily (*JAF*,
66:123) that "The *Flying Cloud*" is a modernized combination
of two lost mid-eighteenth-century pieces about Caribbean piracy.
More arresting, though not quite proved, is William Doerflinger's
suggestion in *Shantymen and Shantyboys* (1951, pp. 135,
334-35) that the ballad was inspired by a twelve-and-a-half-
cent temperance tract "purporting to be the confession of one
of the crew of the notorious Benito de Soto, on the eve of his
execution in Cadiz in 1829." Those who sang "The *Flying
Cloud*" in dockside dives and inland taverns were merely
amused, we may be sure, by the cautionary sting in the tail
stanza.

Text: *JAF*, 35:370-72; tune from unpublished transcript in the Barry Collection, Harvard.

My name is Ed - ward— Hal - la - han, As—

you shall— un - der - stand; I be -

long to the coun - ty of Wa - ter - ford, In—

Er - in's hap - py— land. When

I was— young and— in my prime, Kind—

for - tune— on me— smiled; My— par - ents reared me—

ten - der - ly,— I — be - ing their on - ly child.

1   My name is Edward Hallahan,
         As you shall understand;
     I belong to the county of Waterford,
         In Erin's happy land.
     When I was young and in my prime,
         Kind fortune on me smiled;

My parents reared me tenderly,
  I being their only child.

2 My father bound me to a trade
    In Waterford's own town;
He bound me to a cooper there
    By the name of William Brown.
I served my master faithfully
    For eighteen months or more;
When I sailed on board the "Ocean Queen,"
    Bound for Bermuda's shore.

3 When we arrived at Bermuda's shore,
    I met with Captain Moore,
The commander of "The Flying Cloud"
    Belonging to Trimore;
So kindly he requested me
    Along with him to go
To the burning coast of Africa,
    Where the sugar-cane doth grow.

4 We all agreed excepting five,
    And these we had to land,
Two of them being Boston men,
    And two from Newfoundland;
The other was an Irishman
    Belonging to Trimore.
Oh, I wish to God I had joined those men,
    And staid with them on shore!

5 "The Flying Cloud" was as fine a boat
    As ever sailed the seas,
As ever hoisted a maintopsail
    Before a lively breeze;
I have ofttimes seen our gallant ship,
    As the wind lay abaft her wheel,
With the royal and skysail set aloft,
    Sail nineteen by the reel.

6 Oh, "The Flying Cloud" was a Spanish boat,
    Of five hundred tons or more;

She would outsail any other ship
   I ever saw before.
Her sails were like the drifting snow,
   On them there was no stain;
And eighteen brass nine-pounder guns
   She carried abaft her main.

7 We sailed away without delay,
   Till we came to the African shore;
And eighteen hundred of those poor slaves
   From their native isle sailed o'er;
For we marched them all along our decks,
   And stored them down below;
Scarce eighteen inches to a man
   Was all they had to go.

8 The very next day we sailed away
   With our cargo of slaves.
'Twould have been much better for those poor souls
   Had they been in their graves;
For the plague and the fever came on board,
   Swept half of them away.
We dragged the dead upon the decks,
   And threw them in the sea.

9 We sailed away without delay,
   Till we came to the Cuban shore;
We sold them to a planter there,
   To be slaves forevermore;
The rice and coffee fields to hoe
   Beneath the burning sun,
To lead a long and wretched life,
   Till their career was run.

10 And when our money was all gone,
   We put to sea again.
Then Captain Moore he came on deck,
   And said to us his men,
"There's gold and silver to be had,
   If with me you will remain;
We will hoist aloft a pirate's flag,
   And we'll scour the raging main."

11 We robbed and plundered many a ship
        Down on the Spanish Main;
    And many's the widow and orphan child
        In sorrow must remain;
    For we made them to walk our gang-plank,
        And gave them a watery grave;
    For the saying of our master was,
        "A dead man tells no tales."

12 At length to Newgate we were brought,
        Bound down in iron chain,
    For robbing and plundering merchant ships
        Down on the Spanish Main.
    It was drinking and bad company
        That made this wretch of me.
    Now let young men a warning take,
        And a curse to piracy!

Canaday I O

The informant who sang for Mrs. F. H. Eckstorm the ex-
ceptionally sound text given below (from *Bulletin* 6:10) believes
the ballad was composed by Ephraim Braley, a lumberman of
Hudson, Maine, when he returned in 1854 from his indescribable
suffering in Quebec. The date tallies with the names of the
lumber companies cited in various versions. Pennsylvania lumbermen substitute "Colley's Run I O" and otherwise adjust the
song to local circumstances (Shoemaker, p. 88); in North Dakota
(Rickaby, p. 41) and Michigan (Beck, p. 16) the region
satirized is "Michigan I O." And of course the frontier ballad
"The Buffalo Skinners" is actually nothing but a parody of
"Canaday I O." A short, insipid forecastle ditty about an English girl stowaway who wanted to see "the pretty place called
Canada I O," a piece found in several songsters 1830-50, seems
to have given Braley some strong hints for his song; the musical
set of the sea song is perpetuated in its offspring.

In lumberjack slang, "a preacher of the gospel" is a lumber
company's labor recruiter.

Come— all ye jol - ly lum-ber-men, and lis- ten to my

song, But do not get— dis - cour - aged, the

length it is not long, Con - cer - ning of— some

lum- ber- men, who did a - gree to go To—

spend one pleas- ant win- ter up in Can- a- da I O.

1   Come all ye jolly lumbermen, and listen to my song,
    But do not get discouraged, the length it is not long,
    Concerning of some lumbermen, who did agree to go
    To spend one pleasant winter up in Canada I O.

2   It happened late one season in the fall of fifty-three,
    A preacher of the gospel one morning came to me;
    Said he, "My jolly fellow, how would you like to go
    To spend one pleasant winter up in Canada I O?"

3   To him I quickly made reply, and unto him did say:
    "In going out to Canada depends upon the pay.
    If you will pay good wages, my passage to and fro,
    I think I'll go along with you to Canada I O."

4   "Yes, we will pay good wages, and will pay your passage
       out,
    Provided you sign papers that you will stay the route;

But if you do get homesick and swear that home you'll go,
We never can your passage pay from Canada I O.

5 "And if you get dissatisfied and do not wish to stay,
We do not wish to bind you, no, not one single day.
You just refund the money we had to pay, you know,
Then you can leave that bonny place called Canada I O."

6 It was by his gift of flattery he enlisted quite a train,
Some twenty-five or thirty, both well and able men;
We had a pleasant journey o'er the road we had to go,
Till we landed at Three Rivers, up in Canada I O.

7 But there our joys were ended, and our sorrows did begin;
Fields, Phillips and Norcross they then came marching in;
They sent us all directions, some where I do not know,
Among those jabbering Frenchmen up in Canada I O.

8 After we had suffered there some eight or ten long weeks
We arrived at headquarters, up among the lakes;
We thought we'd find a paradise, at least they told us so,
God grant there may be no worse hell than Canada I O!

9 To describe what we have suffered is past the art of man,
But to give a fair description I will do the best I can;
Our food the dogs would snarl at, our beds were on the
       snow,
We suffered worse than murderers up in Canada I O.

10 Our hearts were made of iron and our souls were cased with
        steel,
The hardships of that winter could never make us yield;
Fields, Phillips and Norcross they found their match, I know,
Among the boys that went from Maine to Canada I O.

11 But now our lumbering is over and we are returning home,
To greet our wives and sweethearts and never more to roam,
To greet our friends and neighbors; we'll tell them not to go
To that forsaken G—— D—— place called Canada I O.

The Jam on Gerry's Rock

Shanties from Portland, Maine, to Portland, Oregon, have resounded to lilting renditions of this "darling song of the woodsmen and river drivers." Gerry's (hard "g") Rock has been most substantially located on the East Branch of the Penobscot River in Maine, but some old-timers place the tragedy on the Connecticut or Miramichi or Androscoggin Rivers or on the Saginaw in Michigan. Mrs. F. H. Eckstorm, who tracked down rumors and reports about the ballad over a period of twenty years, was unable to find any historical occurrence behind the story or to fix the exact scene. It emerges from her researches (*Minstrelsy of Maine*, 1927, pp. 176-98) that the song probably originated during the Civil War, when Canadians were imported as rivermen in the Maine woods. Monroe is of that nationality; moreover, only Canadian lumberjacks would have scruples about working on Sunday. Someone among Monroe's associates seems to have composed the ballad, for undue emphasis is placed on the collection the men took up for Monroe's mother or sweetheart. In the 1890s the song, already several decades old, burst into the popularity it has held since. The rejuvenation may have been due to a new tune, or, more likely, to the ballad's suddenly being featured on broadside slips and in songsters. Only a widely distributed slip could account for the fact that a Maine text of 1904 and a West Virginia text of 1915 (Cox, p. 236) turn out to be virtually identical.

Text and tune: Rickaby, p. 11 (Minnesota).

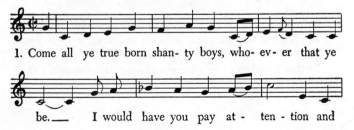

1. Come all ye true born shan- ty boys, who- ev- er that ye be.___ I would have you pay at - ten - tion and

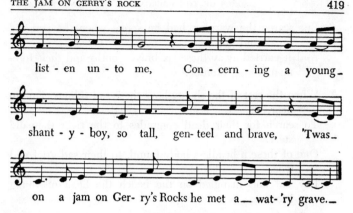

list - en un - to me,   Con - cern - ing   a   young—

shant - y - boy, so   tall,   gen- teel and brave,   'Twas—

on   a jam on Ger- ry's Rocks he met a— wat- 'ry grave.—

1 Come all ye true born shanty-boys, whoever that ye be,
I would have you pay attention and listen unto me,
Concerning a young shanty-boy so tall, genteel and brave.
'Twas on a jam on Gerry's Rocks he met a wat'ry grave.

2 It happened on a Sunday morn as you shall quickly hear.
Our logs were piled up mountain high, there being no one
    to keep them clear.
Our boss he cried, "Turn out, brave boys. Your hearts are
    void of fear.
We'll break that jam on Gerry's Rocks, and for Agonstown
    we'll steer."

3 Some of them were willing enough, but others they hung
    back.
'Twas for to work on Sabbath they did not think 'twas
    right.
But six of our brave Canadian boys did volunteer to go
And break the jam on Gerry's Rocks with their foreman,
    young Monroe.

4 They had not rolled off many logs when the boss to them
    did say,
"I'd have you be on your guard, brave boys. That jam will
    soon give way."

But scarce the warning had he spoke when the jam did
    break and go,
And it carried away these six brave youths and their fore-
    man, young Monroe.

5 When the rest of the shanty-boys these sad tidings came to
      hear,
    To search for their dead comrades to the river they did
      steer.
    One of these a headless body found, to their sad grief and
      woe,
    Lay cut and mangled on the beach the head of young
      Monroe.

6 They took him from the water and smoothed down his
      raven hair.
    There was one fair form amongst them, her cries would
      rend the air.
    There was one fair form amongst them, a maid from Sagi-
      naw town.
    Her sighs and cries would rend the skies for her lover that
      was drowned.

7 They buried him quite decently, being on the seventh of
      May.
    Come all the rest of you shanty-boys, for your dead comrade
      pray.
    'Tis engraved on a little hemlock tree that at his head doth
      grow,
    The name, the date, and the drowning of this hero, young
      Monroe.

8 Miss Clara was a noble girl, likewise the raftsman's friend.
    Her mother was a widow woman lived at the river's bend.
    The wages of her own true love the boss to her did pay,
    And a liberal subscription she received from the shanty-
      boys next day.

9 Miss Clara did not long survive her great misery and grief.
    In less than three months afterwards death came to her re-
      lief.
    In less than three months afterwards she was called to go,

And her last request was granted—to be laid by young
Monroe.

10   Come all the rest of ye shanty-men who would like to go
and see,
On a little mound by the river's bank there stands a hemlock
tree.
The shanty-boys cut the woods all round. These lovers they
lie low.
Here lies Miss Clara Dennison and her shanty-boy, Monroe.

Jack Haggerty

Next after "The Jam on Gerry's Rock" in popularity among
lumbermen, "Jack Haggerty" is an undisputed product of the
Michigan woods. Though one would never guess it from hearing
the ballad, it originated as a spite song. Its author was an
accomplished raftsman and entertainer in the Flat River camps
named Dan McGinnis. Annoyed that George Mercer, a younger
man, had been appointed woods boss over him, McGinnis and
a few other mischief-makers concocted this song in 1872 about
an affair between Jack Haggerty, a good-looking lumberjack
at the camp, and Anna Tucker, the belle of Greenville and
Mercer's fiancée. Haggerty was hardly acquainted with Miss
Tucker. We owe these facts about "Jack Haggerty" to the
diligence of Mrs. G. J. Chickering (see *Modern Language Notes*,
35:465-68).

Text: R. W. Gordon, *New York Times Magazine*, August 28,
1927.

1   I'm a heartbroken raftsman,
From Greenville I came;
All my virtue's departed
With the lass I did fain.
From the strong darts of Cupid
I have suffered much grief;
My heart's broke asunder,
I can ne'er get relief.

2   Of my trouble I'll tell you
Without much delay;
Of a sweet little lassie
My heart stole away.
She was a blacksmith's daughter
On the Flat River side,
And I always intended
To make her my bride.

3   By occupation I was a raftsman
Where the white waters roll.
My name I've engraved
On the high rocks and shoal.
I am the boy that stands happy
On the dark purling stream;
My thoughts were on Mollie,
She haunted my dream.

4   I gave her fine jewels,
And the finest of lace;
The costliest muslins
Her form embraced.
I gave her my wages
All for to keep safe,
I deprived her of nothing
I had on this earth.

5   I worked on the river
Till I earned quite a stake,
Was steadfast, steady,
And ne'er played the rake.
O'er camp, flat and river
I am very well known.
They call me Jack Haggerty
The pride of the town.

6   Till one day on the river
A letter I received.
She said from her promise
Herself she'd relieve.
To wed with another
She'd a long time delayed,

And the next time I'd see her
She'd never more be a maid.

7   To her mother, Jane Tucker,
I laid all the blame;
She caused her to leave me
And go back on my name,
To cast off the riggings
That God would tie,
And leave me a wanderer
Till the day that I die.

8   Now good-bye to Flat River
For me there is no rest.
I'll shoulder my peavy
And go further West;
I'll go to Muskegon
Some comforts to find,
And leave my old sweetheart
And Flat River behind.

9   Now come all ye bold raftsmen
With hearts stout and true,
Don't trust to a woman,
You're beat if you do!
But if you do meet one
With a dark chestnut curl,
Remember Jack Haggerty
And the Flat River Girl!

XIV: COWBOY AND FRONTIER BALLADS

The Cowboy's Lament (The Streets of Laredo)

The sufferings of the cowboy awaiting death in Tom Sherman's barroom or on a street in Laredo, the more usual locale, are mild beside the afflictions of the eighteenth-century Irish rake about whom the song was originally made, for the Irishman was dying of syphilis. "The Unfortunate Rake" was sung in Ireland as early as 1790, though the only part preserved (Joyce, p. 249) is the chorus, in which the rake, obviously a soldier, specifies a military funeral with fife and muffled drums. Derivative English broadsides of about 1850, generally called "The Unfortunate Lad," are ruthlessly candid about the soldier's ailment (see Belden, p. 392). His comrades find him wrapped in flannel down by Lock Hospital, then the London center for treating venereal diseases. He complains to them of his hard fate:

> Had she but told me when she disordered me,
> Had she but told me of it in time,
> I might have got salts and pills of white mercury,
> But now I'm cut down in the height of my prime . . .

and goes on to order drums, pipes, guns, and the dead march for his funeral.

Both in England and America, the sex of the sufferer was occasionally changed by folk singers to yield a widely distributed piece known as "The Bad Girl's Lament" or "St. James Hospital," printed here as a separate ballad. The cowboy adaptation of "The Unfortunate Rake" may owe some details to this bad-girl ballad. Both the girl and the cowboy absurdly request military funerals, a holdover from the songs in which a soldier was the victim. Some versions of the cowboy song, however, correct the discrepancy by arranging a true cowboy funeral:

Then drag your rope slowly and rattle your spurs lowly,
And give a wild whoop as you carry me along,
And take me to the green valley and lay the sod o'er me,
I'm just a young cowboy and I know I done wrong.

The Negro blues "St. James Infirmary" combines elements of the
bad girl's and the cowboy's laments.

Texts: A, Cox, p. 242; B is a lumberjack parody, "The Wild
Lumberjack," from Shoemaker, p. 201.

❦◊ A ◊❦

1 As I passed by Tom Sherman's bar-room,
  Tom Sherman's bar-room, quite early one morn,
  I spied a young cowboy all dressed in his buckskins,
   All dressed in his buckskins, all fit for his grave.

  "Then beat the drum lowly and play the fife slowly,
   Beat up the death marches as they carry me along;
  Take me to the prairie and fire a volley o'er me,
   For I'm a young cowboy and dying alone."

2 "Once in my saddle I used to go dashing,
  Once in my saddle I used to ride gay;
  But I just took up drinking and then to card-playing,
   Got shot by a gambler, and dying to-day.

3 "Go gather around me a lot of wild cowboys,
  And tell them the story of a comrade's sad fate;
  Warn them quite gently to give up wild roving,
   To give up wild roving before it's too late.

4 "Some one write to my gray-headed mother,
  And then to my sister, my sister so dear;
  There is another far dearer than mother,
   Who would bitterly weep if she knew I were here.

5 "O bury beside me my knife and my shooter,
  My spurs on my heels, my rifle by my side;
  Over my coffin put a bottle of brandy,
   That the cowboys may drink as they carry me along.

6   "Some one go bring me a drink of cold water,
       [A drink of cold water," the poor fellow said;]
    As they turned the soul had departed,
       He had gone on a round-up and the cowboy was dead.

✿◇ B ◇✿

1   One day I was walking out on the mountain,
       A wood robin was singing. I happened to spy
    A handsome young lumberjack on the banks of the river,
       All dressed in white linen, and laid out to die.

    So beat your drum lowly, and play your fife slowly,
       And play the Dead March as you carry me along.
    Oh, take me to the mountain, and lay the sod o'er me,
       For I'm a wild lumberjack, and I know I've done wrong.

2   Once out in the forest I used to go slashing;
       Once in the big timbers I used to be gay.
    I first took to drinking, and then to card playing,
       Was shot in the breast, and I'm dying today.

3   Go, some one, and write to my gray-headed mother,
       And also to my brothers and sisters so dear;
    But there is another far dearer than mother,
       Who'd bitterly weep if she knew I was here.

4   Go, some one, and bring me a cup of cold water—
       A cup of cold water, the poor woodsie said;
    But ere it had reached him his spirit had vanished—
       Gone to the Giver, the poor fellow was dead.

The Bad Girl's Lament (St. James Hospital)

This ballad, like the previous one, is an offshoot of the Irish
homiletic ballad "The Unfortunate Rake."
   Text: Mackenzie, p. 301, from Nova Scotian tradition.

1   As I walked out of St. James's Hospital,
       St. James's Hospital one early morn,

I spied my only fairest daughter
  Wrapped up in white linen as cold as the clay.

2 "Once on the street I used to look handsome;
    Once on the street I used to look gay.
  'Twas first to the ale-house, then down to the dance-hall,
    From the dance-hall to the poor-house, then down to my
      grave.

  "So beat your drums and play your pipes merrily,
    And play the dead march as you bear me along.
  Take me to the churchyard and throw the ground o'er me;
    I'm a young maiden. I know I've done wrong."

3 "O come, dear mother, and sit down beside me,
    And sit down beside me and pity my case,
  For my head it is aching, my heart it is breaking,
    With sore lamentations I know I've done wrong.

4 "O send for the minister to pray o'er my body;
    O send for the doctor to heal up my wounds;
  O send for the young man that first came a courting me,
    That I may see him before I am gone.

5 "O send for young sailors to carry my coffin;
    O send for young Ganders to sing me a song;
  And one of them with a bunch of red roses
    To place on my coffin as you carry me along."

Zebra Dun

The Lomaxes (*Cowboy Songs*, p. 78) attribute "Zebra Dun"
to a Negro camp cook for a ranch on the Pecos River, but the
style declares it to be the work of some itinerant white minstrel.
According to Margaret Larkin, the collector of our text (*Singing Cowboy*, 1931, p. 36), the stranger was probably a young
adventurer "who looked like a greenhorn and talked like a dude
but who had learned to sit a horse while riding to hounds in the
English countryside." A zebra-striped dun is an impossibility;

"Zebra Dun" is properly "Z-bar Dun," a dun-colored bronco with the Z-bar brand.

1   We was camped on the plains at the head of the Cimarron,
    When along come a stranger and stopped to argue some.
    He looked so very foolish, we began to look around,
    We thought he was a greenhorn just escaped from town.

2   He said he's lost his job upon the Santa Fe,
    Was going 'cross the plains to strike the Seven D,
    He didn't say how come it, some trouble with the boss,
    But asked if he could borrow a fat saddle hoss.

3   This tickled all the boys to death, they laughed in their
        sleeves.
    "We will lend you a fine hoss, fresh and fat as you please."
    Shorty grabbed a lariat and roped the Zebra Dun
    And give him to the stranger and waited for the fun.

4   Old Dunny was an outlaw, had grown so awful wild,
    He could paw the moon down, he could jump a mile,
    Dunny stood right still as if he didn't know,
    Until he was saddled and ready for to go.

5   When the stranger hit the saddle, Dunny quit the earth
    And travelled right straight up for all that he was worth,
    A-pitching and a-squealing and a-having wall-eyed fits,
    His hind feet perpendicular, his front feet in the bits.

6   We could see the tops of the mountains under Dunny every
        jump,
    But the stranger was growed there like the camel's hump.
    The stranger sat upon him and curled his black mustache
    Like a summer boarder waiting for the hash.

7   He thumped him in the shoulder, and spurred him when he
        whirled,
    And hollered to the punchers, "I'm the wolf of the world."
    And when he had dismounted once more upon the ground
    We knew he was a thoroughbred and not a gent from town.

8   The boss who was standing 'round watching at the show,
    Walked up to the stranger and said he needn't go,

"If you can use the lasso like you rode old Zebra Dun,
You're the man I'm looking for since the year one."

9   There's one thing and a sure thing I've learned since I've
     been born,
     Every educated feller ain't a plumb greenhorn.

The Buffalo Skinners

Professional buffalo hunters from Dodge City, Kansas, first
invaded the Texas Panhandle in 1873, the year given in the
song. Another of the pioneer complaints of deception and discomfort, "The Buffalo Skinners" was adapted from a complain-
ing song of the Maine lumberjacks called "Canaday I O" (see
p. 415). Later the pioneer ballad was itself revamped into "The
Hills of Mexico," a cowboy favorite describing the exaggerated
hardships of men hired to herd cattle "in that God-forsaken
country they call New Mexico."

Text: R. W. Gordon, *Adventure Magazine,* October 20, 1924,
from a correspondent who sang the ballad on the Chisholm Trail
in the early 1880s.

1   Come all you jolly buffalo skinners and listen to my song,
     If you will pay attention I won't detain you long.
     'Tis concerning some jolly bull-skinners that did agree to go
     And spend a summer pleasantly on the Range of the Buffalo.

2   It was in the town of Jacksboro in the spring of seventy-
           three
     That a man by the name of Crigor came walking up to me;
     Says he, "How do you do, young fellow, and how would
           you like to go
     And spend a summer pleasantly on the Range of the
           Buffalo?"

3   On being out of employment, I answered unto him,
     "Going out with you on the Buffalo Range depends upon the
           pay.
     If you will pay good wages and transportation too,

I will go with you to the Buffalo Range and spend a month
or two."

4   "Oh yes, I'll pay good wages and transportation too,
     If you will go with me to the Buffalo Range and spend the
          summer through;
     But if you get tired and homesick and to Jacksboro go,
     I will not pay you wages from the Range of the Buffalo."

5   By such talk and flatteration he enlisted quite a crew, I
          think 'twas twenty-one.
     And when he got to Peas River our troubles then begun.
     The very first tail I tried to split—Christ! How I cut my
          thumb!
     And out skinning those damned old stinkers, our lives we
          had no show,
     For the Indians watched to pick us off out skinning the
          Buffalo.

6   We lived on *rotten* buffalo hump and damned old *iron-
     wedge* bread,
     Strong coffee, croton water to drink, and a bull hide for a
          bed;
     And the way the gray-backs worked on us, God knows it was
          not slow!
     God grant there is no hell on earth like the Range of the
          Buffalo!

7   The season being ended, Old Crigor could not pay—
     The outfit was so extravagant he was in debt that day—
     But among us jolly bull-skinners bankruptcy would not go,
     So we left poor Crigor's bones to bleach on the Range of the
          Buffalo.

8   Now we are 'cross the Brazos River and homeward we are
          bound,
     And in this hell-fired country we never shall be found.
     We will go home to our wives and sweethearts and tell
          others not to go
     To that God-forsaken hell on earth—the Range of the
          Buffalo.

Joe Bowers

The author of this well-known relic of the California boom of '49 was probably one John Woodward, an actor with Johnson's Minstrels at the old Melodian Theater in San Francisco in the early years of the gold fever (see *SFLQ*, II, 131-33). The nominal hero seems to have been not an actual person but merely a fictional representative of the "Pikes" or "Pikers." In the first contingents that trekked over the plains were a large number of men from Pike County in northeast Missouri, and in California slang of the 1850s, a "Pike" was any poor white with backwoods manners and a veneration for Andrew Jackson.

The song was first published in *Johnson's Original Comic Songs*, 1856, and is here reprinted from the edition of 1860.

1   My name it is Joe Bowers, I've got a brother Ike;
    I come from old Missouri, yes, all the way from Pike;
    I'll tell you why I left thar, and how I came to roam,
    And leave my poor old mammy, so fer away from home.

2   I used to love a gal thar, they call'd her Sally Black;
    I axed her for to marry me, she said it was a whack;
    Says she to me, "Joe Bowers, before we hitch for life,
    You'd orter have a little home to keep your little wife."

3   Says I, "My dearest Sally, oh Sally, for your sake,
    I'll go to Californy, and try to raise a stake."
    Says she to me, "Joe Bowers, oh you're the chap to win;
    Give me a buss to seal the bargain," and she threw a douzen
      in!

4   I shall ne'er forgit my feelins when I bid adieu to all;
    Sally cotched me round the neck, then I began to bawl;
    When I sot in, they all commenced—you ne'er did hear the
      like,
    How they all took on and cried, the day I left old Pike.

5   When I got to this 'ere country, I hadn't nary red,
    I had such wolfish feelins I wish'd myself 'most dead;

But the thoughts of my dear Sally soon made them feelins
    git,
And whispered hopes to Bowers—Lord, I wish I had 'em yit!

6 At length I went to minin', put in my biggest licks,
   Come down upon the boulders jist like a thousand bricks;
   I worked both late and airly, in rain, and sun, and snow,
   But I was working for my Sally, so 'twas all the same to Joe.

7 I made a very lucky strike, as the gold itself did tell,
   And saved it for my Sally, the gal I loved so well;
   I saved it for my Sally, that I might pour it at her feet,
   That she might kiss and hug me, and call me something
       sweet.

8 But one day I got a letter from my dear, kind brother, Ike—
   It come from old Missouri, sent all the way from Pike;
   It brought me the gol-darn'dest news as ever you did hear—
   My heart it almost bustin', so, pray, excuse this tear.

9 It said my Sal was fickle, that her love for me had fled;
   That she'd married with a butcher, whose HAR was orful
       red!
   It told me more than that—oh! it's enough to make one swar,
   It said Sally had a baby, and the baby had red HAR!

10 Now, I've told you all I could tell, about this sad affair,
    'Bout Sally marryin' the butcher, and the butcher had red
        HAR.
    Whether 'twas a boy or gal child, the letter never said,
    It only said its cussed HAR was inclined to be RED!

Sweet Betsy from Pike

A companion piece to "Joe Bowers," this song also belongs to
the Gold Rush era and has all the coarse gusto associated with
the forty-niners. Betsy's hailing from Pike (see note to "Joe
Bowers") was a significant fact for the original hearers.

Text: Belden, p. 344, from Missouri. The tune, borrowed from
the sentimental English broadside of "Villikens and His Dinah,"
was fitted to several other Western texts.

Oh, don't you re-mem-ber sweet Bet-sy from Pike   Who
crossed the big moun-tains with her lov-er   Ike,   With
two yoke of   ox-en,   a   large yel-low dog,   A—
tall shang-hai roost-er   and   one   spot-ted hog?

1   Oh, don't you remember sweet Betsy from Pike,
    Who crossed the big mountains with her lover Ike,
    With two yoke of oxen, a large yellow dog,
    A tall shanghai rooster and one spotted hog?

        Eli compoly compoly copelia
        Eli compoly com copleria
        Eli compoly com petheria
        Eli compoly com petheria.

2   One evening quite early they camped on the Platte,
    Close by the roadside on a green shady flat,
    Where Betsy sore-footed lay down to repose.
    With wonder he gazed on his Pike County rose.

3   The shanghai ran off and the cattle all died;
    The last piece of bacon that morning was fried.
    Poor Ike was discouraged, and Betsy was mad;
    The dog wagged his tail and looked wonderfully sad.

4   At length the old wagon came down with a crash
    And out on the prairie rolled all kinds of trash;
    A few little baby-clothes done up with great care
    Looked rather suspicious, though all on the square.

5   They went by Salt Lake to enquire the way,
    When Brigham declared sweet Betsy should stay.
    Betsy got frightened and ran like a deer,
    And Brigham stood pawing the ground like a steer.

6   They next reached the desert, where Betsy gave out
    And down in the sand she lay rolling about.
    Poor Ike, half discouraged, looked on with surprise,
    Saying, "Betsy, get up; you will git sand in your eyes."

7   At length they arrived on a very high hill,
    With wonder looked down upon old Placerville.
    Ike sighed, and he said, when he cast his eyes down,
    "Betsy, my darling, we've got to Hangtown."

8   This Pike County couple attended a dance,
    And Ike wore a pair of his Pike County pants;
    Betsy was dressed up with ribbons and rings;
    Says Ike, "You're an angel, but where is your wings?"

9   A miner says, "Betsy, won't you dance with me?"
    "I will that, old hoss, if you don't make too free.
    Don't dance me too hard; if you want to know why,
    Doggone you, I'm chockful of strong alkali."

10   This Pike County couple got married, of course,
    And Ike became jealous, obtained a divorce.
    Betsy, well satisfied, cried with a shout,
    "Goodby, you big lummix, I'm glad you backed out."

The Arkansaw Traveler

Songs satirizing the crudeness and discomfort of certain regions were a staple of frontier humor. This particular piece resembles the Irish satires on backward counties, and it has been suggested that Irish navvies imported to work on the railroads brought the model with them.

Text: Brewster, p. 265 (Indiana).

1   My name it is Bill Stafford; I was born in Buffalo town;
    For nine long years I've rambled this wide world 'round
      and 'round.
    It's many ups and downs through life, it's many hard times
      I've saw,
    But I never knew what misery was till I struck old Arkansaw.

2   It was in the year of '75, in the merry month of June
    That I landed in Van Buren one sultry afternoon;
    Up stepped a walking skeleton, had a long and lantern jaw;
    He invited me down to his hotel, the best in Arkansaw.

3   I followed that big loafer down to his dwelling-place;
    Starvation it was written on his sad and haggard face.
    He fed me on corn dodger, and his beef I couldn't chaw;
    He charged me fifty cents a meal, way down in Arkansaw.

4   I was to be up early to catch a morning train;
    Says he, "Young man, you'd better stay; I have some land
      to drain.
    I'll give you fifty cents a day, your board and washing all;
    B'gosh, you'll be a different lad when you leave old Arkan-
      saw."

5   I worked for that big loafer, Jess Herald was his name,
    He stood 6-7 in his boots and as slim as any crane;
    And his hair hung down like rat tails on his long and lantern
      jaw;
    He was a photograph of all the gents that I saw in Arkansaw.

6   He fed me on corn dodger that was hard as any rock
    Till my teeth began to loosen and my knees began to knock,
    And I got so thin on sassafras tea I could hide behind a
      straw;
    You bet I was a different lad when I left old Arkansaw.

7   The day I left old Arkansaw (I dread the memory still!)
    I shook both boots from off my feet with an everlasting chill,
    And I staggered into his saloon and called for whiskey raw;
    I got as drunk as a son-of-a-gun when I left old Arkansaw.

8   His wife came into the room, she was just sweet sixteen;
    Her cheeks were red as any rose, she was fair as any queen.

And she put her arms around my neck and kissed me on the
    jaw,
Saying, "Bill, O do remember me when you leave old Arkan-
    saw!"

9 So it's fare-you-well, old Arkansaw, the canebrakes and the
    chills;
It's fare-you-well, old sassafras tea and old corn dodger pills,
For if ever I see that land again, I extend to you my paw,
It'll be by means of a telescope from here to Arkansaw!

The Lone Prairie

As the next few pages demonstrate, the cowboy favorite "The
Lone Prairie" ("O Bury Me Not . . .") turns out to be a reworking of Reverend E. H. Chapin's formal and lachrymose "The
Ocean Burial," contributed to Poe's *Southern Literary Messenger*
for September 1839 (V, 615-16). Ossian Dodge, a Whig song-
campaigner, sang "The Ocean Burial" on the concert stage
during 1845-55; it was printed in songbooks; eventually it passed
into limited oral circulation. Cox, p. 250, recorded a traditional
version of the Chapin–Dodge song in West Virginia. It is con-
trasted here with a Missouri version of "The Lone Prairie"
(Belden, p. 390). A stanza has been interpolated into Belden's
text to make it more typical. It will be noticed that the West
Virginia text retains a certain literary stiffness. Perplexing in the
cowboy adaptation is the line "No sunbeams rest on a prairie
grave," a manifest untruth, but comparison with "The Ocean
Burial" shows that singers slavishly borrowed this line without
realizing that it is applicable only to a grave at sea.

1 "O bury me not on the lone prairie"—
    These words came slow and mournfully
    From the pallid lips of a youth who lay
    On his cold, camp bed at the close of day.

2 He has wasted and pined till o'er his brow
    Death's shades are slowly gathering now.

He thought of his home with his loved ones nigh,
As the cowboys gathered to see him die.

"O bury me not on the lone prairie,
Where the wild coyote will howl o'er me,
Where the wild winds sweep and the grasses wave;
No sunbeams rest on a prairie grave.

3 "I've ever wished that when I died
My grave might be on the old hillside.
Let there the place of my last rest be;
O bury me not on the lone prairie!

4 ["I had hoped to be laid where a mother's prayer
And a sister's tears might mingle there;
By the side of my father, O, let my grave be!
O bury me not on the lone prairie!]

5 "In my dreams I saw"—but his breath failed there.
They gave no heed to his dying prayer.
In a narrow grave just six by three
They buried him there on the lone prairie.

6 May the light-winged butterfly pause to rest
O'er him who sleeps on the prairie's crest;
May the Texas rose in the breezes wave
O'er him who sleeps in a prairie grave.

7 And the cowboys now as they roam the plain—
For they marked the spot where his bones have lain—
Fling a handful of roses o'er his grave
With a prayer to Him who his soul will save.

The Ocean Burial

See note to "The Lone Prairie" (p. 436), which is an adaptation of this song.

1 "O bury me not in the deep, deep sea!"
Those words came slow and mournfully,

From the pallid lips of a youth who lay,
On his cabin couch at the close of day.

2 He had wasted and pined till o'er his brow
Death's shade had slowly passed, and now,
As the land and his fond loved home drew nigh,
They gathered around to see him die.

3 "O bury me not in deep, deep sea,
Where the ocean billows will roll o'er me;
Where no light can break through those dark cold waves,
And no sunbeams rest upon my grave.

4 "Yet it matters not, I oft have been told,
Where the body lies when the heart is cold;
But grant, O grant, this boon to me,
That you'll bury me not in the deep, deep sea!

5 "Let my death-chambers be where a mother's prayer
And a sister's tear may be blended there.
O it will be sweet, ere the heart throb is o'er,
To know that its fountains will gush once more,

6 "And that those it so fondly hath yearned for will come,
And plant the first wild flowers of spring on my tomb.
Let me lie where those loved ones will weep over me;
O bury me not in the deep, deep sea!

7 "And there is another whose tears will be shed
For him who lies in an ocean bed;
In hours that it pains me to think of now,
She has twined these locks and pressed this brow.

8 "In the locks she has twined, shall the sea snake hiss,
And the brow she has pressed shall the cold wave kiss.
For the sake of that loved one that is waiting for me,
O bury me not in the deep, deep sea!

9 "She has been in my dreams—" His voice failed there;
They gave no heed to his dying prayer;
They lowered him low o'er the vessel's side,
And o'er him closed the dark, cold tide.

VQ
82104 ← main
C53e

→ PR
1181
C5
1904

GT
755
M3

82104
G76e

REF
DA
880
A7693

ry and its

two weeks and
another per-
ves, you may
d when it is

the library
ten days (as

10 There to dip the light wing, the sea birds rest,
    And the blue waves dance o'er the ocean's crest;
    Where the billows bound and the waves roll free,
    They buried him there in the deep, deep sea.

The Dying Stockman

Like many of the American cowboy ballads, this Australian stockman song (it has not enough narrative in it to be considered a ballad) is a reworking of a piece from some other sphere of activity—in this instance, the sentimental sea song "Wrap Me Up in My Tarpaulin Jacket," sometimes called "The Old Stable Jacket." Australian stockmen also follow their American counterparts in showing a predilection for singing about melancholy events. There is so little difference among variants of "The Dying Stockman" that one gathers that Australian tradition is extremely weak and uncreative.

Text: *Adventure Magazine*, September 20, 1924, from New South Wales.

1 A strapping young stockman lay dying,
   His saddle supporting his head;
   His two mates around him were crying
   As he rose on his pillow and said:

2 "Wrap me up with my stockwhip and blanket,
   And bury me deep down below,
   Where the dingoes and crows can't molest me
   In the shade where the coolibahs grow.

3 "O, had I the flight of the bronzewing
   Far o'er the plains would I fly
   Straight to the land of my childhood
   And there would I lay down and die.

4 "Then cut down a couple of saplings,
   Place one at my head and my toe,
   Carve on them cross, stockwhip and saddle,
   To show there's a stockman below.

stockman, cowboy. *dingo*, native dog. *coolibah*, Australian tree. *bronzewing*, Australian pigeon.

5 "Hark! There's the wail of a dingo
  Watchful and weird—I must go,
  For it tolls the death-knell of the stockman
  From the gloom of the scrub down below.

6 "There's tea in the battered old billy;
  Place the pannikins out in a row,
  And we'll drink to the next merry meeting
  In the place where all good fellows go.

7 "And oft in the shades of the twilight,
  When the soft winds are whispering low,
  And the darkening shadows are falling,
  Sometimes think of the stockman below."

billy, tin cannister. ***pannikin,*** tin cup.

xv: HUMOR

The Derby Ram

This venerable English lying song—wild exaggeration is a common mode of folk humor—was a favorite of George Washington. The tune resembles the Hobby Horse Dance used in current English folk ritual, and for this reason the song is connected by some folklorists with the "luck-visits" of the animal maskers (*JFDS*, 5:23). Primitively the ram may have been the sacrificial animal killed by the ancient British priests to atone for tribal sins. It is part of such a sacrifice to glorify the animal victim, thus impressing the gods with the offering they are about to receive; and from these ritual praises may have come the fantastic exaggerations of the modern comic song.

The text, from Massachusetts, is recorded in Rosa S. Allen, *Allen Family Songs*, 1899.

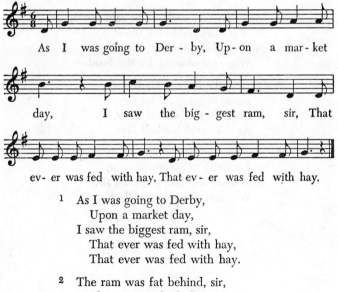

As I was going to Der-by, Up-on a mar-ket day, I saw the big-gest ram, sir, That ev-er was fed with hay, That ev-er was fed with hay.

1   As I was going to Derby,
        Upon a market day,
    I saw the biggest ram, sir,
            That ever was fed with hay,
            That ever was fed with hay.

2   The ram was fat behind, sir,
        The ram was fat before,

He measured ten yards round, sir,
   I think it was no more.

3   The wool grew on his back, sir,
     It reached to the sky,
   And there the eagles built their nests,
     I heard the young ones cry.

4   The wool grew on his belly, sir,
     And reached to the ground,
   'Twas sold in Derby town, sir,
     For forty thousand pound.

5   The wool upon his tail, sir,
     Filled more than fifty bags,
   You had better keep away, sir,
     When that tail shakes and wags.

6   The horns upon his head, sir,
     Were as high as a man could reach,
   And there they built a pulpit, sir,
     The Quakers for to preach.

7   And he who knocked this ram down,
     Was drowned in the blood,
   And he that held the dish, sir,
     Was carried away by the flood.

8   And all the boys in Derby, sir,
     Came begging for his eyes,
   To kick about the streets, sir,
     As any good football flies.

9   The mutton that the ram made
     Gave the whole army meat,
   And what was left, I'm told, sir,
     Was served out to the fleet.

Father Grumble

Like most other American texts of "Father Grumble," this Missouri version (Belden, p. 225) goes back to the Scottish "John Grumlie," first published in Cunningham's *Songs of Scotland* (1825). The comic theme of man and wife exchanging jobs is much older, of course—the sixteenth-century *Wyf of Auchtermuchty*, for example, also had a husband who decided unwisely to play the "hussy" or housewife.

1   There was on old man lived under the hill,
     As you may plainly see, see.
     He said he could do more work in a day
     Than his wife could do in three, three,
     He said he could do more work in a day
     Than his wife could do in three.

2   "Be it so, then," the old lady replied,
     "But this you must allow,
     That you go work in the house today
     And I'll go follow the plow.

3   "But you must milk the Teeny cow,
     For fear that she goes dry.
     And you must feed the little pigs
     That live in yonder sty.

4   "You must watch the speckled hen
     For fear she lays away.
     And you must wind the hank of yarn
     Your wife spun yesterday.

5   "You must go to the dining-room
     And scour up all the plates;
     And don't forget the curly dog,
     Or he'll eat all of the cakes.

6   "You must wash the dirty clothes
     That hang upon the wall;

But don't forget the crooked stairs
Or you'll get an awful fall.

7   "You must churn the crock of cream
    That stands upon the frame;
    But don't forget the fat in the pot
    Or 'twill all go up in a flame."

8   So the old woman she took the whip in her hand
    To go and follow the plow,
    And the old man he took the pail on his arm
    To go and milk the cow.

9   But Teeny she hooked, and Teeny she crooked,
    And Teeny turned up her nose;
    And then she gave the old man such a kick
    That the blood ran down to his toes.

10 He went to watch the speckled hen
    For fear she'd lay away;
    But he forgot to wind the yarn
    His wife spun yesterday.

11 He then went to the dining-room
    To scour up all the plates;
    But he forgot the curly dog,
    And he ate all of the cakes.

12 He went to wash the dirty clothes
    That hung upon the wall;
    But he forgot the crooked stairs,
    And he got an awful fall.

13 He went to churn the crock of cream
    That stood upon the frame;
    But he forgot the fat in the pot,
    And it all went up in a flame.

14 That night he swore by the light of the moon
    And all the stars in heaven
    His wife could do more work in a day
    Than he could do in seven.

Our Goodman (274)

Herd printed "Our Goodman" for the first time in 1776. This Scottish copy was imitated shortly thereafter in a London broadside, which was in turn translated into German and eventually diffused into several Continental balladries. Most American texts follow the original Scottish scheme, though some singers find the old man's gullibility hard to take and have therefore made him a drunkard: "The old man came home last night / As drunk as he could be . . ." Since the rhyme words are set ("he, be, me, see"), improvisation is easy, and the ballad has thus acquired many additional stanzas, some of them unprintably obscene.

Texts: A, Herd MSS., I, 140, via Child, V, 91; B, Cox, p. 156 (West Virginia, 1916).

❧❖ A ❖❧

1 Hame came our goodman, and hame came he,
   And then he saw a saddle-horse, where nae horse should be.

2 "What's this now, goodwife? What's this I see?
   How came this horse here, without the leave o' me?"

[*Recitative:*]

   "A horse?" quo she. "Ay, a horse," quo he.

3 "Shame fa' your cuckold face, ill mat ye see!
   'Tis nothing but a broad sow, my minnie sent to me."
   "A broad sow?" quo he. "Ay, a sow," quo shee.

4 "Far hae I ridden, and farer hae I gane,
   But a sadle on a sow's back I never saw nane."

5 Hame came our goodman, and hame came he;
   He spy'd a pair of jack-boots, where nae boots should be.

mat, may. *minnie,* mother.

6   "What's this now, goodwife? What's this I see?
     How came these boots here, without the leave o' me?"
          "Boots?" quo she. "Ay, boots," quo he.

7   "Shame fa' your cuckold face, and ill mat ye see!
     It's but a pair of water-stoups, my minnie sent to me."
          "Water-stoups?" quo he. "Ay, water-stoups," quo she.

8   "Far hae I ridden, and farer hae I gane,
     But siller spurs on water-stoups I saw never nane."

9   Hame came our goodman, and hame came he,
     And he saw a sword, whare a sword should na be.

10   "What's this now, goodwife? What's this I see?
     How came this sword here, without the leave o' me?"
          "A sword?" quo she. "Ay, a sword," quo he.

11   "Shame fa' your cuckold face, ill mat ye see!
     It's but a porridge-spurtle, my minnie sent to me."
          "A spurtle?" quo he. "Ay, a spurtle," quo she.

12   "Far hae I ridden, and farer hae I gane,
     But siller-handled spurtles I saw never nane."

13   Hame came our goodman, and hame came he;
     There be spy'd a powder'd wig, where nae wig should be.

14   "What's this now, goodwife? What's this I see?
     How came this wig here, without the leave o' me?"
          "A wig?" quo she. "Ay, a wig," quo he.

15   "Shame fa' your cuckold face, and ill mat you see!
     'Tis naething but a clocken-hen, my minnie sent to me."
          "Clocken-hen?" quo he. "Ay, clocken-hen," quo she.

16   "Far hae I ridden, and farer hae I gane,
     But powder on a clocken-hen I saw never nane."

17   Hame came our goodman, and hame came he,
     And there he saw a muckle coat, where nae coat should be.

18   "What's this now, goodwife? What's this I see?
     How came this coat here, without the leave o' me?"
          "A coat?" quo she. "Ay, a coat," quo he.

stoup, pitcher.   *spurtle,* stirring stick.   *muckle coat,* overcoat.

19   "Shame fa' your cuckold face, ill mat ye see!
      It's but a pair o' blankets, my minnie sent to me."
          "Blankets?" quo he. "Ay, blankets," quo she.

20   "Far hae I ridden, and farer hae I gane,
      But buttons upon blankets I saw never nane."

21   Ben went our goodman, and ben went he,
      And there he spy'd a sturdy man, where nae man shoud be.

22   "What's this now, goodwife? What's this I see?
      How came this man here, without the leave o' me?"
          "A man?" quo she. "Ay, a man," quo he.

23   "Poor blind body, and blinder mat ye be!
      It's a new milking maid, my mither sent to me."
          "A maid?" quo he. "Ay, a maid," quo she.

24   "Far hae I ridden, and farer hae I gane,
      But lang-bearded maidens I saw never nane."

❦ B ❦

1   Home came the old man,
             Home came he;
         He went into the house,
             Strange boots did see.

2   "My wife, my beloved wife,
             O what does all this mean?
         Strange boots here,
             Where mine ought to been?"

3   "You old fool, you blind fool,
             Can you not but see,
         'Tis nothing but a bootjack,
             That my mother sent to me?"

4   "Miles have I travelled,
             Five hundred miles or more,
         But spurs on a bootjack,
             I never saw before."

ben. inside.

6   Home came the old man,
      Home came he;
    He went into the kitchen,
      A strange hat did see.

6   "My wife, my beloved wife,
      O what does all this mean?
    A strange hat here,
      Where my own ought to been?"

7   "You old fool, you blind fool,
      O can you not but see,
    'Tis nothing but a dinner pot,
      That mother sent to me?"

8   "Miles have I travelled,
      Five hundred miles or more,
    But crape on a dinner pot,
      I never saw before."

9   Home came the old man,
      Home came he;
    He went into the house,
      A strange shirt did see.

10 "My wife, my beloved wife,
      O what does all this mean?
    A strange shirt here,
      Where my own ought to been?"

11 "You old fool, you blind fool,
      Can you not but see,
    'Tis nothing but a table cloth,
      My mother sent to me?"

12 "Miles have I travelled,
      Five hundred miles or more,
    But sleeves on a table cloth,
      I never saw before."

13 Home came the old man,
      Home came he;
    He went into the bed room,
      A strange face did see.

14 "My wife, my beloved wife,
      O what does all this mean?
   A strange face here,
      Where mine ought to been?"

15 "You old fool, you blind fool,
      O can you not but see,
   'Tis nothing but a baby,
      My mother sent to me?"

16 "Miles have I travelled,
      Five hundred miles or more,
   But whiskers on a baby's face,
      I never saw before."

The Wife Wrapped in Wether's Skin (277)

"The Wee Cooper o' Fife," text A (A. Whitelaw, *Book of Scottish Song*, 1855, p. 333), is the more common title and form of this ballad. The excellent American version (B) from Salem, Massachusetts, first printed in *JAF*, 7:253 (1894), dates from about 1810.

❖ A ❖

1 There was a wee cooper who lived in Fife,
      Nickity, nackity, noo, noo, noo
   And he has gotten a gentle wife.
      Hey Willie Wallacky, how John Dougall,
      Alane, quo Rushety, roue, roue, roue

2 She wadna bake, nor she wadna brew,
   For the spoiling o her comely hue.

3 She wadna card, nor she wadna spin,
   For the shaming o her gentle kin.

4 She wadna wash, nor she wadna wring,
   For the spoiling o her gouden ring.

5 The coopers awa to his woo'-pack
 And has laid a sheep-skin on his wife's back.

6 "It's I'll no thrash ye, for your proud kin,
 But I will thrash my ain sheep-skin."

7 "Oh, I will bake, and I will brew,
 And never mair think on my comely hue.

8 "Oh, I will card, and I will spin,
 And never mair think on my gentle kin.

9 "Oh, I will wash, and I will wring,
 And never mair think on my gouden ring."

10 A' ye who hae gotten a gentle wife
 Send ye for the wee cooper o Fife.

❀◇ B ◇❀

1 Sweet William he married a wife,
 Gentle Jenny cried rosemaree
 To be the sweet comfort of his life.
 As the dew flies over the mulberry tree

2 Jenny couldnt in the kitchen to go,
 For fear of dirting her white-heeled shoes.

3 Jenny couldnt wash, and Jenny couldnt bake,
 For fear of dirting her white apurn tape.

4 Jenny couldnt card, and Jenny couldnt spin,
 For fear of hurting her gay gold ring.

5 Sweet William came whistling in from plaow,
 Says, "O my dear wife, is my dinner ready naow?"

6 She called him a dirty paltry whelp:
 "If you want any dinner, go get it yourself."

7 Sweet William went aout unto the sheep-fold,
 And aout a fat wether he did pull.

8 And daown on his knees he began for to stick,
 And quicklie its skin he thereof did strip.

9   He took the skin and laid on his wife's back,
     And with a good stick went whikety whack.

10   "I'll tell my father and all my kin
     How still a quarrel you've begun."

11   "You may tell your father and all your kin
     How I have thrashed my fat wether's skin."

12   Sweet William came whistling in from plaow,
     Says, "Oh my dear wife, is my dinner ready naow?"

13   She drew her table and spread her board,
     And, "Oh my dear husband," was every word.

14   And naow they live free from all care and strife,
     And naow she makes William a very good wife.

Johnny Sands

A traveling troupe of the 1840s, billed as the Hutchinson Family, popularized "Johnny Sands" on the American stage, from which it seeped into songsters and eventually passed to the folk singers. Our text, from an English broadside of about 1850, in the Harvard collection, differs little from traditional copies except in completeness.

1   A man whose name was Johnny Sands
     Had married Betty Hague,
     And though she brought him gold and lands,
     She proved a terrible plague.
     For, oh, she was a scolding wife,
     Full of caprice and whim;
     He said that he was tired of life,
     And she was tired of him.

2   Says he, "Then I will drown myself;
     The river runs below."
     Says she, "Pray do, you silly elf,
     I wished it long ago."

Says he, "Upon the brink I'll stand,
　　Do you run down the hill
And push me in with all your might."
　　Says she, "My love, I will."

3　"For fear that I should courage lack,
　　　And try to save my life,
　Pray tie my hands behind my back."
　　　"I will," replied his wife.
　She tied them fast as you may think,
　　　And when securely done—
　"Now stand," she says, "upon the brink
　　　And I'll prepare to run."

4　All down the hill his loving bride
　　　Now ran with all her force
　To push him in, he stepped aside,
　　　And she fell in, of course.
　Now splashing, dashing like a fish—
　　　"Oh, save me, Johnny Sands."
　"I can't, my dear, though much I wish,
　　　For you have tied my hands."

The Farmer's Curst Wife (278)

Satan's mention of an eldest son in stanza 3 hints that once
the song had a more serious plot, one in which the farmer, in
paying off a compact with the devil, shrewdly tries to rid himself
of a shrewish wife. At the performance where this text was
recorded, the tune used was "Lilliburlero," a solo voice singing
the story and a chorus of Sussex countrymen whistling the refrain.

Text: J. H. Dixon, *Ancient Poems . . . of the Peasantry*, 1846,
p. 210.

1　There was an old farmer in Sussex did dwell,
　　　[*Chorus of whistlers*]
　There was an old farmer in Sussex did dwell,

And he had a bad wife, as many knew well.
[*Chorus of whistlers*]

2   Then Satan came to the old man at the plough:
"One of your family I must have now.

3   "It is not your eldest son that I crave,
But it is your old wife, and she I will have."

4   "O, welcome, good Satan, with all my heart!
I hope you and she will never more part."

5   Now Satan has got the old wife on his back,
And he lugged her along, like a pedlar's pack.

6   He trudged away till they came to his hall-gate;
Says he, "Here, take in an old Sussex chap's mate!"

7   O! then she did kick the young imps about;
Says one to the other, "Let's try turn her out."

8   She spied thirteen imps all dancing in chains,
She up with her pattens and beat out their brains.

9   She knocked the old Satan against the wall—
"Let's turn her out, or she'll murder us all."

10   Now he's bundled her up on his back amain,
And to her old husband he took her again.

11   "I have been a tormentor the whole of my life,
But I ne'er was tormented so as with your wife."

Blue-Tail Fly

White audiences first heard Negro songs from the blackface minstrel troupes, which from the 1830s on were a staple music-hall attraction in England as well as America, and in the North even more than in the South. Very little in the minstrel repertory was genuine. Much of it in fact was deliberate pro-slavery propaganda, for the picture Dan Emmett, "Jim Crow" Rice, "Pickaninny" Coleman, and Christie's strutters gave of the Negro—indolent, ignorant, slyly thieving, disloyal, bestial, inanely joyful, and boisterous—was calculated to show that the race was happy in its present state and unworthy of a better. One of the few minstrel pieces to survive in tradition, "The Blue-Tail Fly" describes the suppressed glee of a little Negro pageboy when his master is thrown from his horse and killed. Curiously, the text recorded by Miss Scarborough in Texas in 1920 (*On the Trail of Negro Folk-Songs*, p. 202) adheres almost word for word to the *Ethiopian Glee Book* version printed in Boston in 1848.

1   When I was young I used to wait,
      On Massa an' hand him de plate,
      An' pass de bottle when he git dry,
      An' bresh away de blue-tail fly.

        Jim crack corn, I don't care,
        Jim crack corn, I don't care,
        Jim crack corn, I don't care,
        Ole Massa's gone away.

2   Den arter dinner Massa sleep,
      He bid dis Nigger vigil keep;
      An' when he gwine to shut his eye,
      He tell me watch de blue-tail fly.

3   An' when he ride in de arternoon,
      I foller wid a hickory broom;
      De pony being berry shy,
      When bitten by de blue-tail fly.

4   One day he ride aroun' de farm;
      De flies so numerous dey did swarm;
      One chance to bite 'im on de thigh,
      De debble take dat blue-tail fly.

5   De pony run, he jump an' pitch,
      An' tumble Massa in de ditch.
      He died, an' de jury wondered why;
      De verdic' was de blue-tail fly.

6   Dey laid 'im under a 'simmon tree;
      His epitaph am dar to see:

"Beneath dis stone I'm forced to lie,
All by de means ob de blue-tail fly."

7 Ole Massa gone, now let 'im rest;
Dey say all t'ings am for de best.
I nebber forget till de day I die,
Ole Massa an' dat blue-tail fly.

BIBLIOGRAPHY

INDEX

BIBLIOGRAPHY

Sources of texts and music
including important collections not drawn upon

(Abbreviations used in headnotes are indicated in left-hand column)

	Baring-Gould, Sabine, and Sheppard, H. F. *Songs and Ballads of the West.* 4 parts, London, 1889–91.
Barry	Barry, Phillips, with Eckstrom F. H., and Smyth, M. W. *Ballads from Maine.* New Haven, Conn., 1929.
Beck	Beck, E. C. *Lore of the Lumber Camps.* Ann Arbor, Mich., 1948.
Belden	Belden, H. M. *Ballads and Songs Collected by the Missouri Folk-Lore Society.* University of Missouri Studies, XV, 1; Columbia, Mo., 1940, reprinted 1955.
Brewster	Brewster, P. G. *Ballads and Songs of Indiana.* Bloomington, Ind., 1940.
	Broadwood, L. E. *English Traditional Songs and Carols.* London, 1908.
	—— and Fuller-Maitland, J. A. *English County Songs.* London and New York, 1893.
Brown	*The Frank C. Brown Collection of North Carolina Folklore,* edited by N. I. White and others. Vol. II, edited by H. M. Belden and A. P. Hudson, Durham, N. C., 1952.
	Bruce, J. C., and Stokoe, J. *Northumbrian Minstrelsy.* Newcastle-upon-Tyne, 1882.
Buchan	Buchan, Peter. *Ancient Ballads and Songs of the North of Scotland.* 2 vols., Edinburgh, 1828.
	——. *Gleanings of Scotch, English and Irish Scarce Old Ballads.* Peterhead, Scotland, 1825.
Bulletin	*Bulletin of the Folk-Song Society of the Northeast,* edited by Phillips Barry. Cambridge, Mass., 1930–37.
	Chappell, Louis W. *John Henry.* Jena, Germany, 1933.
	Chappell, William. *Popular Music of the Olden Time.* 2 vols., London, 1855–59.
Child	Child, F. J. *The English and Scottish Popular Ballads.* 5 vols., Boston, 1882–98.
Christie	Christie, William. *Traditional Ballad Airs.* 2 vols., Edinburgh, 1876–81.
Colcord	Colcord, J. C. *Songs of American Sailormen.* New York, 1938.
Combs	Combs, Josiah. *Folk Songs du Midi des Etats-Unis.* Paris, 1925.

459

Cox   Cox, J. H. *Folk-Songs of the South*. Cambridge, Mass., 1925.

Creighton, Helen. *Songs and Ballads from Nova Scotia*. Toronto, 1932.

————. *Traditional Songs from Nova Scotia*. Toronto, 1950.

Cunningham, Allan. *The Songs of Scotland*. 4 vols., London, 1825.

Davis   Davis, A. K. *Traditional Ballads of Virginia*. Cambridge, Mass., 1929.

Dixon, J. H. *Ancient Poems, Ballads and Songs of the Peasantry of England*. London, 1846.

Eckstorm   Eckstorm, F. H., and Smyth, M. W. *Minstrelsy of Maine*. Boston, 1927.

Eddy   Eddy, M. O., *Ballads and Songs from Ohio*. New York, 1939.

Finger, C. J. *Frontier Ballads*. New York, 1927.

Flanders, H. H., and Brown, George. *Vermont Folk-Songs and Ballads*. Brattleboro, Vt., 1931.

————, Ballard, E. F., Brown, George, and Barry, Phillips. *The New Green Mountain Songster*. New Haven, Conn., 1939.

Gardner, E. E., and Chickering, G. J. *Ballads and Songs of Southern Michigan*. Ann Arbor, Mich., 1939.

Gray, R. P. *Songs and Ballads of the Maine Lumberjacks*. Cambridge, Mass., 1924.

Greenleaf, E. B., and Mansfield, G. Y. *Ballads and Sea Songs of Newfoundland*. Cambridge, Mass., 1933.

Greenway, John. *American Folksongs of Protest*. Philadelphia, 1953.

Greig   Greig, Gavin. *Last Leaves of Traditional Ballads*, edited by Alexander Keith. Aberdeen, Scotland, 1925.

Henry   Henry, M. E. *Folk Songs from the Southern Highlands*. New York, 1938.

Herd, David. *The Ancient and Modern Scots Songs, Heroic Ballads, etc.* Edinburgh, 1769; 2 vols., 1776.

Hudson   Hudson, A. P. *Folksongs of Mississippi and Their Background*. Chapel Hill, N. C., 1936.

JAF   *Journal of American Folklore*: 1887 to present.

Jamieson   Jamieson, Robert. *Popular Ballads and Songs*. 2 vols., Edinburgh, 1806.

JFDS   *Journal of the English Folk Dance and Song Society*: 1932 to present.

JFS   *Journal of the English Folk Song Society*: 1898–1932.

Johnson   Johnson, G. B. *John Henry*. Chapel Hill, N. C., 1929.

Joyce   Joyce, P. W. *Old Irish Folk Music and Song*. London, 1909.

Kidson, Frank. *Traditional Tunes*. Oxford, 1891.

Kinloch, G. R. *Ancient Scottish Ballads*. London and Edinburgh, 1827.

Korson, G. G. *Coal Dust on the Fiddle: Songs and Stories of the Bituminous Industry*. Philadelphia, 1943.

――――. *Minstrels of the Mine Patch: Songs and Stories of the Anthracite Industry*. Philadelphia, 1938.

Larkin   Larkin, Margaret. *Singing Cowboy*. New York, 1931.

Linscott   Linscott, E. H. *Folk Songs of Old New England*. New York, 1939.

Lomax, J. A. and Alan. *American Ballads and Folk Songs*. New York, 1934.

――――. *Cowboy Songs and Other Frontier Ballads*. New York, 1938 (latest of several editions).

――――. *Negro Folk Songs as Sung by Lead Belly*. New York, 1936.

McGill, Josephine. *Folk Songs of the Kentucky Mountains*. New York, 1917.

Mackenzie   Mackenzie, W. R. *Ballads and Sea Songs from Nova Scotia*. Cambridge, Mass., 1928.

Morris   Morris, A. C. *Folksongs of Florida*. Gainesville, Fla., 1950.

Motherwell   Motherwell, William. *Minstrelsy*. Glasgow, 1827.

Neeser   Neeser, R. W. *American Naval Songs and Ballads*. New Haven, Conn., 1938.

Odum, H. W., and Johnson, G. B. *The Negro and His Songs*. Chapel Hill, N. C., 1925.

――――. *Negro Workaday Songs*. Chapel Hill, N. C., 1926.

Ord, John. *Bothy Songs and Ballads*. Paisley, Scotland, 1930.

Owens   Owens, W. A. *Texas Folk Songs*. Dallas, Texas, 1950.

The Pepys Ballads, edited by H. E. Rollins. 8 vols., Cambridge, Mass., 1929–32.

Percy's Folio MS.   Bishop *Percy's Folio Manuscript*, edited by J. W. Hales and F. J. Furnivall. 3 vols. and Supplement of "Loose and Humorous Songs," London, 1867–68.

Percy, Thomas. *Reliques of Ancient English Poetry*. 3 vols., London, 1765 (numerous later editions).

Pills to Purge Melancholy (*Wit and Mirth*), edited by Thomas D'Urfey. 6 vols., London, 1719–20.

PMLA   *Publications of the Modern Language Association*: 1885 to present.

Pound   Pound, Louise. *American Ballads and Songs*. New York, 1922.

Ramsay, Allan. *The Ever Green*. 2 vols., Edinburgh, 1724.

――――. *The Tea-Table Miscellany*. 4 vols., Edinburgh, 1723–40 (edition of 1750 used throughout).

Randolph   Randolph, Vance. *Ozark Folksongs*. 4 vols., Columbia, Mo., 1946–50.

Rickaby   Rickaby, Franz. *Ballads and Songs of the Shanty-Boy*. Cambridge, Mass., 1926.

Rimbault, E. F. *Musical Illustrations of Bishop Percy's Reliques*. London, 1850.

Ritson, Joseph. *Ancient Songs from the Time of King Henry the Third to the Revolution*. London, 1790.

———. *Robin Hood*. 2 vols., 1795.

Roxburghe   *Roxburghe Ballads*, edited by William Chappell and J. W. Ebsworth. 9 vols., Hertford and London, 1871–1899.

Sandburg   Sandburg, Carl. *The American Songbag*. New York, 1927 (and later editions).

Sandys, William. *Christmas Carols, Ancient and Modern*. London, 1833.

Scarborough, Dorothy. *A Song Catcher in the Southern Mountains*. New York, 1937.

———. *On the Trail of Negro Folk-Songs*. Cambridge, Mass., 1925.

Scott   Scott, Walter. *Minstrelsy of the Scottish Border*. 3 vols., Kelso, Scotland, 1802–1803 (and later editions).

SFLQ   *Southern Folklore Quarterly*: 1937 to present.

Sharp   Sharp, C. J. *English Folk Songs from the Southern Appalachians*, edited by Maud Karpeles. 2 vols., Oxford, 1932.

——— and Marson, C. L. *Folk Songs from Somerset*. 5 series, London, 1904–1909.

———. *One Hundred English Folksongs*. New York, 1916 (English edition is *English Folk Songs: Selected Edition*, London, 1921).

Sharpe, C. K. *A Ballad Book*. Edinburgh, 1823.

Shoemaker   Shoemaker, H. W. *Mountain Minstrelsy*. Philadelphia, 1931.

Smith   Smith, Reed. *South Carolina Ballads*. Cambridge, Mass., 1928.

White   White, N. I. *American Negro Folk-Songs*. Cambridge, Mass., 1928.

Williams, Alfred. *Folk-Songs of the Upper Thames*. London, 1923.

Wyman, Loraine, and Brockway, Howard. *Lonesome Tunes: Folk Songs from the Kentucky Mountains*. New York, 1916.

MANUSCRIPTS AND PAPERS

The texts of Child ballads have been compared with the following manuscripts, original or transcript, in

Herd's MSS.
Motherwell's MS.
Jamieson's Brown MS.

Percy Papers

the Harvard University Library: Elizabeth Cochrane's MS., David Herd's MSS., G. R. Kinloch's MSS., William Motherwell's MS., Robert Jamieson's Brown MS. (songs received from Mrs. Brown of Falkland), Alexander F. Tytler's Brown MS., William Tytler's Brown MS. In the same library are deposited the Thomas Percy Papers and the Phillips Barry Collection of New England Folksong.

GENERAL BIBLIOGRAPHY

Coffin, T. P. *The British Traditional Ballad in America.* Philadelphia, 1950.

Dean-Smith, Margaret. *A Guide to English Folk Song Collections: 1822–1952.* Liverpool, 1954.

Laws, G. M., Jr. *Native American Balladry.* Philadelphia, 1950.

Lomax, Alan, and Cowell, S. R. *American Folk Song and Folklore: A Regional Bibliography.* New York, 1942.

CRITICISM

Entwhistle, W. J. *European Balladry.* Oxford, 1939.

Gerould, G. H. *The Ballad of Tradition.* Oxford, 1932.

Gummere, F. B. *The Popular Ballad.* Boston, 1907.

Hodgart, M. J. C. *The Ballads.* London, 1950.

Pound, Louise. *Poetic Origins and the Ballad.* New York, 1921.

Wells, E. K. *The Ballad Tree.* New York, 1950.

Wimberly, L. C. *Folklore in the English and Scottish Ballads.* Chicago, 1928.

INDEX TO TITLES
AND FIRST LINES